New American Blues

Other books by Earl Shorris

FICTION

Ofay
The Boots of the Virgin
Under the Fifth Sun: A novel of Pancho Villa

NON-FICTION

The Death of the Great Spirit: An Elegy for the American Indian
The Oppressed Middle: Scenes from Corporate Life
Jews Without Mercy: A Lament
Power Sits at Another Table: Aphorisms
While Someone Else Is Eating (editor)
Latinos: A Biography of the People
A Nation of Salesmen: The Tyranny of the Market and the Subversion of Culture

Earl Shorris

New American Blues

A Journey Through Poverty to Democracy

W. W. Norton & Company

New York ▪ *London*

First Edition

Lyrics from "Poor Man's Blues" by Bessie Smith © 1930 (Renewed),
1974 Frank Music Corp. All Rights Reserved.

Lines from "The Well Dressed Man with a Beard" from *Collected
Poems* by Wallace Stevens. Copyright 1942 by Wallace Stevens.
Reprinted by permission of Alfred A. Knopf, Inc.

For information about permission to reproduce selections from this
book, write to Permissions, W. W. Norton & Company, Inc.,
500 Fifth Avenue, New York NY 10110.

The text of this book is composed in Garamond #3 with the display
set in Berling. Desktop composition by Debra Morton Hoyt.
Manufacturing by The Maple-Vail Book Manufacturing Group.
Book design by Judith Stagnitto Abbate.

Library of Congress Catalogiing-in-Publication Data
Shorris, Earl, 1936–
    New American blues : a journey through poverty to democracy/
Earl Shorris
    p.   cm.
    Includes bibliographical references and index.
    ISBN 0-393-04554-4
    1. Poor—United States. 2. Poverty—United States. I. Title.
HV4045.S46   1997
362.5'0973—DC21   97-6834
                                                            CIP

W. W. Norton & Company, Inc., 500 Fifth Avenue,
New York NY 10110
http://www.wwnorton.com

W. W. Norton Ltd., 10 Coptic Street, London WC1A 1PU

1 2 3 4 5 6 7 8 9 0

To Charles, Grace, Jaime, Patricia, Sylvia, and Tim,
who stayed the course;

with thanks to
Starling Lawrence, Rick and Sophie MacArthur, the AKC
Foundation, and W. W. Norton & Company

Mr. Rich Man, Mr. Rich Man, open up
your heart and mind.
Mr. Rich Man, Mr. Rich Man, open up
your heart and mind.
Give the poor man a chance, help stop
these hard, hard times.

—BESSIE SMITH

Contents

Part Two—Public Life

Intentions

ACCORDING TO ISAIAH BERLIN, Alexander Herzen "had a natural gift for criticism—a capacity for exposing and denouncing the dark sides of life." And only a few paragraphs later, Berlin added, "As if to restore the equilibrium of his moral organism, nature took care to place in his soul one unshakable belief, one unconquerable inclination. Herzen believed in the noble instincts of the human heart."

This work seeks to offer an explanation of long-term poverty by placing the unfairness of force, "the dark side of human life," in contrast to the inclusiveness of legitimate power, which is one of "the noble instincts of the human heart." It examines and denounces the dark side and suggests a triumph of the noble instincts.

Part One

Private Life

I.

Happy Pride Day to You! Observations and Adumbrations

Where you coming from?
— S T R E E T   T A L K

WHEN I LIVED IN Chicago's 24th Ward, it was the most beautifully, generously corrupt political jurisdiction in America. In every election the dead and departed voted alongside the winos hauled in for the day and the fearful, sometimes hungry, still-striving citizens of the Great Depression. In our precinct, on West Congress Street, some of those who came to vote in the basement of Marty O'Brien's house had been among the poorest of the poor. Our neighbors, who with such diligence marked their ballots for the Democratic ticket, remembered the food riots, for some of them had fought for the scraps that tumbled out of the garbage trucks and into the starving crowds who gathered like beasts in the city dump.

By 1940, the first year of my memory of our neighborhood, some people had been without money for a long time. A few had tried to open shops, and failed. A man who worked as a tailor lost his eyesight. Mr. Gerber, who worked in a butcher shop, cut off his finger. A lot of men went on the road. I never knew what they did, but I saw that they were not home at night, like other men.

We admired men with steady work: barbers, junk dealers, auto mechanics, cutters, pressers, milkmen, postmen, any salesman with a draw. In most families, one job supported three generations. We lived that way for a long time, crowded into a one-bedroom apartment with my grandparents.

As I remember, the first people in the neighborhood to lose hope were the young men. They fought, they quit this or that, they gave up on school, they went on the road; one boy was sent to reform school, my mother said; another, old enough to wear the blue shadow of a man's beard, went to prison, no one told me why.

My father said that on our block a few people lived with hunger. I did not know what he meant, but I was sure that it was nothing like the hunger I sometimes knew in the early evening before dinner. This other hunger, this saddening hunger came late, in the dark, when good people were asleep.

We never said that anyone was poor, but they were. By any definition, those who were hungry were poor. The others, those with sometime jobs and maybe next-time business plans, may not have been poor, although they had little money and no economic security. To understand them and their place in the world a definition of long-term poverty, the kind that extends over much of a lifetime and often goes on for generations, is needed, something more meaningful than what my father said or the line the federal government imagined. And a thesis. If we throw out the *underclass* and the *culture of poverty*, what can poverty be? And why? A comfortable man who sets out to write a book about poverty in his own country and in his own time surely owes the journey a beginning.

I thought it best to begin the writing where I began, in the North Lawndale district of the West Side of Chicago as it was then and as it is now: long ago in a yellow brick tenement at the weary end of the Great Depression when almost every remedy other than armed revolution had been tried and failed; and now on the same streets, when almost every remedy other than armed repression has been abandoned. Two sets of observations separated by more than half a century—paired and told with little comment, they should adumbrate all the observations, definitions, and ideas that follow.[1] But they will not fit perfectly with the theories, as if the poor were pegs to put into corresponding holes. Divergences, contradictions, disputations occur. Human beings bear no resemblance to Plato's

---

[1] One set of observations came at the beginning of what was known as "the safety net" for the American poor and the second set comes as President Clinton and the Republican-dominated Congress put an end to the safety net with the Welfare Reform Act of 1996. Whether or not this return to life without a bottom limit will send the poor back to rioting over scraps in the garbage dumps of Chicago, as some of our neighbors did before the establishment of a safety net, is not yet known.

Forms; they are not immutable, ideal, or as true as numbers; if statistics can be relied on to tell us everything about all of them, they can also be relied on to tell nothing about each of them.

The other way to know something about human beings is to begin with them as they are, to find in them and what they have said and done something reasonable about the world. The problem of this *bricolage*, making structures of found materials or bric-à-brac, is that a lot will be left over. The author compares what is included in the structures to what won't fit. If the leftovers outweigh the inclusions, another structure, perhaps a replacement, must be conceived. The scientist, on the other hand, makes a theory and shapes the world to fit.[2] Since this work is bricolage, cobbled together out of observations, readings, lies, experiences, stories, events old and new, whatever is at hand, there will necessarily be a lot left over when the structures have been completed.[3]

Here at the beginning it may be helpful to know something about the end; that is, to have some idea of the final structure, if only for the purpose of navigation. It may surprise you as it did me that the people of my old neighborhood were correct about who was poor during the Depression, because their definition of poverty was much more sophisticated than the one I held when I began this work. They knew the difference between *force* and *power*.

They thought only of the legitimate form of power, the kind that comes from the people and includes the people. They called this power by its correct name, "politics." The difference between the poor and all the rest of the people grew out of this distinction between those who practiced politics in their daily lives and those who did not. In this, they were like Pericles of Athens, who thought of politics as a way of living that happened at all levels of human organization, from the family to the polis, which was in his time merely a city-state and not the kind of great continental republic so familiar to us.

Of course, hardly anyone in my old neighborhood had ever heard of Pericles or of Aristotle, who thought of politics as the master art, the one that controlled all the others. Even so, they knew that in America those who did politics were not poor and that the lack of money in their lives would not be an enduring problem.

---

[2] I have used the word "theory" in two ways here: one serves as a synonym for structure, which the assembler makes of what he finds in the world; the other, according to Claude Lévi-Strauss, connected to science rather than bricolage, describes a plan for the world. The reader will understand the meaning from the context.

[3] See Claude Lévi-Strauss, various works, especially chapter 1, pp. 19–33, of *The Savage Mind* (Chicago: University of Chicago Press, 1966) for his views on bricolage, science, games, etc.

In the city of Chicago, as it had been in the polis of Athens, reflection made the difference between the political life, the life of power, and the apolitical life, the life of force. Where force ruled, there was no time for reflection; politics was impossible, people lived in poverty.

The idea that poverty comes of the failure to practice politics, that there is not a culture of poverty or a cycle of poverty or a genetics of poverty, but a politics (or more accurately an apolitics) of poverty, stands at the heart of the structure cobbled from the worlds in which the author has done his scavenging. Everything found did not fit into the structure; only luck or lies could make so perfect a world.

I have included some of the leftovers, enough to show that the world of the poor is not monolithic or even very predictable. Poor people manage, at one time or another, to violate every structure that can be imagined for them. Unlike science, however, the structures of bricolage can accommodate the infinity of unique acts which we know as human life. To the one who arranges this bric-à-brac every apparent contradiction presents the possibility of a better, more accurate structure. The structure he recognizes, the idea he finds, always comes as a surprise.

The one who does this work, the arranger, has no authority over the world in which he finds the materials of his structures; on the contrary, the people he meets determine his work, he is their fellow. In his relation to them he has no expectation of power; the work, which depends entirely upon what he finds, is his act of gratitude to the world.

1940

There were 20 million unemployed in the worst days of the Depression, one out of four, and in the beginning the government did not help them, there was no relief but charity. At Christmas and Thanksgiving, when hunger takes a harder line, flatbed trucks rolled through the streets of the West Side loaded with fresh turkeys, gifts to the people from the Republican Party, compliments of Al Capone.

The Democrats offered relief, too, but of a different kind, one that might be called semi-private. The system was an open secret in Chicago, but I did not learn the extent of it until many years later, when some of the surviving members of the West Side political machine—including my father and Colonel Jacob Arvey, who had all but invented Chicago Mayor Dick Daley, and Adlai Stevenson[4]—instructed me in something they called "politics."

---

[4] Daley worked in various capacities in Illinois county and state government and served for several terms as mayor of Chicago. His son now holds the same office. Adlai Stevenson was gover-

Arvey, who had turned his success as a ward boss into a position of power in the national party, directed me to my father to learn what happened at the precinct level, for there, according to Arvey, one did politics.

"But wasn't it also politics when you sent Daley to Springfield to run the state for Stevenson?"

"That was administration," Arvey said.

Arvey was polite, charming, the veteran of many such conversations; he asked if I remembered Al Horan and Charley Eagan and Jockey Myers, and I said I did, although I could not put a face to Horan's name. Finally, we talked about the pledge cards. He said he remembered the story, but vaguely, wondering if it was true. I said it was.

Unlike Arvey, my father had never been to the smoke-filled room where presidential candidates were nominated; his business was done over hot dogs at Val's on Crawford Avenue (now Pulaski) or during Saturday afternoons at Joe's Barbershop on Harrison. He worked the neighborhood, and in return the party provided a job. He picked up papers in the park, then he moved to the Sanitary District, and finally to a clerical job in Cook County.

Now and again, I went with my father to Joe's, but a kid was not welcome among the horseplayers and tough guys who mixed with the politicians there. Some kinds of business I did not understand—and my father would not explain—went on at the barbershop. In that respect Joe's typified the West Side, which had been jointly held by the Democrats and the gangs—Jews, Italians, and Poles—since Prohibition. I do not think my father was a criminal, but he followed the rules of conduct established by the gangsters. He told me many times of having witnessed the murder of a laundry truck driver in an alley on the edge of the Loop. The story served for a catechism in Chicago life: Before my father could leave the scene, two policemen appeared, drawn by the sound of gunshots. "I told them I didn't see anything," he said; "I didn't even know a guy was killed."

In the precinct a different set of rules applied, in the precinct he knew everyone, he saw everything; he did politics. When the widow who lived on the third floor of the big building on the corner was threatened with eviction because she could not pay the rent, my father intervened, for he was the man from the Machine. He used methods learned at Val's and when necessary a few tactics picked up at Joe's. First, he asked the landlord to

---

nor of Illinois and the Democratic Party's presidential candidate in 1952 and 1956. Arvey drew a sharp distinction between the urbane, charming Stevenson and "Hizzoner da Mayer," as Daley was known: "If I had a choice of dinner companions," he said, "it would be Stevenson. But if I had to choose someone to run the city of Chicago, it would be Daley."

give the widow a little more time, then he insisted, and if the landlord did not grant his request, my father said he would have to "make a call downtown. Then you'll have a visit from the fire inspector and the building inspector and the county assessor, and do I have to go on?"

On the South Side, in the black neighborhoods, there had been rent riots after hundreds of people were evicted. In my father's West Side precinct, there were no riots and no evictions. "It was politics," he said; "you have to understand politics."

Hunger required a different solution. It was my father's job to know when someone in the precinct had no food. In such cases he went to the alderman or to the ward committeeman's office and got either a food basket or the cash to buy what the family needed. That night, after the hungry family had turned out the lights and gone to bed, he left the basket at their door. No card or note accompanied the food, no gratitude was required, but in the same way that he knew who was hungry, the hungry knew who had left the basket at the door: No ward in the history of the United States voted more overwhelmingly Democratic than the 24th Ward of Chicago during those years. Arvey and my father told the same story about the Democratic majority: During one election they had to bribe three people to vote Republican to keep the totals from "looking bad."

Politics did not totally eclipse the daily life of our household, but we never missed a "fireside chat" and no talking was permitted while the thin, elegant voice of the president visited us. In 1940, when I was four years old, my father brought home an FDR poster large enough to fill a living-room window from top to bottom and side to side.

Most of the conversation in the house and at Val's was not about FDR, however; it centered on the enemy, the Republican candidate for governor, someone known as "Curly."

To ensure the size of the Democratic turnout in the ward, the party instructed its precinct workers to ask their constituents to sign cards pledging to vote the straight ticket. The day before the pledge drive, a lead pipe came loose somewhere in the bowels of the city, the Sanitary District, and fell on my father's head. Half blind, dizzy, and nauseated, he needed help to get home.

He and my mother fretted over the bundles of pledge cards. I do not recall just how I announced my intentions, but I offered to canvass his part of the precinct. There was no discussion. They gave me the cards and two pencils, and I began my rounds. For most of the day I climbed the stairs of the gray three-story back porch system of the West Side tenements. At every door I delivered the same story about my father, who I said was too sick to canvass the precinct, and not once did the person who answered my faint knocking—usually a woman wearing an apron, but now and then a man with the two-day beard and fallen suspenders of the unemployed—fail to pledge to vote the straight Democratic ticket. Many cookies were offered, for the residents of the precinct were penurious but not stingy, and all but those containing peanut butter were accepted. At most of my stops I was required to state my age: "Four, going on five."

The people I liked best were those who asked me why they should vote Democratic. Mrs. Burak's daughter-in-law asked that question and so did skinny Mrs. Packer. One woman responded to my answer by inviting me into her house to listen to a phonograph record. The deep tones and thrilling diction of the singer have remained with me all my life; it was Paul Robeson singing about America.

M Y   F A T H E R ' S   H E A L T H   R E T U R N E D; the party moved him to a clerical job; Roosevelt won a third term; "Curly" pulled some votes downstate, but was crushed in Cook County. Soon afterward my father was favored with part-time work on Saturdays as a pari-mutuel clerk at Sportsman's Park. The worst of times were over for us. My grandfather, who had suffered a stroke after losing a considerable fortune in 1929, moved to a small town and began another business. A year later, we left Chicago and the 24th Ward for West Texas on the Mexican border. We were pioneers, among the first people to move away from the block and out of the ward. In deference to the rules of the death of American cities, we never looked back.

1995 & 1940 & 1995

Although I returned to the city to attend the University of Chicago, I did not visit the West Side again for more than half a century. The building we lived in had been razed to make room for the Congress Street Expressway. My relatives had moved from Douglas Park and Lawndale Avenue. In the twenty-eight years following Roosevelt's third presidential victory, the racial makeup of the neighborhood had changed almost completely, so that when the Reverend Martin Luther King, Jr., was assassinated, the new residents of the 24th Ward expressed their sorrow by a terrible rage. The fires and looting destroyed much of the West Side of the city.

When it was over, after the Army packed up and moved out, every level of government abandoned the ward. The looted stores did not reopen. The movie theaters closed. No one rebuilt the burned-out buildings. Only after many years did the fast-food franchises move in. Meanwhile, the gangs grew powerful, as in the days of Capone. Drug dealers vied for control of the streets. One alderman was murdered in gangster fashion, shot in the head at close range while he sat in his office; another was indicted for his alleged criminal activities. The police, all but half a dozen of them white, roamed the streets of the ward like an army of occupation, beating, humiliating, and killing the young men of North Lawndale, provoking a resistance movement founded on hatred and devoted to crime. In the last years of the century, the people of the 24th Ward suffered, as they had during the Great Depression, but the manner of their suffering had changed.

In the first year of Roosevelt's third term a terrible gang fight took place on the corner of Springfield and Congress. My parents pulled me away from the narrow window on the west side of our living room before I could see much, but I remember the men with baseball bats leaping out of the backs of trucks to engage the phalanx standing out in the center of the street under the yellow cone of light cast by the overhead lamp. My father said that the men in the trucks had come out of "the poolrooms on Roosevelt Road."

Fifty-five years later, in K-Town, at the corner of Kostner and 14th, less than three-quarters of a mile from where I had lived, members of two gangs met in the street.[5] They, too, came from "the poolrooms on Roosevelt Road." The confrontation was abrupt, and final. A member of the New Breed stepped up out of the shadow of a basement, walked to the side of a car, took an automatic pistol from his pocket, and shot the Black Gangster Disciple who sat behind the steering wheel.

By the time Anthony Johnson, who lived around the corner, got to the car, the police had arrived and covered the body with a sheet, but Anthony, who is four years old, cannot shake the scene from his consciousness. It describes his neighborhood, the parameters of his world. "Saw a man got shot in the car over there," he said. "Blood was all over the sheet."

Anthony lives in the basement of his grandmother's house, in summer darkness, by the light of the television screen, in the killing heat of Chicago. He makes up stories, often talking about his father, whom he has never seen. He is a wiry creature, with a bony skull and intensely perfect fingers, teeth, eyes, ears, skin, speech. He races honeybees, examines ants, fears guns, and carries a set of handcuffs with him almost everywhere he goes. Anthony does not yet understand the color of his mother and grandmother. His grandfather Berry, long gone, was a G.I. who married a

---

[5] A section of North Lawndale in which the streets running north and south begin with the letter "K." K-Town is the most dangerous area of North Lawndale, which is considered the most dangerous area on the West Side.

German woman and brought her home to K-Town. They had a daughter, Antonia, who grew up with olive skin, straight black hair, and the diction of North Lawndale; among her men were the three daddys of Anthony; his sisters, Antonette and Ashley; and his brother, Anton.

Late in the afternoon, when the sky threatens rain and the big, slow-moving, fat ants of Chicago toddle along the steps of the high stoop, Anthony and his family come out into the waning daylight. They sit on the stoop, arranged according to the hierarchy of the family. His grandmother, Liz Berry, sits at the top, a big woman, with short blond and white hair, red-faced in the heat, red-faced in late middle age, heavy-boned, fleshy, speaking in German, Chicago, and Mississippi accents, as loud as beerhall laughter, as tough as a tank. She tells Anthony: "You make up stories about your daddy. You don't got no daddy."

He turns away to Ashley Elem, his seven-year-old sister, who has a tale to tell about her father: "I only see my daddy in pictures and I only see him two times in jail. He had shot somebody, and every time it time for him to come out of jail, he started fighting." She can sum up the family: "My brother has his own daddy. And I got my own daddy. And my big brother and sister got their own daddy. He's at home. They see him every day."

Killing comes quickly into Ashley's conversation. "I saw one get shot, Jojo. He had got it in the head. My cousin, he was walking to the store and he got shot by a bullet that came up and shoot him in the head."

The incongruity of murder in the mind of such a child disturbs the patterns of human understanding: The killing, the chubby girl with newly emerging front teeth; the gunshot to the head, the chubby girl exuding an almost angelic sweetness, as if petitioning for the love of God. She demonstrates her knowledge of the times tables and finds excuses to embrace whoever sits close by her on the steps of Liz Berry's house. In school, she has been put into an accelerated class, like her older brother, like her older sister, Antonette, the pianist who so loves Schubert and Mozart.

Ashley and Anthony and Antonette and Liz Berry sit in their respective places on the stoop. They glance over at their neighbor, but do not speak to her, not one of them speaks to her, not the children, not Liz Berry who has befriended almost everyone she has met since coming here from Germany.

Their neighbor uses drugs, they say, sells her body, sells her food stamps, sells everything for drugs. She will be murdered one day, and soon, for she has taken to selling at exorbitant prices to white men who come to North Lawndale in search of cocaine; she has become a middleman in a place where no middle is permitted.

Antonette carries a book and walks barefoot, almost dancing down the stairs of the stoop; only Antonette lives above the life of North Lawndale.

She has won an "I Have A Dream" scholarship for her performances of Schubert and Mozart. In autumn, after the end of the murderously hot summer, Antonette will leave the city and North Lawndale, at first for months, and then perhaps forever. She is the flower of the ghetto, the prettiest girl, the reader and the dreamer, the one to whom the gangsters defer, the girl who speaks as if she had been born in Nebraska, the one whose voice somehow speaks music among the caws and drawls of white and black Chicago. Murder is not on her mind; she imagines herself the woman of the forthcoming century.

Her mother Antonia's life belongs to the government; she survives by the system, but less well all the time. When the officials of Project Chance told her she had to go to school or get a job, Antonia countered that she had no one to care for her children. Then, as a permanent reminder of the force of their good intentions, the welfare department cut her benefits from $485 to $318 a month.

No one in this family, where everyone has a different last name, votes. Only Liz Berry has an interest in politics, for it has given her all the comfort of society she has known in her years as the white woman in North Lawndale. In the meetings, among the women of southern style, the genteel angry women, she finds acceptance; she brings great pans of food to picnics and parties and fends off the loneliness of her exile in America.

Politics is so far from the Berry house that Anthony says he has never heard of voting or elections. "I know the fire station," he says. And he almost knows the name of the president. "George Clinton," he says, retailing the lessons of the day-care center. "He stops people from shooting. Send you to the judge to make sure you don't go to prison.

"The President tell people to be quiet. He is not in a gang. He ask what you did bad in jail.

"The President is white, like my momma. He has a big suit. He have on a suit, black pants every day."

Ashley has never heard of voting or elections either. She believes, "The President is George Clinton. He lives in Washington and his job is to keep the place safe. I want everybody to be safe." And then the killings come into her mind again, and she looks for someone to hug, to tell of her successes: "I know my times tables and my take away."

No one walks in the streets. The sound of gunfire breaks into the waning afternoon. It must be far away, probably 16th Street, east of the Berry house, near the place where Gino's people deal. Police cars roar down the streets and into the alleys, screaming into the oncoming traffic, hunting the shooters in the empty lots and the long-dead alleys where the scrap dealers and the vendors once passed in their horsedrawn wagons filled with rags and old iron, shouting, "Rex-al-ion, rex-a-lion."

In half an hour the streets become quiet again. No one died, no one bled. The shooters missed their targets, the police missed the shooters. In the middle of the block, in the meeting room occupied by the supporters of the recently defeated alderman Jesse L. Miller, the women shrug at the sound of gunfire. Rosie L. (Aunt Rose) Brown, who lives on a street that bears her name, conducts the meeting. She wears ankle-length dresses and hats of straw and flowers, a most southern lady now nearing her tenth decade, graceful and ferocious, among the most well-spoken women of the ward in all its long history, and the bravest. A few years ago, she offered to lie down in the street to stop the trucks that hauled broken concrete into the ward and dumped it there, making a great, dusty mountain on Roosevelt Road.

In the meeting room, Aunt Rose and the other women have been planning the annual Pride Day Picnic in Douglas Park. It had been Jesse L. Miller's brightest moment when he was the alderman, his invention, cause for a parade through North Lawndale, reason to cook and eat and celebrate in the streets and in the park. Aunt Rose and Rita Ashford and the other women stood by him even though he had suffered the worst loss of any alderman in the city, but they hadn't been able to manage a parade. This year, Pride Day would be a picnic and only a picnic.

All of the former alderman's supporters did not attend the planning session. A woman who lived on the far side of the park, the most enormous woman, with a pre-adolescent son approaching her girth, did not often leave her apartment. A branch of my family had lived in that place: among them, in the farthest of many rooms, as if in a separate world, the yellow-haired, blue-eyed dowager of Königsberg, my grandmother.

In the rehabilitation of the building the huge old apartments had been chopped into small ones. The obese woman and her child now lived in one of these, sitting on salvaged furniture, sleeping on a legless bed, sickly, eating, bickering, as the former residents had been sickly, eating, bickering, but not immobilized. The obese woman and son did not know the history of their house. She suffered from asthma, a hopeless thyroid gland, high blood pressure, and heart disease. The welfare department demanded that she find work, but did not say where. The welfare department demanded that she become slim, healthy, productive, and sweet. The obese woman remembered when she had known men, worked in an office, sat on other furniture, slept in other beds. Her fingernails were painted, she smelled of perfume, she did not know what to do. The obese son cared only about computers, he thought all day and into the night about computers. He wished for computers in the way that some people wish for heaven or an end to pain.

AT THE CLOSE OF EVENING, in the red sky, black cloud Chicago summer, when the light confounds the eyes, a boy climbed up onto the roof of the condemned building across the street from the alderman's office on Roosevelt Road. Squatters lived in the stripped and rotted rooms below, awash in stolen water and the dim comforts of stolen light. Cars passed on the street, under the scrutiny of the boy on the roof. He looked to the west, to the cars coming out of the light. The boy carried a rifle, stolen, like the water and the light. The alderman's black Cadillac, a rented sedan, then trucks, more cars, then a city bus passed through the sights of the rifleman on the roof. He waited, half hidden by the crumbling yellow brick parapet, until the enemy car came out of the halo of the western light, and he fired, and fired again and again.

One shot passed through the thin metal roof of the car and into the driver's head. The car crashed into the side of the bus, careened off the thick metal, and spun crazily down the street, hitting car after car until all the energy was gone and the driver lay dead in his seat. The boy descended through the building like a shadow, leaving behind nothing but the ejected shell casings the automatic rifle had pumped out onto the roof and the street below.

Before the police arrived, the neighborhood knew it had been a mistake. The dead man was too old, too proper, a black man from Maywood, a suburban man tired from his labors, a black man with graying hair and a car exactly like the one the enemy gangster drove. "Who did it?" the police asked. "Did anyone see the shooting?"

"Give him up!" said Michael Chandler, the newly elected alderman.

Everyone knew, and no one spoke. Within a few hours, even strangers knew, but when the police asked, the response was as it has always been among the poor in Chicago: "I didn't see anything; I didn't even know a guy got shot."

Millie Thomas, who lived in the nest of apartments immediately to the west of the condemned building, had heard the shooting, but she did not get worried until she heard the crashings of the dead man's car. She went outside to see what had happened. The sight of the cars, the bus, the dead man still behind the wheel of his smashed car, and the police and the crowd gathering terrified her. She ran back up the stairs and into her apartment. Her daughter and one of her grandsons had followed her out onto the street to look at the results of the shooting. Her other grandchild, the crack baby, could not follow them. The crack, Millie believed, had caused brain damage and spinal deformations, making it impossible for the six-year-old girl to walk or speak or control her bowels. The child lived in a huge crib in the dining room and made her way around the apartment by holding on to furniture, siblings, and friends, grasping as best she could with her piscine limbs.

Another bad night, Millie said, hot and dangerous, bullets killing the ones the heat didn't kill. She drew the long pale chartreuse velveteen draperies over the windows that faced Roosevelt Road and turned on the air conditioner in the dining room next to the dead console TV that served for an ironing board. The electric bills ate up much of the food money in summer, but she did not want her children or her grandchildren to die of the heat, especially the damaged one, whose limbs flailed like fins or flippers in the heat.

The next morning after she had done the scolding and the bedmaking required to put her house in order, Millie prepared to go to the store. In the company of a friend, she got into her car and headed for the market. Far from Roosevelt and South Kolin, in alien turf, Millie noticed a red car reflected in the rearview mirror. When Millie turned onto another street, the red car followed her. She stepped on the gas, and turned again. The red car was still behind her. When she slowed, the red car slowed; when she drove faster, the red car was still behind her. It was an error, Millie thought, like the error on the rooftop. She drove faster, turning and turning through the West Side streets, and everywhere she turned and dodged, the red car stayed behind her, getting closer. They would kill her, she thought. She and her friend prayed and trembled, and Millie drove faster than she had ever driven before on the city streets. They had mistaken her car for another, she was sure, and now they were going to kill her. She and her friend, expecting to die, decided to go home. Millie drove straight to Roosevelt Road, and headed for her house. When she looked back again, the red car was gone. She parked her car and ran up the stairs and into the apartment. Although it was not yet noon, she pulled down the window shades and drew the heavy draperies closed. After that, she preferred the inner rooms of the house. She said she had lost confidence in the streets.

Millie and the generations in her house had lost confidence in almost everything: husbands, boyfriends, politics, government, justice, mercy, and people on the street. Keith, the youngest of her grandsons, nearly six, had no connection to the outside world, except as it was made of basketball games. He was a troubled boy, difficult in school, not violent but recalcitrant; he stayed home often, although he was not sickly. He did not know the name of the President of the United States or the mayor of Chicago or the alderman whose office faced the front windows of the Thomas apartment. Pride Day and even the picnic did not interest him; he helped to care for his sister, who flopped from place to place around the rooms of the apartment, he watched basketball and thought basketball, and hid.

Nothing describes the streets of North Lawndale so much as the need to hide, to live in the back of the apartment, away from the window, to maintain life as separate as possible from the rest of the world, to be safe. A deadly quiet hangs over the neighborhood, as if it were partly deserted, until a car alarm or the boom and shriek of a radio disturbs the calm. On the street across from Rosie L. Brown's house two women have set up a steel drum barbecue. The first odors of charcoal and pork and spice drift out on the heated air, an advertisement to the neighborhood. Aunt Rose complains that the street vendors have no license, but she does not really mind; they bring life to the empty street.

The ward I knew had never seemed so empty. The Depression drove people out of their houses into the camaraderie of the streets, with the noise of children everywhere and the men in their sleeveless undershirts stretched across fenders tinkering in the motors of old cars. The young women pushed carriages filled with summer babies; the hopscotch players stood on one foot like chubby cranes; the tiny crowds of gossipers blocked the sidewalks. All this passed before the rows of observers sitting on metal folding chairs, the old ones, the women with their stockings rolled and their legs crossed at the ankles, their swollen feet comforted in the ease of carpet slippers, and above them always a woman demanding the attention of an errant child, entertaining the street with family woes, a comic opera sung in the accent of an ancient, soon forgotten life.

After the freeway and the self-destruction and the abandonment of the ward, a distance grew up between the buildings as if to remark the distance between the people. Children played less easily, in nests of siblings, not of neighbors. Empty lots separated the houses. On some blocks the sidewalks had been shattered by time and left unrepaired, impossible places for handball, hit-the-penny, or hopscotch. Yet extraordinary children still live in North Lawndale. Such a child looked out the window of her grandmother's apartment on the first floor of a redbrick building half a block away from the place where Millie Thomas had drawn the draperies to close out the street:

In the summer heat of 1995 Katrina Ashford wore her hair in tight braids and dressed in tiny sunsuits with open midriffs. She was five years old, a child of great beauty and almost preternatural qualities. Katrina had certain rules she made for herself in the life of the three-generational household in which she lived with her grandparents, mother, two aunts, her brother, her sister, and two cousins: She will always be the last one to bathe in the morning, she will get more attention than any of the other children, including the two-week-old baby her aunt brings to visit every day, and no one will ever take advantage of her, no matter how much bigger or older they are. Katrina enforced these rules with the most fetching grin in the household, perhaps on the block, or even in all of K-Town. Unlike most grins, which come to a point at the extremities, Katrina's grin remains round at the corners, the depth the same from end to end, exposing perfect, china white teeth, which she keeps clenched during the most intense smile. The effect, enhanced more than a little by a tiny nose and round, uncommonly bright eyes, is of charismatic innocence.

No one in her family speaks about Katrina's charisma, however. Nor do they mention her innocence or even the power of her smile. Katrina's mother, Sharina, a great, dark-complected woman, with skinned-back hair and the dignity of a lioness, speaks seldom, and always modestly. A scar beneath her left eye serves to glorify her small, straight nose and high cheekbones. Clearly, the physical power of the mother has been invested in the child.

In time, however, the true source of the child's power becomes evident. Neither her grin nor the dark perfection of her features produces the magnetism. In time, the stories of her mind, her powers of observation emerge. When she and her mother were confronted by a gunman on the street outside their apartment, Sharina was so focused on the gun that she could not tell the police anything about the gunman. Not so Katrina, who described the man in astonishing detail, including the colors of his clothing and the fact that he parted his hair on the wrong side. When the man was found, her description proved to be accurate down to the smallest detail.

In a buffet-style, all-you-can-eat restaurant, a jumble of steamless steam tables—with ice cream, vegetables, and chicken at one table; Jell-O and turkey at the next—Katrina leads adults through the maze, pointing them toward this food or that, although it appears that she cannot quite see over the edge of the steam tables. The adults do not question her advice; they have learned to follow.

Did Katrina know politics, too? She answered my question about voting with her characteristic smile, but the word meant nothing to her; nor did she know the name of the president or the mayor or the alderman in the office around the corner.[6] Was that the difference between two quick chil-

---

[6] Katrina was hardly alone in this. After services in the Mt. Calvary M.B. Church in Sun River Terrace, a black community near Kankakee, Illinois, I spoke with the members of the first two grades of the Sunday School. The children, who were all five, six, and seven years old, listened attentively to the Reverend Alex T. Bond, Jr., as he instructed them in the importance of the question.

When it came my turn to speak to them, we laughed a little at this and that, then I asked if any of them knew the name of the President of the United States. One said, "George Bush"; none knew it was Bill Clinton. The word "politics" was foreign to them.

It was not until we spoke of voting that they began to respond. When I asked if any of them knew what voting meant, several hands went up.

dren in separate times? Was that the distance wit could not overcome? Or was it the empty street, the gunman with his hair parted on the wrong side? Her mother said, "Women started making more money than men; that was when the trouble started. The men around here, they're just women, not men."

1995

In the 24th Ward of Chicago, according to Alderman Michael Chandler, 33,000 people have registered to vote. Of these, he considers more than a third "dead weight," meaning a true constituency of no more than 20,000, but fewer than 9,000 actually voted in the last aldermanic election. Chandler managed something of a miracle in that election: he was the only candidate for alderman in the city who was elected without a runoff. But the vote has little meaning beyond the ability to dispense patronage. Given the likely undercount of the population in the ward and the low voter registration, Chandler was elected by less than 10 percent of the adult population of his ward. As an alderman, he has great power, but not legitimate power; 10 percent is not democracy.

The man he defeated, Jesse L. Miller, had no power at all. He won the job because the alderman before him was indicted while in office. Miller belonged to the mayor, to any part of the power structure that wanted him. During Miller's term the debris from the highway demolition project was piled up in the ward. It became a mountain of broken concrete, and the wind took the fine, gray, choking dust of the mountain and covered the streets and clogged the breathing passages of all the people who lived along Roosevelt Road. Even so, Miller had a loyal cadre, women who believed something illegal must have caused the humiliating defeat. He had Aunt Rose and Rita Ashford and all the women on his payroll. Some of them still say drugs were involved in the defeat; others claim Chandler made an agreement with the gangs to intimidate Miller's constituency, the

---

Did they think voting was a good idea?

Yes? No hands.

No? Many hands.

Why did they think voting was a bad idea?

A little girl raised her hand. "Because you could drown," she said. And the others nodded in agreement. The concept of voting was so foreign to them that they had fixed on the closest thing to a homonym: boating.

old people, keeping them away from the polling places. The deeper complaint argues that Chandler will give control of the ward to whites, because he was supported by Acorn (Association of Community Organizations for Reform Now) and the New Party, both of which are white-dominated left/liberal organizations.

Chandler has other ideas. Educated in Catholic schools in the ward, connected to a church-inspired movement to help poor residents beat the redlining practices of the Chicago banks, a former precinct captain, the son of a man who thought little of politicians and a woman who often served as a judge of elections, he is one of the two politically sophisticated people in the ward. Instead of drawing a picture of life in North Lawndale as hopeless, Chandler practices boosterism. He knows the results of talk about the *underclass*: no investment, no jobs, no loans, no hope.

His view of the possibilities of the ward coincides with the work of Joella Williams in the 3800 block of Flournoy. When Mrs. Williams and her late husband bought the building in which she still lives, no bank in Chicago would give a mortgage to a working poor black family in the 24th Ward. The only way they could buy a house was on a contract, paying rates "to the white man twice as much as a mortgage would cost."

Shortly after she and her husband bought the house, he was killed, leaving her with three children, a bad heart, and the contract. When she fell behind on the payments, the mortgage company tried to evict her, but Mrs. Williams held on. When she was at the bottom, she had a visit from a committee of the local Roman Catholic church. Through Presentation Church, the Contract Buyers League was organized. They began to go en masse to real estate offices, demanding fair terms; meanwhile, they put their monthly payments in escrow accounts instead of handing them over to the loan companies.

"They threw eggs on us, they put dogs on us, they called us all kind of names. Mrs. Morris even told me, get that so-and-so out of here; didn't nobody twist her arm to buy a house. When I finished with the picketing I think I still owed twenty-three thousand on my house, but I went to court, and when I finished with that I owed four thousand. I went to court three or four times, but the last time I went before Edith Sampson, a black judge." The judge set Mrs. Williams up with the First National Bank to handle the last part of her mortgage, even going so far as to make the appointment for her.

"It really change a person when you see so much around you that need to be done," Mrs. Williams said. "It give me love and make me want to reach out more and more in the community. You got to work with kids, they need somebody to work with them that's concerned and compassionate. And that's a great step in a neighborhood."

The block, however, does not yet please her. She plants flowers, talks to her neighbors, arranges block parties for the children, pulls the people into community. In the middle of a gang war, no one fears to walk down the 3800 block of Flournoy. Flowers bloom in front of every house. The empty lot near the corner is in the process of becoming a park.

The stoops belong to the gossips in the afternoon; the women crowd together in the shady places. While they talk, others work in the tiny gardens, stooped over petunias and four o'clocks and geraniums, calling out to their less energetic neighbors, keeping up conversation as they garden, using tiny shovels no bigger than soup spoons. Girls turn a long jump rope, chanting new versions of old rhymes, men in sleeveless undershirts lean into the engine compartments of aging automobiles, clanking tools and softly cursing the unfathomable computers in tiny boxes lurking in the shadows. Someone pushes a grocery cart borrowed from a distant supermarket, the indistinct gray or brown Chicago birds call to each other, butterflies inspect the flowers, Mrs. Williams sits on a summer chair, watching over the neighborhood, wrapped in the aching calm of age, and smiles as her tiny dog rolls over in the shade.

Alderman Chandler works the block, shaking hands, asking questions, making a note here and there about something he may be able to do now that these people have given him the power. This is his base, the heart of the organization he has begun to build; he found his campaign workers here, he expects his future here. In his early forties, a big man, at ease on Flournoy Street or taking smiles and handshakes over lunch at Edna's Restaurant, where much of the business of the West Side takes place, Chandler grew up on solid ground. "My dad picked up second jobs, dealt with furnaces, boilers, that kind of thing. He worked at Parkway Gardens out at Sixty-First and Indiana, took side jobs here in the Lawndale area. He kept a lot of different jobs; we never did without. My father was very wise. He had all these sayings, you know, like, 'If you convince a fool against his will, he will have the same opinion still.' He was just real witty."

Chandler has a theory about himself: "A whole lot has to do with your expectations. A lot has to do with being blessed. I'm a Christian. I don't know if it has anything to do with being the seventh child of a seventh child, but I am."

And he has a theory about the ward; he knows the history of the office he holds: "You remember Jake Arvey? You remember that whole time of organized politics? When I became a precinct captain, that's when I learned about politics, really learned what a Democratic organization was: precinct workers, election workers, election judges, going out into each precinct, giving the people information. There hasn't been that in this ward at least for the last four years.

"One thing I plan to do, really because of my upbringing in politics, is build a strong organization. It's the whole theory of politics that I'm trying to bring back. You got to have that. A basic political education has been nonexistent in this community, so we got to—some kind of way—bring all that back.

"When I'm out recruiting people, that's what I'm talking about, that you have a place in this organization, you have a place at the table, whether you're old, whether you're young. We talk about weekly community meetings, meetings for the businesspeople, meetings for the churches, to make you feel, whoever you are, however poor you are, you got a place in this organization. You don't have to make no money to be a part of this. We collectively collect our thoughts and ideas and your thought process will be part of something. It won't be blown away in the wind, so to say; we can take *that* downtown.

"I have to take that gamble, to educate the people politically, to bring them to the table, get them involved, just to try and make something happen, because for a long time there was nothing happening; it was like a dead zone."

But the new alderman could not take his theories to the Pride Day Picnic, for no one had invited him. Pride Day still belonged to Jesse L. Miller, who even at the dying end of a brief career remained convinced that politics and culture are synonymous. It was, as we shall see, an error. It did not occur to him that legitimate power, the circle of equals in which no member may be exploited by the others, could only come out of politics. He relied on culture, not realizing that it contained no defense against exploitation. Culture was his hope, his lonely bunker. He called for his people to gather in celebration of their African heritage, to mass in the park, but the crowd at the south end of Douglas Park that afternoon had not come to celebrate Pride Day; the tents, the music, the vast tables of food, all belonged to a high school class reunion.

Closer to the road, a little knot of people gathered about an hour after the picnic was scheduled to begin. They set up a small tent and filled a couple of plastic trash barrels with ice and off-brand soft drinks. Slowly, through the early afternoon, people arrived carrying food and folding chairs. Jesse L. Miller sat in the shade of the small tent, dressed in more or less African attire and carrying a colorful cane, as if he were a chieftain in nineteenth-century Africa and the cane was his investiture.

Women and children came to pay homage to him, men brought him ice-cold soft drinks to wash down his food as he sat in the shade of the tent, vanquished as no alderman had been vanquished in many years, yet still in the splendor of his error: He had confused culture and politics. Jesse L. Miller had imagined some pre-political world again in North Lawndale, a place of unison rather than dialogue, where the people did not govern themselves but were governed by ancient rules interpreted by an inspired leader.

It was a common confusion: Oscar Lewis posited a culture of poverty; Thomas Sowell thought culture persisted through immense social, economic, and political change. Like them, Alderman Miller could not separate the private from the public life of Americans. Like them, he could not imagine ancient Athens or Rome, except as pots and stones; it did not make sense to him to say that the polis was the Athenians, not Athens.

The former alderman had dreamed (assuming he was not cynical) of ancient Africa in Chicago; he had invited his constituents to put on a mask of culture to make up for the lack of a life of politics. What he wanted, quite simply, was to lift his people out of the shame of slavery by dressing them in the culture of the time before slavery. It was a noble if wrongheaded notion, and as such it merited the noble adjective "tragic." He had made his invitation at the end of many years of failed politics, and it had been accepted as an alternative. But for no more than a season; archeology had been no substitute for the dream of autonomy.

Even so, culture had not disappeared from his retinue. It remained the banner of his most loyal followers, those who showed their loyalty in a cultural way, through emulation of their leader. Like the former alderman, some of the women who came to the picnic also wore African clothing, but only a few of them knew how to make high-crowned hats out of the dress material. The others took the same material and tied it around their hair with a front knot. The effect was unfortunate: They looked more like house servants in the antebellum South than proud Afro-Americans. Aunt Rose disdained such attire. She appeared, as usual, in a nearly ankle-length dress and a round pale yellow straw hat with a perfectly rolled brim edged in dark blue fabric, a design not unlike a nineteenth-century British sailor's hat. She was a small figure among the women, slim, slow and careful in the way she walked on a recently healed ankle, but she commanded that corner of the park. It was as if the dowager of Königsberg had come to Douglas Park again; I recognized the bearing, the indulgence of her smile.

Of all the men who came to cook or eat or ice down soft drinks, only Marcel Walton, a nearly toothless twenty-five-year-old numerologist, Marxist, black nationalist, Egyptologist, Muslim, revolutionary, anti-Semitic welfare recipient, with a sheaf of Xerox copies of newspaper articles spilling out of the crook of his arm, wore a hint of Africa: a dirty black and white skullcap.

Without a microphone or even a platform to assist him, Jesse L. Miller had to come out from under the shade of the tent to speak to his followers. They gathered around him in a strange formation, grouped according to the dappling of the shade trees. "Happy Pride Day to you!" he said, greeting the group as he had greeted each individual, and they responded, in unison, "Happy Pride Day to you!"

He spoke a little about Pride Day and less about the election, shouting his words through the afternoon breeze, losing whole sentences to the rustling leaves above and the music coming from the class reunion at his back. The sun moved while he spoke, driving him this way and that, away from the crowd, to the shade again. He wiped his face, invited everyone to enjoy the ribs, his gift to them, and sat down.

Most of the people who sat in the shade, eating ribs and sausages, had come up the railroad line, straight north out of Mississippi. Selma Pettigrew, the former alderman's assistant, had grown up in North Lawndale, but her parents had come from Mississippi. Anne Lott, who worked in government until she retired, was born in Mississippi. They had fought for the vote in Mississippi; it had been precious there, in the small towns in the pine country and along the Delta. Frances Davis had Mississippi roots and so did Rita Blue. None of them knew for certain what had happened to politics in Lawndale, how the meaning was lost from the vote, except for Rita Blue, who remembered how voting became an insult in her house. She recalled the man from the Machine who came to their house at election time. "He gave my father two dollars for his vote," she said. "He knew my father was a proud man, and it shamed him, selling his vote, so the man from the Machine said it was to buy Kool-Aid for the kids. But it didn't fool my father."

Across the street from the picnic, on Albany Avenue, the 24th Ward's leading political figure had been buying up property, preparing for gentrification or social justice, whichever came first. Michael Scott was still young for a man so influential, with such a long history. He had been shot, badly wounded in his own house by an intruder, and he had recovered. He had worked for Mayor Harold Washington, rising quickly in his campaign organization and then in his administration, and when Mayor Washington died, the political man from the 24th Ward had recovered, working for Jane Byrne, and then for Mayor Richard Daley. He sat on the board of Mt. Sinai Hospital, and he was a Parks Commissioner and the head of one of the city's two cable television systems.

"Happy Pride Day to you!" the former alderman said to Scott, who shook his hand and smiled, but did not return the Pride Day greeting. Scott had been educated at Fordham University in New York, graduating in 1972, and he had been connected to politics and power ever since; he drew an unspoken distinction between culture and politics. Scott had learned the lesson of power a long time ago, and he kept it in the front of his mind, in detail, as if it were a catechism for politicians.

During his last year at Fordham, Scott applied for a job as a policeman in Chicago. He came home to take the written examination, which he passed easily. Then came the physical. Scott said the applicants were all lined up, standing in their underwear, when "a little white doctor came by and touched his stethoscope to each man's chest." He told Scott that he had a heart murmur, and rejected him.

Scott, who had been an athlete, was astonished. In the locker room, where he went to get dressed, Scott spoke to one of the other black men. He had also been turned down because of a heart murmur, and he was just getting out of the military, where he had been examined and found perfectly fit. What Scott had seen was the way in which the Chicago Police Department limited the number of black officers.

Not long afterward, Scott's father, an assistant precinct captain, appealed to the Democratic political organization. Once again, Michael Scott came home from Fordham. This time, "a bagman from the administration" picked him up and drove him downtown to take his physical. This time, the little doctor looked up Scott's record, took out the card, tore it up, and wrote out another one without mention of a heart murmur. The defeat of racism by political power was not lost on Scott.

He could have lived anywhere in Chicago, in any suburb, but Scott stayed in Lawndale. It seems like sentimentality in a hard-edged man, until Scott explains, "I'm the only man in North Lawndale who understands contracts. I'm needed here." And then he laughs, a wise politician's laugh, full of Talmudic irony, more Irish, more ancient, more practiced than black political laughter had ever been in Chicago. Scott harbors old angers, but he is beyond the reach of his tormentors now; like the 24th Ward politicians of old, his anger drives him more toward practicality than rage. He has grown accustomed to winning.

Michael Scott knows what happened to politics in North Lawndale: he attended the death of it. He could recall when the world of political power lost its legitimacy by abandoning its connection to the people. He remembered when all of them came to be treated like the vagrants and winos who had voted the ballots of the dead during the Depression. "No one in the ward understands politics," he said, "certainly not the children. The change came when people began selling their votes. The vote became a commodity; it lost all political significance."

Most of the people at the Pride Day Picnic did not know Michael Scott. They saw only a trim, light-skinned man in his early forties who wore no African clothing and ate no ribs. In less than half a century, the face of legitimate power had become unrecognizable on the West Side of Chicago.

II.

A Game of Poverty: Definitions

Them that's got shall have.
Them that's not shall lose.
— B I L L I E   H O L I D A Y

T HE N AVA H O GAVE LESSONS IN economics, but he did not
hold formal classes. Sometimes he taught in taverns, his voice cutting
through the murmur of English and the Diné of the Navaho, and sometimes he gave his lectures on the barely discernable cuts in the rock that
served as roads on the reservation. He taught strangers how to see the gray-
brown figures of sheep across the distance of the high desert. He recited the
affairs of the Hero Twins. After he went with the strangers to visit in
hogans and summerhouses, he took stock of them, his students, the journalists or bureaucrats or anthropologists who came to the Navaho to do
their fieldwork or satisfy their curiosity in those nearly forgotten times.
Being a good teacher, he could read the confusion in the eyes of his students.

He advised them not to think of Navahos as they thought of whites. "If
you do," he said, "you will think all the Diné are poor, and that is not so.
We do not value things as you do. Harmony, which we value most, has no
use in your world. Money, which you value highly, has little importance in
a traditional Navaho's life."

If the whites did not understand, if they pitied the Navahos for their dependence on sheep and fried bread and pinõn nuts and small amounts of corn and squash, he explained to them the nature of a life prescribed by ritual. He used an expression he had learned from the Pueblos, "Do not raise your head above the others." But the whites could not comprehend his meaning. He shook his head in dismay, for the whites were like his antagonists, the members of the Native American Church, peyote eaters who believed it was possible to tell a good man by the value of his pickup truck.

All the whites who came to the reservation showed great compassion and little understanding. As the Navaho grew older and the search for Harmony occupied more and more of his time, he stopped speaking to the whites.

1

The kind of poverty known in the United States belongs to the modern world. In Neolithic societies, which Rousseau said were "the youth of the world," wealth generally belonged to the entire social unit. Chieftains may have had more wives to enjoy or fewer onerous tasks to perform, but in these societies, governed by ritual, equality rather than inequality was the rule. Bad hunting or drought affected the entire social unit on a more or less equal basis.

As Neolithic societies grew larger and farming and husbandry replaced hunting and gathering, the concept of private property developed, and inequalities became more pronounced. Property extended beyond the limits of memory or common knowledge, and owners had to find some way to describe their cattle and mark the boundaries of their land. This new inequality led to the invention of writing and the emergence of the modern world some four or five thousand years ago in Mesopotamia.

With inequality came other changes in society. Ritual, which had brought people together, binding them by the memory of some common and therefore equalizing experience, broke down and was replaced by contests. The Olympic Games spring immediately to mind, but that formalization came late. By the time of the Trojan War, according to Homer, contests had become institutionalized.[1] Simple board games were played in

---

[1] The solid date in ancient Greece is 776 B.C., the first Olympic Games. No certain date can be given for Homer, although approximately 700 B.C. is now widely accepted. The funerary games described in the *Iliad* may have taken place as early as 1220 B.C. The question then arises whether

Egypt at least a thousand years earlier. The precise timing does not matter so much as the loss of equality inherent in a game: The players begin as equals and end as unequals; games establish differences between the players.

The making of poverty in a rich country like the United States has the same structure as a game, because the players begin as equals in nature and end up as unequals in society. Capitalism probably accounts for much of this, but games played according to slightly different rules exist in all modern societies.[2] Certainly the old Soviet Union was such a place. Thorstein Veblen, who preceded the structuralist Lévi-Strauss by half a century, claimed the rules of American economic society were formed on the playing fields of colleges. Veblen's words echo now in the use of the term "player" among the wealthiest Americans, for whom it describes a man or woman who wins on such a scale as to be able to determine who among the rest of society, including his or her peers, will also win. Or lose.

If the choice of words among the most powerful Americans is apt and the theories of the social scientists are correct—and it surely seems so on the face of it—the goal of modern society is not wealth but inequality.

Lewis H. Lapham, the editor and essayist, once wrote with uncharacteristic bluntness that for every person who eats caviar someone must eat dog food. Lapham, who chooses his words carefully, did not speak of beef or chicken at one end of the continuum and rice and beans at the other; he chose extremes, winners and losers, the game of the modern world, the American way.

Homer's reference to wrestling contests refers to his own time or to the date of the historical event in Troy. In either case, the evidence shows the game as a very early component of modern civilization.

Musical contests probably took place at Delphi as early as 1500 B.C., and Egyptian board games, like Hounds and Jackals, were played at least three hundred years earlier.

It was the athletic contest, however, that most clearly delineated the change in status of the players.

[2] See Lévi-Strauss, *The Savage Mind* (Chicago: University of Chicago Press, 1966). In this, as in much of his social thought, Lévi-Strauss brings to mind the arguments of Rousseau's *Discourse on the Origins of Inequality*.

The game of the modern world as it was played in ancient Greece is revealed in the concept of *pleonexia*, which the OED defines as "covetousness, avarice, greed." Gregory Vlastos, in his *Platonic Studies* (Princeton, NJ: Princeton University Press, 1981) has a more extensive explanation: ". . . gaining some advantage for oneself by grabbing what belongs to another—his property, his wife, his office, and the like—or by denying him what is (morally or legally) due him—fulfillment of promises made to him, repayment of monies owed to him, respect for his good name and reputation and so forth." (p. 116)

In a footnote, he adds: "I despair of an adequate English translation. Its occurrence in [Aristotle's *Nicomachean Ethics*] is rendered by 'self-advantage' in Shorey . . . Cornford's 'self-interest' is intolerably loose: only when self-interest is sought at the expense of others and in contravention of . . . [equity, fairness] would the Greeks speak of *pleonexia*." (ibid.)

According to the Organization for Economic Cooperation and Development (OECD),[3] Lapham knew what he was talking about: The United States had a greater income gap between rich and poor in the 1980s and early 1990s than any of fifteen other industrialized countries the group studied. In the richest country in the world, measured according to gross domestic product, the contest had produced the greatest inequality.

The game of modern civilization does not require that the loser suffer privation. It has no interest in desperate poverty; the OECD studied poverty at the 10th percentile, not the 99th. At the far end of the scale, the 99th or even the 98th percentile, there is no contest, for the winners must assume that those people were never equals, not even in nature; either they were born lacking normal mental, emotional, or physical abilities or they came into the world in impossible circumstances, without sufficient food or even the most meager educational opportunities. According to the rules of the game, the participants must begin as putative equals.[4]

No sense of fairness should be inferred from this, however; equals cannot logically mean exact equals. If that were the case, every contest would end in a draw. And the game of modern society never ends in a draw, even in the most rigorously socialistic societies.

Precisely what do I mean by "equal"? This is not the place to explore the question in depth, but it may be the place to admit the vagueness of the concept and the likelihood that its main use in contemporary America is to validate the game of winners and losers, feeding the pride of the winners

---

[3] Quoted in the *New York Times*, Oct. 27, 1995. The countries studied, from the lowest to the greatest income gap, were Finland, Sweden, Belgium, the Netherlands, Norway, West Germany, Luxembourg, Switzerland, New Zealand, France, Britain, Australia, Canada, Italy, Ireland, and the United States. Even in Finland, however, people at the 10th percentile earned a little more than half the median while those at the 90th percentile earned more than 1.5 times the median. The difference between the United States and Finland was significant: The rich earned 2.59 times as much as the poor in Finland and 5.9 times as much in the United States. It is important to keep in mind that the study dropped out the very richest and the very poorest 10 percent in making the comparisons.

[4] Immigrants who come to the United States for economic reasons have a different understanding of the game. Although they come with little or no money or real capital, they consider themselves winners compared to those they left behind. If this sense of relative wealth and the ability to make a new social contract in a new homeland enables them to move into the middle, where the illusion can be continued, they and their children prosper. If they do not move into the middle within a generation, their children understand themselves as relatively poor rather than relatively rich, and suffer the bitterness of losers in the American game.

and the shame of the losers by keeping the results from appearing to be pre-ordained.

Over the last quarter of a century the game has been played with great ferocity in America; the income gap between rich and poor grew faster during the Reagan, Bush, and Clinton administrations than it had during any period in recent history, reversing the trend of the preceding twenty years when the gap had narrowed.[5] And it is not absolute income that defines the game, but the gap between the 10th and the 90th or the 15th and the 85th percentiles. The middle represents only the inefficiency of the game, which was devised to sort the winners from the losers.[6]

In democratic societies, the middle group creates an illusion of efficiency by allying itself with the rich or the poor. When the middle allies itself with the rich, as in the recent past, members of the group declare themselves winners— perhaps not winners of the blue ribbon, but winners of the red or the gold. During the Depression, what remained of the middle allied itself with the poor, defining anything but the blue ribbon as a loss. This may account for the different definitions of poverty then and now.

Since unequals must be produced in order to have a game, the definition of "winners" and "losers" becomes of paramount importance. As in war, the power to define the terms belongs to the winners. The exact point at which

---

[5] *New York Times*, June 20, 1996, reporting Census Bureau data. Changes in the methods of gathering and analyzing income data may account for some of the rate of increase during the Clinton administration, but the trend remained constant. In one analysis, household income for the highest quintile increased from $73,754 to $105,945 on an inflation-adjusted basis between 1968 and 1994. During the same period, income for the lowest quintile increased from $7,202 to $7,762.

The next day, figures compiled by the University of Michigan in a longitudinal study of 7,000 families were reported. The figures, all adjusted to 1996 dollars, follow:

| | 1984 | | 1994 | |
	Avg. Net Worth	Share of Wealth	Avg. Net Worth	Share of Wealth
Poorest 20%	$-3,282	-0.44%	-7,075	-0.64%
Poorest 10%	-7,777	-0.52	-15,467	-0.70
Next Poorest 20%	12,151	1.64	17,503	1.58
Middle 20%	47,760	6.44	61,777	6.56
Next Richest 20%	114,881	15.49	141,778	12.77
Richest 20%	570,050	76.84	871,463	78.47
Richest 10%	918,633	61.32	1,482,698	66.76

[6] In *The Savage Mind*, Lévi-Strauss equates winners and losers in the game with the killers and the killed in ancient situations. Veblen's use of the playing field seems more correct, especially in the industrialized world where the suffering of the losers has been mitigated to some extent by the welfare state.

a person passes from the middle to winning is of little interest except to those who live near the dividing line, which is always blurred by illusion.

More serious thought has been given to defining poverty. On the one hand, naming the losers has always been one of the comforts, if not the pleasures of the rich, and on the other it measures the extent of the social, political, moral, and economic failing of the modern world. How one defines poverty depends on one's view of the game. There are at least five different ways to understand the origins of inequality in America:

1. If the definer pretends that a game among equals has taken place, he or she may decide that the great variable in the game is moral; that is, the losers are not the moral equals of the winners. The game was played that way long before the birth of John Calvin, and it will continue to be played that way after the demise of Bill Clinton, Newt Gingrich, and William Bennett, but Calvin was the Hoyle of the game, and Clinton, Gingrich, Banfield, Bennett, Auletta, Robertson, et al. have fought hard to maintain the canon.

Played by such rules, the game leads to the idea of an *underclass* or a *culture of poverty*.

2. If the definer pretends that a game of equals produces equal results, he must argue that the losers were unequal in nature. This argument in defense of the game has a long and distasteful history: slavery of various forms, Gobineau, the Nazi philosophers, and in more recent times the work of Charles Murray and William Shockley.

3. The game itself is flawed. But to prove that view, the outcome must be shown to be flawed; the losers will have to be equal to or greater than the winners in every way but the outcome of the game. Socialism, communism, and what is now commonly known as liberalism result from this view. Conservators of capitalism, like Franklin Delano Roosevelt and Lyndon Baines Johnson, subscribe to this view when they believe it is necessary.

4. In the late 1950s and 1960s a syncretic view was widely held by the liberal wing of the Democratic Party. It resulted in the War on Poverty, which was based on the idea that both the poor and the game were flawed, but emphasized the need to improve the former.

5. The belief that the winners are flawed belongs largely to saints, saviours, and a few monks. Communists, socialists, and even liberal Democrats are often accused of holding this view, but one has only to look at the comforts enjoyed by the winners among them to understand the frivolity of the accusation.

Every view depends in large measure upon the definition of poverty and each view has a different definition. Poverty was not codified until the beginning of the twentieth century, when Charles Booth completed his massive study of the poor in London. He concluded that a third of the people were living in poverty; that is, having income below the level needed for bare subsistence. An official poverty level was not set in the United States until the 1960s, when Mollie Orshansky, an employee of the Social Security Administration, put the poverty level at three times the cost of a subsistence diet. She based her formula on a Department of Agriculture study showing that the average family spent a third of its income on food.

Orshansky claimed that her estimate of poverty for the Social Security Administration should never have been used for that purpose, according to Michael Katz in *The Undeserving Poor*. Orshansky said that the number of poor people in 1975 should have been 36 or 37 million, about 10 million more than the commonly used figure. Using the same ratio, the number of poor people in 1992, officially estimated at 38 million, would have been closer to 53 million.

Estimates by established academics and demographers of the number of people living in poverty in the mid-1990s range from 14.5 percent to 18 or 19 percent. As the effects of the 1996 Welfare Reform Bill begin to push large numbers of children and old people into poverty, the number will undoubtedly increase. At the upper end of the scale, some radical groups claim that one third of the entire population lives in poverty, the same proportion that Booth found in London at the turn of the last century. If that estimate seems outrageous, it should be compared with the figures for New York City teased out of Census Bureau reports by the Community Service Society of New York: They found that 27 percent of the people in the city lived below the federal poverty level in 1993.[7]

---

[7] *New York Times*, July 14, 1995. Since the people not counted by the census mainly comprise the very poor, undocumented persons, the homeless, and the physically and mentally disabled, it is probably safe to assume a slightly higher true percentage, bringing the prevalence of poverty in contemporary New York City even closer to London at the end of the nineteenth century.

Projections of the number of people who will be forced into poverty by the Welfare Reform Act of 1996 may be overstated, especially for cities like New York, where local and state governments may attempt to ameliorate the effects of the act. However, there can be no doubt that the number of poor will increase, perhaps surpassing the percentage of poor who lived in London a century earlier.

But the idea of what anybody means by "poor" is still not clear. Did Booth and Orshansky choose to describe absolute or relative poverty? Who determined the subsistence level in London at the end of the nineteenth century or in the United States in the middle of the next century?

If poverty were merely a matter of subsistence, objective means could be used to define it: indoor temperatures in winter, the presence of insects or rodents, the absence of hot and cold running water, and so on, for housing. Minimal proper nutrition can be measured, as can the availability and quality of health care. Clothing, especially for children, presents a problem, because some children outgrow clothes faster than others and some climates require more expensive winter clothing. But food, shelter, and clothing may not be all the components worth considering. We know exactly what a cow needs, but a six-year-old girl and her twenty-two-year-old mother have sensibilities considerably more complex than those of a cow.

The great complication in arriving at an accurate definition of poverty grows out of the uses of the definition, some of which are counterintuitive. For example, to reduce the size of the middle, making the game more efficient, those in power may lower the official poverty level, knowing that reductions in benefits will follow and the number of losers will be increased. Or by raising questions about values, those in power appear to be trying to improve the lives of the poor, but stigmatizing behavior such as out-of-wedlock births merely improves the efficiency of the game by making all single mothers into losers.

Perhaps the best way to define poverty is to listen to people who consider themselves poor.[8] I attempted to do that in 1994 and 1995, working with a group of women from the Young Mothers Program in the South Bronx who agreed to help me with this book.[9] Our first task was to define poverty.

---

[8] For the purposes of this book, the poor are those people who have declared themselves poor, which may be done in various ways. The most common is to associate themselves in some fashion with an institution that attends the poor: church programs, the state welfare department, Medicaid or unpaid emergency-room services, low-income housing, low-income community action programs, youth service organizations, settlement houses, legal services for the poor, homeless shelters, battered women's shelters, public or private food distribution organizations, full-time programs for recovering addicts, jails and prisons, minimum-wage or near minimum-wage jobs.

Some people who declare themselves poor by association prefer to say they are not poor, and that is understandable, for poverty is not considered a virtue in America. Others who have no association with any organization or institution connected to the poor may simply say, "I'm poor."

[9] Most of the women appear in the Acknowledgments, but they asked me not to use their names in connection with their personal experiences. To honor their request, I have used only an initial for each woman. All the women had children and were recovering addicts. Most of them had been homeless at one time, more than a few had worked as prostitutes, and perhaps half of the women in the Bronx who helped me with this book had spent time in prison.

We sat in a circle of folding chairs, and we were all proper people, serious about the work. Sometimes the women were tired, for we met at the end of the day and they had frequently endured the unrelieved stress of a confrontation session. Now and then children came into the room, and there was rarely a time when someone in the group did not have an appointment to keep elsewhere, for the poor, as they said, do not choose their lives. In that way, the conversations we held were extraordinary, for there was nothing mandatory about them.

Over time, the aspects of poverty, as described by the women, fell into categories: *privation* and *oppression*, which produced different feelings in them.

Privation came first, told by H, a big woman, whose hair was dyed in a curious way, tiny blond braids on a cap of black. She had lost many teeth, so that her speech was both slurred and sibilant, and because her back was injured, she could not move with grace. Of all the women in the group, H wore the weariest clothes, the most ill-fitting clothes. In summer, her feet were tucked into ragged shoes, like bedroom slippers, but she gave the appearance of being barefoot.

"Poor is a little girl who worked in the fields all day," she said, remembering Barbados, where she was born. Her words came in the form of a litany, loud at first, diminishing, and finally lost in tears.

"Poor is all day in the dirt.

"Poor is too tired to eat.

"Poor is walking barefoot on a tar road in the hot sun.

"Poor is a house with no electricity.

"Poor is no water in the house.

"Poor is going outside to use the toilet.

"Poor is not having a mother to take care of you.

"Poor is being carried around in a fish basket when you're a baby.

"Poor is a little girl making rice for her grandma, that little, hard rice we have in Barbados, cooking the rice, but not cooking it right. Grandma says the rice is good, but you know it's hard. I didn't put enough water in the pot. The rice was hard."

Sobbing took her breath, and H could not speak any more. The little woman who sat beside her, dark and thin, wizened before she was thirty,

---

If the language they used in discussing poverty seems overly refined, it is not because I sanitized it. Rather, they understood themselves as my colleagues, and spoke and worked appropriately. Two of the women went on to work with me in another project, where they have continued to speak and act politely, and with genuine charm. The one woman in the group who used street language was the best educated, having finished two years at Medgar Evers College. She stayed with the project only briefly.

rubbed her back and soothed her, cooed to her. It was a long time before anyone else spoke.

From the other side of the room, M, a fat-faced, puffy, pallid woman of forty who had lost all her five children to the Child Welfare Agency, spoke. She poured out the words, running the sentences together in a low, thickened voice made coarser by the hard vowels and perverse final consonants of Puerto Rican Spanish violated by the New York streets. "I was so poor when I was growing up that all my teeth rotted by the time I was five years old, because I never had a toothbrush. My ass got all red and bleeding, because I didn't have no toilet paper to wipe myself. At night, in bed, I couldn't lay still, I couldn't sleep, because I had nothing to eat for five days. I used drugs, I sold myself, I did anything just to stay alive."

She, too, silenced the room. Like H, she brought tears to the other women's eyes, but no one touched M, no one soothed her. She sat alone, she made a distance between herself and the rest.

Other women spoke of hunger and crowding, but hunger was the common thread. It sorrowed them, it debilitated them, it left them weeping. Hunger meant tragedy, a fate that could not be overcome no matter how they tried; hunger meant that nothing more could be found, it implied an end to dreaming. They resigned themselves to hunger, in the way that the dying no longer feel their pain.

They reserved their anger for the other poverty: They raged against oppression, which they associated with the game. "It makes me feel low-class," one woman said, as if to describe the rules of the game, "not upper-class, not middle-class, low-class; I can't have self-esteem when I'm low-class."

"Poor is homelessness," P said. She looked around the room, as if to gather the agreement of the others, who set their jaws and looked ahead and nodded, for most had known the streets and the shelters; they could recall a night, a week, a season in the park. Nothing spoke so clearly of the relative world as homelessness; the word itself existed only to remark the existence of something better.

When the silence had made its point, she closed out the others for a moment, and spoke directly to me. She began in anger: "I got a nine-month-old-baby, a nine-month-old-daughter and a twelve-year-old son. I'm fuckin homeless, living in a shelter. All of these things. It's pressure and it's stressful. It's stressful. I'm actually using you, Earl, I'm actually using you to vent, because you know I don't get a chance to say, 'I'm sick of being poor. I'm sick of being a single parent, I'm sick of being an addict.' So, I'm using you, Earl. Help me get my daughter into day care which is safe, get me back into school. I don't want to be on welfare. Can you tell them that I don't want to be on welfare? My life's goal is not to be a welfare bum bitch all my life."

A soldier's anger came into the room, and remained, for relative poverty isolates the rich from the poor, the poor from each other. In the game, everyone plays against everyone else. There was no more touching.

They turned to education; everyone agreed that lack of education was a form of poverty, but it produced no discussion, no passion, for education of the kind the winners know was too far away, which made it cool and beautiful but unreachable.

No matter who tried to define poverty, the welfare department turned up as an aspect of being poor.

"Food and shelter," A said, "because I have a education. I finished high school. I know how to read and I know how to write. I can get a job, but if I don't have food and shelter, even if I have a education, I'm not gonna have what I need. I define poor as being on welfare, because without welfare my rent wouldn't be paid. If I wasn't getting no welfare or anything like that, I wouldn't have no shelter and those food stamps wouldn't be comin to me and I wouldn't be able to eat. That is poor, not knowin where your next meal is gonna come from, havin to depend on society or welfare. For me that's poor."

C carried the discussion of the welfare system on to the issue that wounded most deeply. She spoke, as always, in a blunt, irrefutable way, using words as if they were bludgeons made of mixed languages and Brooklyn streets. She was the one who found the heart of things, the bitter one, the one who had been to prison, who had touched the bottom the others feared. They studied her, as if to see how long she could avoid destruction.

"Right now, I'm living in a place that ain't mine," she said. "Even though I get welfare, it's not enough. What if they cut you off?"

The rest of the day followed her. The others could not let go of the idea of the absurd in their lives: almost everything intended for them was used against them. "What if they cut you off? What if the computer makes a mistake?"[10]

No woman could escape the question of the differential, the relativity described with such eloquence by the counter and the desk in the welfare office.

M said, "They act like they're givin us their paychecks. They look down at you. It's like my worker, she says, 'Well, who knows what you've been doin with that money?' So I says, 'Let me tell you somethin, sweetheart, I worked, I pay taxes just like you're doin right now. You're no better than me. And it don't give you the right to talk to me any way you can. I can

---

[10]Shortly before Thanksgiving Day, 1996, the New York City Human Resources Administration made such an error, mistakenly closing 6,368 cases, immediately depriving them of all benefits. *New York Times*, Nov. 27, 1996.

change workers. I can report you. And if that person doesn't want to do right, I'll report that person.'"

Her voice had risen to a shout by the end, color had come into her pallid cheeks. And then she fell from anger to defeat: "In reality, they treat you like you're a piece of shit," she said, "like you're just a roach, a cockroach. You don't mean shit. They don't care about you."

C rescued her: "For me, I give an example. I'm on my own case budget, that's what it's called. I had my own apartment. They were only give me two fifteen. Where in the hell would I find a apartment for two fifteen unless it's tore up? It would have to be all broken down. I feel that's unfair, even though the welfare is always doin it. By starting us off and paying two fifteen a month, that'll bring down our self-esteem even more. I have to move all the way, way into the ghetto, maybe where it starts." Everyone laughed, even M.

P leaned into the conversation again. Although she was not as large as some of the other women, she gave the impression of weight, like a Henry Moore statue, smooth and dense, the immovable occupier of a certain place in the world. She said, "I know it's big business who's on his [the caseworker's] back, saying we're tired of picking up the slack, we're tired of paying for women laying down having baby after baby for the same old chump. Goin down to these welfare systems and sayin, 'No, I don't know who my baby's father is. No, I don't know this. No, I don't know that.' Because the welfare system is set up like that. You can't go in there and say, 'Yeah, John Brown. I got four kids with John Brown, and me and him is layin up in this Section Eight apartment.' It don't work like that. John Brown has to disappear from the scene, like four years ago. You ain't never seen the niggah, nothing but it ain't bullshit. I need your help, this is how desperate I am. We all know and understand that all that shit is lies. It's lies, but this is what you're forced to do. That's what I mean when I said it's degrading. It does not promote a sense of family. I can't go down to a social worker and say, 'My man did not graduate from high school, therefore doesn't have what it takes to get certain job skills, therefore does not have a job. I love him. He's the father of my children. I would like to keep our family together. Can you please help us?' Look, you can't go in there with that. That nigger got to be twenty miles north of West Motherfuckerland and nobody can't find him. And you have to be totally desperate as to be deprived and degraded."

A said, "I think that poorness have to do with the generations. It start from whoever was way back."

"I say poor is the spirit," D said. "If you feel poor in the spirit you ain't gon do nothin."

The list grew during the conversations: The compassionate union of H's description of desperate poverty never returned; absurdity stayed in the air, always the enemy, attacked by C and others, too. P changed the understanding of absurdity and the thrust of the conversation from then on, when she said, "People don't just wake up with this idea: Oh, I wanna be poor or I wanna get food stamps or I wanna live in the ghetto. Nobody grows up with this idea that you just wanna stay at this one level. You know, there are certain things that happen that set up the dynamics so you stay right there, in the ghetto."

Coercion became the theme. The women would not be dissuaded from it, not by me or by each other. They spoke of it as control, as force. They did not ever speak of it as a restriction of freedom or a lack of freedom; such notions did not interest them. They felt force; they had no experience with freedom.

Over time, the aspects of poverty, as the women of the Young Mothers Program described it, fell into two categories. Their definition was not complete, because they were a homogeneous group with a common set of problems and because they had tried for most of their lives to avoid the pain of thinking about their condition. During our conversations they did not so much define poverty as name some aspects of it, unconsciously following the Marxist notion of quantity becoming quality.

There is some overlapping in the categories they made, for poverty is not as clear as counting:

PRIVATION

1. Lack of money for current needs
2. Lack of capital, both real and intellectual
3. Inadequate housing
4. Insufficient food and fresh water
5. Inadequate clothing
6. Unhealthful living conditions, including lack of heat, hot water, and sanitation
7. No access to medical care
8. Lack of education
9. Unsafe conditions
10. Lack of communication
11. Unsatisfactory social life
12. Dearth of the objects of culture

OPPRESSION

1. Enduring defeat, lifelong and passed on to the next generation
2. Excluded from duties and rewards of citizenship

3. Subject to coercion
4. Without recourse
5. Despised (not hated) by the powerful
6. Death not mourned by the community
7. Limited choice of food, clothing, housing, employment, place of residence and recreation
8. Reduced to pleasures of the body
9. Responses limited to passivity or violence
10. Prevented from enjoying marriage and family life
11. Excluded from education, schooling limited to training
12. Fungible, in economic terms more like goods than persons

If poverty were one thing, indivisible, with many things growing out of it, a definition both simple and accurate would be possible. But poverty in the modern world is a complex quality, made of physical deficiencies and many kinds of moral defeat. The women in the South Bronx were correct, and so was Marx: quantity becomes quality. A poverty line, based entirely on income, cannot adequately sort the poor from those who have found a middle life.

Only a very few who live below the line Mollie Orshansky devised belong to the middle, but some do—the small farmer who rises above the subsistence level through a mix of labor and land, or those who live in the buoyant matrix of a huge family. For the most part, the aggregation of defeats and deficiencies reaches far above the official poverty line into what appears to someone at a distance as safety.

A true definition would have to include many levels of subsistence: education as well as nutrition, hope as well as housing. If one were to make an honest effort to relieve poverty, the aggregation would have to be broken down into its component parts so that each could be dealt with as needed in order to lift a person or a family into the middle, denying the game its efficiency.

Obviously, some moral defeats could not be attended to by means of economics, but they could be ameliorated, perhaps enough to affect the other aspects of the aggregation, eventually changing enough of them to cause the quantity to describe a different quality.[11]

---

[11] The definition of poverty is regularly debated in the legislatures and academic works. Dale Jorgensen of Harvard and Daniel Slesnick of the University of Texas have argued that the number of people living in poverty has decreased greatly, if one considers that families of four headed by single mothers need far less to live on than two-parent families of four. Christopher Jencks of Northwestern answers that single mothers don't live on air. Peter Passell reported on this in the *New York Times* on Dec. 8, 1994, asking what Newt Gingrich would make of

No one but the poor themselves has enough information to decide who should be counted among the poor. Consider the Navaho; he asked only that his people, imprisoned on a reservation, living at the whim of the Bureau of Indian Affairs, be permitted this rag, this last shred of self-determination, to decide the meaning of poverty for themselves.

In his petition for the Diné, he limned the problem for all people who live in the house of defeat: When anyone other than the poor defines poverty, the definition itself becomes a force against them, whether it pronounces them poor when they are not, as the Navaho explained, or it declares the truly poor too rich to need help or too immoral to deserve it.

The two groups of people who lived in the 24th Ward of Chicago in 1940 and 1995 were analogues in many respects, but not in the one that transforms all the others. The blacks were pitted against the browns, the Jews were antagonists of the Poles; thugs came from poolrooms, candy stores, and barbershops on Roosevelt Road then, and they still do; racial intolerance wounds more deeply, but religious and ethnic intolerance also hurt; gangsters killed each other then, and their symbolic progeny kill each other now; hardly anyone had long, deep roots in the neighborhood then or now. The critical difference between the 24th Ward today and the ward where my father practiced politics is the kind of poverty suffered there.

During the Depression, the people of the ward thought they lived in absolute poverty. Franklin Delano Roosevelt told them it was the nation's problem, the Communist Party told them it was the system's problem, and Paul Robeson sang to them that it was everyone's problem. When all the people think all the other people are poor, a sadness comes into their lives; it underlies their every action, and in quiet times, as in the moments when sleep refuses to come or rain has ruined the day, the sadness rises to engulf consciousness. But in other times, on other days, at softball games, in barbershops, when baby carriages pass in the street, or children laugh, the sadness can be put away. Absolute poverty functions like a ritual, conjoining the people in their sadness and even when their sadness has temporarily been put away. In the throes of what they understood as absolute poverty, the people did politics.

No one in the 24th Ward accepts the existence of absolute poverty now; even the hungry and the squatters cannot bring themselves to believe they

---

the Jorgensen-Slesnick argument.

If poverty becomes defined as an aggregation of defeats and deficiencies, as it should, the administration of grants and other programs to bring about greater equity will fall to the bureaucrats, as it has for more than half a century. But it should not be the administrators who define poverty or the many-pronged attack necessary to ameliorate it; that work can only be done by the poor.

are absolutely poor. Like the women in the South Bronx, they think absolute poverty exists only in foreign countries. No matter where they look, or how they think, or to whom they pray, the residents see only less or more: Wealth is overflowing, spilling out of the fat pockets of everyone else, and in the ward people scramble to pay the rent or the doctor's bill and still keep food on the table.

No politics can be done in the ward now; it is every man for himself.[12] Economics rules. The world is as relative as race, and relative poverty is unendurable, an insult to the modicum of self-regard required to participate in the human community. At the end of the game, when the middle has chosen to ally itself with the winners, thereby defining everyone else as poor, envy comes to the ward. And out of envy: isolation, hatred, and rage.

■———————■

A VAST LIBRARY OF INFORMATION about poverty has accumulated since Charles Booth completed his seventeenth volume at the beginning of the twentieth century. Herbert Gans, Andrew Hacker, Christopher Jencks, Michael B. Katz, William Julius Wilson, and many others have studied and interpreted the data. Mary Jo Bane, David T. Ellwood, Mark Robert Rank, and others have made important contributions to the debate about welfare policy. In all, these writers have produced an indispensable library addressing the question of poverty. The devotion of many of these people to the cause of decent treatment for the poor was exemplified in the decision of Ms. Bane and Peter Edelman of Health Education and Welfare to resign their posts in the Clinton administration after the president signed the Welfare Reform Bill in 1996.

In large part due to their work, many of the economic and educational aspects of poverty have become common knowledge, although always subject to interpretation. I have gathered some of the statistics and ideas in Appendix A for the reader who wishes to review them.

---

[12] Alderman Chandler is attempting to change the situation, but he would be the first to admit that he has a long way to go.

III.

■———————■

Born for Each Other

He who considers things in
their first growth and origin,
whether a state or anything
else, will obtain the clearest
view of them.
— A R I S T O T L E ,
Politics, Bk. I

1

THERE IS A TENNIS COURT in the South Bronx. On some days, after school has let out, a social worker from the Neighborhood Youth and Family Services program takes a group of children to the tennis court. Since there are only two tennis rackets and one tennis court to be shared among the children, they must take turns. The worker begins by giving the rackets to two of the children and asking the others to line up to await their chance to play.

The children form a line, but as soon as the worker tells the players on the court that their time is up, the rest of the children break out of the line and crowd around the players, asking, reaching, demanding, cajoling, desperately wanting to be next to use the rackets.

Each time the rackets are exchanged, the line breaks down, requiring the teacher to sort out the crowd, award the rackets, and restore the line before play can begin again. Much of the afternoon is taken up with the complexities of passing on the rackets to the proper players.

A few miles to the north, at a suburban school, the children are also taken to a tennis court. They, too, must form a line and take their turn at hitting the ball up and back across the net. At the suburban school the children also vie for position, but once they arrange themselves, they maintain their places in line: the rackets are exchanged quickly, and play on the courts is almost continuous.

The children at the suburban school know the rules of political life at their most basic level. They have found the middle road between liberty and order. At the beginning, they are at liberty to find their places; but once they find them, they maintain order. Play proceeds according to the rules defined by the group when forming the line, and it goes along efficiently.

In the South Bronx the group does not govern itself; it chooses liberty over the middle road. In the chaos of liberty, force dominates; the bigger, stronger, or more aggressive students get the rackets every time. The social worker must then intervene to establish order in the group.

The two tennis courts do not serve as perfect analogues of states, but they illustrate an important difference between rich and poor in the United States: The poor children are not political. They cannot find the middle ground between order and liberty. Instead, they attempt to exert what little force they can muster. Much of the time that could be devoted to learning to play tennis is lost in the chaos of force. The poor children do not reflect on their situation at the tennis court, so they cannot recognize the folly of their apolitical behavior. They react, following the rules of force rather than the rules of politics, because force is what they know; it is the world that the world teaches to the poor.

The poor children, who may be equal to or even greater than the rich in natural ability, fall behind in the learning of tennis. In the game of modern society they are beginning to lose.

Many explanations have been offered for the losing behavior of the poor, especially the children. Psychological, social, economic, and racial problems all intervene to wound the lives of the poor. But the rich may also be wounded by psychological problems, as well as social and racial problems. Even economic problems may wound the rich, as in the precipitous fall from affluence following a bad investment or the inability to manage one's life in the wake of social, psychological, or racial problems. All of these may be, as Aristotle said, subsumed under the master art, the one that governs all the others: politics. He did not, however, mean politics as it is discussed in the daily newspaper or the corner tavern.

Politics, the lack in the lives of the poor, has come to be understood in America as electoral politics or shrewd manipulation. Those definitions betoken a healthy mistrust of power, but they do not explain the meaning of politics, the *vita activa* or *bíos politikos* of ancient times.[1] To understand the difference between the behavior of the rich and poor children on their respective tennis courts requires that we heed the ancient advice to consider things in their first growth or origin to gain a clear view.[2]

---

[1] Language is too important to be tossed around from century to century, continent to continent. Heidegger was correct when he said, "Language is the house of being," putting the burden of consciousness upon the words we use. He insisted that one could understand the Greeks only in the original. It was a good argument, but Heidegger's critics are forever pointing out the errors in his Greek.

There are other models: Petrarch read the Greeks in Latin, although he was not satisfied with the translations. I have relied entirely on standard English translations by sensible and talented men and women (Cornford, Fagles, Fitzgerald, the Jowett I first read as a student, the new Sterling and Scott *Republic*, etc.). When important disagreement among translators exists, I have generally given more than one rendering for the reader to consider. For the exegesis of single words or phrases, I have relied upon the work of experts. Translations of individual words or phrases are from Liddell and Scott, *A Greek-English Lexicon*, 9th edn, (New York: Oxford University Press, 1968).

This book is not about the Greek language. Disputes over the understanding of the Greeks here should have to do with ideas rather than renderings. For example, a deep schism exists now between the "liberals," who are interested in Protagoras and the Sophists, as well as Plato, and the "fundamentalists," who follow Plato out the window. The fundamentalists will not be happy with the view taken here, but their displeasure should not arise from questions of translation— Bloom or Cornford or Shorey or Jowett. The issues should have more to do with democracy, elitism, and that ever elusive notion—justice.

[2] The advice is from Aristotle (*Politics*, Bk I, ch. 2). For the reader who holds the view that the politics of Athens have no relevance in modern times, because the Athenians held slaves and did not extend citizenship to women or immigrants, I offer two thoughts from M. I. Finley. The first is that we should not be guilty of anachronism, asking the ancient Greeks to accept our modern morality. The second, from *Democracy Ancient and Modern* (New Brunswick, NJ: Rutgers University Press, 1973), is more subtle:

"Before we accept that the elitism of the *demos* renders their experience irrelevant to ours, we must examine more closely the composition of that elite minority, the *demos*, the citizenry." He goes on to describe "a large section of the *demos* . . . the peasants, shopkeepers and craftsmen who were citizens alongside the educated upper classes. The incorporation of such people into the political community as members, an astounding novelty in its time, rarely repeated thereafter, rescues some of the relevance of ancient democracy, so to speak." (p. 16)

Finley is restating the important point made by Pericles, that the democracy includes those who were not members of the aristocracy. Pericles apparently thought them capable of thinking as well as aristocrats, an idea that the Clemente Course in the Humanities (see Chapter XVIII) put to the test in New York City in the 1995–96 academic year.

2

We followers of Socrates—and in the modern world we are all his intellectual progeny—live with the loss or misrepresentation of much of what he said. Plato and Xenophon claim to have noted his thoughts in dialogues and memoirs, and Aristophanes provides us with the contradiction of satire, but Socrates refrained from writing down a word. He did not write, because he thought the written word was dead; it could not be argued, changed, clarified, improved, or denied. The dialectician believed in the living connection between men; using what he called "maieutic dialogue," the midwifery of the mind, the philosopher led his opponents through the maze of argument to the brilliant aporia, the point at which there could be no escape from truth.

In his decision not to write Socrates exemplified the political life; he melded thought and action, the marriage of which politics is born. The political life and the life of the mind followed a similar course and used a similar method: politics is always dialogue; it cannot ever be done alone. Like dialogue, politics does not happen within a person, but in the free space between persons, the political space. There cannot ever be a private life of politics, since politics takes place between persons, in a public way, not public in the sense of broadcast or crowds but as the opposite of private.

The Greek word for private, *idios*, stands in opposition to *koinos*, which means in common, public, and the state. *Koinologia* means consultation, discussion, or philosophical dialogue; the foundation for much of the intellectual and interpersonal activity of the Greeks. This intertwining of thought and action describes the core of the world where politics and freedom were born.

Could Socrates have come out of some other tradition? It is unlikely. By the time he put off the armor of a hoplite and settled down "daily to discourse about virtue," the melding of thought and action in public life was common behavior. Politics had long been established in Athens. In about 440 B.C., when Socrates was only thirty years old, Athens was so taken with a political drama, *Antigone*, that its author, Sophocles, was made one of the generals of the city-state. In the play, Antigone violates the ruling of Creon the king by giving a proper burial to her brother, who had been killed while leading a foreign army against the state.[3] The conflict between her

---

[3] See George Steiner's fascinating essay, *Antigones* (New York: Oxford University Press, 1984).

duty to family and her duty to the state, the latter eloquently set out by Creon early in the play, leads to the tragic conclusion.[4]

The conflict harkens back to the origins of political life in the reform of Cleisthenes, who broke down the traditional clan structure of the *polis* and reorganized it based on *demes*, which were geographically determined political entities. The proximity of the people within the *deme* contributed to the making of a public space where the dialogue of political life could take place.

This change from family to political organization, from the privacy of the clan to the public life of the *deme*, came on the heels of Solon's reforms at the beginning of the sixth century B.C. Solon, the poet who became chief magistrate, had not only codified the laws, he had opened the possibility of the poorest of citizens sharing in the government of the state. Although he had been offered the role of tyrant, Solon had chosen instead to aid the people in finding the middle ground between the fiercely limiting order imposed by a tyranny and the chaotic liberty of people without government. He made self-rule (*auto nomos*) a reality in law, if not entirely in practice. It was to take place in the public space between the people.

Every citizen, according to Athenian law, was permitted to participate in the public world of politics. Members of the most important legislative body, the *boulē*, were chosen by lot—a constant, living proof to the citizenry of the reality of the democracy and of the melding of thought and action through the medium of language. The largest legislative body, the *ekklēsia*, comprised about one-fifth of all the citizens. Together, the election by lot to the *boulē* and the size of the *ekklēsia* gave the citizens of Athens the sense of legitimate power.

Once the legislative bodies were established, the citizens entered the circle of power; all belonged to all, but only as long as the power was active. Power could not be put aside or stored up like grain or the materials of war; it existed only in practice, in the dialogues among the thousands who crowded into the Pynx in Athens to debate the actions of the city; it existed only in the quieter deliberations of the *boulē*, where the five hundred set the agenda for the great crowd of the *ekklēsia*.

Power could be replaced by force in Athens: Thirty tyrants could take over the rule of the polis. But power and force could not coexist as equals; force could be a tool of power, but never its mate. Force could be built up, stored like an army in waiting, but not power, for power was like Socrates's

---

[4] Creon condemns Antigone to be walled up in a cave; she hangs herself; in his grief Creon's son Haemon, who was betrothed to Antigone, falls on his sword; and Eurydice, Creon's wife, commits suicide upon hearing of the death of her son.

understanding of language: The moment it stopped—in silence or the immutability of writing—it died.

The political life was properly termed the *vita activa* because it existed only in action, in the constant search for the place between order and liberty, which is politics, and also temperance.[5] The Greek word *sophrosyne*[6] is generally translated as temperance, but it also describes a moderate form of government and, in a person, self-control, discretion, sanity. Sophrosyne is a description of the state of mind of political life, but it has no place in private life. To achieve sophrosyne, an act that may be translated as "to come to one's senses," requires a plurality of possibilities; a private life offers no alternatives, no other, no possibility, as Aristotle would have it, to find the mean. In a private life there are no boundaries, as in dialogue, to bring the person to his senses.[7]

Negotiation over the conduct of the members of the group, the activity of political life, cannot take place in private; in modern societies, it is replaced by reaction, in the form of lethargy or force. In primitive societies, ritual did not permit the political life.

The Greeks often said a life of leisure was necessary to practice politics, but as Sarah Broadie explains in *Ethics with Aristotle*, leisure meant "to escape the pressure of necessity."[8] The concept of *necessity* meant something quite different to the Greeks than it does in common use today. When Aristotle used the word, he distinguished two kinds of necessity, only one of which did not include violence. Then, as now, to live according to the

---

[5] For a discussion of the *vita activa* see Hannah Arendt, *The Human Condition* (Chicago: University of Chicago Press, 1958).

[6] It is now also an English word. Among many others, I urged the OED to include sophrosyne in its new supplement, giving it equal place with hubris in the English language. On April 16, 1973, R. W. Burchfield was kind enough to write to me that "sophrosyne/sophrosune" would be included, "though our printed evidence is rather thin."

Cynthia Farrar tells us in her illuminating book, *The Origins of Democratic Thinking* (New York and London: Cambridge University Press, 1988), p. 182, that sophrosyne was understood quite differently by the Spartans, who connected self-control to courage.

Thucydides quotes Archidamus, king of the Lacedaemonians (Ch. III), in another connection to temperance: "We are both warlike and wise, and it is our sense of order that makes us so. We are warlike, because self-control contains honor as a chief constituent, and honor bravery. And we are wise, because we are educated with too little learning to despise the laws, and with too severe a self-control to disobey them. . . ."

[7] Cynthia Farrar writes of the role of politics: "Political validity is founded on a decision-making procedure, not on a divinely-ordained truth or order. This is part of the point of politics since . . . the gods may well demand conflicting things. Yet political deliberation cannot in itself *dissolve* a deep and tragic conflict between legitimate claims. . . . The political community must . . . absorb and domesticate conflict. . . ." *The Origins of Democratic Thinking*, p. 36.

[8] (New York: Oxford University Press, 1991), p. 421.

rule of necessity meant to live by the rule of force. In that situation, according to Aristotle, the political life was not possible.

Not that he thought politics was an easy life or a form of leisure, nor even that it was an end in itself, but the pressure of necessity was such that it pushed a person out of the *vita activa* into a grim existence in which the habits that led to happiness could not be practiced. He compared the life of necessity to slavery.

Perhaps no better definition can be made for poverty in contemporary America than to say it is the life of necessity, with all the violence the Greeks found in that word. To live in poverty then is to live according to the rules of force, which push people out of the free space of public life into the private concerns of mere survival.

When necessity rules, there is neither time nor energy to live the political life, to participate in the circle of power, for power, like the philosophy of Socrates, exists only in action; it is the doing of politics, and the moment it ceases it dies.

Long after the fall of Athens, the most political state of the ancient world, perhaps in all of history, came to flower in Rome. It was deeply affected by the Stoic philosophers, who imagined politics spreading beyond the city into a great brotherhood of man, an idea that lies behind Cicero's summation of the political life: "Men are born for each other."

In that plainspoken sentence he tells us that politics is in the nature of human beings, that we are many, not one, public, not private, that we exist in the melding of speech and action, and that we are sufficiently temperate to live together, to absorb conflict through politics. It is his expansion of Aristotle's belief that man is a political animal, but it holds out no promise for those who are born, not for each other, but for the struggle to survive against the force of necessity.

Two thousand years after Cicero, in the richest nation in the history of the world, necessity has been redefined to include color television and hundred-dollar sneakers, but in light of the wealth of the nation, poverty has become as starkly relative as it was in the beginning of the modern world. There are many reasons for the inequality at the conclusion of the game in America, many explanations for the relativity of wealth, but it becomes clear when listening to the poor that politics and poverty do not share the same house.

IV.

Geographies Great and Small

O F ALL THE WAYS in which poverty eludes understanding, none causes more confusion than geography, for the world is of two minds about the whereabouts of the poor. They are here and there, everywhere and nowhere, a demographic conundrum. Poverty cannot be seen and it cannot be avoided.

In the best descriptions, the poor live in one place or make one great journey, enabling a social scientist or a reporter to concentrate on a few people and present them in the fullness of their human lives. The problem comes in the reading, for when the last page has been turned and the lamp has gone cool in the darkness before sleep, the mind will do its work, sorting and filing, abstracting the instances of life into patterns, commonplaces. Then these works become the worst of descriptions, the people collapse into types: blacks or hillbillies or mothers without men. Unlike art, which always tells the truth about itself, these unimagined works eventually become lies about the world.

When a grand geography drives the thinking, as in federal or statewide definitions or the most precise statistical pictures, the descriptions fit like a suit made for all sizes and all occasions. At some moment, for some person, somewhere, the match will be perfect, but for all the rest the tailor will have cut and sewn a mistake.

During the decade or two when the casework approach to relief was current, many people thought the best way to deal with poverty was to make it ever more specific, until each unique aspect of every problem could be dealt with. Because there were too few caseworkers with too little money and time to spend on each case, the theory was never truly tested. One thing was certain, though, the casework theory solved the demographer's conundrum: Every poor person was supposed to get a suit made to measure.

Poverty faded from the public mind for a long time during the last quarter of the century. Social Security took better care of Grandma, and that was all that really mattered.

Works about the poor in one place, mainly Chicago[1] and New York, began appearing in the 1990s. The journalist and critic Michael Massing approved of the respect these writers showed to their subjects; he liked the detail in their work, and what he thought must be their liberal intentions. But "By limiting their scrutiny to the lives and behavior of individuals in the ghetto," he wrote, "they implicitly invite the reader to find explanations there and nowhere else. The larger economic, political, and even cultural factors that lie beyond the ghetto and the behavior of its residents—in boardrooms, say, or in Washington—also lie beyond the scope of these books." The new works were nothing like Agee's *Let Us Now Praise Famous Men*, but Massing maintained that the writers were "infinitely more dedicated and conscientious" than Michael Harrington, who he says just walked around Harlem jotting down notes.[2]

The problem, according to Massing, lies in the inability of the writers to think of theory and practice at the same time; in other words, geography. Poverty is either here or everywhere, and if it is everywhere, who can put his finger on it?

One solution to the problem of geography was tried by Agee and again by Jonathan Kozol: The soul of the writer substitutes for all the rest of the world in a wondrous act of hubris. Agee made a literary pastiche of his thoughts and feelings, often straying far afield of the people he stayed with in Appalachia. Kozol is also the center of his recent work, but he is not so literary and what he tells of himself relates directly to the subject at hand. Another solution may be to use bricolage. The arranger of bric-à-brac goes

[1] Alex Kotlowitz, *There Are No Children Here* (New York: Doubleday, 1991), takes place in a housing project in Chicago. Nicholas Lemann followed a migration from Mississippi to Chicago in *The Promised Land*, published in the same year (New York: Alfred A. Knopf).

[2] *The New Yorker*, Jan. 16, 1995.

along looking for materials to serve his occupation; he is a serious maker of structures, but one buffeted by serendipity and obsession, like the homeless who scour the city streets in search of scraps to fill their purloined carts.

What can be made of his hoard? On the surface, a Jewish single mother in Brooklyn and a marijuana trader in Appalachia have nothing in common with the granddaughter of a murderer in California. Certainly none of the three can be compared to the aging cadre of the civil rights movement in the Mississippi Delta, not on the surface.

Although such disparate families, each with its component of seemingly incommensurate individuals, suggest that poverty cannot be characterized by race, region, or religion, they share many basic attributes. There is no need to succumb to the casework theory of uniqueness or to accept poorly defined notions of class or culture to describe poverty. Structures can be found underlying the lives of the poor, and when no structure can be discerned in the complexity of modern existence, there is still the matter of public or private life to be considered. In the end, the distinction between rich and poor comes down to the most elemental question: Human life or mere animal existence; by which I mean, politics or force?

First, some of the old geography must be put aside. Urban and rural poverty have usually been approached as separate and distinct problems in America, although in many respects they have the same cause: technology. The displacement of workers on farms and in factories can be traced to a change in method.

The effect of force on the poor may have different surface manifestations in urban and rural areas, but an isolated area like the Clear Fork Valley in Appalachia rests upon an act no less sudden or cruel than the one used by real estate companies in the North Lawndale section of Chicago.

Religious affiliation has also been connected to poverty, both positively and negatively. Jews, for example, are often thought of as a group that has escaped poverty, but the Metropolitan Coordinating Council on Jewish Poverty reports that 13 percent of Jewish households in New York City lived at or below 150% of the federal poverty line in 1991.[3] The most interesting aspect of their study shows the change in the composition of the households over the last two decades: The number of elderly poor fell while the number of poor families with children rose—a pattern exactly like that of the rest of the country.

---

[3] Their use of 150 percent is based on the cost of living in New York City compared to most of the rest of the country.

The study showed only a slight (12%) difference between those at 125 percent and 150 percent of the federal poverty level, but a very large (156%) increase between those at 100 percent and 150 percent. Applying the same standards to the general poverty level in New York City would produce similar increases in the number of poor people.

Given that the percentage of blacks and Latinos living at or below the poverty level is much higher than that of whites, one might argue that members of certain Baptist, Methodist, and evangelical churches tend to be poor, but of course the determining factor in such instances is not religion but race.

A distinction will have to be drawn, however, between race and racism. If a person's genetic connection to Africa or pre-Columbian America or Southeast Asia has any bearing on whether or not that person will be poor, I have seen no evidence of it. But racism and ethnocentrism play an important role: They are acts of force. Even so, the geography of poverty in the United States cannot be divided into a quartet (black, white, brown, Asian) of nations. A priori, race will dominate the issue of poverty in a racist country, but the facts do not confirm the deduction. If racism determines economic status, all blacks must be poor and no whites can be poor. But a growing number of blacks live in the second- and third-wealthiest quintiles and the single largest group of poor people in the United States is white. Racism contributes to the high rate of poverty among blacks and Latinos, but it cannot be the sole determining factor.

It has been argued that while blacks and Latinos do not make up the majority of poor people, they account for most of the underclass. Since the commonly used definition of the underclass is *the group of people whom most others fear and despise*, the distinction between the objects of racism and the underclass cannot be made clear.[4]

The old geographies—regionalism, urban/rural distinctions, religion, even race—do not hold. The existence of poverty is either endemic, a natural wrong, or in need of a different kind of examination. The examples that follow begin to show the inaccuracy of the old geographies. At the same time, they point to aspects of poverty at a structural level. Thus, in each one poverty will appear to be both different and the same.

1. A Cash Crop

To get to the Clear Fork Valley from the county seat at Tazewell it is necessary to drive north past Lincoln Memorial University at Harrogate,

---

[4] Herbert J. Gans devoted more than half of a book to the question of *underclass* as a label: *The War Against the Poor* (New York: Basic books, 1995). Michael B. Katz edited *The Underclass Debate*, published two years earlier (Princeton, NJ: Princeton University Press, 1993).

through the Cumberland Gap into Kentucky, back down into Tennessee on the other side of Cumberland Mountain, then follow a narrow road as it winds down the steep side of the valley to Clairfield. Mud obliterates the road in places and for some stretches near the coal operations tiny pieces of coal, like shining dust, turn the pavement slick. Black snakes sun themselves on the road in the day, and at night the mist and the steep drop along the south side make it a dangerous trip, but never so dangerous as when the coal trucks come around a bend as sudden as a wall.

A hundred and twenty-five years ago, before the coal operators came to the Cumberlands, the valley was a clear, harsh place where mountain people lived in pitiless harmony with the land. They hunted and prayed, grew corn and vegetables on patches of flat land, and kept their own rules. Although they owned the land, the barter economy of the valley did not generate enough money for them to pay property taxes. But it made no difference: No one took the land in lieu of taxes, for no one wanted land so steep it would not even support a cow.

Then the coal company came from England and grabbed the land. The American Association, Ltd., the work of the Lord Mayor of London,[5] bought up the life of the valley for a pittance, for back taxes or the price of a gun. The Association bought everything, the entire history of the land back to the flowers that died and were pressed into coal under the weight of mountains. Then it hired the mountain men and boys to dig the coal and cut off the mountaintops, and the lungs of the miners died and the natural rhythms of trees and rain were disturbed forever by the sudden cascades of water that flooded the valley.

Relative poverty did not exist in the valley until the company came. After the company took the land, the barter economy broke down and a new relation between people and money grew up in the valley. The owners, the superintendents, and the shift bosses were different from the men who went down into the mines. It was easy enough to see: coal dust mixed with the sweat of the miners; it said on their faces that they were poor.

A century later the American Association has gone from the valley, exposed, defeated, destroyed in scandal, but there is still no work other than coal. Many of the mines have closed, and Colquest and the other companies that remain are hard and stubborn, like the men who go down into the mines. The United Mine Workers Union came to organize the miners in the valley, promising unending loyalty to the men who labored in the Colquest operations. But in the middle of a long strike the union aban-

---

[5] See John Gaventa's fine book on the valley: *Power and Powerlessness* (Urbana, IL: University of Illinois Press, 1980).

doned the men, leaving them for dead, marked as troublemakers, barred from almost every other mine in the region. Now, there is nothing for those men in the valley where there had been very little. One family in five has no running water. Intestinal ailments, like those in Third World countries, plague the poorest of the people along the Clear Fork. Isolation holds sway. The people get some help to survive, but it is not enough.

In the sixties an ex-nun from Brooklyn, Marie Cirillo, came to the valley to help the mountain people. She started a land trust to take back some of the acreage from the companies and she brought young people from the cities to the valley to join in her efforts. She did good work among the people. She helped the sick and the indigent, and she asked for nothing but cooperation in return. Some said she was saintly. But she was not a mountain woman.

After thirty years, Brooklyn is still not in Tennessee, and the choices of how to keep alive in the valley are still limited to coal mining, Supplemental Security Income (known as "a-drawin"), gathering ginseng root in the mountains, or raising marijuana. No one thinks it wrong to grow marijuana, just as no one thinks it wrong to steal bricks or lumber from a coal company. People do not grow marijuana in the deep woods for the sake of smoking it; they climb up into the seemingly impenetrable forest to plant and harvest the only crop they can sell for cash. They flout the laws the outsiders make and they steal from companies that stole their land and their labor, but they do not steal from each other. Those are the rules. Because of the rules, this happened:

She lived in a wooden trailer situated on a lot that belonged to the land trust. He was a thief.[6] Other men planted and harvested marijuana, and he stole what they had. He took the stolen bales to her trailer, where she hid them until he could deliver the drugs to the dealers who came to the mountains.

One afternoon, when she had gone out, there was a fire in the trailer. It was not an ordinary fire, because it started from both ends of the trailer, and it burned up everything inside and out.

When the thief heard about the fire, he understood from the way it started that it was no accident. He knew it was time to leave. The woman did not leave with him, but she could not stay, either. The trailer was burned beyond repair, which meant she had no place to live, and even though she was a mountain woman, no one took her in. She moved away.

---

[6] Although I have heard about these two people from several sources, of whom Marie Cirillo is the most reliable, I have not met the man or the woman and I question some of the details of what I have heard. For obvious reasons people do not use their names.

After a time, the woman said she wanted to come back. The members of the land trust met to consider her request. They set very strict conditions on her return, "for she brought shame on them," Marie Cirillo said. "Her boyfriend can never come back. If he does, the people will. . . ." And then the ex-nun from Brooklyn, the smooth-skinned, famously compassionate woman with the executive air, made a strange, rattling sound, a euphemism, the closest thing to murder that a saint may be permitted to say.

2. Strippers

On her way home from the Head Start program, Lastarla Brown walked with the exaggerated bustle of a four-year-old at the end of her patience. The cause of her vexation was a toy dog, a ball of fluff so soft it draped over her arm. "He bad," Lastarla said. "When I get home, I'm going upstairs and get the gun and shoot him."

She did not speak of a child's imagined world. There was a gun upstairs; her aunt had bought it after a jealous lover threw a Molotov Cocktail into her house. Lastarla knew how her aunt survived the flames by jumping out of a second-story window and what the jump had done to her. She had seen the scars and heard about the pins that held her aunt's foot and leg together, and she knew that her aunt would never again get up on a stage and dance. And she knew about the gun.

Lastarla had heard the history of her family many times. She could see it in the pictures arranged on the wall of the tiny living room:[7]

In Athens, Texas, in the 1950s, colored girls chopped cotton—all except Joyce Ann Collins. Joyce said she would never go into anybody's fields to work. She was the lightest-skinned colored girl in Athens, very pretty, and she had dreams, very specific dreams, for she loved to dance.

Joyce was the first black girl in Athens to put on high heels and a tight skirt to go walking down the dirt roads of the little farm town halfway between Houston and Dallas. No one in the town had ever seen such a pretty and strong-willed colored girl, so full of dreams. She was a jukebox dancer, a girl who loved dancing so much that she went out to the little

[7] This history of the Williams family is constructed out of many conversations with Margarette Williams, a few brief exchanges with Lastarla Williams, and many conversations with Margarette's friend Monsa Nitoto. I first met Margarette when Monsa and I and several other people were leafletting in the Acorn housing projects in West Oakland. Our conversations began then and have continued over several years.

clubs whenever she could. One night, when she was fourteen years old, she danced and danced until she had danced the night away. Then a young sailor took her home.

Her parents accused her of having sex with the sailor. Why else would she have stayed out all night? And no matter how Joyce protested or the sailor swore they had done nothing more than dance together, her parents would not believe them. There was a shotgun wedding, then the sailor who had been home on leave went back to Germany or some other very distant place that no one from Athens, Texas, had ever seen. Before long the sailor's monthly allotment checks began arriving. Joyce Williams was delighted. She put on her tight skirt and high heels and went to California.

On the West Coast, where careers are made, Joyce felt free to pursue her dreams. She danced and danced, until finally she had an offer to dance for money. She sewed a costume for herself and dyed her hair red. It was a white woman named Joyce who appeared in a California club one night and danced in a most seductive way as she slowly removed her clothes down to a tiny brassiere and a G-string.

The first baby was born in 1954, after her sailor came home from the Korean War. Joyce named her Margarette. The baby was darker than her mother, but beautiful, with the eyes of an Egyptian queen. A routine developed in the household: Joyce worked as a stripper at night and during the day she washed and ironed and cooked for her baby. When she traveled, she took Margarette with her. She taught her to cook and sew, and she passed on her talent for dancing. By then, there were many men in Joyce's life; she and Margarette called them stepfathers.

Joyce gave birth to three more girls by the stepfathers. With the money she earned as a stripper, she sent Margarette and her sisters to ballet school, modeling school, and to a charm school for young ladies. They traveled everywhere, visiting the sailor wherever he was stationed, staying in hotels while Joyce danced in cities far from their home in California.

In 1964, when Margarette was ten years old, Joyce made a long-term arrangement with the Showcase Club in Oakland, and settled into domestic life. She rented a two-story house, and tended to her children, her dancing, and the stepfathers.

Then a series of calamities befell the family. One daughter had a seizure in school and was diagnosed "with tumors the size of potatoes growing on her brain." A second daughter and two other children were killed in a fire in the rented house. Joyce had to go down to the morgue to identify the body. She saw her baby "all burnt up, with cracked teeth," and never recovered from the trauma. Joyce had a breakdown, and when she came out of it, the stripper had become an Evangelical Christian. Soon afterward, she married a man named Brown, a dapper fellow, so well-spoken that people said he sounded like "a white boy preppie." Joyce had two more children, John John and Bettina, but she was not close to them. Margarette raised the children from infancy. When Bettina was three years old, Margarette took her into the room where Joyce lay on the bed and told her, "I'm not your momma. This is your momma."

Margarette remained at home through high school. Then, like her mother, she sewed a costume of satin and strings and went on the road to dance in strip joints and nightclubs. She was fully a woman by then, sleek and firm, a dancer.

John John and Bettina were still very young when Margarette went on the road, and she would regret later that she had not waited two more years before leaving them. But dancing excited her. She formed a troop of six women and two men. Margarette choreographed, produced, and danced. Everything she did was sensual, seductive. She was a stripper, and she was pleased by her work.

When her daughter was born, Margarette called her Lajoya. By the end of 1980 Margarette was back home in Oakland, dancing at the Showcase. She wished she had found a way to get to Europe when she was on the road, or to Canada, at the very least, to Canada. But life hadn't worked out that way. John John was coming up, and he was trouble. Bettina was fourteen when she met a man who turned her on to drugs. Margarette, known to her friends as Cho Cho, took up with Monsa Nitoto, a former Black Panther, who sometimes did political organizing and sometimes was "in the life," running a few women, doing this and that. She liked him because he was very bright, and she fought with him because he was headstrong, demanding, short-tempered, and given to using street language when he talked to the increasingly religious Joyce.

Margarette had moved into the Acorn projects by then. She looked at the rows of tan two-story buildings, the steel clothesline poles, the wide, flat, empty grass corridors and gray concrete walkways, the relentless decay of the walls and walks and windows, and the drug dealers and winos everywhere on every corner, and said, "This is the last resort."

John John stayed there with her when he was not in prison. One night Margarette watched him get arrested. He knew the police were coming for him, but he made no effort to escape; instead, he drove up and down the streets of the project in a stolen car, doing the tight, skidding turns known as doughnuts, as if he were on parade. When the police came, he went quietly. "He likes to be in prison; he has a Ph.D. in prison," Margarette said.

Margarette broke up with Monsa; Bettina fell deeper and deeper into the drug world. When Margarette and Joyce tried to convince her to give up drugs, she responded by sucking her thumb and laughing. John Brown, the well-spoken man, the very black man with white teeth and excellent manners, took up with another woman. She was not his wife, he did not live with her, but he made her pregnant. She was in her eighth month when Brown, high on crack cocaine, beat her to death with a baseball bat. He made a prison confession to Margarette: Crack had been an experiment, he had no idea what it would do to him. Brown admitted killing the woman, but he could not even remember "jumping on her."

John John, always anxious to be part of something, agreed to the initiation rite of a prison gang: He killed a man. His sentence was increased, and he was moved to Pelican Bay, the toughest prison in the California system. What few privileges he had were taken away. He had no money, nothing. Whenever he had the chance, he telephoned Margarette, asking for money, for solace, for visits. She told him not to bother her, that she had enough stress without him; besides, he was selfish, he never thought about anyone but himself. "I did my best trying to take care of you the last time you was here," she said. "All you ever say is 'I need, I need, I need.' You didn't care about us when you was out. You thought being out was like a little vacation from prison. I think you like being locked up."

Her life on the outside was more difficult than his life in prison, Margarette said; she had a little money, and she planned to hold on to it. "The only thing I see for my brother's future," she said, "is he'll be killed, which I don't want to happen, or he'll just end up in prison for the rest of his life. Come out, kill somebody here on the street."

By 1992, her daughter Lajoya was living with a drug dealer who conducted his business in the presence of their son, Margarette's grandchild. Bettina had been arrested, used in a police sting operation, and sent to prison for possession of crack cocaine. Lastarla was two years old. Margarette adopted her, hoping to save this child as she had not been able to save John John or Bettina.

When she was not worrying about Lajoya and her husband, Margarette thought about Bettina, which only made her angry. Out on parole in 1994, Bettina quickly went back to cocaine. "She's out on somebody's street corner, panhandling, with her thumb in her mouth, laughin; probably ain't washed her behind in over a week," Margarette said, and then the time gets away from her for a moment: "My main dream was to go to Europe. I liked pretty clothes, I liked smellin pretty, I liked all them things that women do. And she don't care how she looks, thinks everything's funny. I just look at her and ask, 'What we here for?'"

Past forty now, Margarette thinks often about old age, someone to keep her company. Perhaps Monsa, perhaps not. They say the Housing Authority plans to tear down Acorn and turn the land over for gentrification. The buildings withstood the Loma Prieta earthquake, but the nearby freeway collapsed. It has been a long time since "the Housing," as it is known, painted or repaired anything. The ceiling fell in over the stove, and Margarette fixed it. When the Housing refused to paint her place, she did it herself, outlining the doorways to give the appearance of woodwork.

In the afternoon she stands in the kitchen, which is also the entrance to her apartment, and prepares the next day's meal. She packs chicken into a plastic bag, grating onion, adding soy sauce and garlic to the marinade. When she puts the chicken into the refrigerator, a plastic bucket falls out, spilling garlic skins and an egg. Margarette scoops it all up, pleased that the egg did not break. Perhaps it is a sign.

The kitchen is crowded with a small round table, a child's table, toys, yesterday's wash and tomorrow's wash. In the living room, where Margarette prefers to eat, two videotape machines have been set to copying the movie *Philadelphia*. She has covered each of the tiny glass-topped tables in front of the couch with a paper towel in preparation for dining with a guest. Lastarla plays in the kitchen. When it comes time to eat, the girl will insist on potatoes.

Upstairs in the bedroom Margarette keeps the videotapes and the albums filled with pictures from the years when she was dancing. Two of her favorite pictures have been torn at the corners, victims of a fight with Monsa. The plastic cover of the album was torn off in another fight so that the big book has the appearance of something discarded and salvaged, an afterthought.

As Margarette turns the pages, stiff poses of her dance troupe look out, old pictures in black and white of nearly naked women and two muscular men looking at the camera. In one picture Margarette has her tongue in another woman's ear; in another she appears to be mounting the woman from behind. All of the pictures show Margarette nearly naked, her round, strong body covered only with the tiny halter top and G-string she sewed for herself.

The pictures have an unexpectedly benign atmosphere; the bodies, meant to be sultry, have succumbed to the camera. Motionless, the women cannot practice seduction; they rest, timeless. The pictures look prematurely old; they have a sepia air, like old films and segregation. The world in the pictures is not African-American, not black, not even Negro. Margarette has saved the world of colored folk to show the generations.

Lastarla does not bother to look at the pictures. She plays quietly in the kitchen, then slips out the front door to sit on the concrete stoop. The isolation of the child concerns Margarette. She has begun to take Lastarla to the prison to visit her grandfather, John Brown. She wants the girl to know her grandfather. It is Margarette's way of teaching the child "where she comes from and who she is."

3. In Brooklyn, with Pants

Near the far end of Brooklyn, between Flatbush and Sheepshead Bay, on the way to Brighton Beach, the Metropolitan Council on Jewish Poverty has set up an outpost to serve the homeless and the helpless of farthest Brooklyn. They are often old or foreign-born, many speak only Russian, some communicate in Hebrew or Yiddish, the lingua franca of Jews around the world, and a few are "Americans," the native-born Jews of Brooklyn. Others, the ones the outreach worker finds on the boardwalk or under the boardwalk at Brighton Beach, are not Jews at all, like William Lauritch, the homeless veteran of World War II who was found on Brighton Avenue. The outreach worker knew Lauritch because he was the friend of a legless homeless woman who was murdered not so long before, another of the non-Jews who belongs to the Jews of farthest Brooklyn.

Shaya Kivelevitz (pronounced Kiv-el-ov'-ich) is a rabbi, although not exactly a rabbi as most people think of rabbis. He has no congregation, he does not preach, he is more comfortable as a kosher slaughterer than a man at a pulpit, but he is nevertheless a rabbi, ordained. Kivelevitz himself lives in Far Rockaway, with his wife and five children. He is forty-four years old, with a short scraggly beard, very thick glasses, and the bluntness that came to America from the villages of Poland. It is possible to imagine Kivelevitz killing a chicken or digging the veins from the front quarter of a steer.

The grace of Kivelevitz is not in what he says or how he looks, but in what he does. He walks. They say of Kivelevitz in the Manhattan offices of the Metropolitan Council, "He walks."

Where does he walk? one asks.

"He walks." It is said with a shrug, as if the questioner were a fool to fail to understand that the outreach person at the farthest end of Brooklyn must walk.

But where?

"Everywhere. On the boardwalk he walks. On the avenue he walks. He walks."

And what does he do when he walks?

"Outreach."

It was a dialogue between a fool and a shrug. I went to see Kivelevitz. His office was exactly where he described it to me over the telephone, a narrow door around the corner from the elevated train and one flight up. The building that housed the Brooklyn Homeless (that was all it said, the entire name on the door) was dark, decrepit, made of narrows and plaster-board partitions, darker, disorganized, broken, with a myriad of locked doors, stacks of papers, and little rooms, a food pantry filled with tuna and cornflakes, spaghetti and gefilte fish. While I waited, I heard the rabbi talking to his clients: "Rose, you need food? I'll bring a little gefilte fish, you'll have for the holidays. Miriam, your son eats only yogurt; yogurt I don't have. From Meals on Wheels you'll get yogurt. You can't chew the meat; eat the vegetables. Next week they'll have fish."

He has many cases, clients, old, young, Russians, American blacks, a man who thinks the world stinks and will continue to stink until the next time Jesus Christ comes to earth, but most of his clients are Jews.

And of all the Jews, one is special, an Iraqi Jew, a thin woman, who was as recently as yesterday exotic. I first met her in the rabbi's office in 1993. By then, the metamorphosis had begun. But I am getting ahead of the story.

In 1965 a daughter was born into the family of a taxi driver, a recent refugee in a long line of exiles and refugees. He had entered Israel according to the rules of the Law of Return, yet return had not meant welcome for the Iraqis. Nothing but citizenship had been handed to him on his arrival. But his daughter—there was a gift! From the moment of her birth his daughter had been beautiful and headstrong, born seductive in the fashion of the women of the Middle East. At fourteen she met her future husband. At seventeen she married, and went to America.

And where is America? America is in Brooklyn, where the subway trains come up out of the ground and roar and screech past the two-family houses and the tiny factories and endless rows of shops and stores, where blacks and Jews and Latinos battle over the last scraps of life in a borough increasingly divided among the many poor and the wealthy immigrants from Manhattan who have come to buy up the best of Brooklyn.

In Brooklyn she was beautiful and young, dressed in blue jeans and high heels, like a modern American woman. She had a child at eighteen, and a few years later another child. "For the first five years I didn't know what I was doing," she said of life in America. Then the marriage went sour. "It was the pressure of being in New York without a family," she explained, demonstrating her knowledge of the psychotherapeutic patois of an American girl in Brooklyn.

"My second angel," she said, with all the irony a woman can muster in a language learned late in life; "we went out for eight months. Then we got married and things started to change."

The angel worked, but he did not think he was appreciated at his job. He thought he was worth $16 an hour, but they paid him $8. After a few days he quit. He stayed home. And stayed home. The money ran out. His wife confronted him with the situation: No food, no money for the rent, and no prospects while he sat home. He did not answer with words. He had no words.

"You know," she said, "somebody that is not sure about himself. He realize that he is garbage, so he wants to make sure that I think he is still strong and this is the way that he talks to himself, by hitting me. By hitting me he realizes that he still has power. He really felt bad after he did it. But when we got to the point where we didn't have money—he can't afford clothes, he can't afford food, he can't afford anything; he can't afford to go out—he used to go crazy. He would hit, he can't say. A person that can't talk, he hits."

And she is not alone in this: "I have friends, their husbands aren't working. And once a month, twice a month, they're hitting them."

Sometimes the fights started over her welfare check. He wanted her to cash it and give him the money. It was not much, $360 a month in cash for her, the children (there were three by then), and him. When he got hold of the money, he bought beer, he lived high for a week, and then they were without food for the rest of the month.

Another marriage had gone sour. She went to the police to ask for protection. There were court fights. She threw him out, he broke down the door, and beat her again. Everywhere she went, she was demeaned—in the courts, by the police, at the religious school, Rambam Yeshiva, where she met at the end of the summer with Rabbi Bernstein, who told her he might take her children into the school and he might not. He toyed with her over the tuition.

Although her son maintained a 97 average, it seemed to make no difference. "You know how many cases we have like you?" Bernstein argued. "Where am I going to get the money from?" And she said there were no cases like hers. She fought, until she could fight no more, and when he told her again, "We don't know, we don't know," she shouted, "I'm giving you half of what I'm getting for welfare. Don't think that by waiting until the last minute I'm gonna come up with another thousand dollars. You want to take them, take them. If not, the hell with it."

She was evicted from one place, found another, and was evicted again. In desperation she went to a famous Brooklyn rabbi to ask for help. "He was so busy," she said, "forget it." On her way out of his office, the rabbi's secretary beckoned to her. There was someone who could help, and he was not far away: Kivelevitz.

He wears a battered fedora, blue jeans with his suitcoat. A thousand pieces of paper litter his desk, perhaps not literally a thousand, as he might say, seven hundred. To which he will add a quote from Scripture, speaking it first in Hebrew, then locating the passage in time and place. "This is the portion we read on Yom Kippur, from Isaiah [the Hebrew first], 'You should give the hungry one the bread from the table. . . .'"

Kivelevitz gives charity, he raises money, he gives food, but he remembers always, "Abraham, in the Bible, sets a table by the road, he opens up a restaurant to bring people to God." There is no sin in this, in luring the hungry to the Lord with the gift of bread. So Kivelevitz has not one mission but two.

What touched him about the woman he does not say. She is not so reticent. "I went just for the food, but when I started talking to him, that's when he started to get involved even more than he should have in this story, because it really was just to go and get the food. He did more than he was supposed to do. He's so good in his heart.

"He used to call me at night, nine o'clock, ten o'clock at night. He is like my family. I have nobody here. To me, I'm depending on him. To speak to him, it's really helping me."

More things went wrong for her. Although he did not have much, her first husband had helped her with money, then he was badly hurt and left disabled by an automobile accident. At almost the same time, in Israel, her father's taxi was wrecked, and he too was left broken and weak, unable to work. "Now, I am more close to the rabbi," she said. "A lot of time we speak on the phone and he would tell me things from the Bible and everything. In the beginning, I used to go to the rabbi with pants, and I told him, 'I can't be pressured to do things. I can't have people telling me what to do. When I decide to do things, I'm gonna do it, but you can't tell me you have to do it, because I don't have to do nothing.'

"I started to get a bad attitude when I was with him, my second husband, because he tell me, 'You do this, you do this.' He was ordering me. Now, I got to the point that when somebody is telling me, 'Do it!' I'm doing the opposite.

"That's why with the rabbi, he never criticizing me. He never pushed me to do things. I can't figure it out, but the way he talked to me, he make me do things that he wanted without telling me. That's why I admire him so much. He explained to me why I shouldn't go with the pants.

"For the religious Jewish, you're not supposed to go with pants. Men supposed to walk with pants, not women. To me, it's like all my life I walk with pants. It took a little while, then I asked the rabbi, I said, 'Rabbi, I don't have any skirts,' so he found a woman, she's the wife of a rabbi, she's my size, so she gave me a lot of clothes, and to her she was so happy I was going with a skirt."

Over the months, the jars of gefilte fish (You'll have for the Sabbath?), the cornflakes, the skirts, the Scripture, made their impression: The religious woman emerged, the skirts grew long and the blouses no longer fit her form, only the eyes were the eyes of the languorous woman, the woman of the Middle East.

She spoke to the rabbi every day and every night. She sought a benefactor for her children, she dreamed a saviour for them, but only the rabbi appeared when she needed him. "I spoke to his wife on the phone," she said. "I know his children. He is a good man. He doesn't want nothing from me."

As the years passed, '93, '94, '95, her voice grew tired. She had the same anger. She could still say, "Nobody talks to me like I'm a piece of garbage. I got to the point where I'm saying, 'I don't have to take nothing from nobody.'"

The insults continued; there were court battles over custody and divorce; a welfare worker scheduled her for an appointment at eight-thirty in the morning and did not see her until four o'clock in the afternoon. The "angel," whose father had beaten his wife, broke down the door to her apartment again. He threatened to kill her and her children. She got a restraining order, and he broke it and broke it again. Finally, she got a civil divorce, but she needed a *Get*, a religious divorce, and she did not have $150 to pay for it.

"I don't trust men," she said. "I don't trust anyone." Kivelevitz remained the exception. She listened to him, she learned from him. He was her family and her teacher. She wore long skirts, she walked through the streets of Brooklyn with her child trailing behind her, coughing and covered with chicken pox. At thirty, she has become a proper Jewish woman of Borough Park, Brooklyn, the worn-down ward of the rabbi who walks. In summer he walks in the sun, and in winter he bundles up against the cold of Brighton Beach and he looks on the boardwalk and under the boardwalk where the homeless hide. He does outreach.

She has put the last of the children into school, and she is studying to be a bookkeeper, which has sharpened her gaze. Rabbi Kivelevitz does not insist, he would not tell her to do anything, but he asks in autumn, when a holiday is coming: Will she have her children spend the time in learning?

Yes, she answers, they want to learn.

And although Kivelevitz does not insist, should she marry again, she will take ritual baths and shave her head.

4. Freedom

Something went awry in the Mississippi Delta east of Leland, and I do not know precisely what it was. There are theories; Thelma Barnes of Delta

Resources has a theory. But no one knows for certain. There are two parts to the story, and most of what came between those two parts is missing—hidden, mislaid in damaged memories, or buried.

It began one evening in 1965 (or was it '64? no one remembers the exact date) on the porch of the Wilson house in Indianola, Mississippi. Ora Wilson, her oldest son Sam, and several of the younger children saw them coming up the road: Two people, on foot, emerging from the dusk, a tall, thin young white man, and beside him, hurrying to match his pace, a short white woman. "They was from Russia or Paris or somewhere like that," Mrs. Wilson recalled; "it was for sure they weren't from around here."

The young man introduced himself as Herschel Kaminsky. The woman was his wife, Georgia. He told the Wilsons that he and his wife had come to Mississippi to register people to vote. They were civil rights workers, they said, and it was their aim to get colored people together to work for their equal rights. The whole Wilson family came out onto the porch to listen to the young people. Sam, the oldest son, was the first one to get caught up by them. He joined right then and there. Catherine and Charles Lee were younger, still in high school, but they were anxious to join up, too. And so was Booker T., even though he was still no more than a child.

Mrs. Wilson said she had always been afraid to speak out about anything, but she listened to Herschel and Georgia Kaminsky, and she made them welcome in her house. It was all right with her, she said, for more civil rights people to come to Indianola and stop by her house; she was with them.

The whole Wilson family was with them. It was as if a dream had come out of the dusk, and they were part of it, blacks and whites together in the great movement for integration and voter registration. The Wilsons marched, and sat in, and demonstrated, and went to jail, and came out and sat in and went to jail again. The Wilson children integrated the Riverside School south of Greenville. They marched on Selma. They joined the Mississippi Freedom Democratic Party, they met Fannie Lou Hamer and marched beside her. Catherine taught the alphabet to the children of the civil rights movement. Charles Lee was plucked out of Mississippi, thanks to the civil rights workers, and sent off to college in Washington, D.C. But Sam was the one, Big Sam; it was as if he had been born to lead.

Something like a miracle happened then. Someone in England, a person who wished forever to remain anonymous, sent a gift to Sam Wilson with the expectation that he would use it to build a place where Negroes could fully enjoy their civil rights. The gift was $70,000, a great sum in 1966, greater still in the agricultural economy of the Mississippi Delta. Sam went south of Greenville to buy a piece of land among the few black-owned farms in the area. With more than a little sense of the drama of the historical moment, he announced the establishment of Freedom City.

There was a bit of a disappointment when the county said that a place needed a certain number of people and services, and so on, before it could be called a city. But Sam Wilson was a resourceful man. Freedom, he said, freedom had to stay, but what did it mean to be called a city? He announced the founding of Freedom *Village*.

Perhaps for tax reasons the farmer who sold the land to Sam Wilson wanted only $40,000 down. That suited Sam just fine; he had uses for the rest of the money: housing, farm machinery, seed, and fertilizer. The settlement of Freedom Village began. Eighteen houses were built, and a bean farm was laid out. The people who moved into the village had been among the most oppressed, least political in the state: plantation workers, unlettered and unschooled in economics or the ways of independence. They were exactly the kind of residents Sam had hoped for.

Thelma Barnes said that even then, in the early days of Freedom Village, some people had questioned Sam's dream. A city, they said, should not be made up of people who came from the same background, "the same level."

For the next twenty-five years the people of Freedom Village stayed to themselves. Charles Lee had his first stroke while still in school. He came home from Washington and got a job in Greenville. The rest of the family stayed in Freedom Village: There was an eighty-acre farm to run and a village to administer. Sam went away, leaving the village in the hands of his family and the other people off the plantation. Charles Lee had another stroke; this one grabbed him by the jaw and twisted him as if he had been made of clay.

When Big Sam finally came back home, he was obese, almost immobile. His weight overtook him, breaking down the functions of his body, weakening his heart and all the organs of digestion, driving his blood pressure up beyond the ability of the vessels to withstand it. He had little strokes, larger and larger failings.

In 1994, Big Sam's body could no longer endure its load. The inner workings of the founder of Freedom Village burst, and he died.

I DO NOT KNOW HOW THE WILSON FAMILY lived when Herschel Georgia Kaminsky came out of the dusk to bring the civil rights movement to Indianola, but it could not have been any worse than what has been left to them now. The clapboard house they built with their own hands has not been painted for a long time, perhaps since it was put up. Over the years the walls have lost their square so the sheet of plywood that serves for a door scrapes over the soggy gray boards for a few feet and stops.

In the afternoon in August when the Delta gets hot enough to cook a cake in the shade, Catherine Wilson sometimes sits out on the porch under the tiny rectangle of overhanging roof. A dog keeps company with her, small and black, like a miniature pig, with fallen ears and a hairless pink belly festooned with listless, conical teats. Catherine smiles through protruding teeth, a woman in her mid-forties, not a large woman and not pregnant, but big-bellied as if she were carrying a child, holding it low. She speaks clearly and with the mildest of accents, not at all like the Mississippi mumbles that her mother makes.

The best of the Wilson house is the face it shows to the road. Inside, in the semi-darkness of a shelter completely shaded from the sun, roaches walk up and down the walls; a barbed kitten as thin as a bird weaves among the chairs, raking its sharp claws along the legs of the people; wasps float in the air close to the ceiling, their long legs ominously dangling, promising pain. A blanket separates this room from the others; couches sit at right angles along the outer walls, old things, misshapen, cloth without even a souvenir of the colors that had been.

Charles Lee, who dresses every morning in a clean shirt and neatly pressed trousers, as if he were still able to work, prefers the straightest chair. He sits with dignity, the only member of the family in fine shoes, the cleanest one, the neatest one, although the strokes twisted his lower jaw out to the side of his face so that his mouth is always open, revealing the existence of a single, white tooth. Speech comes with great difficulty, and it is not so much thickened as rounded, the edges of the words smoothed off into an endless meandering vowel.

Ora Wilson has no teeth, which muffles her speech, but at seventy-nine she recalls events close and far with equal accuracy. Booker T. has the most energy in the family. He works and tries to farm, and spends yet another day every day in consternation over the events of the last quarter of a century.

If it were not for medicines and taxes and the telephone and the murderous summer heat that runs up the electric bill, the Wilsons might be able to get along better on the $1,100 a month they collect in pensions and SSI. If the farm produced anything, if the people who lived in the other sixteen houses in Freedom Village paid their share of taxes, if the original people hadn't moved out and left the houses to this new group who were more like squatters than dreamers in the civil rights movement, if and if and if.

In the year since Big Sam died the Wilsons have come under the sway of Booker T., who is an ambitious man and very tired of working six and a half days every week and coming home sweat-soaked and weary to work the farm and fix the half-dead car that rests on the scrub grass in front of Ora Wilson's house. Booker T. is the darkest of the Wilsons, a quick man, with stringy nervous muscles and fingers thickened with the calluses of work. He leads the family now, speaking from behind small dark glasses, talking fast, commenting on his words with a rueful laugh.

With the help of a lawyer, Booker T. and the Wilsons have put together a new dream for Freedom Village: They plan to evict their neighbors, pay the back taxes, and get control of all the houses and the farm. Then, Booker T. prophesied, they will be able to sit back in their house in Freedom Village and live off the rents.

THE HISTORY OF THE WILSON FAMILY raises questions about the thesis of this book: Why did their involvement in the civil rights movement not lead them out of poverty? Why, as Ora Wilson said, did the movement "leave some folks behind"?

Integration had a curious effect on black people in the South. Dr. Goldie Wells, president of Saints Academy in Lexington, Mississippi,[8] watched it happen: "They thought integration was the promised land, but it wasn't that at all." Instead, Dr. Wells explains, integration led to the decline of the black churches, the only place where blacks had truly been in charge, the one area of life where they were political beings.

Well-meaning people came to the Wilsons and mobilized them, but did not politicize them. The Wilsons were not the beginning of anything. They lived in a private world, every bit as private as that of the single mother in Brooklyn or the stripper in Oakland or the marijuana dealer in the Clear Fork Valley. The forces surrounding their lives battered them into thinking of their neighbors in Freedom Village in the same way a British mining operation thought of the people in the Clear Fork Valley.

THE STRUCTURE OF POVERTY in America lies below the physical geography and the racial landscape. There are no types among the poor; no culture made them poor or holds them captive. The poor are neither a class

---

[8] Saints Academy has recently begun holding classes again after a long fallow period that followed integration. Dr. Wells attributes the revival to the rejuvenation of black churches in the South. If she is correct, a new wave of educated, ambitious blacks should begin to appear in the South in five to ten years, and the theory of southern blacks bringing poverty to the North and creating an "underclass" will be disproved yet again.

nor an underclass. They lack the cohesion of a class; they have no consciousness of themselves in opposition to other classes or to the means of production. Class implies politics, and even the people who lived in a village imported from politics did not enjoy a political life. Class implies a social group, commonalities, communication. Margarette Williams, who had spent years in the long rows of apartments of an Oakland housing project, was as isolated as the people of the Cumberlands. She and the Jewish woman in Brooklyn both lived in the shadow of violent men, which has nothing to do with the means of production or any of the other attributes of class. They were poor.

V.

The Golden Age of Poverty

AT THE END OF THE eighth century B.C. Hesiod, a wealthy aristocrat, lost his money and position as a result of a revolution in Boetia, and went into exile. Or so it is said; in truth, very little is known about Hesiod. He may not have been an aristocrat, but something happened to him, some fall that led him to invent the devastating notion of a Golden Age. There is evidence of this in his writings, where he rages against poverty, claiming that it "eats the heart out and destroys."

In his epic poem *Works and Days,* Hesiod confirms the notion of the modern world as a game when he speaks of gods and men beginning as equals, and then goes on to make the first clear exposition of the central myth of the poor of his time and ours:

And now with art and skill I'll summarize
Another tale, which you should take to heart,
Of how both gods and men began the same.
The gods, who live on Mount Olympus, first
Fashioned a golden race of mortal men . . .

And like the gods they lived with happy hearts
Untouched by work or sorrow. Vile old age
Never appeared, but always lively-limbed,
Far from all ills, they feasted happily.
Death came to them as sleep, and all good things
Were theirs; ungrudgingly, the fertile land
Gave up her fruits unasked. Happy to be
At peace, they lived with every want supplied.

Then he spoke of "a lesser, silver race of men." And after them a race of bronze, "worse than the silver race." Then came the race of heroes, "the race before our own. Foul wars and dreadful battles ruined some. . . ."

After the race of heroes came "The fifth, who live now on the fertile earth./I wish I were not of this race, that I/Had died before or had not yet been born." Men are now of the race of iron; they spend their days working and grieving, and at night, "they waste away and die."[1]

The idea of a Golden Age has a celebratory sense when applied to literature or movies, but it has a different meaning when it serves as the central myth of man. Hannah Arendt said that it "implies the rather unpleasant certainty of continuous decline." Hesiod intended a harsher view. He does not say exactly how these ages changed, but he makes it quite clear that man's fall from one age to the next-lower age was not of his own doing. An outside force, nothing less than the gods themselves, caused the fall.

Nearly three thousand years later, the poor in America embrace the same explanation of the world. If it seems an impossible stretch of the imagination to see similarities between Hesiod and an unemployed man in San Francisco or a woman in the South Bronx, listen to this tale of origins by a formerly homeless woman named Hyacinth: "My grandfather bought this land—you'll excuse me—from a white man who thought he was selling him some no good land, but this land turned out to be big, so he lived on it and even had white sharecroppers who worked on it. And my grandfather had so much land even the sheriff had to ask his permission to come on the land. They had everything on the land, even a smokehouse for the pigs they killed, everything. Why, my momma never went into a big grocery store, like a supermarket, until she came up here to New York. Didn't have to. They had everything on the land.

"My momma was one of thirteen children; they all come up here.

"My grandmother could make anything. She could look at a picture of

---

[1] Hesiod, *Works and Days*, trans. Dorthea Wender (Harmondsworth, UK: Penguin Books, 1973), pp. 62–64.

a wedding dress, no pattern, nothing, just a picture, and sew it just like the picture."

She went on to say that the farm was in Alabama, near Mobile. She named all the vegetables that grew on her grandfather's farm, and cotton, too. She said what the sharecroppers grew and picked, and again and again she told of the respect the white sheriff showed.

Yet Hyacinth could not explain why her mother and all her twelve siblings deserted the farm for New York City, or why her mother took to drink. And when I asked her, doing what seems in retrospect a cruelty, why she did not return to her grandfather's farm, she spoke of her mother again, of the clubs in New York City where she was lured by the fast life.

Hyacinth was not simply a liar, nor did she live in addict's dreams. She spoke with a recovering addict's frankness of her own troubles: She told how she had spent a week partying in a motel with a strange man who had a thousand dollars' worth of drugs. "Then he went back to his life," she said, "and left me with this addiction."

Her tale of the farm in Alabama followed the structure of Hesiod's tale of the decline from the Golden Age. Hyacinth's cruel gods were alcohol and crack cocaine. They had brought her down to the Iron Age, when she truly spent her days grieving, often wishing she had not been born.

The bones of Hesiod's tale and Hyacinth's dreamed history occur again and again among the poor. A Mexican American, living in an adobe house the size of a cheap motel room, with his children's beds arranged in tiers, like something in a nightmare, recalled the good life in the mountains, where winged ants fell from the air like manna from heaven on rainy days in spring and his father ruled the town from the Alcalde's privileged place. For him it was a revolution that ruined the world.

A woman in Tulsa, living in terror of an abusive man, locked into a house with broken windows and sagging floors, remembers her rich grandparents, a tiny Oklahoma town, evenings by the lake, and then an aunt come home from the city to tear everything down with cocaine.

The Wilson family remembered the Golden Age of the civil rights movement and the strokes that took one son away and ruined another, ruined them all.

In the Clear Fork Valley the Golden Age existed until the coal company took the land away, leaving the men of iron to grieve and work.

The Golden Age has many names. It can be Aztlan or it can be the Yoruba gods whom the Dominican poet Chiqui Vicioso found in Africa to explain her life before the fall. In parts of the American South, some blacks have begun to think of the time before integration as a kind of Golden Age, taken from them by the force of a court order.

Sometimes the force that ends the Golden Age is a sudden act of physical force, as when Monsa Nitoto, the former Black Panther, lost his successful and influential father. The newest Golden Age occurred before the good jobs went overseas or the computer came to take what jobs were left:

Adrian Langston stands on a street corner in the Hunter's Point district of San Francisco, an unemployed man who learned nothing useful during three years in the Army. His grandfather, he says, "farmed tobacco in North Carolina for roughly about fifty-four years. He stopped in seventy-nine, and right now he farms just nature crops. He's a self-made person: thirty-five years as a contractor in cement, and he was self-sufficient. And there's a lot of rural people in those rural areas who have no education. Grandfather's now eighty-nine years old and he owns roughly about three, four hundred acres of land."

A week later, Langston said his grandfather had five hundred acres, "about fifty chickens, all the corn and vegetables he could ever need." Still without a job, in his mother's apartment, caring for his small son who trembled with the tension of living among his grandmother's fishtanks and plastic-covered couches, Langston said his problem was "the generations of change." He had no formal training, and "it's impossible for a man like me to get into a union."

Often tales of a Golden Age include "the prices back then." A man in Appalachia said it was a good life when "you could buy a dope [soft drink] for five cents." He identified the force that destroyed the Golden Age as "outsiders, the government." Until they came to Hancock County, Tennessee, life had been simple, food had been plentiful, and good.

The structure of the myth is always the same: Plenitude—an act of force—poverty. It is not mere nostalgia, but it includes nostalgia; people feel homesick for the Golden Age.

Like Hesiod's tale, stories of a Golden Age need not be true in the sense that facts are true. They are metaphorical explanations of the history of the world as it made the life of the storyteller. The danger of them, as with all imagined truths, is that they are incontrovertible: Who can deny a metaphor? Once the poor accept the mythical explanation of their situation, it becomes the central myth of their lives, and to overcome it may be nearly impossible.

Having such a myth not only explains the world, it comforts in a cruel way by removing the poor from control and thus responsibility for their own lives. Who can overcome the will of the gods? Who can overcome history? It requires an act of hubris that inevitably ends in defeat or destruction, which of course is the notion of classical tragedy.

Among Americans with African ancestry the myth works perfectly to their detriment. Africa was paradise; slavers came and plucked people out of paradise, putting them into the worst of conditions, like Hesiod's men of iron. If there were no Golden Age in Africa, if blacks came up from slavery, the myth would have the same structure, but it would move in the opposite direction. As one would expect, blacks who have succeeded in America speak of coming up from slavery, while the poor, like Marcel Walton, the man in the dirty skullcap at the Pride Day Picnic in Chicago, preach the fall from the Golden Age.

For those who are not poor in a nation of immigrants the same structure serves, but in the opposite direction: They proceed from a difficult life through the force of their own moral will to a better life.[2] Who has not heard of people pulling themselves up by their bootstraps? What is the story of America but the tale of upward mobility? Even the Pilgrims arrived with so little they had to depend on the largesse of savages to enjoy their first Thanksgiving, so says the myth.

The myths of rich and poor are homologous; one simply has to be turned upside down to show how it resembles the other. The United States may have been founded in a political revolution, but the central myth of America is economic. All Americans, rich and poor alike, subscribe to it. But the poor are ill served by the myth, while the rich are made to feel morally comfortable.

All through history the rich have used myths to control the poor while aggrandizing themselves. Consider the Calvinist notion of "the elect of God." It follows the same structure as Hesiod's tale; Calvin simply turned it upside down. Instead of the gods moving humans into continuously lower forms of life, the one God elects to take them into Heaven, which explains their good fortune on earth: A man becomes rich through God's election. Since such things are in God's hands, the poor may resign themselves to their lot.

This aspect of resignation, based on the comfort of the Golden Age

---

[2] Assimilation and multiculturalism do not appear to be predictive of wealth or poverty. In general, assimilation opens more opportunities than retention of an old country culture and language, but one may succeed without assimilating, as evidenced most recently by some Cubans, Hasidic Jews, West Indians, Pakistanis, and Russians. Members of these and other groups have established themselves in businesses and professions within a small community, or have limited their private lives to a small homogeneous community, with old country cultural traits, while doing business with other Americans outside their communities.

The economic danger in multiculturalism, when it leads to ghettos, is that outsiders will come into the cultural ghetto and drain the money from it. Banks, savings and loans, fast-food franchises, retailers of clothing, jewelry, and household goods have been the most frequent venturers into ghetto communities, with the banks causing two kinds of economic harm by taking money out of the ghettos and then redlining them when it comes to making loans to ghetto dwellers for housing or business.

myth, is not mere speculation. In discussing the nature of the American economy with a group of young adults, all of whom live at or near the poverty line, the common response to abject poverty, even slavery, is that some people can be happy under such conditions, but only when they think it is their lot in life; in other words, when they have a Golden Age myth to explain their situation.

Overcoming the myth—making melodrama rather than tragedy of a life, as Aristotle would have described it—demands a different worldview; that is, a new understanding of the central myth. (Part Two of this book will deal with this question of personal revolution in America.)

In the past, social revolution has served—theoretically—to turn the myth on its head, with the revolution taking the rule of force, and the goal being to turn the game of the modern world into a ritual, with the revolution as the unforgettable equalizing act. In states founded on such revolutions, like Mexico or the former Soviet Union or Cuba, remembrances of the revolution become the ritual.

The problem for the poor in a country where revolution is unlikely, if not impossible, is how to overturn the central myth. If they abandon the Golden Age, they lose the comfort of it, and if they hold on to the myth, they remain poor and in need of the comforting explanation. The effort to rise from multigenerational poverty, to break the double bind of the central myth, requires a heroic risk, one that often results in tragedy, for the courage of the valiant poor may be great, but it is the nature of myths to endure.

VI.

The Surround of Force

THE GOLDEN AGE OF POVERTY, the central myth of the multigenerational poor in America, like all myths, has worldly origins. Force, which plays the determining role in the myth, holds the same key position in the daily lives of the poor. But without the revealing clarity of the myth, the role of force can be difficult to recognize:

First, there is not one force, there are many. Twenty-five different forces will be listed and put into context in the following pages, and the list could easily extend to thirty or forty.

Second, the observer's distance from them transfigures the lives of the poor: Their own acts of force become salient, while the forces that act on them fade into the background. It is exactly the reverse of the beautifying effect of distance on New York or Chicago viewed from an airplane at night.

Third, observers look from the wrong direction: the forces that act on the poor often come from the direction of the observer. Attempting to look at the poor in what we think of as objective fashion, i.e., from the wrong direction, requires a certain arrogance and invariably leads to deceptions. In the case of the multigenerational poor, it leads to the appearance of the poor bringing their troubles on themselves.

Fourth, forces do not exist in the abstract. Like transitive verbs, they need objects to make sense; objects are the human context that makes them understandable.

Fifth, recognizing the forces that act on the poor often entails counter-intuitive thinking; for example, helpers, social services, marriage, and the law do not usually present themselves as negative forces.

Sixth, it may not be to the advantage of the observer to understand the role of force in the lives of the poor, because it would change his or her understanding of the way the game of inequality is conducted.

Finally, the observer may think that force is something else entirely, because force can have various meanings, ranging from the definition used in the physical sciences to that used by the military and the police. Force is sometimes used as a synonym for power or violence, but that leads to confusion, as in the work of the early twentieth-century Marxist Georges Sorel.[1] In relation to multigenerational poverty, force has a clear and specific meaning, which distinguishes it from violence to a large extent and places it in opposition to power. Moreover, force initiates a predictable and circular pattern of response not unlike the one Michel Foucault describes for prison inmates in *Discipline and Punish*.[2]

Force is not negotiable, nor can the object of force agree with it; the object can only succumb or react. Although force need not be physical, it produces the same state in the object as physical threats or acts and an equally limited choice of responses. A bureaucracy, which Hannah Arendt calls the "rule of nobody," exemplifies force in modern society. The bureaucracy does not use violence to exert control, but it does not permit negotiation. Some bureaucracies have elaborate appeals systems through which they feign negotiation, but everyone who deals with bureaucracies soon learns that the force they exert is non-negotiable.

Force cannot be withdrawn once the act has been done; the arrow cannot be returned to the bow and the word cannot be unspoken. Like the arrow loosed or the word said, force occurs, and everything that follows is contingent.

Unlike argument, which has a dialectical shape, involving thesis and antithesis, and lies at the heart of political life at all levels of society, force closes off dialogue. It is not like the endless rope of social discourse; force presents itself as a wall.[3]

---

[1] Isaiah Berlin said of Sorel: "How the use of violence in practice can be distinguished from the use of force is never made clear." *Against the Current* (New York: Viking Press, 1980) p. 322.
[2] (Paris: Gallimard, 1975; first American edn, New York: Pantheon, 1978).
[3] In Chapter XII it will be shown that the function of this sometimes metaphorical, but often

Since force can neither be negotiated nor withdrawn, it cannot occupy a middle ground. In an abusive marriage, for example, the man tells the woman, "You're an ugly whore." He cannot, like a congressman or a corporate officer, say, "I misspoke," nor can the man and woman find a middle ground, such as, "You're ugly, but chaste." Similarly, once it occurs, the experience of eviction cannot be withdrawn, and there is no middle ground between eviction and occupancy; the door is either open or closed.

Isolation, racism, theft, insult, disease, hunger, fear are all forces, and none can be withdrawn after they are loosed. Nor can they be negotiated. Diseases can be cured, but a person either has AIDS or asthma or high blood pressure or he doesn't. Racism is, by definition, immoderate. A television set cannot be more or less stolen. Insults and imprecations do not lend themselves to negotiation (a person cannot be slightly damned), and silence is not an antidote: The wordlessness of isolation, which also leaves no middle ground in which to execute human maneuvers, may be one of the most dreadful of all the many forces people use against each other.

The exertion of force happens so frequently that it might appear to be part of what defines us as human, but that is not the case: various species use force as well as violence to maintain their existence. Everyone has seen films of lions and wolves and so on in which they use force, in the form of shaming, isolation, threats of violence, or withholding food, to manage the pride or pack. What distinguishes us from the other species is that we have an alternative to force, not that we so often employ force instead of killing.

1. Force and Violence

When force and violence are confused, as in the work of Georges Sorel, who said that force was used by oppressors and violence by the oppressed, the moral value of the concepts seems to get lost. Sorel argued at one point that violence was everywhere, using the police as an example. But it made no sense within Sorel's larger definition, for the police were employed by the oppressors, who used force; violence belonged to the oppressed, it was their form of resistance.[4] Sorel's confusion of means and motives—giving the

---

very real, wall is to exclude the poor from the life of the citizen.

[4] Sorel believed that violence would lead the producers (the oppressed) back to a Golden Age like the one that existed before Plato and Aristotle and all the "corrupt intellectuals" ruined the world of creativity. Although I am not sufficiently conversant with the genesis of Sorel's Golden

same act a different name and moral value according to who committed it—may not have been his only error, but he eventually lost control of his ideas about labor, creativity, and violence, and descended into fascism and anti-Semitism.

The temptation to differentiate force from violence according to an ethical prescription did not die with Georges Sorel. In the movies, television, and the press, violence continues to be associated with the poor while force belongs to the rich; and just as Sorel can be a villain or a hero to those on the left or on the right, the poor appear as violent in *The Nation* and *The National Review* while force belongs to "the establishment" according to both ends of the spectrum.

A recent case of the confusion of motives with means can be found in the pronouncements of Louis Farrakhan, the leader of the Nation of Islam. Farrakhan deplores racism when blacks are the objects, but adopts racist language and tactics when speaking of Jews. Like Sorel, he wants to believe that the same act is moral in one situation but not in another. Interestingly enough, Farrakhan seems to be following Sorel in his interest in fascism, which may grow out of the same confusion: In 1996 Louis Farrakhan traveled to Africa and the Middle East, visiting, embracing, and soliciting money and moral support from Fascist regimes in Nigeria, Libya, Iraq, and Iran.

Instead of moral origins, which can only lead to confusion, force and violence should be defined as they appear in the world. In other words, if a striking worker shoots a capitalist or a policeman hired by a capitalist shoots a worker, it is an act of violence. On the other hand, if the capitalist locks out the workers or the workers close down the plant with a picket line, it is an act of force. The motive does not define the act and the act does not imply the motive.

Force describes a condition in which a person or group of persons coerces another. In most cases, force is an ongoing relation in which the one who exerts the force compels or obliges the object to behave as the forceful person wishes.

Violence is a kind of force, a subset in the logical sense; it is quick, physical, savage, and of furious intensity. Violence or the threat of violence accompanies virtually every act of force; it is the physical strength that gives force its authority.

Force constrains its object, defining the object and his or her life condition; it creates suffering and pain through demeaning the object, debasing and shaming him. Violence does not constrain or shame its objects, it is not

---

Age theory to make a judgment, it appears that he adopted the structure common among the multigenerational poor—the oppressed producers, in his view.

ongoing. Violence strikes; it has echoes but no duration. Murder is an act of violence. Imprisonment is an act of force.

Some acts prove more difficult to define; hunger, for example. It has many of the characteristics of violence, but it does not become violent unless it is an ongoing condition. Missing dinner does not constitute violence; going to bed hungry every night does terrible violence.

Since violence is a subset of force, force and violence must be essentially the same, even if they are formally distinct. Once we know the essence, the two acts become homologous: The one who exerts the force or does the violence is the subject and the other is the object. The subject creates, defines, controls, and the object reacts, accepts, obeys.

Here again distinctions can be troublesome, but not impossible. Who is the subject of ill health? When the cause is malnutrition or toxic waste or unsanitary conditions, the subject is clear. When the amount of salt in the drinking water of the city of Greenville, Mississippi, is five times the national average and the incidence of disease caused by hypertension is greater than the national average, there truly is no subject. The subject/object relation here comes in the nature of health care. The lack of medical insurance is a force, and the subject of that force is not only known, it appears to be proud of its role.[5]

Force seems most often to be the work of institutions and government and violence the work of individuals, but the distinction does not hold in all instances. The rogue cop who kills an innocent child represents a group, as does the rioter who shoots a cop in the street. We may think of one group as heroic and the other as villainous, but no matter which side we choose, it is a side, a group that can be defined and counted.

The moral distinction between force and violence does not hold when Sorel makes it from the left or when Charles Murray and Ken Auletta make it from the right. Violence does not belong to the poor any more than force belongs to the rich. Power is another matter.

---

[5] I refer, of course, to those members of the U.S. Congress and the various state legislatures who want to reduce medical care for people in the bottom economic quintiles, whether they are working or receiving entitlements. Legal immigrants were advised early in 1997 that they were no longer eligible for SSI payments. About 1 million people suddenly found their meager benefits cut to zero.

2. Force and Power

The Pueblos of the American Southwest drew a clear distinction between force and power, according to the historian Ramón A. Gutiérrez.[6] The Inside Chiefs held power in the form of authority granted to them by the gods and the members of the pueblo.[7] Within the pueblo itself, neither acts of violence nor any other acts of force were permitted. A second group lived outside the pueblo. These were the warlike Outside Chiefs and their band of hunter/warriors. Although the Outside Chiefs had the greater physical strength and ability, the Inside Chiefs held the power of the pueblo. They directed the Outside Chiefs to hunt, make war, and defend the pueblo using whatever force was required. The Outside Chiefs could not conduct raids, hunt, or even defend the pueblo without the consent of the Inside Chiefs.

Using this convention, the Pueblos were able literally to maintain a wall between force and power. It was this Pueblo wall that led some early and very romantic anthropologists to think the Pueblos were pacifists when, in fact, they had developed something even more important: the ability to separate force and power.

In modern democratic societies, at least since Periclean Athens, the distinction has been as clear as the Pueblo wall. Force remains an instrument of power, a means. Legitimate power is still an end in itself, a way of living, and force can never be an end, only a means. Force can serve as an instrument of power, as in the case of the Pueblos, but power can never serve force. When there is no legitimate power, however, force fills the vacuum.

Power differs from force in that it is self-contained, both the subject and the object. Force is always lonely, while power never occurs in isolation; one person alone among others cannot have legitimate power. At the extremes, ultimate force is one against all, as in a tyrant against the people, while ultimate power is all against one, as in the people against a tyrant.

Force increases by destroying the humanity of its object, but power, having no object or other, can only grow by inclusion. If force and power were turned into simple illustrations, power would appear as a circle and force would be an arrow.

The nature of legitimate power and its relation to democracy will occupy Chapter XII, but there is at least one question about the distinction

---

[6] *When Jesus Came, the Corn Mothers Went Away* (Stanford, CA: Stanford University Press, 1991).
[7] Cicero described this as "power in the public [or people], authority in the senate."

between force and power that has to be considered here. A real instance will serve better than an abstraction in posing the question.

Perhaps the worst housing in the entire United States is in Belle Glade, Florida, in what is known there as "Blacktown." The main street of that part of town is so dangerous that people are afraid to walk by the gambling houses because stray bullets so frequently come through the doors and windows. As an act of force, an ongoing condition that hurts people by shaming and demeaning them as well as subjecting them to filth, rodents, infestations of insects, and some of the most disgusting sights in the entire country, the one-room apartments in Belle Glade have no peer. They rent for $200 a month to people who earn their money laboring in the fields. One toilet for men and another for women, one shower, a filthy stove in an unlit room, and one sink serve an entire floor of more than forty rooms, most of which are occupied by at least two people. Garbage is piled up five to seven feet high in the spaces between the square blocks of rooms.

Many of the people who live in these blocks of foul housing are Haitians who work in the cane fields around the central Florida town near Lake Okeechobee. American blacks, many of them drug addicts, also live there. The Haitians, who have the immigrant's desire to strike a new social contract in a new country, despise the housing and are ashamed of having to live there. They say that housing was better in Haiti, although the government was worse. Everyone who lives in the blocks of housing fears the landlord, who is quick to punish by eviction. And as one of the tenants explained to Sauvern Pierre, a Haitian employed by Florida Rural Legal Services, the new landlord has been far more humane than his predecessor.

The housing was built during World War II at the insistence of Eleanor Roosevelt, who thought it would improve the living conditions of foreign workers who were brought into the country to replace Americans who had gone to war. Mrs. Roosevelt may have had the best intentions, yet these redbrick, three-story blocks of rooms did not have enough showers or toilets or cooking facilities on the day they opened.

Not to be unfair to Mrs. Roosevelt, she apparently considered the housing temporary when it was built more than half a century ago. But the government did not destroy or refurbish it; instead, the poor-quality temporary housing has been turned into an act of force against everyone who has occupied it for the last forty years or more. Thousands upon thousands of people have suffered, grown sick, and been shamed there.

Is this inexcusable act of force what is meant by legitimate power? After all, the governments of the United States of America, the state of Florida, and the city of Belle Glade have all been elected by the people.

The question suggests several different answers. When an instrument of a duly elected government breaks the laws of the government by committing an act of force, the distinction between power and force holds. The illegal act by an instrument of the government is an anomaly, tantamount to a self-inflicted wound. That may explain a rogue cop, but it does not explain Eleanor Roosevelt's housing in Belle Glade.

Legitimate power is also capable of error. Innumerable laws have been enacted that turned out to be harmful to the holders of legitimate power and had to be repealed. That may explain some foolish traffic laws, but not the longevity of the temporary blocks of housing in Belle Glade.

Belle Glade points to something very different about America and the poor. Acts of force directed against the poor do not lead the rest of the nation to question the legitimacy of the power of the government. An act of force against the poor does not compare to a self-inflicted wound, because the poor are not considered to be among the holders of power in the United States. They are illegitimate, outside the self-contained circle of power, nothing more than the objects of force.

In the abstract, some of the conditions in which the poor live seem pleasant enough. What could be the force in neighbors or luck or law? For the rest of society, pregnancy is a blessing, law is a protection, helpers are appreciated. But in the context of poverty, everything changes.

In Chapter IX, twenty-five of the forces that affect the poor will be shown in human context. None will appear alone, for the poor do not often deal with one force or two or half a dozen. They live in a *surround* of force, which differentiates them from those inside the circle of power and determines the outcome of the game.

Instinctively one thinks of a surround, any enclosure, as forcing people together, binding them, like the casing of a sausage or a belt around a bale of cotton. If that were the case, the surround would be the genesis of political life, a kind of polis created by force in which the poor would live public lives . But the forces of the surround do not affect *the poor*, they affect poor persons, not even families, but persons, one at a time. Everyone who lives within the surround lives alone. The weight of the forces separates them, splintering the body of the poor like glass underfoot, driving the shards of family, community, society into feckless privacy.

VII.

The Mirror of Force

*. . . this irrepressible violence is
neither sound and fury, nor the
resurrection of savage instincts, nor
even the effect of resentment: it is
man recreating himself.*
— J E A N - P A U L   S A R T R E ,
Preface to Frantz Fanon,
The Wretched of the Earth

1. The Problem of Anomie

WITHIN THE SURROUND OF FORCE, people live in
poverty and panic. They scurry, going from place to place, looking for food,
a new apartment, medical care for a child. The iron wall of the surround
pens them into a limited area, but the panic inside the surround has no limits; they may do nothing and everything, suffering from excesses of both
order and liberty.

This state of affairs, in which the rules of life make no sense, currently
has no widely accepted name or clear definition. "The underclass" will not
do, for it is more pejorative than descriptive. There is a word, however,
which has a history, both ancient and modern, and goes a long way toward
clarifying what happens within the surround.

A hundred years ago, Emile Durkheim revived a Greek word *anomia*, meaning "lawlessness" or "negation of law."[1] *Anomia* has a cousin in language, *anomiletos*, which means "having no connection with others, unsociable." It is also useful to keep in mind the context of this revival: Durkheim's famous study, *Suicide*.

Durkheim said that anomic suicide "results from man's activity's lacking regulation and his consequent sufferings." This happened, he said, during crises, especially economic crises. But he did not limit such crises to declines in a person's fortunes. Sudden improvements could also lead to anomie. It is the disjunction between a person's desires and abilities that brings about the crisis, according to Durkheim: "No living being can be happy or even exist unless his needs are sufficiently apportioned to his means."

It is restraint, regulation, that is lacking in a state of anomie, he declared. Dire poverty does not lead to anomic suicide, because "it is a restraint in itself." Durkheim gave the examples of Ireland, Calabria, and Spain, all very poor areas at the end of the nineteenth century, and concluded, "nothing excites envy if no one has superfluity."[2]

Anomie, the crisis that precipitates suicide, occurred in the case of relative poverty, but not when poverty was absolute. Durkheim's theory proved out in the North Lawndale district of Chicago, which remained tightly organized and political during the Great Depression, but has become a classic case of anomie at the end of the twentieth century when television daily drives home the relative nature of poverty.

Half a century later, Robert Merton revised Durkheim's definition, continuing to understand it as the inability to accommodate desires to the means for satisfying them, but introducing the idea of anomie as the result of failing to conform. Merton showed how people adapt to anomie, however, describing theft, for example, as an innovative way to satisfy a desire by abandoning legitimate means. He also described drug use as a retreat from the desire to achieve goals.

While Merton said anomie was the result of the inability of people to achieve the American dream of success at the end of the 1950s, others were beginning to use the word in conjunction with juvenile delinquency. Anomie was becoming the crisis rather than a reaction to crisis.

In its new incarnation, anomie became a synonym for the underclass and the culture of poverty. In both the underclass and the culture of poverty, the

---

[1] *Anomia* translates into the English anomie or anomy; both spellings are acceptable.

[2] Emile Durkheim, *Suicide* (New York: The Free Press, 1951), pp. 254, 258. The first quotation is correct; the infelicity is the work of the translator.

poor, especially the young, did not obey laws or behave according to accepted social norms. The connection of anomie to suicide faded into the background and Merton's innovation—crime—came to the fore.

Life within the surround, however, began to lose its likeness to the world Durkheim or even Merton used as a basis for understanding anomie. The game of modern society continued to produce unequals, but the crisis in many parts of the country had become endemic: The multigenerational poor lost before they could even attempt to compete; for many poor people the crisis was born with them, and ongoing. Still, it differed from life in absolute poverty. In America, every poor person knew he or she was poor in comparison to Bill Cosby or Donald Trump, the corporate executive Michael Jordan or the basketball player of the same name; every poor person knew that somebody could buy new sneakers or an automobile or a house in the country—in fact, according to television programs and advertisements, practically everyone but the real losers could afford such things.

This kind of ongoing crisis had less connection to the rest of America than to the colonies of the Third World, those places where relative poverty is expressed in the relation of natives to settlers (or conquerors) rather than to each other. In 1961, a young psychiatrist from the island of Martinique, Frantz Fanon, published his view of life within the surround of force as it was lived in Algeria under French colonial rule, *The Wretched of the Earth*. A preface to Fanon's book, written by Jean-Paul Sartre, elaborated on some of Fanon's observations about the character of life within the colonial surround. Addressing Fanon, he wrote, "You said they understand nothing but violence? Of course; first, the only violence is the settler's; but soon they will make it their own; that is to say, the same violence is thrown back upon us as when our reflection comes forward to meet us when we go toward a mirror."[3]

Sartre had found the beginning of an endless series of reflections: the mirror of force. The response to force, as Sartre read it in Fanon, was exactly as Hannah Arendt and others understood it: "If he shows fight, the soldiers fire and he's a dead man; if he gives in, he degrades himself and he is no longer a man at all; shame and fear will split up his character and make his inmost self fall to pieces."[4]

The third option, to use greater force to overcome the oppressor, is the advice of Fanon and Sartre to colonialized peoples. Fanon the psychiatrist argued from this third alternative that man re-creates himself through vio-

---

[3] Frantz Fanon, *The Wretched of the Earth* (Paris: François Maspero, 1961), Preface by Jean-Paul Sartre, p. 17.

[4] Ibid., p. 15.

lence, adding yet one more to the standard list of such re-creations: Christians hold that man re-creates himself through the love of God; Hegel thought it happens through the power of mind; Marx said labor was the way. The Greek concept of autonomy may also be considered a means for man to re-create himself.

Fanon spoke of violence as a unifying force on the national level and "At the level of individuals . . . a cleansing force. It frees the native from his inferiority complex and from his despair and inaction; it makes him fearless and restores his self-respect."[5]

In his comments on Fanon, Sartre recognized one other aspect of violence: "If this suppressed fury fails to find an outlet, it turns in a vacuum and devastates the oppressed creatures themselves. In order to free themselves they even massacre each other. The different tribes fight against themselves since they cannot find the real enemy. . . ."[6] In the United States, this is the only possible response for the poor. They cannot mirror force with overwhelming force. Even if Sartre's notion of man re-creating himself through violence in a colonial situation was reasonable, it would not apply in the United States. Even if the poor are considered an internal colony, they cannot re-create themselves through feeble acts of violence against their powerful oppressors; they can only turn the violence against each other and themselves, isolating themselves from each other and the world, inviting a lonely death.

A structure of force begins to emerge:

In a society that operates like a game, turning equals into unequals, the crisis of change produces a state of anomie where the rules fail to hold.

The poor, those who lose in the game of modern society, are thrust into a surround of force. Inside the surround, they experience anomie: panic is limitless action within a surround, but the surround ruthlessly limits the freedom of its objects by enclosing them. In other words, there are no constants within the surround, no reason, no stability, and no rules; there is only force.

The one who experiences force within the surround mirrors it; that is, the object of force reacts instantly, at the speed of light, if you will, like an image in a mirror. And there can be virtually no end to these reactions. As in any set of facing mirrors, the images bounce up and back to infinity.

When those inside the surround cannot effectively mirror the force exerted on them, they turn it on themselves; they become the object of their own rage: Durkheim's anomic suicide, Merton's innovation (theft) or

[5] Ibid., p. 94.
[6] Ibid., p. 18.

retreat (drugs), and Sartre's devastation of the oppressed. Of these, drug addiction, which has lately been described as "self-medication," comes closest to a pure act of suicide. Drug addiction, generally includes both the death of the conscious rational person that occurs following the administration of the drug, and immersion in a drug culture, which may lead to actual death resulting from a drug overdose, disease, violent confrontation, or a dealer/customer relationship more like indentured servitude than a business exchange.

Since the poor are rarely able to turn the tables on their antagonists in America, to mirror force with force, the keystone of the structure is the act of suicide, which takes many forms: drug addiction, alcoholism, poor-on-poor crime, or withdrawal from society into slavery, gangs, cults, homelessness, hypersexuality, violence, or depression.

The alternative to life within the structure is to create a new structure— one that interferes with the mirror of force at its inception. It too begins with reflection, but of a very different kind, one that leads to the light of political life rather than the darkness of self-destruction. Man, who enters the world alone, more fearful than any other creature, has but this one opportunity to re-create himself in the modern, secular world; that is, to go among men, which the Romans thought of as a description of life itself. It is this going among men, this profound step out of the private world into the public space in which politics occurs that enables the lonely organism to re-create itself as political man, the one who participates in governing himself.

2. The Example of the Prison

The surround of force appears in a highly evolved miniature in the prison. It begins at the outer boundary of the institution with the wall, which may be made of stone or concrete, rising to the height of the rooftops and beyond, or constructed of chain-link fence and razor wire. The force represented by the wall is enhanced by the guard towers and the men who stand watch with weapons loaded and ready, threatening the prisoners with the violence of the rifles and automatic weapons while constantly exerting the force of surveillance.[7]

---

[7] During the 1995–96 academic year, I spent some hours in the Bedford Hills Correctional Facility in Bedford Hills, New York, teaching a course in the humanities. Bedford Hills is a maximum-security prison for women. It is a model institution, run by Elaine Lord, one of the most enlightened prison superintendents in the United States. An extraordinarily intelligent

Prison operates as the purest surround of force. Inside the prison every inmate lives in panic, unable to discover a single face to present to the world. The prisoner who turns force against force at one moment, acts as a supplicant the next; growling and making a show of teeth in the morning, and in the afternoon peeping in a mendicant's voice and humbled stance. The demeanor of the prisoner, the set of his shoulders, the timbre of his voice, betrays the shift from one reaction to the other. And the reaction is always quick, almost instantaneous: suicide or murder; submit and be destroyed, attack and be destroyed.

Within such an anti-political world, the solution suggested by Fanon and Sartre makes sense to the prisoner. Even the confused terms and definitions of Sorel come to have a certain clarity. Violence seems the only rational as well as the only emotional response appropriate to the situation. Anything else requires a surrender to fatalism or an otherworldly martyrdom.

No prisoner dares to trust another, even if they are of the same "family" or they are long-term sexual partners; the only relation is to those who are in control, the hierarchy of force. And in such circumstances, the prisoner may only resist and be punished or submit to the ongoing punishment. Deceit would appear, at first, to offer a way out of the dilemma, but it is merely a form of submission.

All the prisoner sees is hierarchical, force responding to greater force. In a prison setting legitimate power does not exist, since power must be given willingly by those within the circle, and there is no circle, only a rigid hierarchy of force. There can be no public life in a prison, only the privacy of isolation within the surround of force. No model of the *vita activa* exists within the prison.

---

woman now serving a life sentence there said, "If I have to be in the joint, this is where I want to be." Nevertheless, Bedford Hills is a prison. Many of the redbrick buildings are very old, some of them built in the nineteenth century. The heat is poor in many of the units. Ice forms on the walls of some of the cells in winter.

Some of the ironies of prison life, even in this prison, are nearly unbearable. Judith Clark wrote of one such irony in a prize-winning poem describing the construction of death row on top of the nursery where the children of inmates are raised until they are eighteen months old.

Women's prisons are far less violent than the prisons for men, but the separation of women from their small children is in itself an ongoing act of terrible force. Women are less likely than men to force each other to endure sexual acts, but the rape of female prisoners by male guards is a commonplace. In an extraordinary case at the Bedford Hills prison in Westchester, New York, a woman who was forced to perform fellatio on a guard held his semen in her mouth until she could spit it out into a cup and bring it to the guard's superiors as incontrovertible evidence of the act and the identity of the attacker.

The person who leaves the prison knows less about politics, if that is possible, than he or she did upon being forced inside the wall. When the prisoner finally goes outside the wall, the experience of prison has sealed him inside the surround. He is poor, an ex-prisoner, and inexperienced in the art of politics, condemned to loneliness and the bitter speed of the reactive life. By destroying their political life, the prison farms the poor, raising its own crop of prisoners through recidivism and infection.

The prison world not only mirrors the world of the poor, there is a constant exchange of persons, language, and style between the prison and the poor. Among non-whites—and to a lesser extent among whites—the prison system, which extends out into the community through the probation and parole officers, the courts, the police, and the criminals, exerts force against every person, beginning with young children.[8]

When a person enters a prison, the sudden fall, the situation Durkheim said would produce anomie, takes place. In terms of relative poverty, nothing drives the point home more effectively than the restriction of the prison. Inside the walls, prisoners speak of "the free world" that is denied them. To counter the anomic state of the prisoner, the prison exerts terrible and constant force through surveillance and punishments; the suicides of prisoners take place in symbolic fashion, in the form of drug use or depression.

When a person leaves a prison, the sudden rise creates another spawning place for anomie, and in the world outside the prison nothing can counter the anomic urge so well as politics, for politics is the polar opposite of anomie. But the prisoner comes out of the prison with no sense of politics, a creature of isolation, jobless, penniless, confused by the sudden shift in the kinds of force that form the surround. It would be difficult to imagine a more perfectly anomic situation.

In effect, the prison system has exported anomie into the outside world, seeded it again among the poor, whom it farms to produce more clients.

[8] As it moves deeper into American society, the prison system seems to me to be an increasingly important aspect of racism.

VIII.

The Theater of Force

Ɪɴ 1598 ᴀ Sᴘᴀɴɪsʜ ᴇxᴘᴇᴅɪᴛɪᴏɴ led by Juan de Oñate made its way north through the pass between the two great continental mountain ranges, the Sierra Madre and the Rocky Mountains, crossing a wide, fast-flowing river into what is now the United States. As the conquistadores moved north through the high desert, they treated the natives, whom they found living in strangely constructed villages of many apartments, to a reenactment of the bloody conquest of Tenochtitlán by Cortés in 1519.[1]

Oñate and his men were quite certain that the little drama would be respectfully if not happily received, because news of the conquest had reached the Pueblos by the time the Spaniards arrived. Without this basis in accepted fact, the drama of the conquest would have been perceived very differently by the audience. The Pueblos would most likely have put the pageant of banners and swords in the category of dreams or arguments, and ignored it. After all, other people's dreams do not interest us and we tend to dismiss arguments that do not agree with our view of the world.

We can assume that the goal of the presentation was not the amusement of the audience, because that is not the business of conquerors. It also seems very likely that the Spaniards knew exactly what they were doing when they presented the play, since they used such dramatic presentations on many occasions. Perhaps they had borrowed the idea from Athens or Rome

---

[1] The description of the play is taken from several sources. The primary source is Gaspar Pérez de Villagrá, who wrote about the Oñate expedition, of which he was a member, in the closing days of the sixteenth century. See also Gutiérrez, *When Jesus Came, the Corn Mothers Went Away.*

or from some unknown source. Perhaps it originated with them, an insight of conquest. However it came about, the idea of using theater to change culture and character succeeded; even the inventors of the form could not have imagined the depth of its penetration into the soul of the audience. In his history of the Pueblos, Ramón A. Gutiérrez describes the long-term effect of the drama:

> In time the actor-audience relationship of the 1598 conquest drama was reversed. The Indians became the actors and Spaniards smugly looked on. When the Indians performed the dances, dramas, and pantomimes of the conquest, they continually relived their own defeat, their own humiliation and dishonor, and openly mocked themselves with those caricatures of Indian culture the conquistadores so fancied. Today in many Pueblos these conquest dramas are still enacted in seventeenth-century attire. A highly ideological view of the conquest thus became an integral part of what we now brand native culture.[2]

The Spaniards had created a special kind of theater, an American Theater of Force. Over time, it became the original American contribution to theater, eventually expressed in music, films, television, and videos as well as on the stage. The uniquely American character of the form depends upon the commonness and therefore the credibility of the incidents portrayed.

Unlike Homer, who mixed gory, realistic battle scenes with visits from the "gray-eyed goddess," and then imagined a fanciful voyage home for the wily wrestler, the Spaniards followed reality with a theatrical reproduction of it: The showing of violent acts entered the consciousness of the audience, where it was converted into force. The degree to which this kind of theater converted violence into an ongoing exertion of force shows plainly in the Pueblo conquest dramas. The force has been so deeply implanted that the Pueblos now display it as a part of their own culture.

The argument against this American Theater of Force always accuses it of leading to violence, especially among the young. And that may be so, but no convincing evidence has been offered so far, only vague correlations. In New York City, a classic *post hoc ergo propter hoc* argument was made about the robbery of a subway token booth. During the robbery, the criminals poured a flammable liquid into the booth and set it on fire. Newsprint moralists quickly compared the method to that of a killing in a recently released movie. In their minds it was obviously a case of *after this, therefore because of this*. The fallacy of their argument became evident to everyone

---

[2] Gutiérrez, *When Jesus came . . .* , p. 48.

when the robbers were caught: They had not seen the movie.

In creating the form of the Theater of Force, the Spaniards knew, by means of reason or instinct, of the necessity of a real analogue, not the "objective correlative" of T. S. Eliot's set of assertions made in his (1919) attack on *Hamlet,* but action for action. Contrary to Eliot's idea of an external correlative for a necessarily internal state of mind, the Spaniards envisioned two externals (event and drama) producing a specific state of mind: The force of Spain becomes a part of Pueblo culture.

Using the Pueblos as a testing ground from which we have sufficient distance both temporally and culturally, a theory of the Theater of Force emerges and finds application in contemporary life. The historical act and the theater exist interdependently; that is, one feeds on the other. Even so, we are not left with a chicken and egg argument. The Spaniards based their play on a real incident; the Theater of Force imitates a part of life and extends its sway through artistic means.[3]

So much has been written about the depiction of violence in the media, from television pictures of war in Vietnam to the lyrics of rap songs, that it would serve no use to repeat a long list of examples here. Social scientists, artists, churchmen, and civil liberties advocates debate endlessly over the chicken and egg argument about violence in America. Most of them agree that violence is bad in any form, but they cannot agree on what to do about it, other than to bemoan its existence.

To conclude that violence in theater begets violence in the streets requires one to believe that life is a form of war in which the only response to violence is violence, which, of course, is not true. One widely known alternative to that belief would be turning the other cheek. Another more complex alternative to violence in theater was recognized at least as early as 1598, perhaps thousands of years before: the conversion of violence into force.

When violence in the contemporary media follows this path rather than simply producing more violence, the media assume a different role in society—but not, as I shall argue, for all of society.

The Theater of Force cannot succeed unless it has a double in the real world. For example: a cartoon of a woodpecker flattened by a steamroller or a cat hit over the head by a mouse does not have a real-world double. For the affluent, who have no experience with it, a shooting in the street or a beating in the schoolyard also lacks a real-world connection; it functions like a cartoon. For the poor, however, the same shooting or beating often

---

[3] It could be argued that the style of the conquest of Mexico had historical antecedents in the Spanish wars against the Moors, as well as in Egyptian, Hebrew, Roman, Greek, Persian, and Aztec wars, but the defeat of the Aztecs was as close to being truly unique as a war of that era could be.

has a real-world double, and this reality gives the Theater of Force the means by which to create a different effect. In such circumstances murder means something.

Violence on film or videotape or in songs of one kind or another has little effect on children (or adults) who have no experience with violence. Televised news footage of war in Vietnam did not make jungle fighters of children in the suburbs of Minneapolis, for they knew no comparable reality; Vietnam was very far from the breakfast table or the living room. The argument to the contrary follows the same logic as the subway token booth fire that must have been incited by the movie; the sequence is apparent, but no causal relation can be proved. On the other hand, hundreds of thousands of young people who saw the same movie did not copy the crime.

Only a specific kind of violence affects the audience: the violence they know. Ask a person who has had a heart attack how it feels to see someone realistically have a heart attack on the movie screen. When there is no dissonance, the theater works.

The Theater of Force resonates perfectly with the real world in the North Lawndale section of Chicago or in Little Creek, in the mountains of eastern Tennessee. In those places almost every person has seen the wounded, watched the police ambulances haul away the dead. Like the Pueblos who watched the Spanish pageant in 1598, they have heard the news, theater means something.

The violence seen and heard by the poor does not, however, necessarily produce violence; the audience understands that it lacks currency. It was not always that way. When the military men who made the Mexican Revolution of 1910 were shown a film which included pictures of some of their enemies during the Constitutional Convention in Aguascalientes at the close of the war, they took out their pistols and began firing at the screen. In 1916 it was possible to mistake the image for the reality and react to it. Contemporary audiences, like the sixteenth-century Pueblos, know better. All they can do with the experience of the analogous violence of the Theater of Force is accept it.

The Theater of Force, which exists only for the poor, cannot be dismissed or even negotiated by the poor. Unlike the rest of society, the poor cannot move to a "better," less violent neighborhood or send their children to private schools. To an audience of the poor, the Theater of Force is a demeaning mirror. It goes on and on, not because the poor are violent, but because they live, inescapably, in a violent part of the world. The Theater of Force multiplies the violence suffered by the poor, so that the occasional becomes the commonplace becomes the norm. It is a common mistake to think the Theater of Force engages a poor person in a contest of violence; on the contrary, it administers an unforgettable beating.

It does not matter in the contemporary Theater of Force who is depict-ed as the subject or object. America operates according to the rules of games, and in the Theater of Force the poor among the audience arrive hav-ing lost the game. Violence as theater may amuse or delight or terrify them, but it will never be only a dream for them, for they know who really suf-fers. The theater tells them only to expect more. That is the nature of los-ing in America. The Theater of Force makes money for some of the winners and amuses the rest of them in the way that fairy tales and daydreams amuse. Only the poor lose: They buy the ticket and take the beating.

The Theater of Force takes its place in the surround, increasing the panic. Only as it contributes to the surround and the panicked life within does the Theater of Force lead to acts of violence, for life within the sur-round leaves the poor without the possibility of politics, hurrying, helpless to do anything but react, with no time to reflect, no time to do anything but react. And sometimes, as the surround presses them into extreme responses, the poor do violence to each other, becoming a force against themselves, as if the only proper complement to a Theater of Force is an audience of suicides.

A Note on Method

Hip-hop and rap have achieved a position of eminence in America. No other form of expression earns the same amount of invective. Gangsta rap in particular has been vilified by practically everyone who has not yet found out how to make money from it. The response of the Hip Hop Nation and the gangsta rappers to their critics has been chilled disdain, except in the case of the black musician currently most admired by whites, Wynton Marsalis. His theory of the lack of invention in hip-hop and the dangerous nature of any music so mechanistic sends the Hip Hop Nation into a rage.

Yapos Sopay, born Matthew Washington, produces tracks for hip-hop groups. He owns an SPS machine for sampling and an EPS machine for sequencing. The machines, which he bought on credit, cost nearly $5,000. When he sells his tracks, he gets as much as $1,000 for them. He also earns money as an emcee and a deejay. Yapos Sopay had this comment about Wynton Marsalis: "Hip-hop differs from jazz. But Wynton Marsalis is full of bullshit, because there's a lot of jazz where there's only minor changes, and we ask the hip-hopper also to make minor changes. We're not as limited as Wynton would want people to think. I don't think he listens to rap enough to have a fuckin comment, so he should shut his fucking mouth. If I see him, I'll slap him in his mouth, because I betcha if I went to his house I wouldn't see not one rap CD. If I did, it'd probably be somebody like MC Hammer."

To make a comparison of the Marsalis theory and Yapos Sopay's response requires some understanding of the way hip-hop music is made and how it differs from jazz, which is not to say that hip-hop musicians dislike jazz; in fact, Yapos named his son Jazz and uses jazz albums as source material for the tracks he builds.

Since I am not a musician or a member of the Hip Hop Nation, I have relied entirely on Matt's explanation.[4] It begins with definitions. The *beat* is the music track, which is built from a *bass line*, usually produced from recordings of a bass fiddle, but not necessarily; the sounds on a hip-hop track can be taken from anything or even made (by moving a record up and back while recording the sound). The melody is called the *riff*. Then come the *drums*. The bass usually comes first in building the beat, but not always. Sometimes the riff gets *laid down* (recorded) first.

Matt prefers making the drum track first, then the bass, making his own "little riff."

Using the sampler, he pulls out a two-bar piece from a record. This two-bar section can be repeated for eight or twelve bars or it can be varied from piece to piece. A *segment* is two bars on a 4/4 time signature. A song can be anything from two bars on up. Matt says his songs are usually eight two-bar segments or sixteen bars. Most often hip-hop music is constructed that way.

While hip-hop has emcees, deejays, and so on, live hip-hop music is impossible, because of the tedious technological construction of the music. *Freestyle* is unwritten rapping, but it is performed to mechanical beats and electronic sounds, like playing music in keeping with the beat of a metronome.

According to Matt Washington, hip-hop came about because the kids who made it were so poor they couldn't afford instruments or music lessons. That unlikely explanation is not, I think, original with him. He knows full well, since he made the down payment and pays the monthly installments on some of the machines he uses, that the turntables, sampling and segmenting machines required to make hip-hop tracks cost as much as ten or twenty guitars adequate to a beginner's needs, or many saxophones, trumpets, and even a couple of playable old pianos. Hip-hop does not belong to poverty, like a slave's work song, but to technology, like a computer-programmed machine.

From the first sample to the completed beat (music track), everything

---

[4] Matt is the name used by his family and some friends. I find it more comfortable than the acronym Yapos (for Young African Prophet of Soul) or the complete palindrome Yapos Sopay, and more fitting to the person. To use his "stage" name would, I think, be misleading.

More about Matt and several generations of his family in Chapter XIV.

about a hip-hop track follows a technological imperative. Unlike music played or sung, the sample cannot be invented; it can only be chosen from what exists. The technological imperative begins with limiting the music to what has been made: no birth of the new will be permitted.

Hip-hop beats differ from music, which is played ensemble, in what may well be one of the most cooperative, most political human endeavors. The beats differ most from improvised music, like jazz, which when played ensemble comprises both invention and political activity. In making a hip-hop beat, only one person can operate the sampler, and even then it must be done sequentially rather than concurrently. Ensemble performances are impossible. It is factory music, made in loneliness, as in a factory, where a person obeys the dictates of a process. Hip-hop is not based on the principles of art but on method, as it was devised by Descartes. The limitations of the method dictate every aspect of hip-hop beats, creating a mechanistic form, anti-human at its core.

Matthew Washington argues against this aspect of his music and the effect it may have on the listener. Aristotle would not have agreed with him. In the *Politics* (Bk. VIII, Ch.5), he wrote that "even in mere melodies there is an imitation of character, for the musical modes differ essentially from one another, and those who hear them are differently affected by each. . . .

"The same principles apply to rhythms; some have a character of rest, others of motion, and of these latter again, some have a more vulgar, others a nobler movement. Enough has been said to show that music has a power of forming the character. . . ." [5]

Aristotle, like Wynton Marsalis, would have us believe that the mechanistic rhythms of hip-hop affect the character of the listener, and I think they have a point. Such music—not music at all, but a technological imperative accompanied by words—has a place in the surround of forces. Rap beats do not amuse or entertain so much as they defeat their listeners. The character they imitate is the character of the machine, which in turn forms the character of the listener, driving out the human sense of possibility and politics. Rap beats are the victory of method over man, and they have no greater audience than the poor.

---

[5] Aristotle, *Politics*, trans. Benjamin E. Jowett (New York: Random House, 1941).

IX.

Contexts

Force is used not by those who have become weak under the preponderance of the strong, but by the strong who have emasculated them.
— P A O L O   F R E I R E,
The Pedagogy of the Oppressed

T H E   S U R R O U N D

Public Housing   Hunger   Helpers   Luck

Other Men's Eyes: Intellectual Muggings   Feudalism   Law

Guns   Hurrying & Pressure   Isolation

Government   Family Violence

Neighbors   Graffiti

Landlords   THE POOR   Meanness

Drugs   Prison

Criminals   Illness

Other Men's Eyes: Media   Other Men's Eyes: Racism

Police   Selling   Abuse   Ethnic Antagonisms

IN AMERICA BEFORE THE EUROPEANS and the Africans came, the natives hunted and made war using the same tactic: the surround. Buffalo, deer, small game, and human enemies could be killed or captured most efficiently within a surround. Isolated, with no place to turn, no place to run, they panicked, and then the killing began. Over the course of history many variations of the surround have been employed in killing. The pincer movement is among the best known of the military tactics, but any plan that prevents the escape of the enemy, or even reduces the enemy's ability to maneuver, is likely to produce a victory.

The Germans nearly changed the course of World War II by using that tactic during the Battle of the Bulge. If Patton's tanks had not arrived or the weather had not cleared, permitting air drops, the German surround would have annihilated an important American military force.

Sometimes a wall, a mountain range, a river, or a cliff will serve as part of a surround: the Jews at Masada and the native people of Illinois at Starved Rock capitulated to cliffs. And not only humans use the surround. Wolf packs kill that way, and so do other predators. The tactic has two advantages: First, of course, it isolates the prey and eliminates the possibility of escape; but perhaps more importantly, it changes the behavior of the animals or humans caught inside the surround. The moment the prey recognizes the surround, it becomes desperately lonely, raging or suicidal, unable to think. With no hope of escape, it succumbs to the notion of fate; the modicum of hubris that enables a person to rebel against the deadly promise of fate dies at the instant of recognition of the surround. Only the heroic do not die, and they are few.

RECOGNITION OF THE SURROUND came late to this work. I had not expected it. My intention was to concentrate on force as an alternative and a deterrent to political life. Forces did not seem to me then to be arranged in any way. I imagined a random distribution, each poor person with a specific problem that, once solved, would allow the person to quickly improve his or her economic and social life.

Taken out of context, any force could be blunted, any problem solved. But the poor live in context. Different assumptions had to be made, expectations of order within the context, but not of order independent of context.

Here, then, follow examples of each of the forces in the surround and some comments about forces that do not necessarily belong in the surround. A few require explanation but most do not. I hope I have provided enough context in most cases to show that these forces do not exist alone, but as part of a surround in each life.

The examples have not been squeezed into a single form. Instead, each one follows a form dictated by the content, and since the ideas in this book all depend upon the recognition of the distinction between force and power, I have not skimped in the portrayals.

1. Drugs: If It Isn't One Devil, It's Another

This is the story of Señora Estrelita Cordoba, widow of Hernández, and her daughter Leticia Amador, and I think it is entirely true, even though Mrs. Hernández has been under the care of a psychiatrist, because the widow and her daughter told it at different times and different places in Spanish and in English.

Estrelita Cordoba vda. de Hernández is a slim woman now, given to deep depressions and occasional euphoria, but up until the time when the devil appeared, she was very plump. For occasions such as storytelling or lunch with strangers she wears a suit with a paper flower in the lapel. She lives in El Paso, Texas, now, but her story begins in Mexico:

In 1945, the year my mother was in bed with the paralysis, we had a crime in the family. Gregorio Cordoba killed José Hernández. I was a little girl at the time, just eight years old. Only later, after my mother recovered from the paralysis, did I learn who it was.

When I grew up, I was friendly with a woman who was a prostitute. My mother didn't like me being with her. I was with her when I met this guy. He made a good impression on me. He asked if I wanted a beer. I said, "No, we're already drinking and eating enchiladas." But my friend said to him, "Why not, son, why not send over a couple of beers?"

So, in a short while, a couple of beers arrived. We went on talking. I was twenty-two years old then. In a little while he came over and asked if he could sit with us. We started talking, and then he asked if we wanted to leave there, but we said we lived there, in the front of the cantina. So he asked my name, and I told him, and he said his name was Roberto and that he liked me very much.

He used to knock on the door of our house every afternoon, but I didn't answer. One day he saw my little sister over there in a *vecindad* on Paisano Drive and he asked her if a woman named Estela lived there, one with long, curly hair and with eyes of color. And she said, "No, son, there's no one named Estela."

Well, I had some interest in talking with him because he was very handsome, so I answered the door, and I went out for a walk with him, talking, talking a lot.

Well, one day he asked my name, and I said that the name of the father is Cordoba, and he said, "Cordoba?" And I said, "Yes," and I told him that my name is not Estela, it is Modesta Cordoba.

And he said, "That's very nice."

We went on talking, we went to look at the views, we went downtown to look at the stores, we went to parades. We went on like that, until one day he asked if I was part of the family of Guadalupe Cordoba, who I said was my father's first cousin.

He said he knew the Cordoba family, and we left it at that.

But every time we met, he talked about the Cordoba family. Until we were married. Then he asked me, "Do you remember in 1945 there was a crime in your family?"

And I said, "Yes, why?"

And he said, "Your father's cousin killed my brother, José." And then he said, "I have you in my hands now. You're going to pay for the death of my brother." And that's how it all started.

Leticia interrupts: "My dad's family were all prostitutes, madames, the worst. His family never accepted her. From the time they got married, they spoke ill of her, they damned her unto the fourth generation. That's why we've been unlucky."

My husband had a lot of hate, he hated everyone. And anyone who likes me, he hates. He doesn't want anyone to like or even be around me, he has so much hatred. One night I went to a cantina with my husband and his brother-in-law. When my husband went to get a drink, his brother-in-law asked me to dance. The scene started then. He cursed me, and even took away my passport.

When we got back to the house, and the in-laws left, he beat me, then he tore off my clothes and threw me out into the street naked. He came after me, saying he was going to kill me with a dagger. My parents called the police, who picked up my husband and put him in jail. I didn't want to press charges, so they let him out. Then I stayed with my parents for two days until he came and asked for my pardon. After a while, I gave in, and went back with him.

It was hell after that. Life became very bitter. He was polite, not affectionate, very polite. He even helped me to get a crossing card. He was a good father, except when he was drunk, he was filled with anger.

We lived in the Second Ward after we came to this side. Our house had four rooms. The girls slept on a sofabed in the living room, then came our bedroom, then the kitchen. In the back was the room we called the Big Room, where the boys slept. After seventeen years in the Second Ward, we moved to the Salazar Projects.

"When we moved into the Salazar Projects," Leticia said, "they were new, so we

thought we were moving up in the world. Now, it's like, Oh, God, I lived there! When we first moved there, we bought some furniture, including a bookcase. It was made of paper over wood, real ugly, but we still have it. When people walked by and looked in the window and saw the bookcase, they thought we were rich. We were like the rich family there because of this bookcase, and that's why we don't get rid of it."

My husband got his leg into an accident on the job, and he lost his leg. He didn't lose his leg, but he lost the use of it. He got a lot of money for his leg.

He was schizophrenic, and he started to get more schizophrenic. One night, the boys were in bed and I was in the bath when I heard my husband in the boys' room. He was red in the face and all sweaty. He said the devil got out and he was battling with the devil. He asked, "Who do you think won?" And he said, "I won! Look!" It was only his son who was in the room. I told him. I swore to him it was only his son.

I was afraid that one day he would kill me, or kill someone. He was this way after he lost his leg. A curse was put on him.

Then I got sugar [diabetes].

One night in the projects a woman looked out the window of her apartment and she saw her son in a fight with another boy. The other boy had a knife. The mother shouted at him, begged him, pleaded with him not to kill her son, but the boy was in a rage, so he couldn't stop. He killed her son while the mother looked on.

My son, Juan, was not a gang member, but he had friends outside the projects. They were all involved with drugs.

My husband died, and the curse of schizophrenia died with him. But the curse of heroin put my son, Juan, in prison. And soon Leticia's husband, too. I went to a woman who tells fortunes with cards. She said, "If it isn't one devil, it's another."

2. Public Housing

Roaches

Before Shirley Crane gave up her job to care for her grandchildren, she had tended to the dying, and among the dying only those who died of cancer; it was her chosen work. A very thin woman, with the thinnest lips, and a wide mouth, like a cut in the smooth skin of a melon, she smoked and hacked a smoker's cough between the deep inhalations. Her hair had been dyed blond, perhaps to mask her Cherokee ancestry, as if it mattered to the dying, even in eastern Oklahoma, where Native Americans still endure the prejudices that attend reservation towns.[1]

It had been a long time since things had gone well for her: Her daughter danced naked in a bar in Tulsa and her son-in-law had gone to prison. There was no money and no one to take care of the children, so she gave up caring for the dying and took on these babies. But all the money had come from the dying. When that was gone, Joyce Crane moved to the southernmost end of Tulsa, to a housing project with rotted doors and dying grass, and nothing around it, not a shop or a store, nothing but green fields of isolation.

She put the best face on it. She wore lipstick, and dyed her hair now and then, and gave the babies little wax bottles full of sweetness to taste. When the glass top of the coffee table broke, she found a piece of smoked glass almost the same size, and made do. The tiny living room of her apartment was as clean as a place full of babies could be, cleaner, immaculate, nothing but a couch and a big television set, the coffee table, and one chair.

The rest of the apartment was even cleaner than the living room, in fact, too clean. The shelves were empty in the kitchen and the clothes were packed away in the bedroom. There was no trash and no trash can. The pantry was empty and the floors were swept.

She had begun the retreat into cleanliness when the next-door neighbors moved out. That was when the roaches came. Not one came, not ten, but hundreds, perhaps a thousand. She sprayed them and squashed them, but there was nothing she could do to keep them out of the cupboards and the pantry. They got into the children's clothing and the furniture. Finally, she put all the food into the refrigerator, the only place too tightly closed for them to enter. But she had to open the refrigerator often during the course of a day. It was only a matter of time.

Although the roaches frightened her, because she had found them crawling in the babies' ears, it was not the roaches she feared most. After the roaches, the rats came. They lived in the pantry. At first, they were frightened when she opened the door. They scurried into the darkest corner, and disappeared into a hole. She plugged up the hole, but they came back the next day and the next. And they were no longer frightened. They looked at her in the daylight. Before long, they would venture out of the pantry into the rooms where the babies slept.

The roaches and the rats came in spring when the neighbors moved out.

---

[1] For an appraisal of the special problems of the Native American poor, see *The Death of the Great Spirit: An Elegy for the American Indian* (New York: Simon and Schuster, 1971).

In the beginning of summer, Dwight, the big, soft, puff pastry boy who managed the Parkview Project, came to look at Shirley Crane's apartment. He saw the roaches and the apocalyptic cleanliness. He opened the door to the pantry, and quickly closed it when the red-eyed rats turned to stare at him.

Then he said that there would be pest control in autumn.

It was the beginning of summer.

The new head of the Housing Authority in Tulsa, Linda DuPont Johnson, said she had noticed the infestations when she came to Tulsa. She said there would be pest control in autumn. "The problem is the seventeen-year-old single moms who never learned how to keep house," she said.

In autumn, with money from the U.S. Department of Housing and Urban Development (HUD), she planned to clean up the projects. There would be frequent inspections, she said. If the apartments were "messy," the residents would be "counseled." Then inspected, and counseled. Inspected. Counseled. And evicted.

Snitches

In El Paso, Texas, where relative poverty settled in at the very end of the sixteenth century when Gaspar Pérez de Villagrá came back from the Oñate expedition, there is an old joke told by people in the housing projects. They say that moving out of the projects into the real slum of Chihuahuita is like going from Guatemala (Guate-bad) to Guatepeor (Guate-worse). In other words, the housing projects of El Paso, like those around the country, are bad places to live, but not nearly so bad as the other housing available to the poor. That makes eviction from a project the only fate worse than staying in a project, and the threat of eviction a terrible force bearing down on the poor.

Although the HUD money that built and supports most projects allows the federal government to oversee the operation of the projects, the reality is that every public housing authority is a fief, a kind of Wild West of lodging where no rules apply but those of the head of project or the local housing authority.

Housing authorities not only have their own police departments, they generally have an investigative branch that works with the housing police and a certain class of residents known as spies or snitches. According to Enriqueta Peña, a social worker who grew up in a project, snitching is informal. Neighbors are only too glad to reveal each other's violations of the rules of the project or, more precisely, the project manager.

The kinds of acts that can result in eviction vary from town to town, project to project. In the Salazar Projects in El Paso, for example, a tenant can be evicted for using too much water. Or for having a pet canary. Fish are acceptable, but not cats or dogs.

It cannot be proved, of course, but in the Salazar Projects, as in many others, certain tenants perform small tasks around the buildings and grounds, not real maintenance or construction but little things, inconsequential things, for which they receive free rent or reduced rent. How these payments affect the bookkeeping of public assistance is unknown, but the function of manager's pets is common knowledge in the projects. They are the ones who tell of a cousin staying too long in an apartment or a kitten living there. The snitches keep the managers informed of gang activity and arrests that do not get reported to the housing authority. They monitor water use and noise levels. When the investigations begin, they are almost always instigated by the snitches.

Although HUD finances most of the housing projects in the United States, the rule of force rather than the rule of legitimate power applies. Jack Marshall, a retired police officer who works as a case enforcement investigator in El Paso, said, "We can evict a family if family members or guests are involved in criminal activities. If our investigation shows this, or one of them is arrested, we evict them.

"This short-circuits the due process procedure. All we have to do is prove that criminal activities are going on. An arrest is sufficient grounds. We are not required to wait until the case goes to court and is judged yea or nay."

On March 28, 1996, President Clinton announced a "one strike, and you're out" plan for federal housing projects. In 3,400 federally funded projects, entire families will be evicted if any member of the family or a guest commits an act deemed criminal by the housing authority. No provision for due process was announced by President Clinton or his Housing Secretary, Henry Cisneros. The only comment by Mr. Cisneros reported in the press was, "Public housing is not a right in the United States. It is a privilege." If that were true, and the courts will eventually decide, due process would not be necessary in evictions.[2]

Most of the quick evictions come out of the criminal trespass section of the Texas Penal Code. On occasions when tenants have guests who engage in criminal activity in the view of the housing authority, the family can avoid eviction by signing an agreement saying that the "criminals" cannot visit in their apartment.

Then the snitches do their work; they are the monitors and the enforcers of the agreements, and they are always in attendance. Since due process does

[2] Reported by various broadcast media and newspapers, including the *New York Times*, March 29, 1996.

not apply, no one can monitor the monitors, no one can come between the force of the housing authority and its objects.

The Belle of Belle Glade

Few towns in America have been subjected to more bad publicity than Belle Glade, Florida, but very little has been changed by the light that has been let into the city. It is as if someone deliberately set out to prove that publicity is not the test of morality, that John Rawls was wrong in his view of ethics in the modern world.

Belle Glade first came to light with Edward R. Murrow's famous documentary, *Harvest of Shame*. In its ugly history Belle Glade has been, most recently, described as the AIDS capital of America. When the disease was first studied, scientists came to Belle Glade to find out how it was transmitted. The Haitian theory developed in Belle Glade because of the large population of farmworkers from Haiti. The possibility that the disease was spread by mosquitoes was also studied in Belle Glade, because the infestation of the blood-sucking insects in summer is nightmarish and the incidence of disease is so high.

Nothing in the political economy of the town appears to work except the sugar cane and vegetable farms that support it. Even the prison is a failure, best known for the murderers and armed robbers who dug a tunnel under the fences and escaped at the beginning of 1995.

Approaching the town in winter when the cane fields are burned, one sees a holocaust on the land, everything blackened by fire for miles and miles around, and some fires still raging, black and red against the blue sky, sweet-smelling and strangely beautiful, like a foretaste of the subtleties of Hell.

After the crossroads and before the town turns sour in the center, there are some shops and a few prosperous-looking blocks belonging to the steadily employed, the schoolteachers and state and federal workers. There is no movie house in Belle Glade. Like many American towns, it no longer has a center. Lake Okeechobee provides the recreation. The promoters say the fishing is good and the water sports are better, but it has gained a reputation as a place where great loads of illegal drugs are dropped from the sky.

The composition of Belle Glade is perhaps 75 percent black, but blacks have been unable to gain political power in the town because the white power structure has done some imaginative gerrymandering. There are two Farmers Home Administration– financed housing projects in Belle Glade, both operated by the Belle Glade Housing Authority. One, the Osceola Center, is mainly Latino (in Belle Glade, Latinos are considered white), and the other, the Okeechobee Center, is almost 100 percent black. By arranging the city limits for voting purposes, the residents of the white or Latino center have been included in the city's voting rolls, while the residents of the black center have been excluded even though they pay taxes to the city and receive city services. Gregory Schell, a lawyer for Florida Rural Legal Services, believes that inclusion of the Okeechobee residents in the voting rolls would enable those one thousand-five-hundred voters to change the administration in the town from white to black.

Court tests are pending, but the process is long and very complicated. Meanwhile, the mayor appoints the people who run the Belle Glade Housing Authority. Interestingly enough, the head of the housing authority, Fritz Stein, also employs many of the people who live in the Okeechobee Center project. If he is unhappy with them on the job, he can evict them from the project, and if he is unhappy with them in the projects, he can fire them from their jobs. He has the power of a feudal lord. As his employees say, he has them coming and going.

Stein also serves as vice chairman of the sugar cooperative and owns some of the largest cane fields and farms in the area. James Smith, Jr., the only black on the board of the housing authority, was appointed by the mayor, and simply does his bidding. The tenant representative for the Okeechobee Center, Mildred Thornton, was not elected by the tenants; the mayor also appointed her.

Lois T. Davis, a white woman who might be mistaken for grandmotherly, runs the Housing Authority as its executive director. The tenants say that Davis has complete control of the projects and especially the staff: "The managers of the projects cannot allow anyone to move in or out unless she gives her permission. Anyone who defies her is gone the next day." And they offer examples to prove their case.

To consolidate power over the tenants, Davis no longer offers them one-year leases in the Okeechobee Center projects; they now live on a month-to-month basis. The rent—$329 a month for a small house—does not include utilities, and the tenants must supply their own furniture and appliances. A recent rent increase (about $18 a month for a small place) was explained to the residents as the result of an unexpected loss of income to the city caused by the withdrawal of the sugar cooperative from the water system. The tenants wondered how the Housing Authority had been surprised when the chairman of the board of the Housing Authority was also vice-chairman of the co-op.

After the sugar co-op began using bagasse, a waste product of the sugar-refining process, as landfill on Okeechobee Center land, the chemicals in the bagasse polluted the environs. Some of the bagasse dried into a powder and became airborne. Residents reported strange infections in their children, new kinds of impetigo and herpes. A lawsuit is working its way through the courts.

The planning of the Okeechobee Center itself leaves something to be desired. The playground for young children stands at the edge of a four-lane highway. To pay the rent, a resident must get to the office on the one and a half days a month it is open, unless he or she is elderly. The elderly, some of whom have difficulty getting around, must travel all the way across town to the office at the Osceola Center to pay their rent.

To most people in the Okeechobee Center, the worst part of living there is the management—and that despite the rats, roaches, snakes, pollution, and general decrepitude of the buildings. All it takes to bring out the vindictiveness of Lois Davis is a complaint. She acts swiftly, according to the tenants, and with brilliant indirection. The secretary of the residential council, which has no official standing, irritated the executive director, and Davis responded by initiating eviction proceedings against the secretary's sister. In another instance, the recording secretary of the council is under pressure because one of her grandsons got into trouble.

A few years ago, Linda Robinson, who lived at Okeechobee Center, complained to state Representative Addie Green about conditions in the project. Representative Green came to Belle Glade, talked to the tenants, and wrote a letter to the Housing Authority, which sent her a nasty, arrogant response. Green, perhaps intimidated or without the power to affect a federally sponsored project, let the matter drop.

Not one word about Green's visit or her letter appeared in the newspapers, on the radio, or on television. The media has also been silent on the voting rights suit and the bagasse dumping case. The tenants say the sugar and farming interests have powerful connections to the South Florida media, which keeps them from writing about conditions in Belle Glade.

When Lois Davis turned her attention to Linda Robinson, the media took no notice of that either. How Davis connected Robinson to the visit by the state representative is not clear. Perhaps Representative Green told her. Perhaps she simply chose to make an example of Robinson, to exercise her authority. But the moment Robinson became vulnerable, Davis moved.

I met Linda Robinson in the home of the head of the tenants' council, Albert Petersen. She had not come to complain, but just to talk, for Petersen is the staunchest man in the projects. During the day he does construction work on the farms and in the processing plants around Belle Glade. At night, he comes home to study the court papers and letters and copies of letters that pile up in folders and fill cupboards in his house. He has become sophisticated in the convolutions and failures of the law, but he still speaks with the slow, heavy drawl of farmhands in the South, and when he must turn his mind to legal matters after a day in the fields of construction, he has to search for the language.

In his house, nervously, at first timid, almost whispering, looking to Petersen and his wife for confirmation at the end of every sentence, Linda Robinson spoke of her battle against Lois Davis. She began with a shrug, for she had nothing more to lose; she had been evicted. In three days they would move her furniture and clothing and all her dishes and pots and pans and her stove and refrigerator and her family—whom she described as "seven heads of children"—out onto the street.

She was as thin as a rope, perfectly formed but somehow mismatched with the loose, flimsy dress that hung from her shoulders, exposing the hollows of her collarbones and the washboard beginning of her chest. She had the thin, bare legs of a little girl and no shoes at all.

She placed her beginnings in a cabin in North Carolina on a tragic day in winter. Everyone was outside the cabin but one baby. There was a kerosene heater inside. They all saw the fire. Linda Robinson's mother went inside to rescue the baby. When she was dragged out of the flames, she was nearly dead. "The last thing I heard my momma say before she died was, 'Somebody please help me.' I was thirteen."

When one of her own children was born prematurely, Linda Robinson watched the baby's progress in the hospital as the organs failed to develop. Months went by, then the baby seemed to her to be asking to come home, to be free of the tubes and needles. "I had learned CPR to be ready for her," she said. "I brought her back from dead three times, but I knew she had come home to die. She told me so."

Death, loss of one kind or another, occupied her thoughts, although the days among her seven children, several of them still in diapers, left little time for contemplation. She married the father of her seven children after the last one was born, and the marriage broke up soon afterward. When he moved out, he stopped by the housing authority office to tell them to take his name off the lease.

That was Lois Davis's opening. She did not tell Linda Robinson that the rent had not been paid, and she immediately instituted eviction proceedings. Since Linda Robinson's name was second on the lease and she was not herself a farmworker, she had no official standing with the Farmers Home Administration. And she had missed a payment.

Linda Robinson had the rent money, and offered to pay it, but Davis wanted her out. Davis had been harassing Robinson in one way or another ever since Representative Addie Green had come to town. The eviction proceedings went quickly and the court costs were added to Robinson's debt. She feared that if she paid any money to the Housing Authority they would apply it to the court costs and continue the eviction process, leaving her with no place in the projects and no money to pay on a rental somewhere else. She and her children would be homeless.

I found Linda Robinson's story incredible. Why would the Farmers Home Administration and the Belle Glade Housing Authority evict a woman who had seven children, had just been abandoned by her husband, and was still willing and able to pay the rent? It made no sense, even if Robinson had called Representative Addie Green. Nothing had come of the call or the visit. The cruelty was beyond the limits of revenge. Davis was attacking the children.

To be sure that Linda Robinson was not exaggerating her situation or Davis's penchant for cruelty, I offered to go to the Housing Authority with her. I called the executive director's office and asked to speak to her. She was not in, but an assistant listened politely to my request and made an appointment.

An hour before the appointment, I picked up Linda Robinson at her house. Most of the children were there when I arrived. One little girl looked so much like her mother that I laughed aloud when I saw her. Linda Robinson laughed too, for my reaction was apparently not uncommon. It was the first time I had ever seen her smile.

She arranged for a neighbor to care for the children, then she put on shoes and we went to the Housing Authority office. While I drove, she applied lipstick and arranged her hair. She did not quite tell me that we were on a fool's errand, but she explained that she had found a small apartment in town, only three bedrooms, that she could afford. The landlady hadn't finished renovating the place, but she felt sorry for the Robinson family, and she was willing to rent to them even before the work was finished.

I did not listen very carefully to this proposed remedy because I was certain the eviction would be reversed. If Mrs. Robinson did not have enough money to pay the rent and the court costs, I resolved to help. It was, after all, only a matter of a few dollars.

In hope of cutting the whole process short, I went inside the housing authority building with Mrs. Robinson, and standing with her, I introduced myself, gave my credentials, including a business card, and said she had come to pay the rent. She reached into her purse and took out a cashier's check to show that she did, in truth, have the money.

The receptionist, who also served as cashier, went off to look up Mrs. Robinson's papers. When she returned, she said that Mrs. Robinson had been evicted, and she reminded us that we had an appointment with the executive director. "But she has a check with her," I said.

The cashier said, "You'll have to speak to the executive director."

We waited in the small anteroom, chatting to pass the time. We spoke of Albert Petersen, but because we praised him, we did not say his name for fear we would be overheard and inadvertently cause trouble for him. It surprised me that I had so quickly adopted this way of thinking.

At precisely the appointed time we were ushered in to see Lois Davis. I had expected to meet in her office, but we were taken instead to a conference room. On one side of a long table, arranged like judges in a Kafka novel, sat the executive director flanked by her senior staff and one member of the board. Lois Davis was introduced by the receptionist. We did not shake hands, nor were there any other signs of equality or association. The seating had been designed to express force, and Linda Robinson and I were the objects.

To begin, I offered my credentials; I said that I was writing a book and this meeting would be reported in it. Then I said that I had come with Linda Robinson, who wanted to pay her rent.

Lois Davis said that Mrs. Robinson had been evicted and the eviction order had been signed by a judge.

I was surprised by her grandmotherly demeanor, although the white hair and slightly puffed cheeks would soon take on the appearance of a punishing schoolteacher and the soft voice would develop cruel and cutting overtones in the timbre, like a loosened string on a steel guitar.

At first I spoke too quietly, surprised and confused, like a man falling into sudden darkness. I allowed them to question Linda Robinson, to ask if she had seen the court order. One of them asked her if she worked, another wanted to know why she had not paid the rent on time. "I didn't know," she said. "I have the money with me."

They had intended a hanging—the Cuban head of maintenance in his coveralls, the black woman in the prim white blouse, the fat black man who had been appointed to the board of directors, and Davis.

"Do you know that this woman has seven children? What is your responsibility to them? We're not talking about rent, the subject is little children."

"I'm a grandmother," Davis said. "I care about children."

Then the Cuban attacked. He spoke of "these people," the ones who didn't work, who wanted a handout.

"You mean something like the Cuban loan?"[3]

"They don't want to work."

"This project is the property of the Farmers Home Administration, a

---

[3] Many anti-Castro Cubans who chose exile in the United States received grants from the U.S. government. The grants are known as "the Cuban loan."

part of the government of the United States of America. Isn't that correct? Do you mean to tell me that it is the policy of the federal government to turn out a woman with seven children, throw her and her family and all their belongings into the street, to do that instead of accepting her payment of rent? She has the money. Here's the check. It's up to you, Grandmother Davis. What do you want to do about the little children?"

Linda Robinson had been correct. It was a fool's errand. I could not have imagined anyone as steadfast in her cruelty as Lois Davis. It was her pleasure to evict the woman. She exhibited no shame, no remorse. It was an act of force, a corruption of legitimate power, a challenge to the idea that legitimate power could exist in the real world. I looked at Linda Robinson, who sat next to me—thin, ropes and bones in a shapeless dress, with her little girl's legs—and the lesson I had feared to learn written on her face. No tears, no rage. The face of the object, the one who cannot begin.

Her head was tilted slightly toward me. I think she suffered for me as if I were her child in America. I knew what she meant when she said her baby of nine months told her that she wanted to come home to die. It occurred to me then; I heard once more how she had spoken of the child, the sound of her voice, how she understood the world. The hope of Heaven, I thought, the hope of Heaven.

Not yet.

"If you want any more information, you can talk to our lawyer," Lois Davis said. She was about to adjourn the meeting.

"About those grandchildren of yours," I said. "I'll tell them about you. They'll know what you did."

The room was quiet. There were no secrets. She knew how deeply I despised her.

As we were leaving, I looked over at the young black woman sitting next to Davis. I thought she would have more compassion for Linda Robinson, if only because she was also a black woman in the South. She stared back at me, and her eyes were cold.

I drove Linda Robinson into town. We did not talk much. The young black woman had told me something about isolation. I had no hope for Linda Robinson, much less for her children, as long as they remained in Belle Glade. When I dropped her off, I said that I was going to the lawyer's office, but we knew, she and I, that nothing would come of it. On her behalf I had engaged the cruelest woman in the cruelest town, and lost. I was ashamed and angry, and for a long time afterward I was not able to love my country in the same full-hearted way.

3. Government: Welfare Tales

The welfare system has two distinct effects on the poor: It alleviates some of the dire symptoms of poverty, and it causes poverty. Since welfare, in one form or another, can be found in all modern societies, arguments about eliminating it would seem, at least on a historical basis, moot. The Old Testament describes the Jubilee Year and the rule of the "corners of the field," both times when the wealth of an agricultural society was shared with the poor. The economic theories attributed to Jesus of Nazareth are, if anything, more radically communitarian.

Changes in the welfare system, including the amount allotted to the poor, the categories of poor who deserve welfare, and the method of delivering welfare, have been under discussion since the dawn of the modern age, for the moment society evolved into a game that produced losers as well as winners, something had to be done about the losers.

Motives play the key role at this point. Capitalists and conservatives believe aid to the poor is a moral obligation, alms to the deserving: widows and orphans, the aged and the infirm. In their view, all others should be made to work or . . . The alternative is never spelled out, but most people presume that it refers to life on a lower level of subsistence, and not death by starvation or exposure. Socialists and liberals have long argued for a theory of the use of welfare to maintain the stability of capitalist economies. Frances Fox Piven and Richard Cloward have written a well-known book, *Regulating the Poor*, making the case that civil unrest or the threat of it leads to increased welfare.[4] It is a good theory, but it has not shown up well in practice, especially during the last two decades, since it no longer appears necessary, in the age of downsizing and internationalism, to keep large numbers of poor people on hand to provide wage stability.

Reasons for delivering welfare are most likely far more complex than either the left or right would have us believe: a combination of compassion, the need for social and economic stability, and the desire to maintain a workforce in reserve. It may also be the case that welfare figures into the structure of the game, serving as official recognition of the outcome. The need of such validation on the part of the winners may be unseemly, but what else can account for the obsessive preoccupation with the tiny amount of the national budget paid out in Aid to Families with Dependent Children (AFDC)?

Motives may also account for the second effect of welfare, when it func-

[4] (New York: Vintage Books, 1993).

tions as one of the forces that surround the poor. Some of these motives may be personal, having to do with the feelings of the people who make the rules and those who apply them in face-to-face situations. Racism, sexism, economic and social snobbery, the welfare worker's own personal life, and so on may affect these situations. As everyone knows, the delivery system needs improvement. For the poor, however, the motives have no meaning. They do not understand the system as a palliative; they encounter it as a force.

Whether "the safety net," as liberals like to call it, or "the dole," as conservatives say, properly delivered, should exist at all is not the issue here. The question is what the poor see from inside the surround, and how a system intended by government for the poor functions as a force against them.

In Mississippi, monthly welfare payments in 1995 ranged from $96 a month for a mother and one child to a maximum of $192 a month for a mother and five children. Each additional child brings a woman in Mississippi $24 a month (80 cents a day).[5]

New York City, by contrast, offers one of the most generous welfare packages in the country. The welfare system in Mississippi exerts force against its objects simply by depriving them of enough money to live on; in New York the payments are less than what is needed for a decent standard of living, but women and children there feel the force of the system in other ways.

The women of the Young Mothers Program in the South Bronx, who defined poverty in Chapter II, also define the force of the welfare system, as did many others, including a Jewish single mother in Brooklyn and a snaggle-toothed woman and her strawberry blond sister in Oklahoma and a woman preacher in California. Race may play a role in the tone of the delivery of welfare, but recipients and bureaucrats are now so often of the same race that racism cannot be the determining factor.

Much of the force of the welfare department is expressed through timing, either waiting in the office or waiting for the check. Neither the worker nor the check can be affected in any way by the welfare recipient. She is entirely helpless, anxious and afraid. The bravado of our conversations becomes meek in the waiting room of the welfare office, until it turns into uncontrollable rage.

G:* "They think you have nothing else better to do but to sit in there

---

[5] In one of the other contexts in this chapter, Gloria Browne, who lives in Greenville, Mississippi, will give some idea of rents and other costs in the Delta, making clearer the limits of life on welfare in Mississippi. Payment rates were supplied by Phyllis Epp, a caseworker in Lexington, Mississippi.

* The women in Young Mothers asked that their names not be used in context with their remarks.

and wait for them till they get ready when they want to. You call them and be just as nice as you can be and they talk to you like you're nobody. Like you're nothing!"

The largest woman in the group, Big A, agreed with her, but in a voice that shook the room. "If the computer goes down, I don't get my money. Nowhere in the city can I get my money. I'm at the will of that machine. And that's no way to live. My children have to eat."

Nevertheless, she argued, God was in control of her life, not the welfare department.

A new woman in the program said: "I feel that they have more control over our lives than people want to give them credit for. When you are forced to have to fill out these forms and go to this face to face or we're cuttin you off, yeah, these people have control."

Big A tried to argue, but the new woman came back with a vehemence that overwhelmed even her gigantic voice and dominating personality. "It's not dealin with the CWA [Child Welfare Agency] like you can say, 'Tomorrow I'm not dealin with em, because I don't feel like dealin with em.' Don't deal with em and they'll take your fuckin kids. That's control! And there's not a damn thing you can do about it!"

In the end, it was Big A who summed up the meaning of the loss of control: "If you keep thinkin that they in charge, that's where you gon stay. You cannot stay stuck on people are in control; that's where people stay at."

R OXANNE PARKS HAS THE MANNERS of a Wellesley girl, as such women used to be in the time before the manner of elegance turned blunt and businesslike. She attended the Fashion Institute in Los Angeles for a time, studying clothing design and then interior decoration before she returned to the family tradition and finished her degree at a Bible college.

Her family came to California from Monroe, Louisiana, by way of Arkansas, bringing with them a complex, uniquely American heritage: Creole, Cherokee, Dutch West Indian, German, and African-American. She has a stately air, at once humble and patrician, as one might expect from a woman who had more than once gone overseas on her "missionary journey." She married early to a military man, and followed him, and followed him, until she grew weary of that life. But when she did not follow, he found another woman. She called it adultery, and left him.

A second marriage did not go well at all. The man abused her. He complained against her manners, he accused her of thinking she was white. His family joined in the abuse: They insulted her and took her furniture and many of the things she had gathered on her missionary trips abroad.

Roxanne Parks and her husband separated. Left with two children and no money, she went to the welfare office. No one in her family had ever been to a welfare office; she did not know the rules or procedures; she had never heard the gossip or the rage.

"In my initial interview," she said, "they informed me that San Bernardino County is the number-one county in the country for arresting moms on welfare fraud. When you are having marital problems, that wasn't my focus. I was just trying to get some financial aid from my government.

"I learned later that they have trained the accounting workers to look at your hand gestures, see if you make eye contact, all to see if you're going to perpetrate a fraud. And women when they're battered have low self-esteem. Who says, 'I'm going to look at you, I'm going to make eye contact'?

"They told me that San Bernardino was one of the few counties that sent a home worker to your home. I knew someone was coming, so when they knocked at the door, that's who I thought it was, but when the door opened, it was a fraud investigator who was accusing me of collecting welfare in two different cities— Rancho Cucamonga and Riverside. He was tall, cowboy boots, typical redneck. His attitude was, he was in control. He was trying to manipulate me, get me to say what he wanted. He came in and saw my furniture, my vases, the things I had acquired. He said, 'Why would you need to be on welfare?' He made all kinds of slanderous comments. By the time he left, my daughter and I were in tears.

"I had to go to Riverside and find this other Roxanne Woods. I did. The other Roxanne was white. I'm black. Her maiden name was Woods, my married name was Woods. Our middle initials are different. Our birth dates were the same month, but different years.

"It was supposed to have been cleared up. My worker called and said later, 'You're working, where are the check stubs?' I didn't know I had to turn them in, so I did.

"Three years later, I'm driving down the street in Fremont and a highway patrolman pulls me over. He said, 'There's a warrant out for your arrest.' He took me in. I spent one day in Fremont jail and three days in Santa Rita [prison].

"I won the case. The problem was that they had lost the check stubs. It was a mistake. They had put the income of two different people, with different employee numbers, on my form."

In the Santa Rita prison she was put into a large holding area, peopled mainly with drug addicts, prostitutes, and women accused of welfare fraud. There were murderers in the area, too, women who had killed their husbands or lovers. She thought of it as a nightmare. At first, she observed, keeping her distance, not frightened, watching the women who suffered withdrawal symptoms and the women who had sex with each other.

She found her calling again with a woman in the prison. The woman, a prostitute, was nine months pregnant with her fifth child, the first one she wanted to keep. In the holding area of the prison, amid the screams of the addicts and the whispers of the women who touched each other in the corners of the great room, Roxanne Parks, the missionary, and the pregnant woman prayed.

On the fifth day after her arrest, bail was posted for her, and she went home. Her children were gone, taken by her ex-husband. She had no money, the landlord had begun eviction proceedings, and there was yet another case to fight. By then, she had found Ethel Long-Scott and the Women's Economic Agenda Project (WEAP). She had help, but no money, no work, and two children, one of whom was seriously disturbed and in treatment.

The charges against her were dropped, but it took a long time, and the fight had left her weary. All the things of her life were gone; the rituals of memory had no triggers. She thought of Portugal, of islands off the coast of Africa, of a tiny town in Greece, a theater owner there who had wanted to marry her. Memories of her grandfather flooded her mind. And her mother; when she was a little girl, her mother had picked the cleanest cotton of anyone in the family. That was why they put her cotton on the top of all the bags.

She sat in weariness, older than the oldest women. She had overturned the mistakes, won the cases, but to the object of force, winning is merely another form of defeat. She had been left with nothing; she survived on God and anger.

4. Helpers: The Road of Good Intentions

The confrontation session had been going on for nearly forty minutes. The small, very delicate black woman sat in the center of the room. Attacks came from every side, in the foulest language. She responded in a harsh caw, a bird of the Bronx caught in the net of helpers.

"Bitch! Do-nothin! Bullshit! BullshitBullshit! Why you let that man do you? Pitypot junkie bitch!" They tore apart the details of her life, her child, her Jamaican husband. She fought them, but she was no match for the crowd or the stunning verbal blows of the counselor. They did not know that she was dying. Her T-cell count had fallen to nearly nothing. The diseases of opportunity were growing in her body, filling up her lungs. "Bitch! Selfish, lazy, junkie bitch!" She fought back, she had been the feistiest of them, the fighter. They did not notice how her voice had grown thin. They did not know that she would soon have her first hospital stay. They did not know that this might be the last time she straightened her hair or put rouge on the smooth dark African beauty of her cheeks.

Among the forces that batter the poor, none is more insidious than the helper. The voice of the helper changes from place to place, but it always follows the structure of the game: Helpers have won through moral superiority, which gives them cause to exert control over the losers. For example, who has not heard some good person with straight hair and a firm step say, "I never give money to homeless people. I'll buy food for them, but I never give them money. They just use the money for drugs or alcohol."

One of the distinctions between winners and losers in the game is that the losers have no options. A dollar may be spent in ten thousand ways, from crack cocaine to caviar, but a ham sandwich will always be a ham sandwich. Control belongs to the winners; when helping becomes a means of control, it turns into a victory celebration.

School: Not teaching sends the children into the world help-less, illiterate and enraged, without options. But nothing so controls poor children as the force exerted by the advisers who say to the brightest as well as the slowest: "Learn a trade, become a sweeper or a cleaner, cover yourself with grease, dig trenches, inhale pesticides or paint; consider fast-food ser-vice an opportunity at five dollars an hour, twenty hours a week."

If labor had dignity in America and everyone earned a living wage, the teachers would not be damning their students; but setting limits on a life is an act of force, and teachers do it every day. Schools for the poor have become a contest between forces: The teachers damn the students and the students damn the teachers in return. At night, the teachers take their headaches home to safety in the suburbs; the students stay in place. All the options belong to the teachers. That is the only lesson they teach.

5. Family Violence: Red Christmas

Over time, an act of violence undergoes a metamorphosis. The speed of it decreases, like a toy winding down or a truck coasting to a stop. As memory, the suddenness is ongoing; the violent moment then serves as the soldier of force, the promise of all that can go wrong, everything that hurts. In memory, violence becomes a subject, seated somewhere inside the object; not the brilliant union of subject and object that comes with legitimate power, but an alien subject situated within its object, unshakable, unavoidable, like a failing heart or a withered hand.

The excision of an alien subject has been, at times, the work of shamans, churchmen, psychotherapists, and friends. It may be that poets do the work as well; at one time, in innocence or hope, it was the business of philosophers. The point is that such work cannot be done in isolation; the cure must come in society.

Perhaps no cure will ever happen to Carolyn Fillmore. Or perhaps when I met her she had already banished the violence of family life to the irrelevance of a dream. It would be sweet if it were so, but the alien subject implanted by violence tends more toward metastasis than disappearance, as in Carolyn Fillmore's life.

She is HIV-positive. When she was twenty-six years old, the virus had been growing in her body for five years. It came about, she knew, in an ordinary way: "My mother remarried and my stepdaddy was making passes at us, the girls in the family, and my mother wouldn't believe us and he kept doin it, so we managed to just leave the house at a early age. I was sixteen.

"We went on the streets, sleepin with different men. Get a motel room for the night and sleep, take a shower, buy me some different clothes every day. And what happened to the clothes? I don't know, cause you change in the room, leave your dirty clothes there, go back and do another man the next night."

Carolyn Fillmore is a big woman, with full lips and slightly Asian eyes. She chews a wad of gum as baseball players do, grinding away the thing she calls stress. Sobriety, the end of the cocaine high, fattened her face, which is dominated by a wide, flat nose, and high cheekbones blurred by flesh. To protect herself she displays a sullen facade, verging on anger. It is a presentation learned in the street, protective, unwilling, disengaged, the face of a hooker when the money is due. When she grows easy in conversation, the sullenness gives way to a sweet smile, a girlish laughter that comes across her mouth and closes her eyes with almost religious ecstasy.

She lives now with a man she does not love or even like. At the age of twenty-six, after three years without drugs, she got her first job. She hopes to get another, so that with two jobs she can get out of the welfare system. If she can just get up to $600 a month, she believes, she will be able to pay half of it for rent, and live and save out of the other half. "I'm gon open a bank account for them next week," she said, speaking of her sons, "because if I pass away, I want them to have somethin to fall back on."

In her life there are but few memories. One is of the police who arrested her, insulted her, threw her up against the patrol car, and smashed her crack pipe, turning her treasured Uzi (crack pipe) into shards. She was a scrawny, senseless thing then, sleepless and sick, but nothing they said has faded, no place where they touched her has ever felt the same.

There is an older memory, and stronger, for it comes up time and again in her conversation, more often than the Bible or music or HIV.

"My younger sister, her name's Erica; she's twenty-three now. Her daddy died. My mother killed him one Christmas night for giving me some wine. They was fighting and she grabbed a machete, a big, old-fashioned machete. I guess she got mad and she swung it and it slice him all across here," she said, touching her belly. "I remember that. That was when I was very young, cause that was on Christmas Eve night. My mother just came back from the hospital—it was too much blood—and told us he was dead.

"They took my mother to jail. My grandmother had the best lawyers to come out for her. My grandmother and the lady that pierced our ears kept us. And she said, 'Your mother be okay,' just like that. And that's all I can remember.

"It was so much happened in life that you keep it so bottled up that you never talk about it. But you know it happened, so when we got older, like I am today, we talked to Momma about it. I asked her about it, 'Momma, what happened that night, that Christmas night? I remember all them toys in the front room. We had a red wagon.' And I said, 'Momma, what happened? Why you slice him?'

"'We was fightin. It wasn't like it seem, and I didn't try to kill him, but my temper just blew on me, and I just slung the knife and he was in the way. It wasn't because he gave you no wine, it was because we was fightin, just like that.'"

6. Abuse

CharleZ's Dad

On summer afternoons a group of aspiring hip-hop musicians met in a warehouse building in the industrial section of Oakland, California, to talk and smoke, and sometimes to sit in pleasant stupefaction watching cartoons or talk shows crazily reproduced on a television set without an aerial. The studio belonged to Trixie Garcia, a pale, pretty girl in her twenties whose father, Jerry Garcia, was the lead member of The Grateful Dead. On some days and nights the young men worked on the electronic equipment in the back of the huge warehouse room, producing tracks for hip-hop records. When they were lucky, they sold the tracks to established groups, but really, truly, they wanted to become rich and famous on their own.

CharleZ and Jamal lived in the studio with Trixie. They paid no rent, contributed no food, and were not then her lovers. They floated, penniless usually, sometimes earning a little money from "selling a little weed" or this or that. They had no connection to Trixie's famous father, and Trixie herself had no interest in becoming a musician; the warehouse was her studio, the walls were decorated with her paintings, which were then in an early stage of development. Among the young men who worked and waited in Trixie's studio were Yapos Sopay, Jamal, and CharleZ. Yapos and CharleZ were theatrical names. CharleZ had been changed from Charlesie, in the way that common names are misspelled on soap powders (DUZ for does) to make it possible to copyright them. Yapos was an acronym, originally Young Asian Prophet of Soul, but later changed to Young African Prophet of Soul when Matthew Washington (the name on his birth certificate) left the Muslims.

Yapos is one of four generations of the Washington family who appear in this book. He is a short, burly man of spectacular intelligence. In his early twenties he had already endured virtually every aspect of poverty and racism in America. But his place in this chapter is only as a member of The Sanitation Department, which is the name he and his colleagues had chosen for their production company.

CharleZ and his father also have more to teach than this brief scene. Here the father appears only as a subject who lies inside CharleZ's mind, who speaks to him always about the world, defining it, instructing him in the need "to always be packing."

The surprise of CharleZ's father grows out of his demeanor. He shuffles and scuffles and forgets to shave. He drives around in a five- or seven-year-old Volvo that Jamal and CharleZ sold to him for only $500, something like a gift. White people, rich people, doctors, lawyers, even store clerks frighten him. He works, always at odd jobs, scuffling, but he does not collect welfare.

When CharleZ thinks of his father, he thinks first of their enterprises, the failures, mistakes, foolishness, and then of other times, of childhood. "He was a hard man," CharleZ said, "hard as anybody. He used to whip me. He didn't stop until I could relate to him."

The memory came out of nowhere, while he sat in the backseat of a car, going over a hill, on the road to the freeway, in Oakland, in summer. "He used to spank me with everything. I mean not everything, of course. For the most part anything. Real whips, like horsewhips. One time he sprained his back. He was confined to the couch and he had his little horsewhip right beside him and he started liking it after he got it. He could reach out with that little whip and get us anywhere in the room. He didn't use it like all the time, but while his back was sprained and when he got really mad he would probably use it.

"I didn't like it."

Later, when he was nearly grown and Charlez and his father "got to relate to each other, he stopped using it," CharleZ said. He did not know why he wanted to help his father now or give him gifts; he thought it might have something to do with the horsewhip.

Of all the members of The Sanitation Department, CharleZ was the gentlest and the most well spoken. He viewed the world in an analytical way, commenting often on such things as the difference in the strength of family ties among blacks compared to Latinos or Asians or the relation of graffiti styles to the social movements prevalent at the time. He lived suspended between jobs and dreaming. He navigated by landmarks, one of which was a whip, and did not go out unarmed.

Delta Blues

Tchula, Greenwood, and Lexington, Mississipi, had been difficult for me, but much more difficult for Frank. Perhaps it had to do with race; the consciousness of race is so pervasive in the Delta. Perhaps it was a kind of embarrassment, for we had been only with black people and they had been so poor. The problem of race had not been an issue between us since we had met. He had looked at me then, with a sense of mild amusement lurking in his face, and asked, "Why do you think all the great violinists are Jews?"

"Because we got rhythm," I said. And we have been friends ever since the moment of shared laughter that followed.

In Lexington, Frank Clarke had been unable to enter the dilapidated trailer where the Holmes family lived. Tchula, where the black farmers had been squeezed out of the cottonseed mill by the whites with their Memphis Cotton Exchange connections, had been painful proof that racism was alive and largely unchanged in the Mississippi Delta. The kids in Greenwood who talked about the pump guns and three-eighties used in gang warfare there had not been cheering either.

After days so painful that Frank, a retired Army captain, a man who had been wounded in battle, could no longer enter the houses where the poorest families lived, the applause served as medicine.[6] All the men and women in the teacher training program cheered Frank Clarke and his Educate the Children Foundation. They had used the books and computers and school supplies the foundation brought to the Delta.

The response confirmed the value of Frank's work and lifted him up out of the sadness of the Delta. As the applause echoed through the long halls of the Mound Bayou High School, it pleased me, too, because Frank and I have been friends for a long time, more than thirty years. At first glance, however, we are as different as two men could be. He was a captain, I was an airman second class. He plays tennis, I prefer poker. Frank has retained the bearing of an officer and a gentleman from Boston and I resemble nothing so much as an unmade sleeping bag.

After the applause, we went to Florene King's house in the projects south of the high school, and without thinking, Frank came in with me. We had agreed after the first places we visited together, in Tchula, that we would not judge the people we met, no matter what they said. And that was hard for Frank. He is a man who solves problems. During one conversation in Tchula, Frank had been appalled when a high school girl told him she did not have a library card. He marched her and her mother down the block to the library to get them signed up. And while he was there, he inspected the library, found it deficient, and got the librarian started on repairing and updating the computer system. In the same fashion, if he entered a house and found it less than spotless, the captain was likely to pick up a broom or a mop and start preparing for a white glove inspection at dawn.

Mrs. King's house was darkened to keep out the August heat of the Delta and to improve the picture on the television screen. Five children played in the front of the main room of the house. Behind them, on a table surrounded by plastic chairs, the dishes of the day had not yet been cleared and stacked in the sink of the cubbyhole that served as a kitchen. We exchanged greetings and explanations, then Mrs. King cleared the dishes from the table and invited us to sit with her for a while.

She was a heavyset woman with a handsome, battered face, like a club fighter in retirement when the swelling won't go down any more and the disappointment shows like a scar. She spoke in the low, insinuating voice of the Delta, a blues shouter's voice, tired of day, ready for bed. Grandma King now, keeping the kids, smoking, although her asthma was bad and her blood pressure high, enough so that she lived on disability and food stamps. She said her favorite food was greens made with ham hocks and salt pork: "My

---

[6] More applause for Frank and Faye Clarke came a year later, in 1996, when they received the President's National Service Medal Award in a ceremony at the White House.

mother taught me how to eat em with your fingers. Mash them up together with the bread, but you have to be careful not to eat em that way in public. That's why I never order greens in public, because I might forget myself." Then she smiled, not like a young woman but like a little girl.

The children would not be quiet while we talked. I said that it was no problem, and Frank agreed, but she would not have it. She sent the six-year-old, the oldest of the children, to fetch a belt. The little girl ran to another room, returning with a wide, tan leather strap.

Mrs. King hit the two-year-old boy with the strap. The sound of it shocked the room into silence. The boy stopped for a moment, silent, staring up at her, then burst into a screaming rage. She hit him again and again, until he fell quiet.

She had turned back to us and begun talking again when the two-year-old picked up a small child's chair and threw it at her. The chair missed her, skidding across the table between us. She beat him again with the belt, but this time he made no sound in response.

Frank asked why she had to hit him.

"If they get in somethin that's no business, I punish them. If they don't understand, you have to stiffen the punishment." She looked over at the boy, who stood between her and the alcove kitchen, defiant, staring. "Now, he don't understand. I have to be tappin on him all day."

She gave the belt to the oldest girl, who walked over to the little boy and began to beat him. "See there," Mrs. King said, "now she's tappin on him. Uh-huh. She's not hittin him hard, not as hard as I would."

The boy laughed, and the girl hit him harder and harder, until he cried.

As far as Mrs. King can remember, people have always beaten each other in her family: "Grandma was real mean. She was a black Indian, always whuppin us." The girl continued hitting the baby with the belt. "She whipped people a lot. I guess we was always bad. She whipped us with a peach tree switch."

The boy cried loudly. Mrs. King took the belt, hit him once, hard, then handed it back to the girl. "Mother whipped us, too."

Frank asked who the children belonged to. There was a daughter in Memphis, another in Nashville, sons lived here and there. Mrs. King had not heard from the mother of two of the children for several months.

We listened, Frank and I, not hearing her, watching the child and the girl, hearing the sound of the leather against the boy's skin, sometimes through his clothing, sometimes against bare flesh. He was the fifth generation to be beaten with a switch or a strap, and he responded, at the age of two, like a beast. He sulked or raged; he did not speak or simply cry like a child.

We did not stay long in her house. It was the last time Frank went into a poor person's house in the Delta. In Lamont, Freedom Village, Egremont, Greenville, he went elsewhere; he did the work of the foundation.

I FELT SUPERIOR SOMEHOW, stronger, perhaps because I was younger than Frank, until the day we went to Lamont, where life is as rotten as it can be in America. Tony Mitchell, a young black man in Greenville, told me about the place, and two trustees from the state prison at Parchman Farms confirmed it. "The town is called Lamont [pronounced with a hard a, "Lay-mont"], in Bolivar County, and the place up there is behind the general store on a little hill people call Nigger Ridge." Mitchell, the young college student, laughed with nervous embarrassment as he said the name.

"Does it have another name?"

He shook his head. "That's what people call it. You can tell the place by the smell. There's raw sewerage running out all over. Everybody who lives up there is sick, everybody. You just go around the bend in the road past the abandoned blue bus, and you'll smell it. Ask for Bill King, Lee May, Katie Pearl Smith, or Bertha Adams. They all know me."

We drove around for a long time in Lamont until we finally found the place. It was my fault, because I refused to ask for the place by its common name, asking instead about the blue bus, the sewerage problem, and the collection of names Mitchell had given me. A farmer on the far side of the tiny town finally helped us out with precise instructions.

THE FIRST HOUSE after the blue bus was not a house any more but a conglomeration of unpainted wood and salvaged plastic nailed over the places where the windows had been. It had lost its houseness, becoming more like a shelter or a lean-to. I looked for dogs, saw none, and went up to knock on the door. After a long time, a tall, thin, very pale woman in a housedress opened the door a crack and asked what I wanted.

I explained that I was writing a book and that Tony Mitchell had said she might be willing to help me. She nodded. "I'll ask my mother," she said, and closed the door.

A long time passed, and no one came back to the door. I knocked again. There was no answer. I knocked harder, then called out the name of the old woman. There was no answer.

"Let's go," Frank said. "Can't you see that's a white woman and she does-n't want to talk to me? Can't you see that?" He was as angry as I'd ever seen him. We had gone through a similar scene at a steakhouse in the middle of the black section of Greenville. Now, here we were again. The pressure of visiting with poor black people in Mississippi was tearing us apart, each of us and both of us. It was like attending a lynching every day, day after day after day. And it was not a death solely of men we watched, it was mostly women and children who twisted in the wind in Mississippi.

I said to Frank that it was not only racism we saw. I argued that I had been traveling the country for years by then, that this was, as he knew, the end of my travels, the finishing up of that part of the work. It had been as bad for whites in Tennessee and Florida and Brooklyn and Oklahoma and New England, I said. There had been no political life for the poor in any of those places, either, just the surround of force, nothing but force, for whites and browns as well as blacks.

He is a reasonable man, but this was rural Mississippi, and all that had changed was on the surface. What had the young woman at the clinic said the other day? "Yes, white clerks wait on black people in the stores now, but you can tell when they give you change, they just drop the money in your hand; they don't touch your hand, like you were dirty or diseased."

"I don't know if she was a white woman, Frank. There was strong sun outside and the house was dark inside. She was a light-skinned woman, but I don't know if she was a white woman; I couldn't tell."

He said that she was a white woman and that we should forget about it and go on.

"Okay," I said, although I felt the evil in the air, and I feared that some-one would say the name of the place where we stood. I had not said it, for I knew it would hurt him, and that was the last thing I wanted to do.

Down the road, perhaps fifty yards, the King family sat together in the front yard of their house. Leonard King, his adopted daughter and her hus-band, his grandson, and an old woman. Although Leonard King had no teeth and he had lost all but the last faint echoes of his hearing in his eighty-eighth year, he was the one who chose to speak. The old woman who sat next to his son-in-law has no mind, he said.

I asked what he meant, but he did not hear me or he did not choose to explain. We all looked at his sister for a moment. She is a grayed lady in a gray dress with gray hair, and she sat in a colorless, unclear stillness, a woman faded to gray, so that her presence was not quite real, not fully alive, but in some area between life and death, far away.

While we talked, he and his daughter and son-in-law and their son peeled and sliced pears that had fallen from the tall tree at the eastern end of the little yard in front of his rambling, unpainted wood house. They did the work with kitchen knives and jackknives, peeling and coring and slic-ing. They let the peelings fall into a metal washtub along with the whole pears, while the woman cut up the peeled and cored pears and dropped them into another washtub. Everyone's hands were filthy, and the water in the tubs was filthy too.

We no longer cook and can the pears, they said; we just put them into plastic bags and freeze them until winter. The pears are not so soft or sweet as canned pears, but the work is not so hard as canning.

Mr. King remembered how he worked when he was a young man. He chopped cotton on a plantation, he said, and the work was very hard. His uncle had become an overseer who rode on a horse carrying a rifle and whip. When the men worked too slowly, he whipped them. If they rebelled against the whip, he showed them the rifle. Leonard King said his uncle had shot more than a few men; they knew he was serious. "He was a good man," King said, "but he was too cruel. He horsewhipped me until I bled."

As a father, Mr. King said he was not so cruel as his uncle, but "I beat my children. And my children beat their children. We don't spank them. We use switches and ironing cords and belts."

Everyone in the family has been poor for generations, all the way back to slavery, and everyone in the family is sick, especially those who live in Lamont. The only property anyone in the family has ever owned is the ramshackle house and one pear tree in Lamont. The central myth of the King family, its Golden Age, is a black overseer sitting tall on a horse, with a whip in one hand and a gun in the other.

BY THE TIME WE LEFT the King house there were two cars parked outside the first house on the row, the one next to the abandoned bus. I asked Frank if he would mind if we stopped again. He said it would be all right with him, but he would not get out of the car. I said that it might be a long time. "Let's go," he said.

This time the door opened at the first knock and I was invited in. Although I had grown up in the deserts of West Texas and Arizona, I had never been in a hotter place. The windows had all been boarded up and covered over with thick plastic. There was no paint on the walls, inside or out. The bare boards allowed the heat to come in and kept it there. Although it was 98 degrees outside and the heat index was 110°, according to the radio, it felt cool compared to the temperature inside the house.

An entire family, three generations, had come to stay up on the ridge in the great-grandmother's house. Some had gathered in the front room where she sat. An ancient woman as pale as bone, dressed in a colorless shift, her arms and legs exposed, she stared at a ghostly picture shown in negative on the television set across the room. She said she was dying. That was all she said, there was nothing more.

Across from the dying great-grandmother, a contrast to the bleached bone gray of the old woman's figure, her dark-skinned granddaughter sat slumped in what had been an easy chair; her clothes were as bright as

Christmas wrapping, but lifeless. She had just come home from San Diego, where things did not work out. For a while she stayed with cousins in Greenville, moving from house to house, as long as they would keep her, until now, at the end, she had come to Lamont, to this dead oven on the ridge where the sewerage has made everyone sick. It was the end, she said; like her grandmother, who sat across from her, sick to dying, she had come to the end.

We talked for a long time, the itinerant granddaughter from San Diego and I. She was as hard as any person I had ever met. The sound of the smack of a hand on bare skin was in her voice. She wrote welts and bruises in the air. I felt battered by her conversation:

"What you want to know for? You got any money? Get me a place. I need a place. Get me a place right now. Don't ask her; she don't know anything. She's dying. Ain't you dying, Grandma?"

Could anyone, I wondered, survive this woman's delight in verbal abuse? The sound of arguing came from another room, curses and shouting muffled only a little by the blanket that served for a door. The heat in the house was unbearable. My sweat dried before it could cool me. I did not understand why we did not all die.

I heard a sound beside me, and when I looked around, a little girl had appeared there, next to the door. She held a book and a ballpoint pen. "My name is Bettina," she said, "and I am ten." She was a chubby little girl, with soft, curly hair, and dreaming eyes. "I heard you are a writer," she said.

"Yes, it's true."

"I write poetry," she said. "When we were in San Diego, my teacher told me that I write very well. I am the best writer in my class."

"Do you like to read?"

"Yes."

"And who is your favorite poet?"

"Maya Angelou."

"Anyone else?"

"Yes, I like Mister William Shakespeare."

"When I was your age, I liked Mister William Shakespeare, too."

"I have a little typewriter," she said, "and I am writing a book. Do you know a publisher?"

"Yes," I said. "If you'll write to me when you get settled in San Diego or Chicago, we can talk about it. Take this card. It has my name and address and telephone number."

We went outside together. It was so much cooler there that I trembled as if from a chill. Her brothers had gathered around their car. One had a split lip and a bruised cheek; he looked as if he had been in a fight. The boys were older than Bettina, city boys acting hip, showing off for each other and for Frank and everyone on the ridge. I introduced Bettina to Frank, who gave her his card and wrote the name of a school counselor in Greenville on the back, in case her mother decided to stay home.

She leaned against the car, as if by doing so she could hold us there. Finally, we had to go. We shook hands very formally, as literary people are thought to do. She walked beside the car a little as we pulled away.

On the drive back to Greenville I told Frank that when I was ten years old I was a chubby kid, with lots of curly hair. I loved Mister William Shakespeare very much, and I, too, had a little typewriter on which I was writing a book. And that was all I could say.

We drove in silence for a long time. Every now and then Frank commented briefly on a low-flying crop duster or an experimental field. He did not expect me to talk. He understood. I thought how different we are, the captain and I, and how much we are the same.

7. Graffiti: In Your Face Forever

As the D train comes up out of the ground in Brooklyn the blank bare brick walls of the subway tunnel disappear, replaced by a long concrete barrier that rises with the train to the level of the elevated track. No matter how many times a person makes the trip, the sight of the wall delivers a sudden and momentarily stunning blow. It has been signed with graffiti from top to bottom in a scream of garish color that goes on for hundreds of yards, an angry, demanding wall that controls the eye of the observer, and batters him.

There was a time when graffiti were thought to be a form of art, a conversation with the beholder, but that was long ago, before the act of writing on walls separated into art and anger, offering and demand.

Signs are not architecture; they have no reason for existence other than to speak to whoever can read them. Originally, graffiti marked out territory, like a dog urinating on a fire hydrant or a tree. The markers intended to intimidate everyone who saw their signs: If you are not one of us, you are against us, and you are in danger here. Crossing out a sign symbolized murder.

Graffiti epitomized the phrase, "in your face," which means confrontational, forcing the observer to pay complete attention. In the language of popular psychology, "in your face" means to invade another person's space, that area the person considers private, personal, safe. Graffiti do so violently, at first, but over time resolve into force, controlling the viewer's perception of the world and its dangers, threatening.

In some places, graffiti have evolved into a form of poster art, both decorative and didactic. The famous wall in Los Angeles outside the abandoned streetcar tunnel is perhaps the best example. There is another, less sophisticated graffiti wall along the railroad tracks in Oakland. But even these walls carry with them the confrontational character of graffiti, for the artists cross each other out, painting over each other's work, competing in destructive fashion, mimicking the warfare of the streets. And all around the walls, in Oakland and Los Angeles, the spraypaint cans litter the tracks.

Graffiti sometimes appear in the lives of people who are not poor: on subway trains or the sides of trucks and vans or the walls of buildings in higher-income neighborhoods. When people who cannot read the signs confront them, they see ugliness, acts of vandalism, irritants. Or if they are slightly nuts, they may see the beauty of the expression of the masses. Only the poor, who live among the signs and survive by obeying them, must endure the full force of graffiti.

8. Selling: Until the Water Comes, Television

In the summer of 1994, somewhere in Buffalo Hollow near Clairfield, Tennessee, a man lived by madness. I cannot tell you his name, for fear is the great part of his madness. He does not often leave the one-bedroom trailer in which he lives with his wife, two sons, a daughter, and an aunt. He never enters an automobile, for it was after an automobile accident that his strange agoraphobia began.

In the Cumberland Mountains madness in any form is a blessing and an occupation, for there is no work other than a few mining jobs, and no prospect of work, especially for a man who did not go beyond the eighth grade.

Madness serves the people of Appalachia or the West Side of Chicago as blindness or the loss of a limb serves the poor of India or Mexico; it provides a means of survival. The difference between the mendicants of those societies and the United States is that here the state, however inefficiently, gathers and distributes the alms, allowing the disabled and demented to retain some shred of dignity.

The family of the man who claimed madness, which is known as "nerves" in Appalachia, has a total monthly income of $856, comprising $446 in SSI payments to him, $185 in welfare for his wife and children, and $225 in food stamps.

Other than the fact that the family in Buffalo Hollow does not have to display its suffering in public in order to collect $4.77 a day for each of them, they live in conditions associated with the underdeveloped world. They have no sewerage, and they have either been unwilling or unable to dig a cesspool on the steep hill, which means they live with raw sewage seeping down from an outhouse above the trailer. Sooner or later, they will be sick.

Until the summer of 1994, they did not have a bathtub. They took pan baths, which are good for conserving water, but not for getting clean. After the installation of a tub, Felicia the seven-year-old daughter of the agoraphobic man, took up soaking in the water. She said she liked to be all covered up with water. The trailer belonged to Felicia's grandmother, and they had lived in it since 1980, but it was only in the summer of 1994 that they were able to purchase sheetrock to make interior walls. Until then, they endured the mountain winters with nothing but thin sheets of plywood to shield them from the cold.

Living at such an elemental level, surrounded by so many forces, a family would seem impervious to the salesmen who manipulate the desires of the rest of the population. But poverty is no protection. Felicia's mother, a bulky woman with a long chin and prominent eyeglasses, dressed for summer in black and yellow thigh-length Spandex exercise shorts and a long, loose T-shirt that said across her bosom: "HELL-RAISER." Her brown hair had been dyed blond, but she had grown tired of the process and let it grow out so that the only vestiges of the dye were yellow tufts above her ears.

Although the family had only sporadic running water, getting by on the overflow from a spring up in the hollow, they bought what the salesmen told them they needed: a new television set. A comparison of the cost of running water and the new television set makes clear how the force of selling affects them. To bring water up to the edge of the property would require a cash payment of $300 to the water district. By contrast, the new television set cost $399. But $399 was just the beginning. In order to buy the set on credit, they had to take out a two-year insurance policy for $98. Sales tax was added to that, and the whole thing was sold to them at a high rate of interest. For a small television set worth perhaps $200 in a chain store, they had to pay $40 a month for sixteen months, plus a final payment of $28, for a grand total of $668, more than twice the cost of bringing running water to the house.

The difference between fresh water and a television set is the salesman, that pervasive creature who enters the lives of people to tell them of a thing to satisfy their desires, a thing more satisfying than fresh water or an indoor toilet. The salesman comes between the customer and the world, making the world over as he wishes it. He does not sell them the television set, he sells them information about something they cannot know: the quality, durability, and convenience of the television set. In this case, the salesman recognizes that their desire is as much for the possession as the use of the thing, and he is able to provide the information to satisfy them: "If you got the good credit," he told them, "you can git anything you want."

Salesmen do not make mendicants of the poor, not directly, but selling operates as a force in their lives as it does in the lives of all Americans. The difference between the effect of selling on the lives of the poor and all the rest of society comes in the ability to buy. The salesman may corrupt information, distorting the world for the rich and those in the middle, but the salesman makes a wound in the poor; he leaves a hole where desire flourished and died.

No one makes the hurt of poverty so real as the salesman, and he is always there, on television, in the newspapers, in the stores; he is the new car in the garage of the house next door or the fashion of the day in the wardrobe of the children down the street. Sometimes he comes knocking, a deceitful neighbor at the door. At every opportunity he remarks on the failure of the poor. The wound he leaves compares to impotence, barrenness, stumps, and dead senses; the work of the salesman cannot be forgotten. He is the subject in a thousand forms who enters the object through the wound, and endures, as everlasting as shame.

9. Neighbors: A Knife at the Door

In old movies and novels now mostly forgotten the poor know hunger and sometimes cold, but they do not know loneliness. In the 24th Ward of Chicago, when poverty seemed absolute, life flowed from one family to another, reached beyond the walls of any house, into the streets, across the back porches; a neighborhood in that time was the name of a collection of neighbors. Nothing like a neighborhood exists in a world of relative poverty. Snitches live in the housing projects, a woman visits another in the afternoon to sell a little dope, no one can be trusted; the children are always in danger.

Relative poverty changes the role of neighbors. The game of modern society converts them from allies to adversaries; they become a force, equals against each other, violent or threatening violence, lurking, bound to the rules of the game. The poor do not live in the comfort of neighbors, but in fear of them. Someone or something bad, dangerous, lives next door to the poor; they must always be ready to deal with it. To let down one's guard, in a moment of trust or a sigh of weariness, invites disaster.

This conversion, from a city of neighbors to a world of adversaries, perhaps more than any other single factor, affects the ability of the poor to break out of the surround. It figures in almost every life that appears in this book, but never more dramatically than in the life of Lucia Medina.

When I first met Lucia Medina, she was still obese. Since then, she has lost over a hundred pounds, and in the last year or so a beautiful young woman in her early thirties has begun to emerge from the blurred flesh. When she smiles, deep dimples occur in both cheeks. Her skin is as smooth as that of her five-year-old daughter and it is the color of milk touched by coffee. In her apartment, on a computer so old that its contents cannot be extracted but lie inside as still as if they were carved in stone, she has written the first chapters of a novel. "A romance," she said, "a fantasy romance," and laughed.

No one in Lucia Medina's family, in all the history that can be remembered, has ever been anything but poor. They have lived for generations, perhaps centuries, in the surround. She uses other words to describe her situation, but there can be no doubt that it is the surround. "It's like you're contained," she said of life among her neighbors in the projects and the hotels. "You can't go out, let your kids to play or anything, because you're always worried: Who's out there?

"I don't think you ever get over it. When you look at it, you might put it in the back of your head, but I don't think you ever get over it."

She began as an equal despite her history, a pretty girl and a straight A student until she had a miscarriage, followed by dangerous hemorrhaging. Her teachers told their straight A student that she had spent so much time in the hospital that she would have to repeat the year. With the stubborn sense of honor that deflects the lives of Latinos, especially the poor, she dropped out of school rather than repeat the year.

She lived with a man for eight years before she married him. "And it still turned out bad," she said. "After we got married, he got possessive. Everybody had to go like under his command: You're my wife and you have to do this and you have to do that. And if I didn't do it, he would get upset and he would go out drinking with his friends."

They separated, got together again, lost their bearings in the city. "We wound up in a hotel," she said, "the whole family, me and the kids and my husband, because we couldn't find a place. It was hard. We were in the Prince George, a lot of different ones. And then the places they put you in, you'd rather sleep in the street than in the hotel. It's drab, there's dealers and prostitutes and you name it, they got it. We had one room. It was about the size of my dining area. We had bunk beds. There was two bunk beds here, two bunk beds there, then the baby in the crib. A little chair, a little table. And then they steal everything you have. Everything I owned they stole, the people who have passkeys. They watch you and somebody else steals your stuff. You complain. You go to the cops, and they can't do much. I tried.

"When someone knocks at the door, I open it a little and show them a knife, a big knife. I think if I had to protect myself or my kids, I would use it. At night, because I'm scared, I sleep with the knife under my pillow and I push the dresser and the chest up against the door so I'll hear it move if they try to get in."

About that time, her oldest daughter, Yvette, a plump child with heavy eyebrows and dark skin, brown painted over gray, decided that she was white. No matter what her parents said, Yvette could not be dissuaded from her new image of herself. She was a difficult child, headstrong, beginning to show signs of something strange. Her father responded angrily. He "hit her on the butt," according to Mrs. Medina. In school the next day Yvette told her teacher that her father had punched her in the stomach and beat her with a belt buckle.

The teacher called the Child Welfare Agency (CWA), who put Yvette in a foster home. Then Mrs. Medina was told to bring the other children in to be examined. It was merely a demonstration of good faith, the child welfare worker said. If there was nothing wrong, she would be allowed to take the children home. But there was no good faith on the part of the CWA. "They kept them," Mrs. Medina said. "My other children were fine, and they went into the system also, because we were living in a hotel, and they considered anybody who was in a hotel bad. The system is in charge of your life. It gets to that point. They do things. Your life is worth nothing. They own you. You're just a number."

After that, she entered into a half-crazed routine, up all night in the hotel, fearing that at any moment she would hear the dresser pushed away from the door as someone entered their room, and "All day I kept trying to get the kids back, going to the child bureau agency, and to find out why it happened.

"There was not enough to live on, you live on cold cuts. We used to pick up cans. It helps a little bit. There was a time when I carried my hotplate with me, because that was the most valuable thing to me at that time. They can't take your spoons and forks and pots, but the hotplate they could sell it on [to another person]. I had a little one and I carried it with me everywhere. And then I would buy whatever I needed that day, come down here [to the Lower East Side where she was raised], walking, where the food is cheaper, and take it with me.

"I used to make stew, steak. With a little oil, you fry it. Soups. But you only buy so much. You have a little refrigerator, but then if you buy meat, they're gonna take your meat. There was a lock. When we would come back it was still locked. They had a key. That's what you call an inside job.

"It's like you got your back against the wall and let em all throw stuff at you.

"Then somebody from the hotel asked my husband if he wanted protection or whatever, join them and they won't be stealing our stuff no more and he would be getting money or whatever. He thought about it, but I wouldn't have it.

"After being hungry and eating sandwiches for months, he said, 'Yeah! You know, it's money to eat. You won't have to be eating sandwiches every day. You could go to the restaurant to eat a steak once in a while.'

"When you're hungry, you think that's like gold, but I wouldn't have it. He was upset. He would get loud. Can't do nothing else but get loud. I told him it's not worth it in the long run, it causes more problems.

"They just asked him once, because they kept stealing from us, stealing our hotplates, and stealing our food and everything we had."

In the end, her moral stance made no difference. "He went to jail," she said. "He took a loan or something, and they said he stole the money when we were in the hotel. He took a loan of money, and I don't know. He didn't tell me. And the person had said he took the money from them. Somebody in the hotel. There were loan sharks. He was sent for a year. It was the first time he had been in jail."

"I just had Monica [her youngest child]. She was an infant, and I was trying to protect her so they wouldn't put her in foster care, so I was like on the run all the time. Then I'm carrying my hotplate, carrying my daughter in the pouch and going to different hotels."

When at last she was able to arrange to move into an apartment rented by her aged uncle, the Child Welfare Agency returned her children to her. The oldest girl, Yvette, had been molested while she was in the foster home. The boy, Jeremy, was in worse condition. "My son was two and a half and he only weighed twenty pounds," she said. "And they had told me he was gonna be crippled, he wasn't gonna be able to speak or hear anything, because he was really bad. He kept bleeding from his nose. I think they were hitting him. He wasn't getting the food, the nutrients that he needed to get."

While she was in foster care, Yvette began to have seizures. By the age of thirteen, she had been diagnosed as epileptic, asthmatic, and schizophrenic. There is no doubt that she is a difficult child, sometimes unmanageable, biting, and threatening to kill her mother, but whenever I saw her, which was only three or four times, she was neat and cheerful. Once, when we went to the store together to buy doughnuts and coffee, she talked about her love of mathematics. She is a big girl for her age, and at times her dark eyes and heavy eyebrows have the intensity of a Frida Kahlo portrait.

By 1994, they had settled in with Mrs. Medina's uncle, who had an apartment on the first floor of a project on the Loisaida.[7] The family does not know the neighbors there, except to fear and despise them. They gather in the hallway outside the apartment, shouting and banging against the door, big men, threatening, and children out of control, while the women pass through the gauntlet carrying bundles or dragging children by the hand.

Instead of a dresser, Lucia Medina has a huge iron plate braced against the door. Whenever the door is opened, the iron plate must be pulled aside and dropped to the floor. The clang of the iron against the concrete floor reverberates through the apartment, stopping conversation, laughter, crying, even movement.

Once, in winter, when a sudden warm spell came over the city, all the flies hatched early and filled the apartment. Every night, outside their windows, garbage piles up on the grass. It is the work of their neighbors. The Medinas keep cats in defense. At evening, the children see the rats scurrying through the trash that piles up on the little plot of grass between the project and the sidewalk. They ask about them. They ask about drug dealers, numbers runners, gunfire in the streets.

Lucia Medina said that when she was a girl, she liked to draw and write poems. "I like Elizabeth Browning," she said.

"Even now?"

She nodded.

On afternoons when she and the children and I talked while her uncle traveled about the apartment on his electrically powered wheelchair or when we met over a lunch of *mofongo* or *pernil* at a little restaurant called Adela's, she sometimes dreamed aloud: "I was thinking of going to Arizona. I would like to go to California. I would like to go into a different scenery to see how it goes. It's far away. I like Arizona, because I hear the air is dry. I've seen pictures. A lot of stuff they show on the History on TV about the Indians and stuff is beautiful."

When she spoke so, she often looked away, not to a window but to a corner of the room near the ceiling, as if infinity were there. She dreamed only of places she had never seen and of people who had long since died into history.

10. Police: Claiborne County Jail

At night, on the West Side of Chicago, the police stop young black men on the street, drag them over to a police car, tell them to drop their

---

[7] A pun used by people of Puerto Rican descent. Loíza is a river in Puerto Rico named after a princess. The district called the Loisaida is known formally as the Lower East Side.

trousers and underpants, and "lift their nuts." Then they shine a flashlight on their naked bodies, claiming that they are looking for drugs that might have been hidden under their testicles. If the men protest the public humiliation, the police threaten to drop a packet of cocaine or a few vials of crack on the street beside them, and arrest them for possession or sale of narcotics.

To understand humiliation rather than violence as the force the police exert on the poor is counterintuitive; virtually everything published in the popular media describes police brutality as the issue. The Rodney King case became famous, partly because it set off a riot, as an example of the way police treat the poor, particularly blacks. But the videotapes of the Rodney King beating did not cause a great reaction when they were first shown; it was only the obviously unfair verdict of the jury that incited people to riot. The racial composition of the group that rioted makes an interesting point: Although King is black, browns and blacks rioted in almost equal numbers, suggesting that poverty or anti-white feeling rather than racial identification with King defined the issue.

In delivering the verdict, the white jury showed its contempt for blacks and browns, changing the King case from violence to humiliation. That was cause to riot. A man can endure a beating, if it is not too severe, and come away angry, resentful, in some respects strengthened by the ordeal. The same man may not be able to survive a humiliation, especially a public humiliation. To the poor, the police are a threat of violence, always, but it is the nature of police; they carry guns and clubs, which threaten everyone. Humiliation, however, is reserved for the poor, and this humiliation exists simply because the poor and the police exist; it is the relation of the police to the poor, and as such it is a force applied almost constantly in the lives of the poor.[8]

The common view now is that only black men and Latinos feel the effect of this force, but it is not so. Some poor women understand the police as a force against them, either directly or through suffering caused to husbands, sons, or lovers. It is true that a disproportionate number of the men in prison are black and that the percentage of young black men who are either in prison or on probation or parole is nearing one-third of the entire cohort, but all poor men are not black. The color of a man's skin, if it is white, does not spare him from this aspect of the surround, as it did not spare Robert Taylor in Tennessee.

Taylor is a petty criminal. He has no other view of himself. If he feels

[8] Another example of the lastingness of humiliation by the police appears in section 22 (pp.185–88) of this chapter.

remorse, he cannot say it. If ever he was innocent, he cannot recall it. Nevertheless, he has a sense of how the world ought to be, and he believes that it has never been quite that way. He associates the police—and his judges and jailers—with humiliations, accusations, unfairness, deception, corruption, anything but justice.

Taylor does not pretend to be a likable man. He sees the world as a collection of flawed men, forces arrayed against him. Especially the police. And no matter who he is, there is no justice in that.

I MET TAYLOR THROUGH A CIRCUITOUS ROUTE. One afternoon I was just sitting around at Philip Noah's Cedar Fork Market, talking, listening to the local gossip, when Taylor's brother-in-law, Wayne Long, burst in. Long was covered with grease and sweat and dragging a pale, thin, redheaded woman half his age behind him. He scurried through the store, rat-eyed and skinny, picking up a package of chips and laying down money for the chips and two dollars' worth of gas for his truck. Phil Noah introduced us, Long showed a flash of yellow teeth, and scurried out. His arms and legs waved, and he talked so fast I couldn't understand him.

After Long left, the gossips sitting over in the corner in front of the wire rack of chips said he was a-drawin, but he was also working with his auto wrecker, hauling things up to his property on Hoop Creek. Nobody knew exactly what he did up there, but he always seemed short of money and in a hurry. Since Hoop Creek was the area where the few blacks and the very poorest whites in Hancock and Claiborne counties lived, none of the men knew much about Long, which made them suspicious of him.

The next time I saw Long, his brother-in-law, Taylor, was with him. Taylor was naked except for a pair of swimming trunks and work shoes. His long red hair was matted with sweat, and a thin red beard grew in patches on his cheeks and hung in wisps from his chin. He was a big man, at least half again the size of Long, and heavy, with a fat chest and belly. He talked slowly and easily, inviting me down into the hollow to visit with him and his family.

I drove down to the hollow a few days later. Taylor was naked, as usual, but for the swimming trunks and work shoes. There had been a death, he said. A friend was gone. We would have to visit another time. He spoke in a terse, unmannerly way, as some people do when death has come close by.

For a while I did not see him. And then Taylor appeared at Noah's store. We talked for a long time, then we went up past the old house to his new place on Hoop Creek near the top of Little Ridge and talked some more.

It was a hot, damp August evening up along the creek, and the air was filled with swarms of termites. Taylor brushed them away or picked them off his naked chest and arms. He pulled them one by one out of his hair and crushed them between his fingernails.

His new house, a trailer, was green, more than twenty years old, reached by a step made of piled stones. "I'm buyin it from a colored guy," Taylor said, "cause he give me a good deal is the only reason I could afford it. He told me two thousand two hundred dollars for the trailer, 6 percent interest, which he was nice about that. He don't charge me no lot rent. I can leave it sittin right there until it's paid off.

"Ain't too many people that you can go out and buy a trailer and not a penny down. Moved in, already got my electricity and everything, and ain't even paid him a penny down yet on the trailer. He's a pretty good guy."

We had been up at the house for a while when Long pulled up in the tow truck, driving off the rough road onto the land with a flourish of clangs and roars. He jumped down out of the cab of the truck and scurried across the yard, past half a dozen wrecked cars, demanding to know which of his children had been playing on the small trailer he had left in the yard. The children, a boy of four and a girl of five, paid no attention to him. They were blonde, with dead white faces, barefoot and filthy. The boy lay in the dirt, wrestling with a black and brown dog.

Long's wife stood on the porch of the Appalachian-style house. Her mother sat in a chair beside her. The younger woman complained that she had smashed her thumb with a hammer while trying to tack down the carpet "where it's tore up, so it don't get more tore up."

The unpainted house had no screens, windows, or doors. Trash had collected in piles below the porch: beer cans, soft-drink cans, pieces of scrap metal, plastic bags and wrappers. Behind the house lay Powell Mountain, covered with trees in late summer, the deepest green, the green that comes before the frost.

Mrs. Taylor, a fat woman of about fifty, held a coffee cup in her hand. She wore a shift and showed crooked teeth and empty spaces when she spoke. She said that earlier in the afternoon there were so many termites in the air that they fell into her coffee and she had to pour out half the cup. She smiled. Her hair was still bright red, like that of her daughter and her son, Robert, and her skin was so pale that her veins read like Vesalius.

She said how much she loved corn chips. Robert went up to the porch and gave her half a bag of them; he had eaten the rest along the way.

This is what Taylor said about the police:

I've never been arrested before for nothing, not even public drunkenness. We just broke into this little ole arcade. It was a little store and at the end of it they had a pool hall. We stole $84 worth of quarters, six cue sticks, and a set of pool balls off the table. So I figured at best, breakin and enterin, misdemeanor shit.

No. I get charged with grand larceny, concealin, receivin. Stuck me in jail under $35,000 bond. I got a court appointed lawyer. Then I went to bond reduction hearin. The judge reduced it down to $25,000.

They kept jerkin me around on probation and all that bullshit, so I went to Knox County and got me a damn job. I said, piss on this shit. Had a job workin forty hours a week, everything. So he [the probation officer] comes by my cousin's house where I was stayin at, and I wasn't there at the time. According to his rules that violated me for not bein home when he showed up, so he tells her to have me call him within twenty-four hours or he's gon violate me. So I call him. So he says, "Come up here to my office. I need to see you now."

I says, "Well, have you violated me? Am I goin back to jail?"

He says, "No. If you'll come up here and see me, I won't violate you."

I walked in his office. You know what he done? Click, click. "Sit down there over in that chair and don't you get up," with his hand on his pistol. "You're goin to jail."

I said, "You lyin son of a bitch, you told me you wouldn't violate me if I come up here to see you."

He says, "Well, if I'd a told you I was gon violate you, would you come up here to see me?"

I looked at him. I said, "Mister Christian feller, I hope you know you can go to Hell for lyin."

Shit! I stayed in there five months waiting trial. Then, when I finally did go in front of the big judge, criminal judge, you know what he told me, "Son, sign an OR [own recognizance] bond and go home." I signed a $2,500 OR bond and went home. After they kept me up there for five fuckin months! County prisons draw so much every day that you stay in there. They get paid from the state for that. So that comes back into the county funds, which county funds goes in a judge's fuckin pocket, so he's basically gettin paid to keep you in jail.

I only seen him [the lawyer] like fifteen minutes before time to go to court. He won't even come upstairs to see you. You come down to court and he's in the office a-waitin on you. That was it. The sentencing was right then. He said, "If you don't plead guilty, we're gon charge you, grand larceny, second-degree burglary, concealin and receivin." That's what they already had me charged on for breakin into the store. Four charges, all of them were felonies.

Well, see, I escaped from the jail right there in the process of all this shit. You know, I tore the air conditioner duct up, cause we're starvin to death. They bring us half a biscuit, half a spoon o eggs and a half a spoon o gravy. That's all we got fed, cause we was raisin hell cause they wouldn't feed us. And the respected sheriff that I was in there under, he says to cut us to half-rations.

I seen so much shit go in that fuckin jail out there. This old man, I guess he was in his sixties. I seen em sodomize him with a goddamn broom handle. The old man that was in jail, they run a broom handle up his ass. They put a copper ring through his ears, tied a string around his damn pecker and pulled it down and was makin a woman out of him. The inmates right there in jail. And the sheriff knowed the shit was goin on and wouldn't do a motherfuckin thing about it.

They had to take him [the old man] to the hospital to have the string surgically removed.

The chief jailer, he'd get the girls up there and unlock em out of the women's cell and have em in his office drinkin. I seen that with my own fuckin eyes. I ain't got nobody to ask for that. He'd tell em, if they'd give him some pussy, he'd get em out, he'd get their sentence reduced. He'd go talk to the sheriff: And I think this girl's learnin this, you know. Okay, send her home.

So when I escaped from the jail out there, kicked the air conditioner duct up and went up through the roof, kicked the roof out and run off, they caught me and brought me back and shit and shit.

And another boy in there, we had some trouble, and an assault charge came up over that. When I went in for sentencing they had me charged with grand larceny, second-degree burglary, concealin and receivin, felony assault, felony escape, destruction of county property, fleein from an officer and resistin arrest, and said if I didn't plead guilty to it, you know, take a lesser charge and plead guilty, they were gon stick me with all those charges and throw in habitual criminal. Habitual criminal carries life, and you have to do thirty-three.

The state prison was a picnic. If I had my choice of do three years in the state penitentiary or do eleven months and twenty-nine days in this county jail, I'd say, send me to fuckin penitentiary. I'd rather do state time, because in the state at least you're treated halfway fuckin decent.

I did three years over Mickey Mouse bullshit. You know what's screwed up about it? The boy that I broke into the store with the first time, he gets caught later on for eleven different charges, and one of em was for theft over ten thousand dollars. So he goes and gets him a real lawyer, not from this county, not a court-appointed lawyer. He gets three years probation on eleven fuckin charges and they only convicted me on one charge.

This is one of the most corrupt counties I know of anywhere. They don't give a fuck. The school board, Denny Peters the superintendent of school, he bankrupted the fuckin county. That's the reason they voted in a goddamn twenty-dollar wheel tax. What did they do to him? Not a mother-fuckin thing.[9]

You got the Hurstes, the Brogans, the Rays, Anders, Evanses,[10] the ones that runs the damn county, ninety percent of em in the county is related to em, and that's some of their family. My family's not related.

I went to the last half of my junior year of high school, then worked on a farm, tried to get public work. I got lucky just through a friend of mine, he talked to his papaw, and he got me a job at the sawmill makin three dollars and somethin a hour. Hell, I was on top of the world. Then my ear got bad and I had to go in the hospital, have surgery on it, so I had to take off time for surgery. He said, that was all right, "I was aimin to lay you off anyway," so he laid me off. Couldn't draw unemployment benefits. They said that I hadn't worked the right quarters.

I bummed around here, left, and went to Indiana and got a good job, and then I came back, and that's when I got into all this trouble, cause I was used to havin money all the time, but not down here. I'm alcoholic, I was broke, needed a drink, no money, couldn't buy a job. I broke into the place to get money for a drink. That was about it, and since then I been pillar to post. I been on the streets, left this county for a while, went to Knox County. It got so fuckin bad I'd rather be in Knoxville on the fuckin streets, sleepin in a cardboard box, sleepin under a bridge, as to be in this county.

My dad farmed about all his life. We'd raise baccer. He'd go in debt up to his ass. We'd work like fuckin niggers to pay us out of debt. We'd get paid out of debt, he'd pick up and move and go somewhere else. Sell what we had for what he could get out of it, run through with the money.

We had our ups and downs, me and him, actually fist fight at times, and at times we got along, but mine and his affairs was mine and his affairs, you didn't stick into it. If me and him was fist-fightin and somebody walked up and cracked me in the head with a pop bottle to get me off of him, he was the kind that would turn around and shoot him over it for hittin me. That's the way it was.

My dad killed hisself a little over a year ago, committed suicide. I'm still under investigation for the murder of my dad, and I was in Knox County

[9] Peters was actually demoted from school superintendent to principal after the system showed a $900,000 deficit, according to local historians.

[10] Political and economic leaders in the county. Bill Hurst, for example, had been the most powerful elected official in the county for many years.

when it happened. They still got his pistol at the courthouse, Kelly Ankers has. He asked me, did I kill my dad? and I called him a stupid son of a bitch.

11. Landlords: A Game of Euchre

In America, where 65 percent of households own their homes,[11] only the poor know landlords. There are exceptions, of course, mainly in New York City and a few other very large urban centers. Outside those cities, the word "tenant" remains synonymous with poor, as it has since the British settled along the eastern shores.

Seen through modern eyes, the argument against extending the vote to people who do not own property is a blight on the history of the country, but it may not be so simple as that. The founders suspected something about the relation of landlords and tenants and the force it exerts upon the tenant's life and thought. In the Constitutional Convention of 1787, on August 7, when questions of suffrage were debated, Gouverneur Morris and John Dickinson argued that extending the vote to people without property would eventually lead to the establishment of an aristocracy.[12]

James Madison summed up the debate: Freeholders "would be the best depositories of republican liberty. In future times a great majority of the people will not only be without landed, but any other sort of, property. They will either combine under the influence of their common situation; in which case the rights of property, and the public liberty, will not be secure in their hands; or, which is more probable, they will become the tools of opulence and ambition, in which case there will be equal danger. . . ."[13]

---

[11] U.S. Department of Housing and Urban Development quoted in the *New York Times*, Feb. 9, 1996.

[12] This was the point at which the founders debated the question of how to count Negroes for the purpose of apportioning representation: as whole persons or three-fifths.

In the course of the debate that day, Morris also said, "The time is not distant when this country will abound with mechanics and manufacturers who will receive their bread from their employers."

[13] From notes on the Convention quoted in *The People Shall Judge* (Chicago: University of Chicago Press, 1949), an anthology by the Social Sciences Staff.

It has been argued that an aristocracy or oligarchy based on money and influence has been in power in the United States from the outset. When Steve Forbes, one of the wealthiest men in America and a lifelong defender of the prerogatives of wealth, presented himself as a populist during his campaign to win the Republican presidential nomination in 1996, the alliance feared by Morris and Madison seemed possible.

From the vantage of two centuries, the founders were wrong about the establishment of an aristocracy, but they knew something important about the landlord/tenant relationship and the effect it has on the tenant, not merely the physical condition of his or her life but the politics. They recognized the existence of the surround, and they feared it. To carry on the anachronism, if the founders remained consistent in their thoughts, they would now argue that poverty in the United States must be alleviated, if not eliminated, to preserve the liberty of its citizens. Furthermore, they would probably begin by finding an alternative to the current way of providing housing for the poor.

For the poor, tenant shelter is not a comfort but a force. Landlords operate as if by divine right. There is no Magna Carta for poor tenants; they cannot negotiate their situation. If they fail to satisfy the landlord's demands, they will find themselves in the street, with their children and their belongings, unless the landlord chooses to lock them out, in which case they will have only the clothes they are wearing and the children they must feed and shelter. For anyone living in poverty, eviction is a constant threat. It may end in homelessness, doubling up with family or friends, or a step down into even worse housing.

Landlords, who know very well the vulnerability of the poor, exert force against tenants in many ways. Miserable, unhealthy conditions are common, but some demonstrations of force make the relation even more clear than a fallen ceiling or the lack of heat in winter:

IN A TINY TOWN just south of the Cumberland Gap, a young woman, her husband, and their infant child moved into a trailer court. He had a minimum-wage job in a pizzeria; she stayed home with the child. Her parents lived nearby, but they had virtually no money and no room in their tiny place to put up three more people.[14]

Sally, the young woman's mother, took charge of her twenty-one-year-old daughter as if she were still a child. At a yard sale on the hill above the center of town, she and her daughter, Erin, looked at all the baby clothes piled on a wooden table, touching them, holding them up for size, studying the colors as if the shades of yellow or pink were a serious matter, pretending that the sloping front yard was a store, like the Kmart or Penny's down in Knoxville. When they finished, Erin went over to the old Chevy

---

[14] Because I could not substantiate the statements made by the young woman and no legal action was taken, I cannot use her real name or that of the landlord, or otherwise identify them.

where the baby slept in the car seat, and Sally nodded to the woman who ran the sale that it was time to talk. They argued over what was worth fifty cents and what was worth three for a dollar. Sally, known as Mamaw before she was forty, had long ago lost her looks; her skin had the consistency and color of the pale pieces of hide sold in pet stores. She lacked three of her top front teeth, which took the sharpness out of her words, but she showed no sign of self-consciousness. She fought over every item. In the end, she spent all the money she had, $2.50, and came away with a small armload of baby clothes.

Erin did not accept the clothes as if they were a gift, but took them in a casual way, as young children do. She was a pretty girl, long and slim, with light brown hair and the tragic eyes of Appalachian women. The baby was pretty, too, although she was not clean. Later, in a Burger King, smeared with catsup and part of a milkshake, the baby was suddenly in clown makeup, a funny, beautiful new generation.

Erin said that the trouble began when they could not pay the rent on time. She asked her husband to talk with the landlord, because "he was a man and I was a woman and I didn't feel that was right. It was my husband's job. So my husband went next door to let him know we was going to be late with the rent.

"He come back over, and told me, 'The landlord said it's okay, don't worry about it or nothing like that.' Well, my husband left, and before he left, I told him, 'I need a mop. I don't have a mop and I'm gonna go next door to Ted's and see if I can borrow one.'

"I went over there, and Jerry [the landlord] was sittin there on the couch. And he asked me what I needed and I told him a mop and he said he wanted me to set down fer a minute. And they had beer all around em and everything. After that, my husband had left and Jerry asked me to play cards, and he was a little drunk at the time. But see, he had been over there [next door] before and he had never tried anything on me or anything like that, you know.

"He asked me to teach him how to play—what was it—euchre. And Ted and everybody was there, so I figgered there's no harm in it. And Ted said his girlfriend was gonna be comin over soon. So I set there and I was tryin to teach im how to play euchre and it was like he wasn't payin attention to the cards. He was makin me feel uncomfortable.

"Well, Ted walked into his back bedroom and Jerry and me was settin over here. I got up and moved to the couch. Jerry come over there next to me. And he goes, 'I like what I see.' I was wearin jean shorts at the time, so I thought maybe it's just me. Well, I asked Ted if it would be all right if I went over to the house, you know, and I would come visit him later, because I just felt really uncomfortable by the way that he [Jerry] was lookin at me. I was just real uncomfortable. I said, 'I think it's about time that I leave.'

"Well, I went over there to the house and I got to thinkin about it and I thought that wasn't right the way he made me feel. I need to go talk to Mom about it. And I didn't want to go next door, cuz, see, the reason I knew Ted next door was because he had a phone and I went over to borrow his phone to call my mom or my mom would call me or somethin. Well, I got to thinkin about it and I thought that wasn't right. I'm gonna go talk to Mom.

"Mom and Dad was out on the flea market at the time, but I went next door across the street to my neighbor's house and I used her phone. Well, when I called there I was cryin and everything and I told my little brother, 'Could you please tell Mom and Dad as soon as they get home that the baby needs some milk?' You know, I was trying to think of something that everybody wouldn't know. And me and Mom could talk about it. So I told her the baby was out of milk. She was screamin. She needed some milk.

"Anyway, the message got to my mom. The situation was that my mom thought that I really needed milk, so she went to the grocery store, so that's what took so long.

"Well, when I got back over there to the house, the door was kind of open and I thought, What in the world? He was inside the door. There wasn't no locks on the doors. And I said, 'What are you doin here?'

"He goes, 'Nothin.' And I was scared to say anything, you know. I thought, Well, if I say something to him, then he could kick me out, or if I make him mad he'll kick me out. Just listen to what he has to say. I walked in the house and he shut the door behind me and the baby was in the house sleepin at the time.

"I went to go check on the baby and he followed me into her room. And he goes, 'Boy, I really like what I see.' He goes, 'How come you left?'

"I said, 'I just felt uncomfortable.'

"And he said, 'There's no reason to be scared of me. I wouldn't do anything to hurt you.'

"Well, I walked back out of my baby's room and I walked into the living room and I set down for a minute and I thought, Well, maybe he's gonna apologize for what he did, you know, cuz he was real real quiet. He just kept lookin outside and he was real quiet. My husband was already at work. I didn't have a phone. You know, I didn't know what to do.

"He kept just makin real rude remarks to me. I felt that they were rude, you know. He kept tellin me how sexy I was and at one point in time I was settin down in a chair and he come over there and was tellin me how nice my body is and if I'd just go in the bedroom with him, he'd forget about it and I wouldn't have to worry about nothin anymore. He'd never bother me again. I wouldn't have to pay rent.

"What I was so scared about was we had no place to go. I had a little baby already. Mom and Dad didn't have enough room for all of us to live with them. See, he knew exactly what kind of financial problems we were havin and he said, Oh, how he was gonna help us, you know. He cares about people like us, he just gave it all to us.

"He set there and he put his hand down my shirt and I tried to push him away and he wouldn't listen to me, so I ran in the baby's room and I got her up, cause I was scared to be by myself, but I figgered maybe if I got her he would leave me alone. And I got the baby and he took her out of my hands and said, 'I own his life,' and I told him to put her down and he put her down. He come back over there, followin me again.

"Finally, I didn't know what to do. I thought, I'll just go use the rest room. That's all I could think of was to get away from him. So I walked into the rest room and while I was in the bathroom I was gettin ready to pull up my britches and he walked in there and he said, 'I like what I see,' and put me up against the sink and started to touch me there. I pushed him as hard as I could push him and I grabbed my baby and I ran out. And I called my daddy, and when I called my daddy, my daddy come over there and he was gonna kill him.

"When my daddy walked in there—this is how much of a slime this guy was—he was sittin there still on my chair and he was leanin back, and my daddy says, 'What are you doin here?' "And he said, 'This is mine and I don't have to leave if I don't want to.' And my daddy said, 'I think it's time you do leave. My daughter and my granddaughter's goin over to my house and they're not gonna be here.'

"And he said, 'This is my f . . . . n place and I ain't goin nowhere.' Jest settin there in the chair. And my daddy said, 'When you leave, you lock the door and you turn off the TV,' cause he had the TV on and just laid back as drunk as he could be. And he was still there when me and my daddy left.

"We went over to my mom's. My mom right away called the cops and they told us that we had to come up with so much money to file a claim and to call em back tomorrow and let em know. It was a warrant. To take out a warrant you have to have fifty dollars. So they told us to call em back tomorrow and I talked to my papaw about it and everything. Well, that next day, Jerry called, five, six times on my mom's answerin machine thing.

"At first, I didn't want nuttin to do with him. I wouldn't talk to im. Only thing I kept thinkin of was, I'm gonna take this guy to court. But where was I gon git fifty dollars?

"Well, Mommy had gotten on the phone with him and asked him what he wanted. He was settin there cryin and sobbin, sayin how sorry he was. He was drunk. He was married. The whole time I was tellin this guy that

I was married and everything, and he said, 'So what? I am too. What's it matter?'

"He was sayin how sorry he was for touchin me and how could he make it up to me, if only I wouldn't take him to court, that I've been through a rough time and he's been through a rough time. Can I just forgive him?

"So what happened was I ended up talkin to him on the phone. We put guidelines down such as he has to put locks on the door. See, I didn't have no locks on my door the whole time I lived there. I didn't have a phone, didn't have no locks, there was nobody there I could really trust or talk to or anything.

"One day my husband went home—it was two weeks after it happened—and found an eviction notice on our door sayin that we were kicked out and we only had ten days to move at the time. He went behind our back. He wouldn't even give us back our two-hundred dollar deposit. We had to borrow two hundred dollars from my papaw in order to move to Birchfield.[15] We didn't really want to move, but we didn't have a choice, you know. We had ten days to get out, and we had no place else to go.

"Jerry called my mom one night. He said, 'You better tell your kids to come out and get their hundred dollars. If not, I'm gonna go out and get drunk on it.' She said he better go out and get drunk then, cause he owed us two hundred dollars.

"We never did get our money back."

All the while that Erin spoke, her mother listened. She was a woman from Indiana who had met a mountain man there, married him, and come home with him after he lost his factory job. She smoked long, thin cigarettes, holding them in the corner of her mouth, away from the missing teeth. If her daughter's terror upset her, she did not let her feelings be known. The tragic rawhide look never left her face, but her eyes lost focus now and then, as if she had gone to another place.

Later, we talked about people we knew in common—Bill Hurst, who had run the county for so many years, people in the Birchfield Camp—but Sally did not show her usual angry energy, she did not take charge of anything, not the conversation, not even her daughter. Suddenly, apropos of nothing at all, she said, "I had the same thing happen, sort of. They try to take advantage of you. They say you don't have to pay the rent or nothin, just be there for me."

---

[15] On one of my visits to the Birchfield Trailer Court, Sally and Erin accompanied me. We talked with some of their neighbors and went into the unlocked trailer Erin and her husband had lived in after Jerry evicted them. The trailer had no screens on the windows; flies and wasps circled lazily in the rooms. The door was broken, the floor was rotted in the kitchen, and the carpeting was thin and torn. The Birchfield Court was a step down from anywhere. At night, drunks wandered through the rows of trailers, shouting and fighting. There was gunfire almost every night.

12. Criminals: An Orthodox Beating

Most violent crime involves people who know each other, often from the same family, or poor people; for the rest, the economically comfortable and those without a personal rage, crime is more chimera than reality. It stands to reason. After all, the first requisite of violent crime is proximity, and the proximal place for crime in America is the surround.

There can be little doubt that the surround has some relation to violence, since most violent crime involves poor people attacking each other. Within the surround, proximity again proves a requisite: blacks commit crimes against blacks, browns against browns, whites against whites, and so on. Poor people seldom cross into the lives of the rich, and when they do, it becomes news: the delicious excitement of the great chimera invigorated, proof that the beast of our dreams is to be feared after all. Truman Capote's *In Cold Blood*, in which two drifters murdered a middle-income family, had such excitement. I do not think it would have interested the public in the same way had it not been about the crossing of the boundaries.

Crime has opposite effects on the rich and the poor. The poor witness crime early in their lives. They see violence or suffer it; in either case, violence enters their consciousness, becoming an inner subject, making them its object, exerting force. This force determines where they live, what they keep in their houses, how they lock and bar the doors and windows, whom they speak to on the street, how they raise their children, and so on. It exerts force against them precisely because they cannot limit it to the unusual, which would leave it in the realm of violence.

Rich people and those in the middle use crime as a force against the poor, not only blacks and Latinos, but mountain people, Asians, Italians, Jews, Russians, whoever can be put to use in the economic enterprise of those with money and property, no matter how little, as long as they are not poor, as long as they have some alliance with or allegiance to the winners in the game.

How the rich make the fear of crime into a force was demonstrated by Abel Lomas,* a nineteen-year-old student in an experimental humanities program, who said he believed he could get a job because he was able to say to an employment counselor: "I'm goin to school. I never did no jail time

---

* Not his real name.

or nothing." Needless to say, only the poor must assert their innocence.

The unspoken accusation against the poor works in two ways: It enables the rich to avoid associating with them in business, social, or educational situations; and it strengthens the fearful subject already existing in the poor. They become the objects of criminals and of the fear of criminals.

Although the rule of crime (the poor against the poor and the rich against the poor) would seem to exert enough force of itself, the situation of the poor magnifies the effect of crime. Those who are burglarized or robbed or cheated generally have neither the capital nor the insurance to replace their losses, and those who suffer violent crime often cannot get proper medical attention or fair treatment in the courts. The poor know from the anecdotal sociology that floats on the air of their neighborhoods that any crime against them will almost inevitably begin a chain of troubles.

S HE SENT HER SON TO SCHOOL that morning. He was all she had: a college boy, scholar to be, a library in its youth. He wore a virginal beard, black hat; signs of his love of God hung outside his coat. Nothing else mattered to her now but the boy. Her mother was dead, her father full of darkness, the father of the boy so long gone she had forgotten his face; nothing remained of him but her memory of the stench of his rotted gums.

Nothing went well for her now but the boy. She worked, she earned a little. Her spine had begun to deteriorate; the doctors did not know why. She went to work despite the pain, all for the boy. His cheeks were so innocent, the color of rose, more delicate than the cheeks of any girl. In the evening, when he sat at the little desk, hunched over the narrowness that had been designed for a child, she peeked at his cheeks as she walked by. Sometimes she made up reasons to speak to him, just to hear his voice, and perhaps to bring him around to look at her, to allow her to see for a moment the slightly myopic eyes of one who loved God more than the world.

She sent him down the flights of stairs, through the halls smelling of fried whitefish and brisket already cooking at the breakfast hour, out into the streets of Brooklyn, along the boundaries of the ghettos, where the warring nations of blacks and Jews and Italians touch. All mornings were the same: She had no fear because she prayed, she prayed because she was terrified. The woman and her son had asked God's blessing on the day, on themselves, on the bread of the breakfast. He put on phylacteries, she thanked God.

Four boys—or was it six?—beat him over the head with two-by-fours, and left him for dead.

His eyeglasses were broken, his myopic eyes were stilled, blood ran onto his virginal beard and turned black and solid in the oxygenated air.

Four boys were arrested, white like her son, but not with delicate cheeks or the eyes of one who so dearly loved the Lord.

Love gained a sibling in the woman's world. She hated the four thugs, hoodlums, criminals, lowlifes, more than she had ever hated anyone or anything in her life. They were, she said with her sense of history, like Brown Shirts—not Nazis, not yet, Brown Shirts—so senselessly brutal even a Hitler could not tolerate them.

The stilled eyes moved, but they were, the doctors said, to be forever glazed.

Blind?

Not blind.

So, he can see?

Not exactly.

He can't see, but he isn't blind; what is this? A joke? A game you're playing on me?

We told you what we know.

And his mind?

Perhaps in time.

Why?

They broke the bones of his skull; his brain swelled.

Why?

We told you.

No, no. I mean WHY?

His assailants were presented to him in court. The boy took off his glasses, fogged them with his breath, cleaned the lenses with a handkerchief while the jury watched. He could not recognize them. In a test, he could not see the clock on the wall.

Case dismissed.

I'll sue, the mother said.

She found a lawyer, she lost her part-time job. She lost the lawyer. The rent came due. The doctors demanded payment. He needed therapy for this and therapy for that. She moved in with her father; a widower needed someone to care for him.

Now, you want to take care of me! he shouted. Your son is an idiot. He'll never get well.

You have always been a cruel and abusive man, she said in her best having attended briefly Brooklyn College tones.

Get out! He was eighty-one years old and his heart was failing, but he picked up everything that belonged to her, including chairs, suitcases, and the small desk, and threw it out into the hall.

In time, she found rooms again for herself and the unseeing, unthinking boy who was not officially the victim of anything. On many days she cannot leave her bed, for the rage she feels seems to have settled in the vulnerable place in her spine. The tint of rose has returned to the boy's cheeks and they pray together again; but she no longer believes he is a library in its youth.

13. Health: Life Among the Guallamallahs

Poor people get sick, and when they get sick, they stay sick. Poverty causes sickness and sickness causes poverty. Attempts have been made in America to provide medical insurance to the poor as a way of breaking the cycle, but with only limited success. By 1995, 43.4 million Americans under sixty-five did not have health insurance. At that time it was estimated that more than a million people lost their health insurance every year.[16]

Poor people who collect Aid to Families with Dependent Children are covered by Medicaid, a benefit so vital that many women on AFDC say they cannot afford to work, because they will lose health-care benefits for their children. If one or more of their children have chronic illnesses, the period between the end of Medicaid coverage and the beginning of medical coverage through an employer can be a major problem. If the prospective employer does not offer medical coverage, the problem is insurmountable; getting off welfare means endangering the lives of children.

Among the poor who work, health care is the number-one problem, according to the Henry J. Kaiser Family Foundation.[17] In 1995, more than 20 percent of the residents in thirteen states were without health insurance.

---

[16] Employee Benefit Research Institute statistics quoted in the *New York Times*, Aug. 27, 1995. A study conducted by the Harvard School of Public Health and reported in the *Journal of the American Medical Association* in October 1996 said that 45 percent of the uninsured had difficulty getting needed medical care during 1995. In other words, the commonly held notion that the poor can get free care in emergency rooms and other facilities is not true. According to the survey, reported in the *New York Times* on Oct. 17, 1996, these problems had serious "consequences" not only for their health—mental as well as physical—but for every aspect of their lives at home or on the job.

[17] Quoted in the *New York Times*, Jan. 4, 1993. The same study showed that crime, drug abuse, and violence were not among the top ten issues in importance for poor people. Finding a job was second, paying the rent only eighth.

No state had less than 10 percent of its population without coverage. In Florida, 24.1 percent of the population did not have any kind of health insurance, although the state had passed legislation extending medical coverage to all pregnant women and poor children.[18]

Teresa Wilhoit and her sons in Belle Glade were among those Florida residents who lacked coverage, even though her husband worked full time for the city of Belle Glade as an Equipment Operator No. 3, driving a large truck and picking up trash. His gross earnings came to $17,732 a year or $341 a week, enough to keep the family above the federal poverty line, but barely enough to live on. His health insurance was paid by the city, but to add his wife and two sons to the policy would have cost $260 a month, about 19 percent of his take-home pay. And like all insurance policies, the one offered by the city did not cover everything; there were deductibles that would have brought their total annual cost up close to a fourth of his net income.

Had the Wilhoits chosen to buy medical insurance, his take-home pay would have fallen below the federal poverty level; he would then have been poor by even the most stringent measure. Instead, the Wilhoits took their chances, and lost. Nothing catastrophic happened to them; compared to people living in the slums of Buenos Aires, they were rich. They had a television set and a pushbutton telephone. They owned the trailer they lived in, although not the ground on which it stood. But medical care and its cost dominated their lives.

In the area of Belle Glade where they lived, on the west side of town, there were only three native-born white families. Teresa Wilhoit defined the others according to the kind of agricultural work they performed: "Guallamallahs wants to work in oranges, the Haitians works in cane, Jamaicans works in cane; the Mexicans is only here for the season. Nobody hardly associates with each other. These people next door to me, they been here for about a year now, I haven't spoke to them since they been here. I think they're Guallamallahs." In fact, Mrs. Wilhoit did not like any of her neighbors. She thought the Mexicans tried to take advantage of her younger son, she did not like blacks at all, and the Guallamallahs had, in her view, settled in and taken over. Shopping in Belle Glade bothered her, because there was "no place to go but Jew-stores."

She did not like her family, either. "I have one aunt that was living around me three years ago," she said, "and she passed away when she was forty-six. And I have cousins and uncles around here, but I don't associate

---

[18] National Institute for Health Care Management cited in the *New York Times*, July 2, 1995.

with em. They're the type of people that thinks they're better than you are, and some of em thinks that you do em a favor or they get in a bind and they expect you to help em, and when you get em out, well, then they don't need ya. They like to use you.

"My uncle that lives here is on disability. He has two kids. His son got arrested and put in jail and after he got out of all this trouble, then he quit comin around. He went to jail for burglarizin about eight cars. He's eighteen."

Life for Teresa Wilhoit has become a mix of hatreds, dreams, troubles, and illnesses. If there are comforts, they come as food, for she is obese, a great mound of a woman, sitting. She speaks of food, she thinks of food, she buys chickens and hamburger in five- and ten-pound packages, and she cooks and sits. For recreation, she goes fishing. And sits. Her older son, a wiry blond adolescent with a dozen illnesses, stuffed with Ritalin and still jumpy, sits beside her. Her pushes her, rolls her, moves her about as if she were a sow or something larger.

She has lost confidence in the world, beginning with the lie about Elvis: "I still say the man's not dead. If he could be like these stories and stuff, just die out and change and everything. He could of done left town or anything. I don't think he's really dead. I don't think they buried anybody."

She felt deceived by employers; rivals; and lawyers, too: "I was managing a convenience store, and we had a lot of trouble with people comin in and shopliftin and stuff like that, and then when they started the inventory, it started comin up short real bad, and so they came in one day. . . . And the supervisor was goin with the cashier, so she wanted my position, so they decided to fire me, sayin that I was stealin from em. And they had cameras and everything, and I asked em, 'If you're gonna fire me, why didn't you call the police?'

"I even went and hired a lawyer, and the lawyer that I got waited until the company filed bankrupt, and then he told me there was nothin I could do about it."

Medicine seems still more unfair to her: "They told me that I needed to be under a doctor's care all the time, and how can you be under a doctor's care when you don't have the money to go? Since they changed the law now, with the health care and stuff like that, you can't get to the health department, because they say you're not eligible for it. They say my husband makes too much money.

"I think that people that has illnesses, I think they should be able to see a doctor, get more help than some people can get. I mean you can go out here to HRS [Human Resources Services] and tell em a whole lot of lies and get anything you want. I don't do that, because I don't like jail. I don't think I would want to be behind the bars."

She looked over at her son, who crouched on the floor beside the couch,

tying wires into the telephone jack, attempting to hook up an old telephone. He had been working on it all afternoon, since he had come home
from school claiming illness. "It was enough when I was going to see him
in the detention center in West Palm [Beach]. That was enough for me. If
you've never seen your son locked up or if you never seen your son in
whatchacall uniforms, it's like, it just like tears you apart. I mean it hurts
you so bad, you can't stand to keep from cryin. And you only get to see him
three hours a week and get to talk to him nine minutes a week; three hours
and nine minutes a week is all you get to socialize with your kid, and you
have to drive all the way to Palm Beach to see him.

"And what really bothered me a lot about him bein in the detention center in West Palm, what if he goes and has trouble with his stomach which
he has all the time or what if he has a migraine headache?"

No matter what we talked about, either in the trailer or on the telephone, Mrs. Wilhoit brought the conversation around to one of two subjects: sickness or violence.

Illnesses

Mrs. Wilhoit: Obesity, unstable blood pressure, deteriorated discs or other
inoperable disabling back problems, emphysema, gallbladder removed, kid-
ney stones removed, as well as some less clearly defined problems such as:

"I've had two surgeries on my eyes. I had a real high fever one time to
where the fever was so high it made my eyes go crossed.

"And back when I was a little kid, I guess maybe two or three years old,
I was so sick to where I couldn't even get up off the floor. I never walked or
crawled, talked or nothin, and they had to take me to North Carolina, and
the doctors treated me up there."

Her sons: Hyperactivity (both treated with Ritalin), migraine headaches,
anemia, dyslexia, bronchial asthma, hernias, hearing loss, "Old Timer's disease with tremors in the hands." One son is in classes for the emotionally
handicapped.

She has become used to their illnesses, however: "When I take one of
them to the hospital with their stomach, I can tell the doctors what to do.
All you have to do is put em on the bed and hook em up to I.V. machines
and let the I.V. run through for a while, and they're well.

"They have stomach cramps around navel parts, which is the wall of
your stomach, and there's really not much they can do for it. They put em
in the hospital, keep em in the hospital for twenty-four hours, two days.
My youngest son has been all the way over to Miami Hospital. They did

like a research on him. They wanted to do the sleep study test. What they were lookin for was what was causin the tremors in his hands and why he sweats so much.

"And one time when he was losin weight, they found out that he had parasites in the colon. They said you get it from dirt. They get it from the cows."

Her husband is fine.

Violence

Mrs. Wilhoit was severely beaten by her father when she was a child. She said he often beat her until she bled. Her grandmother, with whom she often stayed for years at a time, forced her to sleep on a concrete floor and beat her severely with switches and belts.

Her husband was also beaten when he was a child. He has difficulty controlling his temper now, a situation she describes euphemistically as hyperactivity.

Her younger son was sexually molested twice by some Mexican boys in the neighborhood.

Her older son was severely beaten by an eighteen-year-old boy when he was in junior high school. After the beating, he began suffering from headaches, hearing loss, and nausea.

Her older son attacked another boy in school, punching him in the face with a pair of brass knuckles. He attacked the same boy again at a dance a few months later, beating him in the head with a padlock, which he used as a weapon. After the second attack, her son was imprisoned in West Palm Beach.

How the Wilhoits came to have so many illnesses is impossible to know. Did the beatings generate the pattern? What happened in her infancy? What fever? What lack of nutrition? Even if hypochondria plays a part in her problems, there can be no denying that the organism has begun to break down; it appears so in her face, in the puffed-out flesh of her hands and feet, in the laborious breathing. Illness does violence to the body in a cumulative way, but illness itself cannot be a force, for it comes about naturally and most often is distributed across the whole of humanity. It must be classed with absolute poverty.

The force the poor endure is the lack of treatment in a society that offers the rich the best medical care on earth. Nothing so separates the losers from the winners as the inability to care for their children or themselves.

Mrs. Wilhoit and her family seem to be consumed with rage: They sue, they hate, they complain against the system. She says that her husband cannot trust himself to control his temper in a confrontation with any of the teachers or other public officials the Wilhoits deal with. And that is understandable; relative poverty produces a rage against the game and all the players.

The diagnosis of illness, even a terrible, deadly illness, produces a different reaction in the poor: Dr. Kathy Sugarman, a young physician who works with poor women in the Bronx, finds quiet acceptance the usual response when she tells poor women they are very sick. She does not think it is merely the momentary numbness upon receiving bad news, for the response does not change over time.

Dr. Sugarman compared the response of a young woman in her clinic upon learning she is HIV-positive to the way a woman who is not poor, one like her own mother, might behave. Her mother, she said, would demand a second or third opinion; launch a great campaign to get well, save her life. Poor women never ask for another opinion. Dr. Sugarman thinks so many bad things have happened to her patients that they learn to accept them, even the news that they are going to get very sick and die.

This distinction the poor make between the relative poverty of economic and social life and the absolute poverty caused by a virus or bacterium or the failure of an organ tells the subtlety of their understanding of the world: All that is absolute is as bearable as the fated changing of the days, but no relative agony can be tolerated.

14. Meanness: Some Men Preaching Are Not Preachers

She stood in the orange light that comes in summer at the start of evening on Frankel Street. Night begins that way along the Mississippi. Before long, the sun falls into the river just beyond the end of the street, and the light gets red and as palpable as mist, and darkness settles over the Delta. In these last moments of light, the women of Frankel Street come out to gossip or collect their children or just to watch the figures of the walkers waning into the distance, like the light.

They do not stand in the street after dark: A boy was murdered in the blue house around the corner last week. Another shot his grandparents to death the week before. And something might be hiding in the tall weeds that grow like a green forest on the corner, shielding rats, hiding guns or even men. Killers might be there. Surely snakes live in the tall grass. The women have seen them there in daylight or in dreams.

Laughter dies politely in the reddening sun on Frankel Street. Sounds of sisters giggling, children calling out a game, a mother gathering in her brood, all grow soft in the summer air, gently fading, like the light. No men are expected on Frankel Street, or so it seems in summer, for the women stand in their dishabille: carpet slippers, loose shifts, T-shirts, papers tied in their hair, clothing chosen for the heat.

She had come out of her house to stand in the orange light and take the first cool breath of evening air when I spoke to her. She is a big woman, tall and wide, and very dark. Her skin shimmered in the Mississippi heat. Her face was handsome in the way of sculpture, without the busy detail of an old painter's work, pure form, not yet abstraction: a modern face, heavy, metallic, glistening with gravity, yet wholly innocent.

She stood to the sun. The color of the light yellowed her eyes. For a long time she did not speak to me. She looked into my eyes with such intensity I thought she must be reading my soul. The light had changed from orange to red before she decided to speak. Then there was a sudden frankness, as if we had become family.

Her name is Gloria Brown and she speaks the language of the plantation where she was born. The voice is not melodious, but a quick step, like running in open country, full of turns and jumps, and as private as poetry.

"This time, like slavery time, carry me back where my parents come from, slavery days. We didn't have shoes or nothin like that. It was barefoot on the ground.

"It's like that now. The white people, some of the black people, you can't get what they got.

"My father worked for ten cents a day on the farm. He's eighty-three now. He talks, but it hurts him.

"They had fourteen heads of kids. He had to do what the white man said, because he was livin on the plantation. [If] he didn't work for that man, what could he done? Didn't have no money, didn't have no education. Back in them days people didn't have no education.

"Before I'd go through what my daddy went through, I wouldn't do it. I got kids of my own, but if I think I got to lick up to a person just to do what they say to do, I would not do it. Me and my kids, we would just starve. My daddy was a helluva good man to put up with it.

"Some mans just walked off and left their kids, but my daddy didn't do it. I just love him from my heart. I feel grateful and proud, because he stuck with us kids, and after my mother died, he stuck with us kids. I love my daddy. I love him to my heart."

She had worked hard almost all her life, on plantations and in kitchens, in the backs of restaurants, but she had never been to a restaurant as a customer, seated and served. So, a few days later, we went. It was not easy to convince her, but Juliette Thomas, a young schoolteacher with marceled hair in the style of Jospehine Baker, helped: "Come on, girl, get changed, and let's go." The conversation took place in Gloria Brown's house, in the tiny living room, where she sat on the couch facing the television set. Behind her, on the wall, was a black cloth with three tigers silkscreened on the face of it, and next to the tiger cloth a small colorful basket on a stick.

In her own house in the hard light of day she looked younger, more vulnerable, girlish, a bigger woman than she had been at last light, filling a chair to overflowing. She wanted to sit for a while in her house, which she called her pretty house. She had been there for less than a month. And for a year before that, she had lived a block away in another kind of house. "It's sad the way us people has to live," she said. "The house where I used to live was too bad for anybody to stay in. That house was so raggedy it's a shame. I used to sit up there at night and cry. 'Lord, if you just bless me to get out of here, I do your power that you want me to do.' And he blessed me.

"That roof was comin out the top of the house. I wouldn't put a dog in that house. And it was pitiful, my own black guy I was renting from. He supposed to have been a preacher. Don't get me wrong, I believe in preachers, but some men are preachin are not preachers.

"He tried to get smart. You know, I'm not a violent person, but it's like my momma says, 'Sometimes you push a dog in the corner, he's gon come out and bite.' If I had to live in Hell, I would just go."

The old house had also been a financial problem. "My water bill came out seventy-eight dollars every month because the toilet was leaking," she said. "When you flush the commode, it was just like turnin the hydrant on. Two months' bill came out one hundred fifty-seven dollars. I talked to the water department. They said they was gon take action. Porter Davis, a black man [in the water department], he said he was gon get after [my landlord] about this.[19] They come out and looked and still don't do any-

[19] George Bacon, a sophisticated black man nearing forty who had come home from the North to stay with his family, said that Davis had been active in the civil rights movement at one time. Bacon was with me when I first met Gloria Brown. He and his sister, Corliss Goree, a registered nurse, are the children of schoolteachers. Their mother, Mrs. Barbara Bacon Quinn, is an officer in several statewide civic and teachers' organizations.

Ms. Goree offered to help Gloria Brown to get the weeds cut down in the lot next to her house. One of Ms. Brown's children has severe asthma, which is aggravated by the pollen from the weeds. To recoup some of the money she had spent on water bills when her former landlord failed to repair the leaking toilet, I suggested that she call state Senator Johnnie Walls, who was also the head of the Democratic Party in Mississippi. At dinner the previous night, I had spoken to Walls, an attorney, about the possibility of her suing to recover the excess costs, and he agreed to look into it.

thing. It's like we get money, we change. We forget where we come from."

No matter what we talked about, killing came into the conversation. To explain why she had never married, she said, "These days people just killin people. Too much happen. You can't just put anybody in the house with you.

"I'm scared to talk to anybody," she said, "because people come into your house and kill you. It's scary to trust folks now. You got to be feared now. Don't let nobody tell you the devil's in Hell, the devil's on earth."

And yet another time she said she was afraid that she might kill somebody.

I asked if she would go by the old house with me, just to look at it, and each time I asked she demurred, saying she did not know if she could control herself around the man who had made her and her children suffer for an entire year. Then one day she changed her mind, and I drove her around the corner to the house.

We found her former landlord lying under a car, dressed in mechanic's coveralls. I called to him, and he slid out from under the car, looking hard at me, trying to understand why a white man in a rumpled summer jacket had come to this side of the tracks. He was short and stocky. His hands were black with grease and he had a yellow gold tooth. He said he was a preacher. And he could talk! Words came pouring out of him on any subject: race, poverty, books, civil rights, preaching, God, justice.

He said he was outside the System: "I depend on God," he proclaimed, "not on the System." He spoke in a combative tone, even when he said how deeply he believed in God. "These houses was a gift from God," he said, waving his hand at the row of shotgun houses, where the paint peeled and the roofs sagged and the windows hung loosely in the walls. Gloria Brown had lived in the nearest of the houses. It was still empty. When I asked if I might look inside, he walked over to the front steps with me, opened the door, and left me there.

I have seen worse places in America, several of them in the Delta, but I do not believe I could find many other landlords to stand with me in sight of such housing and speak proudly of it, calling it "a gift from God."

The heat inside was breathtaking. Apparently the house had been closed for more than a month during one of the hottest summers in the history of the Delta. If there had been no holes in the ceiling and had the windows fit firmly in the walls, I think it might have burst.

My footfall on the spongy floor rocked the structure. Windows rattled. Insects were awakened, appearing as if by magic to buzz in corners or drift lazily in the air, circling around the string that hung from the light bulb in the center of the front room. I went immediately to the bathroom to see the toilet that had leaked away Gloria Brown's food money. He had repaired it. No doubt the work had been done as soon as she left and the bill reverted to him.

When I came out, he was waiting for me under a shade tree. "How much is the rent?" I asked.

"It's one fifteen, but if I fixed it up, repaired the ceiling and put sheetrock on the walls, I would raise it to one sixty-five."

"And the plumbing? The toilet?"

"Toilet's fine," he said.

"Thanks for the tour," I said. "I have to go now."

He smiled, holding me there with the gold of his tooth. "So you writing about poverty. You know why people are poor? Chance and greed. Poor people do not take the opportunity when the chance comes, and rich people take more and more because of greed."

"Which are you?" I asked, and he responded with a golden smile. We walked toward the car, which was parked in the shade at the side of the property. He saw the woman sitting there, tight-lipped and as still as a stone. His face did not change, but he moved forward balancing on the balls of his feet. We said good-bye.

As we drove away, we passed a long blue ranch-style house. The paint was fresh and clean on both the siding and the white trim. Flowers grew in gardens all around. A woman in a wide straw hat walked in the garden. Small children played in a plastic pool. It was the landlord's house, Gloria said, evidence that the devil was here on earth.

15. Luck: The Coal Miner Takes a Wife

There was a story known to all the men who worked in the Colquest mine and to their wives. Junior Perry told them. A miner from the time he was twelve, unschooled and yet sometimes moved to preach, the white-haired husband of a deeply ill woman, the old man of the mine, with his handsome senatorial visage, Junior Perry had been there when the roof bolts came loose and eight tons of rock fell in seventy-nine:

"My buddy was killed there. The rock roof fell on us both and it caught me in the back and put me to the ground. And my 'miner'* caught it up off of me and held it. And when it broke the jacks on my 'miner,' then it let it come down against me. And when it come down against me, I went out. Well, when I come to myself, the men done had me out, laying over on the rib.† And I thought that I wasn't hurt, I said, 'Get my buddy out.'

---

* An augur and transport device used in deep mining.

† The vertical support or "wall" of the mine. Perry was actually laid out *against* the rib rather than *on* it.

"So they laid me over on the rib, covered me up and laid me over on the rib, and I could see my buddy layin there. I knowed he was dead for he didn't even make a sound as I heered of. But I did hear another boy got his foot caught in the rockfall. I heered him scream twice. And that's all I heered him scream. So I must of blacked out. There must have been a period there that I was out.

"They got me on out. They come and asked me to move my legs. Took my shoes off. I was trying to move my feet, but I wasn't. And they told me they'd get me on out of there, an I told em to let me stay and to get my buddy out. 'No,' they said, 'you got to get out o here.'"

Junior Perry was fifty-four years old when the next accident happened. The roof fell in on David Hatfield, a young miner who was popular with the men. The accident and the subsequent treatment of Hatfield by the mine owner precipitated the strike. A United Mine Workers organizer signed the men up and promised to back them for as long as necessary. Mine Workers officials came to the Clear Fork to swear their allegiance to the men, promising strike pay and hospitalization until the mine owners gave in. Even Richard Trumka, president of the union, came to Tennessee to promise the men that the union would not back down, "not ever."

After that, the two sides settled in. Summer came. Thanksgiving. Junior Perry's first wife lay ill and slowly dying. His stepchildren had long since gone away. His brother, who had returned from the war in the Pacific with incurable diseases, was dead. Perry said that sometimes he felt afraid of himself.

His wife died. He had raised her children as his own. He had cared for her through years of sickness. And then he buried her.

Cora slept and worked in a set of small rented rooms above the apartment where her parents lived. She took most of her meals with her mother and father, although she thought they ate too much greasy food. Cora was not an uneducated woman. She had been to college, she had worked in Washington, D.C. She knew it was unhealthy for a woman who had diabetes and high blood pressure to eat greasy food. Nevertheless, she took almost all of her meals with them.

For a long time Cora lived on only $20 a week, but her fortunes improved after she was able to demonstrate to the Kentucky Welfare Department that complications from diabetes had made her too ill to work. SSI paid over $100 a week and Medicaid covered her drug bills, which came to more than $500 a month.

Although she had no formal training, Cora thought of herself as an artist. The medium she chose was the discovery of pictures in rocks and stones that she found in the woods. She believed that the pictures were put there by God, and that it was her task to find them out, trace the outlines in black paint, then color in the faces or scenes. Many of the scenes she found in the rocks were of a religious nature, but not all. Sometimes she found black people, often in African dress, and sometimes she found animals, rabbits and deer.

One evening, at the end of April 1994, a neighbor asked Cora if she would like to accompany her to the Rooster Scratch, a grocery store during the day and a bar and pool hall at night. Cora agreed to go. Being a religious woman she was not sure she wanted to go inside, but when they arrived, she said, "Well, I'm thirsty, so I'll go on in."

Cora and her neighbor bought Cokes and sat down. Her neighbor's husband sat across the room. After a while, he crossed the room to where Cora sat, and he said, "There's three widowers in here, and I'd like for you to meet one of em. I've known him for a long time. He's a real good man, and I think you and him would match up real good."

It was a nice thing to do, Cora thought. "He knowed that I stayed by myself all the time and I needed someone."

Her neighbor's husband went into the next room, where the widower and a woman were shooting pool together. He brought the widower out to meet Cora. They greeted each other, then he went back to the poolroom. The widower said he liked Cora, and Cora told her neighbor, "I liked his looks right away."

After he finished playing pool, the widower came back in to the room. He sat on the far side, and looked at Cora. She told her neighbor's husband, "Get over there and get that man to come over here. He's just gon keep sittin over there."

He spoke to Perry, who crossed the room and sat down beside Cora. The widower and the lonely woman talked and laughed and were immediately comfortable with each other. Afterward, Cora said, "I loved his personality. He's a very gentle man, but he's a nervous man. I thought he was very good-lookin. He is an ordained minister, too, but he doesn't preach unless the spirit gets on him, so that's very rare. I am very fascinated by him."

On May 8, 1994, Cora and Junior Perry were married. Although she could no longer collect SSI payments or Medicare, she was not concerned, because he collected strike pay and she was included on William "Junior" Perry's medical insurance through the union. Her blood pressure went down and her sugar fell to 115, which is in the range of normal. Cora moved her things out of the rooms in Kentucky to Junior's double-wide trailer down below the graveyard in Jellico, Tennessee. She said, in her high-pitched, sometimes formal voice, that she was "on cloud nine."

They had been married for a little more than two months when the union broke its promise to the strikers. A letter came to every striker along with the last check for strike pay. It was addressed TO WHOM IT MAY CONCERN:

> Please be advised that members of UMWA Local Union 3009, previously on strike benefits against Colquest Energy, Kopper Glo Fuel and Four Leaf Coal Company, are no longer on these strike benefits and the strike has ended effective July 15, 1994.
> James F. Wright,
> Deputy Director UMWA Region II

No one was hurt more by the sudden withdrawal of the union benefits than Cora and Junior Perry. A year after the union abandoned the men, she and Perry were desperate. "I was on cloud nine," she remembered. "Then all this trouble and both our blood pressures went up. This last week, it was a hundred and ninety over a hundred and somethin. My heart's been hurtin ever since.

"It has put so much stress on us, we've both become sick, and it has put a damper on any kind of marriage situation. We have become very desperate to the point where I'm kind of a suicidal person."

When she reapplied for SSI, she was told that her benefits would resume only if she promised to pay them back when she sold the broken-down building in Kentucky that her father had signed over to her. Cora wrote a long letter in response:

> Number One. I cannot promise to pay back SSI, because I don't know how much that would be or how long I may need SSI.
> Number Two. This is a double wide trailer I'm living in. It will be around $17,000 to finish paying it off to the best of my knowledge. We cannot pay this and live on SSI.[20] The floor in both bathrooms has to be replaced and the hall and under the hot water tank. I'll be glad to have an official to see the problems we have. It needs a new roof also. I have a $5,000 mortgage on a heat pump.
>
> I will have to pay off money which people has loaned us to survive on. So far, as of this writing, it's $2,050 and we have had only basics. After this, I think we will have borrowed out, so I don't know what we will do. Our friends and family cannot keep helping.

---

[20] The monthly payment on the trailer is $420.05. SSI paid $446 a month in 1994.

William, my husband, still owes $3,000 on his truck. I cannot drive his truck because I cannot reach the pedals. I feel I have a right to my old car, which I have had since 1984.

The letter went on, page after page after page, written in a careful hand in a spiral-bound notebook.

Cora and Junior watched television. They ate what food stamps bought. Junior's teeth, which were very white, did not fit precisely. Now and then, he lost control of them when he spoke. He had taken to long silences; she could not stop talking. Their double-wide trailer had a well-made redbrick wall around the base. When they dressed for church on Sunday, they were among the handsomest couples.

16. Hurrying: Pickin Chickens

In the treatment of mental illness prior to the discovery of tranquilizing drugs, many institutions dealt with patients by a method known as "pickin chickens." Patients were given a square of cloth and instructed to take it apart thread by thread; that is, to reverse the work of the loom. According to the theory of pickin chickens, the patients were calmed by this activity, because it occupied them totally, deterring them from the roiling effect of thinking. As long as they did not think, the theoreticians of pickin chickens believed, the patients could be controlled.

Pickin chickens belonged to the folk medicine of mental hospitals. Its proponents were not the highly trained professionals, but the attendants, the people who had to live with mental patients eight hours a day. They knew that leisure was the enemy of order: if the patients had time to reflect upon their lives, they often became uncontrollable. In the view of the attendants, useless activity was preferable to physical restraints or steel bars; it was not an alternative to force, but another kind of force, a mental restraint.

In the world presented to the poor, a similar technique prevails. The highly trained professionals do not often advocate it, although some officials, newly sworn to cope with the poor as if they were more a nuisance, like vermin, than persons, have suggested outfitting them in orange suits and setting them to any tasks to occupy their days.[21]

---

[21] Such a proposal was seriously considered by members of the administration of Mayor Rudolph Giuliani in New York City.

The occupation of the minds of the poor happens almost inadvertently, almost as if it were part of the natural state of poverty. Contrary to the general understanding of poor people, especially those receiving some form of welfare, life in poverty is not a matter of having nothing to do. Merely to survive in poverty in the United States requires constant attention to details that have been eliminated from the lives of other people in America.

Keeping clean, for example, requires great effort for people who may have trouble buying toilet paper or getting enough money to use both a washer and a dryer for their clothes. In Appalachia, it costs about sixty cents a load to wash clothes and the same amount to dry them in bad weather when sheets and towels can't be hung out on a line. According to Kay Rose, a social worker in Tennessee, washing the family's sheets and clothes, especially in winter, can take up a large part of a poor family's income. The alternative is to wash the clothes by hand, if the family has enough clean water. Either way, the wash takes up a considerable part of a person's life, either in time or figuring how to stretch the money to cover the cost of the coin-operated machines.

The working poor, including those who collect some form of welfare benefit, almost always have several jobs.[22] They may collect bottles to turn in for the deposit money or prepare scrap metal for junk dealers. I have seen men spend hours tearing the metal away from pieces of wood, using no tools but their hands, only to sell a day's work for the price of a package of cigarettes.

Women without jobs or even those who have low-paying jobs may work as baby-sitters or do other forms of domestic work. Begging, which has become increasingly common in the United States, is among the most time-consuming occupations. Not only does it take longer and longer to earn the price of a bed or a bottle of wine, as the society loses its sense of compassion, beggars must work in the cold, even in the snow or rain when they are desperate.

To get close to the poverty line, a person supporting a family of four on

---

[22] Since it is virtually impossible to survive on welfare benefits at current levels, it can generally be assumed that poor people who do not live in shelters, wear decent clothing, and do not appear to be undernourished have found means to supplement their benefits. Often the help comes from relatives or from selling off their few possessions, but more often it comes from working off the books. Almost all poor people work.

Much of the work is done without notifying any government agency, including Social Security, the IRS, or any state welfare department. As a percentage of the uncollected taxes or taxes not levied because of the ability of the wealthy to manipulate the tax laws, this "off the books" income of the poor is insignificant. As a percentage of the income of the poor, however, it often means the difference between subsistence and suffering.

minimum-wage jobs would have to work over 58 hours a week ($15,600 divided by 52 x 5.15), probably at two jobs, since employers who pay the minimum wage rarely offer overtime work.[23] But 58.3 hours a week would only gross $15,600. To net $15,600, he or she would probably have to work closer to 65 hours a week. In a major city, like New York, Boston, or San Francisco, even Chicago or Minneapolis, the cost of living is about half again as high as in smaller towns, especially in the South. To eke out enough money to support four people on minimum-wage jobs in those cities, a man or woman would have to work about 100 hours a week, fifty-two weeks a year! There are only 168 hours in a week.

Even so, work does not entirely occupy the lives of the poor, not work as it is commonly known. The poor who seek any kind of public assistance, including medical care in emergency rooms or even from local centers of health maintenance organizations, must spend hours almost every day waiting for someone to tend to their needs. An appointment with a welfare worker in many cities often means traveling to the welfare office, then waiting for three to five hours for the worker to see them. Hospital emergency rooms, where poor people without medical insurance must go for treatment, are not at all like those portrayed in evening soap operas on television. People may have to wait all day or even more than a full day for treatment.

After the work of waiting comes the travail: The poor are beset by a haunting, like anxiety, differing mainly in that it is not grounded in the past but in the present and the future. What the poor suffer comes much closer to fear, for they cannot ever be certain that there will be food on the table or heat in the radiators or that their children will come home safely from school. They may also suffer anxieties for the same historical reasons

---

[23] In many instances, minimum-wage jobs do not provide full-time work. Jobs in stores and restaurants generally begin with 20 hours a week, then increase slowly, if ever, to 40 hours. Employers who work people at the minimum wage avoid overtime by keeping their employees at less than 40 hours. In the event of an emergency (someone failing to show up for work, for example), they can work their part-time people an extra 10 or 20 hours without incurring any additional costs.

In the past, unemployment was used to hold down wages, as Piven and Cloward and others have written, but the new method at the low end of the wage scale is part-time work. For many people, the minimum weekly wage is not the $206 earned for 40 hours at the federal minimum of $5.15. If they are limited to 20 hours, their weekly pay is only $103. Since the purpose of minimum-wage laws is to enable people to earn a living wage, half-time work leaves people in exactly the same economic predicament they would face if they were paid only $2.57 an hour. Even adding the earned income credit to a part-time minimum-wage worker's pay does not bring it up to the federal poverty level. Moreover, part-time workers seldom receive benefits.

as other people. Either one can be debilitating and time-consuming, but the combination, common among the poor, devours days and nights, leaving little time for any other activity. In some places it is called "stress," in others "nerves." Some poor people are completely paralyzed by it, but every poor person suffers from it.

Like the mentally ill who are made to pick chickens, the poor have no time to reflect on their actions; they become incapacitated by the force of busyness, weighed down by the work of worry, immobilized, in restraints. And when for a moment, in reaction to their lives, they break out of the restraints of busyness, they all too often let loose havoc in their world.

17. Guns: Shootout at Little Creek

Guns are not for killing. They have a different use among the poor. Murder happens now and then, but not as often as the tabloids on television or in print would have us believe. A gun is an act of force, not in waiting, not potential, but real, an act by its very existence. Where the gun exists, fear of the gun also exists, whether the gun is visible or not.

It is not so with a knife or a club, weapons of proximity. The gun kills from a distance, often unseen, but among the poor, never unexpected. This force, which suffuses the world of the poor, does not permit negotiation, not ever. The gun cannot be made into a plowshare; it will always be a weapon. The bullet loosed cannot be turned from its path; aimed, it wounds or kills. The rage that controls the gun does not present itself for discussion; from the foundry to the wound, the gun produces the single most apolitical articulated series of actions on earth. No one can reflect upon a gun. It requires reaction, and even for reaction to work in the context of the gun it must be instantaneous, a reflex of murderous intent, equal to or greater than the force that produced it.

Guns lie in wait in every corner of America, but never closer to the surface of life than in Little Creek, an area of narrow ridges and steep hollows in Claiborne County, Tennessee, just south and east of the Cumberland Gap.

Although it is at the western edge of the time zone, evening comes early to Little Creek; the sun falls suddenly behind the steep hills, the mist rises from the bottom of the hollow, and the fireflies come signaling from out of the trees. The road to Little Creek runs along Forge Ridge, down past the old schoolhouse, doubles back on itself for a quarter of a mile, climbs to the top of the ridge, then begins a steep descent down toward Possum Road and the creek.

Willie Ellison lives in an unpainted gray house on a small but nearly flat piece of land just above the beginning of the steep drop into the hollow. A cat lies alongside the rutted driveway from the road up past the house. Dogs wander slowly across the half-naked ground strewn with cans and bottles and pieces of board. A nursing bitch, fat in the belly and narrow in the haunches, pushes her pups aside and waddles, black and brown, down through the ruts to growl at passing cars. Ellison is not at home. Since he divorced his wife and moved her out, Willie spends much of his time down in the hollow at Mamaw Ellison's house, where he grew up.

Willie has a story to tell about guns, and sometimes in the evening, when he goes down to Mamaw's place, and his daughter, Peggy, brings her boyfriend down from Middlesboro, and Willie's old friend, David, comes with them, he tells about the night it happened. Everyone knows the story by now; a stranger is an excuse to tell it again. They hoot and shriek at the proper places, except for little Beatrice, who wanders about the room, a gargoyle less than three feet tall, grunting out inhuman sounds and grinning Hell's own smile.

Everyone in that part of the county and half the population of Middlesboro on the other side of the Gap, in Kentucky, knows about Little Creek. Most people, unless they are newcomers, have heard of the Ellisons or read about them. Little Creek is the setting for feuds and violence of all sorts, the place where people get shot or burned out. In Little Creek, people hurl insults or shoot a neighbor's dog as they drive by each other's houses on gravel roads so steep a car loses traction even with the brakes on and the transmission in the lowest gear.

Mamaw Ellison's dog was killed by someone driving by after the fire in the rented house down by the creek, and she has been thinking about it ever since. She keeps a rifle in her car, which is parked outside her house, halfway down the steep driveway that leads to the steep road, and when the opportunity comes, she intends to use it. "I'll shoot em," she says simply, without laughter or rage, an old woman in a faded shift, pulled over her head and worn without thought, like the gowns she wore in the hospital where they opened up her chest and repaired her heart. "I'll shoot em," she says, and no one laughs or pretends to humor her. Everyone is afraid of Mamaw, even her great-granddaughter, Beatrice, the child formed with a gargoyle's face.

THE ELLISONS HAVE LIVED IN LITTLE CREEK for generations. Mamaw Ellison remembers her grandfather, but she never knew her father. Whoever it was that fathered her left Mamaw Ellison with the same problems of blocked arteries and congeries of tiny strokes that destroyed the rest of the family. The names and generations get confused in Mamaw's head now, but she knows that she decided as a girl not to make her mother's mistake. She married Ferdie Ellison at sixteen and stayed with him through construction work in Indiana, long years of living off the few dollars they could make by raising their full government allotment of four-tenths of an acre of tobacco, then through emphysema, cancer, and the heart problems that finally killed him.

Ferdie Ellison was a good husband, but a harsh father. He thought the best way to raise children was to beat them with a hitch lead. Once, when he was whipping the younger ones with the hitch lead, Willie said, "Daddy, what you whippin them fer? They didn't do nothin."

"Keep yer mouth shut!" Ferdie shouted, and turned the hitch lead on Willie.

Other than the beatings, life in the mountains was almost idyllic. The boys hunted and helped work the tenths of tobacco, the girls prepared for early marriage and childbearing. School did not attract any of the Ellisons; six or seven years was all any of them could endure. Willie was a serious young man who got drunk once when he was eighteen years old. "Lord, let me live, an I won't drink no more," he prayed, and never took another drink.

He is a long and narrow man, deeply tanned, who peers at the world through black and shining ascetic eyes. His cheekbones, carried to this place from the Scottish Lowlands and Cherokee hunting grounds, stand out like ledges below the deep sockets of his eyes. He takes his place in the failing light, in the precise clutter of the house, amid the gewgaws of a thousand useless trades, the religious paintings and patriotic slogans that hang among the family photographs, the great white, trumpet-shaped piece of pottery that weighs down one side of the room. Were it not for a missing front tooth, he might be the hero of an old cowboy movie, one of those skinny-armed mountain men of confused moral ferocity, the kind of sweet-souled gunfighter who settled the West.

Like everyone in the house, Willie is a formal person. He wears his hair long and neatly combed. When he speaks, his hair sometimes falls over his face, and he combs it back with his fingers. He enters Mamaw's house through a screen door that has no screen in it, carefully opening and closing the empty frame. He stands posed against the light. He looks down at the gargoyle child without beneficence or anger. "I got custody of her," he says, "cause my daughter didn't want her, cause she's got brain damage. I went down there to four different doctors. They run the test on her, say she's got brain damage.

"She's four. She can't talk. She just grunts. Doctor said he didn't know she'd ever talk. He said one side your brain that made you talk; that side was messed up, too. My daughter, she smoked pot and everything before she was born; they say that's what messed her brain up.

"My daughter, right after she was born, she wanted to put her in a dumpster. I told her, 'No, you won't put her in no dumpster.' I told her, I said, 'I'll put you in jail if you put her in a dumpster.' And she got up about a week later after that and she said, 'Daddy, you know, I figgered out last night how to get rid of the baby.' And I said, 'How's that?' And she said, 'I'll just put a pillow o'er her face while you and Mommy's asleep.'

"And I said, 'No, you won't. I'll just take the baby to sleep with me now. Now, that baby, nothin's gon be done to that little thing." And he meant it. He hired a lawyer, took his daughter to court, and won custody of the baby, which he has since adopted.

Perhaps there is some connection between the baby and his own problem in Willie's mind. "I take fits," he said, "I been takin them ten years. I had a operation done on my head, on my ear. Had a cancer by my eardrum, an I took to fits ever since they took that out."

He takes large doses of phenobarbital and drinks coffee to stay awake. No beer or whiskey ever comes into Mamaw's house; she does not permit it. As the extended family begins to gather in the late evening, those who want to drink have to stay outside the house. She does not even permit them to sit on the porch, in one of the chairs with the yellow plastic seats that are grouped around her wooden rocker. As night comes, the yellow plastic shines; everything around the three patches of brilliant color is gray or the deep green of the woods around the house and down the steepness on every side.

Willie's old friend, David, arrives first, crazy-eyed, talking at incomprehensible speed. He is so thin and his arms and legs are so long and loose that he gives the impression of an insect gone mad, dying in a frenzied buzz. He bears an uncanny resemblance to the child Beatrice—the pointed teeth, the angry eyes. David and Willie do a dance of greeting. Willie picks up the huge trumpet-shaped piece of crockery, motioning with it toward David's head. "It won't hurt him," Willie says. "It'll just make him mad."

"Won't make me mad, because I'll be tryin to put my head back together." He laughs. "I been hit with bigger things. I had a cop do it. Broke my neck."

The dance goes on for a while. David speaks of his accidents. "I'm a one hundred percent disability. I fell fifty feet off a high rock and broke my back. My spine was all curled up."

Willie's daughter Peggy enters. Her boyfriend, David's nephew, has remained outside in the truck drinking beer. Peggy does not greet anyone. She finds a place on one of the chairs. Peggy has bushy red hair, like the gargoyle child. Her fat legs bloom from under a short black dress, shaped like a monochromatic cheerleader's outfit. Her second child, a boy of two, has been placed in an institution for the profoundly retarded. The man she lives with supports them with his disability payments. After several attempts at suicide, the state has declared him alcoholic/suicidal. He quit school in Middlesboro, he says, "because teachers picked on me. Niggers picked on me, pushed me into lockers."

He lies in bed late at night, with Peggy beside him, sometimes sleeping, sometimes listening with him to the police radio that he keeps beside the bed. "I'm livin in Hell," he said. "Hell can't be no worse. I'm willin to go at any time at all. I'm ready to die. I ain't kiddin. I tried to kill myself, two, three times. I just overdose.

"Ain't nothin here, bunch o drunks and drug addicts. In five years I'll probably be in jail. I know. My house got broke in the other day. Sister's house was broke in last week. Broke in, tried to get my police scanner. I catch him in my house, he won't walk back out alive. I'd kill him. I ever catch a man in my house, I'll kill him. I keep a gun. Loaded."

Peggy shrugs. She does not look at Beatrice, who moves constantly through the room, grunting and squealing. "Won't get nothin off me," she says, "cuz I ain't got nothin. I got nothin in my house."

Once the house is full, attention turns to Willie. He talks for a little while about the feud. His ex-wife was living in a rented house down near the creek. Willie and his son went down to move her out, but she and his son got into a fight. To show her displeasure she burned the house down. That angered Willie's neighbors, who owned the house but had no insurance. Since then, Mamaw's dogs have been shot, and whenever the neighbors drive by, they shout curses and make obscene gestures. Then Mamaw runs out to the car where she keeps the rifle, but by the time she gets the weapon the neighbors have driven up or down the mountain out of sight.

Mamaw Ellison says she intends to shoot them, but everyone in the room knows the task will fall to Willie. As if to show his ability to handle the situation, as well as to entertain the family, he tells the story, with Peggy's help. It all began when a fellow who lived down closer to the creek wanted to date Willie's youngest daughter. Willie refused to allow it, and the boy swore he would get his revenge.

Peggy broke in, "He said to me, 'Did you get a last look at your daddy?' I said, 'Why?' He said, 'I'm gon kill that sumbitch.' Cuz of my lil sister. He thought he could date her, lil kid."

"I have a pistol and a shotgun," Willie said. "One guy came in here one night." Willie was in the back room, down a narrow hallway from the front room.

"Next thing I know, he was comin through the door," Willie said. "He shot at me that night. He missed me.

"He shot three or four times, and missed me. I shot at him with the twelve-gauge and missed him. He was down the hallway and I was in the kitchen. He hit the floor. He come runnin down the hall with a .22 pistol and put it right up to my boy's head. And he said, 'You put your shotgun down, buddy, or your boy's head gon be blowed off.'

"I just poured a box of shells out on the table, broke the gun down, and took the shells out, put the shells back in, walked around the table, and stuck it right there under his chin. I said, 'Now, your brains are gon be up here on the ceiling if you don't put your pistol down.' He took his pistol away from my boy's head and put it on the table."

There was laughter and the strange screeching of the child. Mamaw laughed until she had to hold her hand to her chest where the incision was still healing. Even the alcoholic/suicidal boy laughed. After a while, the family settled into silence. The story had been told; they had no more to say. Outside the house, beyond the empty screen door frame, fireflies illuminated portions of the night. Somewhere down below, near the burned-out house, where the forest was fed by the creek, a chainsaw tore into the silence.

18. Isolation: Delta Loneliness

In a community, information has increasing value as it is broadcast to the members of the group. As a simple example, imagine the tribe of Lakotas who hunt buffalo using the method of the surround. If they attempt to make the surround with only a few members of the tribe, they may not have sufficient forces to pen in, panic, and then kill the beasts. The best way to make the surround is to notify all the members of the tribe, getting the greatest possible number to participate, increasing the absolute wealth of the tribe.

The distribution of information in a Neolithic society, based on ritual, serves the members of the society best when the distribution is perfect; that is, when everyone knows. If the same group of Lakotas followed the rules of modern societies, the example would be very different: A Lakota comes upon a herd of buffalo. Instead of spreading the information to the tribe so they can make the surround, he follows the herd until a buffalo calf strays, kills the calf, and brings the meat and skin home without telling anyone else about the location of the herd. By keeping his information proprietary, he wins the game, because he has fresh meat and the others don't, making him relatively rich.

Whether the ritual or the game is ultimately more efficient is not at issue here; the point is that modern society values information in two ways, either by making it proprietary (You know the price of gold in Hong Kong before I do and can make a profit by trading on that information) or by disseminating it (You tell everyone that your new soap removes wrinkles from women's skin so that they will all buy it). The political life, which takes place in dialogue in the public world, values the dissemination of information over the proprietary value of it; the life of the poor takes place in a private world of persons isolated from information and from each other, of secrets and mistrust.

The woman in the Young Mothers Program who said she could not tell the truth about her man to the welfare worker is isolated from the public world of her government, an outlaw by virtue of living with the father of her children. Can she afford to trust anyone to know her? Will someone tell the welfare department? Similarly, the person with a sick child, a second job, a progressive disease, may not want to tell an employer for fear of losing his job. In a poor neighborhood it is dangerous to say what treasures reside in one's house, even if such treasures are no more than a video cassette recorder or a camera.

In the surround of force, isolation becomes a defense and the defense becomes another force. Anne M. Harvin, the executive director of Women Service Network, Inc., in Riviera Beach, Florida, describes isolation as a primary attribute of poverty. She says that, in her experience, poor people have no friends, are often separated from their families, and do not participate in any activities outside church. When they do go to church, she says, it is not in the way that she remembers as a young woman growing up in a large family in central Florida.

In 1995 the Women Service Network had fifty-two people, including a few men, hoping to get a high school equivalency certificate through a GED program in their small facility housed in a nest of abandoned buildings. Both Anne Harvin and the woman who taught the GED course wanted the students to become friends to get over the sense of isolation they suffered. One reason for this attempt to bond the students to each other was to solve the problem of theft within the school. The students not only stole from each other, they had taken the teacher's purse as well.

Isolation need not involve such direct acts of force as theft. It can occur in what appears to be perfect calm inside a household, within a family. Television, especially national network television, which has been defended as a medium that creates a community of information, is a primary force of isolation at the family and community level.

This isolating character of television hardly needs proof, but the depths of the isolation it causes can be surprising. One afternoon in the Geneva Towers Recreation Center, part of a large project in the Visitation Valley section of San Francisco, Vernon Long, who runs the center, gathered a group of children in the meeting room to talk about such things as family and community. Most of the children were between ten and thirteen years old and all were residents of the project. They do a lot of giggling at that age, which makes any conversation both funny and tedious. But I think they do not dissemble as much as older children, even when the group is large.

When asked if they regularly ate dinner with their families, not one child raised his or her hand. When the category was broadened to ask if they ever ate dinner with their families, only one girl raised her hand. Then where did they eat? They all described the same routine. Each child got his food in the kitchen and carried it to a bedroom or living room to sit in front of the television set and eat in silence. If there was more than one child watching the same television set, the only conversation was about the choice of channels, and even that was rare, for such disputes had generally been settled long ago.

A similar sense of isolation existed among the adult students at the Mississippi Delta Farmworker's Council GED Program. We met, in part, to talk about services that were available to people in the area: medical care, economic assistance, the federal Legal Services program, and so on. But the conversation quickly turned to members of the class helping each other.

One woman, perhaps the best-dressed person in the class, explained how she had gotten a divorce through the Legal Services program. When I asked if she had told other people about the program, she shook her head. "I'll pass the word on," she promised, "but a lot o people that know somethin don't pass the word on. They don't want to give no directions to nothin."

This proprietary view of information extended to virtually every person in the group. It even included one man who bragged that he always won when he went down to the gambling boat anchored in the river: He refused to share his secret, even though he and the others in the room were not playing against each other, only against the house.

If anyone in the room, including the man who was moderating the dialogue, held any quaint notions about the friendliness of the South compared to the North, one woman dispelled them: "It's hard to find a friend. Neighbors is hard to find. A neighbor is like the older people, like my granny. You know a neighbor come by and help you, like my father. It's gettin hard in Mississippi to find a neighbor. It's hard to find a friend in Mississippi. I been living here thirty-some years and I would still rather go back to the North. This is the worst place to live and try to be friends with people down here."

The woman sitting next to her concurred: "All of us here look like we neighbors, but we not neighbors. Half of em here don't like each other." And yet one more woman agreed: "Somebody may look better than another person here. Somebody may wear shoes that another person can't afford, and they get jealous, somethin simple to get jealous of."

As the conversation engaged the group, often with everyone or at least ten or twenty people talking at the same time, the isolation of people from each other within the same room became apparent. The men, who were thin and bedraggled and without the energy of the women, sat apart from each other, most of them with their backs to the wall. The sense of having lost dominated the room. The posture of the women, the secondhand T-shirts, heavy arms, puzzled faces, all spoke of the insurmountable loss, the damning cruelty of the game. The men appeared to belong to another age, prison or the plantation, the forced labor that bends the spine.

Everyone in the room shared in creating this ambiance of defeat, but for two women: the one who had learned how to get a divorce through Legal Services and one other, a woman with pretty posture and neatly done hair (perhaps a wig) who sat against the wall dressed in a green shirt, the most vibrant, saturated color in the room. She disagreed. "I feel you should put love first," she said. "I love everybody in here. If they don't love me, I love em anyway. I shouldn't be hating anybody. I love em all. If they don't love me, that still hurts, but I love em anyway."

Next to her sat the worst-dressed, least attractive woman in the room. Neither fat nor ugly nor unclean, yet defeated, she had chosen to damn herself in the relative way by sitting next to the woman in green. "I come to class," she said in response to the lecture on loving. "I know some of the peoples in here, but when I leave out that door, I don't have any friends in here. I'm on my own. We're not together, and that's just a fact." Then she lost control; she fell to sobbing, hunched over in her chair, more like a puddle than a person.

I said to the woman in green: "Will you be friends after class today?"

"I don't know her," the woman in green said. "She don't know me."

"But you said you love her."

"God said to love everybody."

The room grew quiet. For the first time no one talked over anyone else. The students looked sheepish, not guilty but worn down, older than the memory of plantation life, timid. They beheld the difference between the love of God and the loneliness of man.

19. Hunger: In Brooklyn Also

One morning in Mississippi I met a woman named Sophronia who gave food away. We do the same in New York City, I said, and told her about the Food & Hunger Hotline, which is a silly name, but not of my invention even though I was for a time a member of the board of directors. We talked about her organization, which was very small compared to things in New York City and also had a somewhat silly name, FEED, which was an acronym at the head of a series of convolutions. We talked about her own name for a while. I said it sounded as if it might have come from the Greek word for temperance, which was very highly valued among the ancients. We talked a little about sophrosyne, which interested her very much. Then she said it would be a good idea if Frank Clarke and I met the Weedens.

The street on which the Weedens lived was not remarkable in any way: a gentle street, if that can be said of streets, a bit run-down, the houses a bit too close together, but not remarkable; tired perhaps, but American, a street of brick and stone and wooden houses and too many cars. The cars were all middle-aged and clean, but not shiny. There was something businesslike about the street, as if the people who lived there lacked the time for ostentation or decay. Robert Weeden was born on that block, in the house next door.

The house the Weedens rented was neat, but on close inspection more worn than the others. Inside, it was more worn still. The couches were sprung, the large living room was mainly empty. A child sat listlessly on a couch. Robert Weeden had just awakened, although it was the middle of the morning.

He had long sideburns and a neat little mustache, like a nineteenth-century riverboat gambler. His wife, Barbara, was twice his size, and loud, all brass, like a marching band. Robert spoke softly, almost inaudibly; his head hung down. He said that a few days before, they had run out of food. That was all. He said it flatly, without apology or anger, but he did not look up.

Completely out?

There had been nothing left.

His wife nodded.

We talked for a long time. At first, Frank and I looked at each other and said, without speaking, that we thought something might be wrong in the Weeden house. Drugs, something; it made no sense for them to be hungry, not in that house on that street.

He worked on the gambling boat on the river; she worked twenty hours a week, all the time she could get, at Wendy's. To avoid the cost of child care, she worked days and he worked nights. When they were home, they cared for the children.

They did not hesitate to recount the economics of their lives. They did it gladly, as if the explanation could alleviate the shame. He earned $5.50 an hour and she earned $4.25. Six people lived in the house and he paid child support to his ex-wife in Kansas City. Barbara had medical bills; the children needed uniforms for school. According to federal guidelines, they did not earn quite enough money to support a family of four at the minimum subsistence level. There were six in their family.

He said several times about the food, "We just ran out." He recounted all the things they did not have on the day they ran out: cereal, milk, bread, rice, lard, beans.

Was it the first time they had run out of food?

He shook his head.

She had gotten food stamps until they were married. He said he would not have married her if he had known the problems it would cause with food stamps and such, but he loved the children and he thought they needed a father. Although he was not able to care for them as well as he wished, he believed his love for them meant something. The burden of caring for the children and for his wife, who had recently undergone major surgery, seemed to satisfy him, as if burdens made a man. But it was clear that he had not expected hunger.

He said he was tired, but not in a complaining way. Only when he spoke of his love for the children did he abandon the low monotone that characterized his speech, as if to say that all but love was fact, flat and fated, like a road in the dark.

Barbara Weeden had all the anger in the house. She knew the ironies, and she retailed them in brass. She said she could not bring food home from Wendy's. The rule was that employees had to buy whatever they ate, although they got a 50 percent discount if they ate in the restaurant while wearing a Wendy's uniform. She could not take out food unless she paid full price, and she could not buy food for her husband or children at discount.

"They throw away leftover food," she said. "With the patties that are left they make chili. With the chicken, I makes the chicken salad. Chicken that be cooked and left over, I go to the freezer and get it and I boil it about thirty minutes, then I take the skin off of it and make chicken salad."

Until the previous day in the late afternoon, they had been without food in the house.

How many days?

A few, he said. We ran out, completely out.

And before that?

There wasn't much.

For how long?

Ain't never very much.

Will it get better soon?

He looked at me, and then at Frank, and back to me again. It was the first time he had raised his eyes. He was a gentle man, according to his eyes; he did not live at the extremes, but he had too far to go.

IN THE LATE MORNING RABBI KIVELEVITZ had begun his rounds as outreach worker. People came up out of basement rooms to greet him. He found others preparing lunch in a soup kitchen. An amateur butcher, a Russian who had little Yiddish and less English, explained the world in words the great cryptographer Turing himself could not decipher. As he spoke, the amateur butcher held up his bloody hands, showing us the black-rimmed fingernails, swollen joints, palms crumpled into cups.

We did not know exactly what he meant to say, but it was clear that he hoped for someone to intercede on his behalf with God. And if not God, then economics, the demiurge that had made this suffering of the butcher's life. Rabbi Kivelevitz wrote the name of a Russian-speaking outreach worker on a card and gave it to the butcher, who looked at the card, stuck it into his pocket, and went back to butchering. He did not have to speak his response; it was written on his face: A Russian—what good was a Russian? The Russians lost on both fronts; they did not know God or economics!

From there we went to Brighton Beach to walk the Esplanade, where the Russian immigrants sat with their faces turned up to bask in the wan winter sun, except for their noses, which were hidden under white plastic shields. While others walked on the boardwalk, we went down the steps to the sand, where we continued on under the boardwalk, seeking the homeless who lay huddled in makeshift rooms of cardboard or old blankets.

In the middle of the afternoon we stopped for lunch in the rabbi's favorite cafeteria on Brighton Beach Avenue. We had just begun our meal when a woman came to stand beside our table. She was very short. By leaning forward slightly, she put her head at a level with ours. Her face was round and fat, yet it appeared to be slightly shrunken, as if it had been recently deflated by age or illness. She had a surreptitious air.

The rabbi introduced us. She gave me her hand, which was small and fat. She spoke in bursts, tiny paragraphs punctuated by wheezing, then longer pauses in which her watery eyes closed momentarily as if to consider something—I did not know what. Perhaps these were moments of anger or regret. This is her side of the conversation:

Rose.
Who thought? Happens.
What should I do?
Thank God for rent control.
In my building . . . it's still a nice building.

Look here! A goiter.
Something new.

What should I do? I don't have what to eat.
On Shabbos a piece fish; that's all I ask.
Now, nothing.
Meat I can't eat. Chicken, a little.
I'm diabetic, too.

Rose. My last name, what difference?
What are you? Writing a book?

Children, yeah.
In Brooklyn also.
Rabbi, you have something for me?
Again the cereal!
So what else is new?
All right.
You'll come by later, the neighbors shouldn't see.

At the appointed hour, we went by the building where Rose lived. Quickly, like thieves, we transferred bags of food from the trunk of the rabbi's car to the trunk of another car, which I presume belonged to Rose. She thanked the rabbi, he said a blessing for her, and we sped away.

ARISTOTLE'S COMMENT ON DURATION, "One swallow doth not a summer make," describes the nature of hunger: One day without any food at all constitutes a fast, but not force. Hunger gnaws; it does not strike. And it is never hunger unless it is non-negotiable. No one chooses hunger, not the obese or even the neurotically fashionable. Hunger is not an option; it mimics the pattern of disease, causing weakness and promising death.

It also mimics the shame of certain diseases, and like AIDS or cancer or some deadly airborne disease, the shame of it is both social and juridical. The social shame takes place in the presence of neighbors, whose gossip overcomes their neighborliness. For Rose, it is the problem of her children, who also live in Brooklyn; why have they failed to help her? For Robert Weeden, it is the people with whom he grew up on that Mississippi street.

Juridical shame comes in the form of isolation for the sick; for the poor, juridical shame is made of questions, prying, judging, by social workers or any other person who offers food, even a rabbi or a writer.

Although few people die of starvation in America, the shame of being hungry, of having to confess to the world a parent's inability to feed a child or an old person's failure to have established a loving and caring family, exerts a terrible force. Unlike most other forces, it indicates a failed life at the most elemental level. In a society structured like a game, where only relative poverty exists, hunger is the most devastating emblem of losing. And even if the person survives—and virtually all do—a scar will remain, and it will defy the laws of genetics, for the shame of hunger is one acquired trait that is invariably passed on to the next generation.

20. Feudalism: Telling the Man

Feudalism may be the wrong word to assign to the working conditions of many poor people in the United States. There are no lords or barons here. Enfeoffment, that awkward name for investing the land in fiefs, really never existed here, even where sharecropping was common; but the relation of the workers to the owners has a feudal aspect about it, especially in the agricultural areas and some parts of the inner cities. The American form of feudalism has to do mainly with the enforcement of the relationship and the ability of the owners to convert feudal practices to industrial and information-processing tasks, as well as to agriculture.

The aspect of feudalism still applicable at the end of the twentieth century grows out of what may be described as the privacy of the relation between the serf and his master. As medieval monarchs were separated from the private relations between serfs and masters, so the landowners or businessmen now engage in private relations with their employees, unregulated and unobserved by government or union. These contemporary feudal lords may do what they will with their employees, who are beholden to them through an often illegal arrangement that includes enforcement procedures far beyond the normal instruments of management: reprimand, demotion, dismissal.

In the situations most like the feudal arrangements of the Middle Ages, the owner/employer not only controls a person's work for wages, he controls his living conditions as well. Sharecropping in Appalachia and the rural South, as well as some kinds of agricultural work, give the owner this kind of sway over the worker. The most extreme conditions involve fruit pickers and other agricultural laborers in South Carolina who live in barracks and pay their employers most or all of their wages for housing, food, sometimes drugs, and a real or trumped-up debt that never goes down. Some of these people, according to news stories and reports by Legal Services Corporation lawyers, live in a situation somewhere between feudalism and slavery.[24] As I understand it, feudalism is the less accurate term.

Appalachian feudalism usually involves working shares in tobacco, a crop requiring so much labor that farmers call it a thirteen-month-a-year job. In this system, an entire family—parents and children—may have to work a whole year to earn a share worth $5,000 or $6,000 less the cost of a ramshackle house and utilities. Since the family works as a contractor rather than an employee, the arrangement need not include benefits or even Social Security payments. Several such arrangements will be described in detail in Chapter XI.

To maintain the feudal relation with undocumented workers in California, Texas, New York, and all through the South, the owner/employer utilizes the threat of deportation to control the laborers in fields and factories. He may or may not provide housing as well as materials for work. With the threat of the Immigration and Naturalization Service available to control employees, the threat to withdraw shelter becomes unnecessary. Needless to say, undocumented workers have a very private relation with their employers, both parties agreeing to avoid the public world in which law and legitimate power affect their relationship. Owners who are unsatisfied with the quantity or the quality of the work turned out by their undocumented employees often use another method left over from the Dark Ages: They punch them or kick them or beat them with sticks.[25]

In the Mississippi Delta the plantation system still operates, even though much of the work has been mechanized. The few people who live in plantation housing now fear "the Man" in the same way that they feared the Man a hundred years ago. Yet, hardly anyone who lives and works on a plantation dares to complain, even to a friend or neighbor, about working or living conditions. As the workers on the Lyndale Plantation southwest of Rolling Fork in Sharkey-Issaquena County say, "We don't stick together. Someone will always tell the Man."

The mercurial charisma that Max Weber considered a part of the dominating character of feudalism still exists in America, where the struggle over rents often occurs in a bizarre fashion. A group of workers who tried to organize a union at a sawmill in the Delta were taught a quick lesson in charisma by the Man, who tore down his own mill rather than let the union in.

Near Tchula, Mississippi, "Knot" Young belonged to a group of black men who were trying to build a cottonseed oil mill. White farmers in the area had formed a co-operative, and built a mill, which they refused to

---

[24] Florida Rural Legal Services workers in Belle Glade and West Palm Beach offices made these allegations in 1995. In 1997, three men were arrested for enslaving workers in South Carolina, according to the *New York Times*, May 8, 1997.

[25] I quoted a description of this in *Latinos: A Biography of the People.*

make available at any price to the blacks who owned small cotton farms. The whites had a simple plan: By refusing to mill the seed, they hoped to force the blacks to sell their farms. The whites could then buy the farms and hire the blacks to work them for shares, reproducing the old private relationship.

The privacy necessary to feudalism did not fit well with the huge factories of the Industrial Age, where men and women worked in large groups and shared experiences, making them more likely to organize to negotiate for a greater share of the value of their labor. With collective bargaining in the workplace, the last vestiges of feudal privacy all but disappeared.

Industrial work retained its public, political character in the United States through a combination of unionization and government regulation until the advent of home-labor systems, beginning with garment workers, who could stay at home and do piecework sewing, basting, and so on. The home worker, often an undocumented person, had no public work life. The raw goods were carried to his or her house and the completed work was picked up and delivered to the next worker or to a warehouse. Home labor could not easily be organized by unions or overseen by government regulators. It was impossible to enforce health and safety codes or laws banning child labor, and so on. Through home labor, the owner/employers had discovered a way to reproduce feudal conditions in Industrial Age work.

Information Age labor was far more easily adaptable, because computer entry work lent itself to the privacy of distributed processing. The assigned work could be delivered by an express company in a large envelope, and the completed work could be sent back by modem, with the raw materials following later. Every vestige of the compulsory community of the Industrial Age was wiped out by distributed computer entry work in the Information Age. For all practical purposes, the political life of work disappeared for the information laborer at the home terminal.

Only the poor enter willingly into the private relations of "contemporary feudalism." The owner/employer's offer attracts only desperate people, because the force inherent in the relationship cannot be disguised. Once begun, however, the relation maintains the poverty of whoever enters into it, because it excludes the public life of work, leaving the person isolated inside the surround, like the serf encompassed by the forces of his lord, with no connection possible either to king or countrymen.

21. Law: A Suckling Criminal

Her voice is low and soft, made into singing by the sounds her mother brought from Alabama. She sings a woman's song, but heartbreaking, like the blues.

"You think: So far, they haven't come. Then you have to think maybe they are gonna come, so I have to go both ways. I would love to say, No, they're not gonna come to my house. My girlfriend tells me, 'Don't worry about it; the Lord gon take care of you. Watch! The paperwork'll get lost, and you don't even have to worry about it.' And I believe in that. I tried to make it all the other kind of ways, and I've gone back to the Lord. And it's helped. I don't care what nobody says, God is good."

She underscores her words with the expression of her eyes, like an orchestra playing the music for a film.

Miss Russell is a big woman, with legs as heavy as stone statuary, and she does not walk easily; the grace of her is all in repose. Nor does she smile with ease; her face crumples into a smile, becomes a basket when she laughs.

So there are several women here: the laughing woman, a basket of discomfort; the seated woman, a statue; the walking woman, without grace; the woman near weeping, an elegiac verse, as regretful as the blues.

When I met her she was a fugitive, convicted of a felony and sentenced in the California courts. She should have been in the women's prison at Santa Rita. We spoke by telephone and arranged to meet in Oakland, in the offices of the Women's Economic Agenda Project (WEAP).

"What now?" she said. "I don't want to go to Santa Rita. I don't want to go to nobody's jail, no county, Santa Rita State Pen; I don't want to go to none o that mess."

It was the winter of 1994, and the state of California had announced a "crackdown" on welfare fraud. There was a plan to put the District Attorney's Office in charge of welfare in the city of Oakland, a plan many poor women understood as the first explicit act in the criminalization of welfare.

Leticia Russell listened to the anger around her, but it was not her concern. She had left theory behind. Jaywalking, a traffic ticket, any random contact with the police, would trigger the information about her in the computer system and send her to prison. She had committed the poor woman's crime. While collecting welfare, she had worked.

"As of February of ninety-three, I was called in by the investigator of welfare fraud," she said. "I was working temporary, not a full-time job, maybe two weeks out of a month, two days out of a month, nothing so fantastic where I was making a lotta lotta money. I was making anywhere from five to seven dollars an hour. It would vary, because I would do receptionist work, data entry, clerical. My grant then was four fifty, plus they were still taking out from the last time, from ten years ago, so I wasn't getting a full grant anyway.

"Rent was five fifty, PG&E ran between fifty and sixty, telephone bill about twenty dollars a month . . . was runnin a little bit more, because my son was in the service, in Fort Hood. Food, transportation, school clothes, my clothes, stockings, things for work, whatever. A good nine hundred a month. It was just the two of us then, just me and Curtis—he's eight now. I was still strugglin then, not making a lot of money, so if I didn't work I wasn't able to pay all the rent. That's how I got farther and farther behind. And by the time I was evicted in November of ninrty-one, I owed Mr. Wong two thousand dollars.

"Medical was the main thing, havin it for Curtis. Other than that, the check went on rent. Food stamps helped out for maybe two weeks and I still had to come up with the rest of the food and money to get around and get back and forth.

"During that time I became pregnant, and I didn't have any Medical, so I thought I better go ahead and turn myself in, because I was pregnant with diabetes.

"When I went to court, the Public Defender said to me, 'You're skating on thin ice now. The probation officer said you didn't show any remorse.'

"When I was tellin the probation officer, was I supposed to cry because this has happened to me? If I thought about all the things I'm going through, I would cry twenty-four hours a day, seven days a week. This welfare thing. I have no job, no money. I have an abusive mate, mentally and physically now, two kids. I would cry. Maybe I didn't show any remorse. Well, I was, what?, nine months pregnant. I was tired, I was irritable, I couldn't sit up, and then she told the Public Defender that I didn't show any remorse about this happening to me. How was I supposed to act? Like jump for joy or cry?

"And I said, 'I didn't show any remorse? Well, I didn't kill anybody. I didn't harm anybody. I didn't do any kind of bodily harm to anybody. Was I supposed to be sorry because I was trying to survive? Was I supposed to break down and cry because I was trying to put food on my table for myself and my son?' I didn't understand that, and I still don't understand that.

"Fred Schneider, the Public Defender, told me to plead guilty. The next court date was December 15, and that's when I was told, 'I got it down from six months to sixty days.' But it was still a felony, still pay the money, and five years probation.

"So I could of got six months, and I was pregnant, so when the Public Defender went before the judge, he said, Your Honor, Ms. Russell is pregnant, diabetes, and we want to set the court date after she have the baby. So I had my son January 22, went to court February 7, and that was the sentencing. [She was to begin serving her prison sentence when the child was six weeks old.]

"My boy's a month and two weeks," she said, referring to the day on which she made the decision not to turn herself in, "and I have a eight-year-old. I don't want to go. I don't want to go to jail. You can't take the baby to jail. That's why I didn't turn myself in. I don't want to go to jail. I don't see what the purpose, I don't see what the use.

"What if I'm not there? Then who's gonna hear him cryin at two or three o'clock in the mornin? The judge is not gonna hear my baby cryin. The policeman that comes to get me is not gonna hear my baby cryin. Who's gon take care of him?"

She sat heavily, leaning, a big-eyed brown-skinned woman, with shaved eyebrows and skinned-back straightened hair. She had been to college, held good jobs, owned a house, lost it all. "Bad choices," she said. "Some choices were good, some were bad, but you can't think of it as a loss, you have to chalk it up to experience, and you have to move on. A lot of choices I made weren't good choices. A lot of things I did, I didn't do right. I was raised to do the right thing, but sometimes when you're grown and gone, you forget about all the things you were taught.

"I think about a lot of things now that I'm forty. Forty years of wandering around. Who's that wandered around? I just read that last night in the Bible. Moses! The Hebrews! Wandered for forty years, and that's just how I feel. I wandered around for forty years, and now that all these things are right here and I have to face em, it's kind of devastating. I'm not where I should be, I know. This is where I'm at right now: Not wanting to go to jail. I shouldn't be in this predicament I'm in, and I wish that I hadn't been. I wish that I wasn't."

22. Ethnic Antagonisms: A Low Rider's Wife Assumes the Position

We set the rendezvous for an abandoned gas station out on Alameda Avenue on the east side of El Paso in the lower valley. I arrived early, and went to a fast-food place across the street to watch the assembling of the members. In the light of the high desert sunset, the white stucco arches of the gas station looked ancient, rouged, the corpse made up for a rosy death.

The first cars arrived about fifteen minutes after the rendezvous had been called. Only one was a low rider, a brilliantly maroon old Chevy. A tall man with a big mustache drove up in it, stopped under the adobe and stucco canopy, gunned the engine, then turned on the motor that lowered the body of the car to no more than a few inches from the ground.

Another car came in a few minutes later, a Buick cut down so low it had the lines of a Lamborghini roadster. It was the beginning of an art show, one car more beautiful than the next; each one unique and perfect in its own style, but all according to the same low-rider aesthetic of folk art adapted to the Industrial Age.

On the street, in the world outside the paint booth and the garage, low riders represented rebellion, a statement of ethnic differentiation, the flaunting of Mexican roots, the nativistic sense of color and design; the cars paraded through the streets of East L.A. and El Paso like angry flags. At their inception, low-rider cars belonged to the members of the earliest gangs, to young men who wore them like tattoos, to *vatos locos, pachucos, eses*. Over time, age and the codification of folk art had changed the character of the low rider, if not his car; the leader of the Latin Pride Car Club was a fireman, and among the members were store clerks (groceries and flowers), a forklift operator, a machinist, and a U.S. Marine.

No member of the club would deny his history. One man beat his wife, three were on probation, others had been in jail. But maturity had overtaken the rage of earlier times; they were married men, and except for the one in gangster clothes, fathers. The club belonged to esthetics and ethnicity, not to war. Or so they would have liked the world to be. In Texas or California, when ethnicity flaunts its Mexican face and walks among the poor, it invites nothing less than war.

When I walked across the street to the gas station, a young Chicano followed me. I had been watching them, trying to decide whether they were a gang or a car club, and he had been watching me. We laughed a little about who had been watching whom, but not comfortably. David Gonzalez, whom I had arranged to meet, had not arrived. The others wanted to know if I was from the police.

"No. *No soy de la Jura, ni la Migra, ni el FBI.*"

Several men had brought their wives and children along in the low-rider cars. They seemed uneasy. The men stood between me and their wives, as if to protect them. I did not understand. It would be a long time before I learned the meaning of this gesture of arrangement.

Hector Gonzalez, the older brother of the man I had expected to meet, took charge of the conversation. He waved his arm at the wide, ugly street in front of the gas station, "Alameda, count em, pawnshops, liquor stores, and car lots, that's what poor people live with," said Hector Gonzalez. "Car lots, you know what car lots are? Money laundering."[26]

"We better get out of here before the cops come," someone said.

They moved quickly. The women and children climbed into the cars, the Buick and the Chevys, the Plymouth made as gorgeous as neon art.

---

[26] It is widely rumored on the Mexican border that the inordinate number of used-car lots function as a means to transfer drug profits to the legal banking system.

They slid onto the leopard-skin seats, zebra-striped seats, pin-striped seats. The sound systems opened up, a Tejano Cantata! Accordions and brass in polka time. All the big engines rumbled, fifties music, dressed in chrome. Then the cars lumbered off, one by one, the gum-chewing mothers in skintight pants going as slow as Sunday ladies leaving church.

"We'll get some beer!"

Steve, the one in suntans and a black T-shirt, with his cap turned backwards, rode with me. We stopped at a supermarket to pick up a case of beer. "We can't stay long at the gas station," he said. "The guy who owns the place gave us permission, but the police don't care. They see the cars, and they try to bust us for something."

"Do you have a car?"

"I don't even have a driver's license," he said. "They stop me because I wear these clothes. I don't even belong to a gang, but they stop me, because of my clothes."

We drove south of Alameda into a cul de sac, where Hector and the others had gathered in the garage of his house. They sat in a circle, drinking beer, talking about cars, drinking beer. "The police can't come in here," Hector said, "but if we go out on the grass or even in the driveway, they'll bust us."

"For what?"

"For being low riders, man."

"Just for that? Nothing more."

We agreed that the police were unfair. Then we drank some more beer, and we agreed that gringos were unfair. The vato with the tattoos of the Mexican colors on one arm and a girl in *ranchera* costume on the other said that he learned the difference between gringos and Mejicanos when he used to get thrown in jail for drinking. "A Mexican gets thrown in with whites, they'll beat him up. But a white, he gets thrown in with Mexicans, after a little while they'll welcome him; they'll be playing cards or dominoes with him."

The tattooed man had fought blacks and whites all his life: in Bisbee, in prisons, in El Paso. He told of running out of gas and trying to borrow a can from a gas station owner, of the racism in the man's eyes. He showed the palms of his hands, which shone in all the places where he had been burned. "You remember the hottest day this summer? The cops stopped me. Put me up against the car, told me to put my hands on the car and keep them there. It was burning up, man. I could feel my hands burning. I said to the cops in a real polite voice, 'Officer, my hands are burning up, could I please take them away?' And he told me to shut up or he would kick my ass."

The Marine said he had grown up in a shack made of cardboard with a firepit in the middle of the dirt floor. He couldn't forget it; he showed his fists, which were scarred from hitting them against walls or people when he could not control his rage.

At some hour, very late that night, when we had drunk a couple of cases of beer, a car went by very slowly on the road just across the strip of sand and greasewood at the end of the cul-de-sac. "Jurajurajura," someone said, in a low voice, half strangled with anxiety, warning that the police were near. I had heard that sound only once before, in a different language, in 1970 in East Berlin, when a dissident writer, declared a non-person by Eric Honecker himself, had seen a police car as we were driving from Grunau into Berlin.[27]

The laughter ended then in El Paso, as it had in Berlin. Before we left the garage, Hector the fireman had one more thing to say. We were all very drunk before the police passed by and we were all very sober when Hector finished speaking. "You know what they do to us?" he said. "When they see us in our low riders, with our wives and children, they stop us anywhere, all the time. They make my wife get out of the car and get down on her knees in the street and put her hands behind her head.

"'Assume the position!' they tell her. And she does it, because she knows what they'll do. And that would be all right, if they said to my wife, 'Get down on your knees and lock your hands behind your head.' That would be all right. But they don't say that. They say, 'Assume the position.' And my wife knows what to do. Why does my wife have to know that? Why?"

23. Other Men's Eyes: Intellectual Muggings

Better than any other device, the computer explains the intellectual mugging of the poor. For all its increasing power, the computer cannot think at all. It doesn't really know where it is in the world, or if there is a world at all, and it cannot tell who, if anyone, kicks it in its metaphorical shins. As a result of its stupidity, the computer issues a never-ending stream of imperatives. For anyone who disputes this imperative character of computing, a look at the computer section in a bookstore should end the debate.

---

[27] The writer was Stefan Heym, a naturalized U.S. citizen and former U.S. Army officer who had defected during the Korean War. Earlier that day he had showed us his old U.S. Army issue .45 caliber pistol. He said that when the Volkspolezei came to get him, he would not go without a fight.

The number of books on how the computer user must behave in order to satisfy the imperatives of the uncomprehending and unfeeling machine has by now reached well into the thousands.

Whoever fails to read these books or otherwise learn these lessons on how to follow the imperatives of the computer embarks upon an inexorable decline toward chaos or many calls to the customer service line at $2 per minute.

The point the computer makes so well is that a person must choose between a life of freedom and one of imperatives—the master builder or the bee. In human terms, education produces master builders and training produces bees. The poor are generally thought to belong among the bees, where imperatives rule.

Education, unlike the imperative of the bee, entertains many alternatives. No better definition of dialectic can be given than to say it is a process of considering alternatives. Would the same definition not also apply to the scientific method? Thinking involves freedom, accepts the existence of alternatives. The more elegant the thinking, the greater the freedom and the fewer the imperatives.

When the poor are consigned to training programs, with no intention other than to convert them into bees, they lose their freedom. However, they do not lose their freedom because of the work they may do, but because of the limiting of the alternatives in their lives and in their thinking.

Those in power—teachers, counselors, clergymen, social workers, even parents—tell the poor by consigning them to a life according to imperatives that they are less than fully human, incapable of freedom. Reflection has no place in such a life; without alternatives, reflection is futile, an act without meaning. Contemplation loses its quality of action; the poor may only vegetate or react. Like the man or woman who sits before the computer screen and reads the messages written there on how to proceed, the poor person can only obey the imperatives or destroy the machine.

After a few months in the Clemente Course in the Humanities, a student said, "They told me I couldn't go to college, but I got enough hubris to tell them, 'No, I want to go.' "[28]

He had by then learned that a certain amount of hubris, enough to challenge the imperative of fate, implies the existence of alternatives and the possibility of freedom. He no longer saw himself through other men's eyes.

---

[28] The Clemente Course in the Humanities is a demonstration project that arose out of work on this book. A report on the course appears in Chapter XVIII and in Appendix C.

24. Other Men's Eyes: Media

Near the end of *Discipline and Punish*, Michel Foucault wrote of the person he names "the delinquent," comparing him to "the offender." Although he did not bother to write exacting definitions of either group, what Foucault meant by the offender was one who committed an illegal act, compared to the delinquent who had a criminal character. According to Foucault, the carceral system creates delinquents; that is, former prisoners who have been organized into "the milieu of delinquency" while in prison, endure continued surveillance once they leave prison, and finally, cannot find work in the world outside the prison, throwing them and their families into destitution. Hence recidivism.

Michel Foucault worked at the extremes, attempting to understand the world from its farthest edges, but his work applies now to the poor in America, for they have been pushed out onto the edges of society in this last decade of the century. Those people Foucault calls "delinquents" now go by the name "underclass," and more and more underclass comes to include all the poor.[29]

His apparatus of prison, social workers, psychologists, doctors, welfare agencies, and so on, remains in place, continuing to produce delinquency by carrying the aspects of incarceration into the general community of the poor. Foucault does not neglect the longtime ally of these "carceral" agencies, the press. He concludes his book with a quote from an anonymous letter published in 1836, suggesting with juicy irony that the poor, the sick, criminals, and mad persons be kept in an enclosure in the center of Paris, and that it be ringed by its suppliers, including "the press, with its sophisms."

A hundred and sixty years ago, even twenty-five years ago, the press—now the media—did not hold the same power to determine society's vision of itself. It affected the poor, but less as a distorting mirror to the poor than as an informing portrait for those other than the poor. Now, the poor can hardly see themselves except as they are seen.

Wherever a space exists in the surround, the media seek to fill the gap, finish the enclosure. And by "the media" I do not mean here only the inventive media, such as films or television series or novels, but the partially invented media as well: newspapers, radio and television news, magazines,

---

[29] Foucault, working nearly a quarter of a century ago, moved toward this concept at the end of his book, *Discipline and Punish* See part IV, particularly section 3.

and books of non-fiction (including this one). In these putative representations of reality the poor find themselves transformed into delinquents, if not offenders. The media perform much of the function of prisons, not only making the poor unemployable, forcing them into a milieu (made of words and images) of other unemployables, but criminalizing them.

Consider crime in the media. The reporting follows an immutable economically based rule: Treat crimes of the poor as routine and crimes of the rich as extraordinary.

On the cheap imitations of *Oprah* that are broadcast on television in the afternoons and evenings, the poor appear as violators of social convention rather than the law. No rich people, nor any who live in the economic middle, come to display their infidelities and other sins before the leering audience. The theme of the programs is not art or even prurience, but the game of the modern world: These are the losers who step out onto the stage. These are the poor, displayed like rouged meat in their hiked-up skirts or muscle shirts. No crimes are attributed to them, but the sly asides of the hosts, spoken to the camera in coded winks and barely perceptible leerings, make clear that the poor are different from you and me, delinquents.

When some federal legislators argued that in our "permissive, liberal society" the kind of behavior thought of as deviant had become too rarefied, it did not occur to them that the phenomenon they were talking about was the normalization of crime among the poor, what Foucault called the making of delinquents.

Largely because of the media, delinquency has become the fate of the poor in America. They have been judged in an exceedingly public trial by the media, and found guilty. In this time, other men's eyes have become the media rather than the family, the community, or even the state, but one thing has not changed: The face one sees in the mirror of other men's eyes is an imperative; the mirror may be distorted, but the image cannot be set free. As Foucault would have us believe, a prison in the world reproduces a prison in the mind.

25. Other Men's Eyes: Racism

When a poor black man learns that more poor people in America are white than black, he usually greets the news with a sigh. On first hearing, the sigh seems to mean something like, "So what? I'm still poor." Only after many such reactions did I finally understand that the sigh means, "Thank God, there is a difference between race and racism," for that is where the battle line is drawn, between nature and perception, between truth and other men's eyes.

The line of demarcation is very important, as Bruno Bettelheim claimed to have discovered when he was interned in a Nazi concentration camp, for that is where a person crosses over into thinking of himself as deserving of the worst.[30] Bettelheim said that he survived the camps because he did not permit the views of the Nazis to corrupt his understanding of himself. But Bettelheim, as he readily admitted, was one among thousands; for the rest, truth was no match for perception.

There is very little that has not already been said several times about racism, except to note in relation to the poor that racism forces entrance into its objects and weakens them at the deepest levels. Most people, subjected to this force, prove to be as permeable as cheesecloth. If they do not die, they weaken, so that they can no longer conceive of themselves except as they are reflected in the mirroring eyes. When that happens, the ability of a person to be a beginning in the world, the miracle of human natality, disappears.

Who becomes the object of racism depends entirely upon other men's eyes. Since race is merely an identity constructed by society, any set of characteristics may identify a race or a racelike group. Blacks, Asians, Latinos, and other natives of the Americas are most easily and most commonly defined as races, but history tells us that almost any identifiable group may be defined as a race—Jews in Germany, Ainus in Japan, Muslims here, Samoans there, Portuguese somewhere else.

Most racism in America takes for its objects blacks, Latinos, Jews, Arabs, Native Americans, Asians, and people of the Indian subcontinent. In local variations, Italians, Poles, Hungarians, and others may become objects of racism.

The American need to hold racist feelings is so great that it often takes bizarrely inventive forms. In Hancock County, Tennessee, where the population is almost entirely white, an unclearly identified group of a few hundred people, with no specific racial or national origins, known locally as "Melungeons," suffer race prejudice. In appearance the Melungeons call to mind the people of the Mediterranean rather than the Lowland Scots who settled much of Appalachia, but they are lighter-skinned than some people whose ancestors intermarried with the local Cherokees. They have been in

---

[30] See *The Informed Heart* (Glencoe, Il: Free Press 1960), and others of his works. The veracity of Bettelheim's autobiographical material is now in doubt, but the point of his apparently invented experience remains valid, in the way that the material of any fiction is valid.

the county for as long as anyone can remember and they speak no language but the heavily accented English of the mountains.

The Melungeons, almost all of whom live in that one Appalachian county, exhibit many of the characteristics of other oppressed groups in the United States: lower income and purportedly higher rates of all forms of activity considered immoral in Hancock County. The few Melungeons who have managed to rise into better social and economic positions in the county are always singled out as examples of racial tolerance.

The case of the Melungeons illustrates the force of racism in the surround of poverty. By almost any measure other than racism, there are no Melungeons; they exist only in other men's eyes. But that has been more than enough to lower the quality of their lives and reduce their participation in the economic, educational, political, and social life of the county.

With very little evidence in nature and less in reason to give cause to its existence, the concept of race has always been malleable: the human race; the "mud race" of Englishmen described by Ralph Waldo Emerson in *English Traits*, published at the height of his abolitionist fervor in 1856; a race of giants, a race of women, a race of pygmies. Since the 1960s, the poor have been seen more and more as if they were a race rather than an economic group. The term for this race, "underclass," has some relation to economics, just as the terms "white" or "black" have some vague relation to skin color (blacks are not black, whites are not white, reds are not red, browns are not brown, yellows are not yellow).[31]

The evolution of the concept of the poor as a race may falter over the next several decades or the multigenerational aspect of poverty may bring codification and an unfortunate permanence to the concept. Much will

[31] Even if the concept of race were limited to groups easily discerned on sight, the poor would be good candidates. It is far easier to pick out the poor people in a crowd than to decide who has Native American ancestors. For those who think Jews constitute a race, movie stars like Kirk Douglas, Paul Newman, Tony Curtis, et al. make the problem of identification on sight extremely difficult. So many people of mixed ancestry have passed into the "white race" that a "white" can only be properly defined as a person other persons say is white.

Claude Lévi-Strauss considered the question in *The View from Afar* (English trans., New York: Basic Books, 1985): "It does not behoove an anthropologist to try and define what is or is not a race, because the specialists in physical anthropology, who have been discussing the question for almost two centuries, have never agreed on a definition, and nothing indicates that they are any closer to agreement today." (p. 3)

All of this is not to deny that in the United States people with certain physical characteristics, mainly skin color, become classified as belonging to one "race" or another. It is to demonstrate that the poor may more easily than one would suspect become defined as a "race." The race of paupers, the indigent race, the impoverished race, or merely the underclass.

depend on the state of the economy, the integration of upwardly mobile blacks and Latinos coming out of poverty and into the prosperous majority, and the rate at which the population continues to move away from the dominance of people of European origin. For the poor, a little less than half of whom now live as the objects of racism, the dimunition of self-regard forced upon them today could become broader as well as deeper. Poor whites would be exposed to the disabling weight of racism, while those who now suffer from racism face the possibility of looking into other men's eyes and seeing themselves twice despised.

M ORE THAN TWENTY-FIVE FORCES surround the poor, many more. The number may be as high as thirty-five or even fifty. Some forces are peculiar to the poor; others are common at all economic levels. For example, the poor live with absurdity. When the poor within the surround can no longer muster what Albert Camus called "the courage to live in an absurd world," they may have passed beyond the threshold of panic:

A woman sent by the welfare department to a hotel at a cost of $3,200 a month cannot reconcile the rent with the unwillingness of the same department to spend $600 a month to rent an apartment for her. She does the arithmetic of her situation over and over and over. It becomes a mantra of unreason. She does something foolish, turns to drugs or beats her children; in an unreasonable world, everything is equally senseless.

Although they sometimes do not know the word, the concept of absurdity becomes apparent to the poor in such situations. Awareness of the larger absurdities of poverty in America requires reflection, a philosophical conception rather than an angry reaction, and the poor do not have the luxury of leisure required to think reflectively; poverty happens at an unstoppable, unmanageable pace.

Another force the poor must endure—pregnancy—does not function in the same way for the rest of America. For those among the poor whose connection to agricultural roots makes children a form of wealth, pregnancy still seems the economic success of women; but for those who have generations of city life behind them, children bring only the sounds of hunger and the clanking of the chains of child rearing. Despite demagogic reports to the contrary, additional children do not make women on welfare rich. And for teenage girls, pregnancy is the announcement of a force that will not relent for the rest of their lives.

Three young women dropped out of the Clemente Course because they were pregnant. One of them, no more than a girl, with the tiny voice of a sad kitten, thought about having an abortion. She would have done it had it not been for the advice of an older sister who said she cried every night for three years after aborting a pregnancy.

Another, a nineteen-year-old woman, was pregnant by a young boy. She told me the boy had never been with a woman before he made her pregnant and that she did not want to hold him responsible.

The third young woman simply drifted off into sadness. In no instance was it necessary for the young women to leave school. All of the babies were due after the course would have been completed. Pregnancy, a miracle to most women, an economic advantage on the farm, was an unbearable force to these young poor women. The very fact of it sent them into panic; it completed the surround.

Marriage often has an equally contrary effect upon poor women. Instead of the emotional and economic security marriage brought to previous generations, it produces force. Not long after the first child arrives, the marriage becomes an implied threat: any misstep by the wife will cause the husband to abandon her and their children to a miserable and lonely life. For an educated or even highly trained woman, the lack of commitment of contemporary marriage may produce a response ranging from anxiety to the pleasures of freedom; but for a poor woman, what had once been a lifetime bond has been turned by a change in mores into a force against her and her children. Nothing need ever be said by the husband for this force to exist. The threat to the poor woman in marriage is implicit in the marriage.

Prison holds another kind of unsuspected threat. For the prisoner, the prison is intended as force, but the family of the prisoner also feels the force of prison, as Foucault asserted in *Discipline and Punish*. Why it should happen that way does not leap into the imagination of people who have no experience with prisons; after all, the intention of prison walls is to separate the worlds, not to liken them. But the system has unintended effects, beginning at the earliest stages of incarceration:

The aunt of a young student telephoned me one Saturday morning to say that her nephew, whom she had legally adopted,[32] was being held in the detention cells below the Brooklyn courthouse. The judge had remanded him the previous afternoon. Neither his adopted mother (his aunt), a woman in her late seventies, nor his biological mother, who had six other

---

[32] Since the student committed the crime for which he was put on probation before he reached maturity, his record will be sealed, unless he commits another crime while on probation. In keeping with that policy, which I think is a good one, I have changed some details and not used his name.

children and an unemployed husband, could afford a lawyer. The boy's probation officer did not answer telephone calls. (I later found out that her phone number had been changed and that she had neglected to inform any of her clients of the new number.) No one in the Public Defender's Office had picked up his case.

The adoptive mother telephoned me several times a day. She had no idea why the boy was in prison. Instead, she talked about his appearances before large crowds at the Jehovah's Witness church: "He was just a little boy, and he talked to hundreds of people right there in Kingdom Hall. They came from all over to hear him."

His stepfather, a street hustler from the Caribbean, could not help. No one in the family knew exactly why the boy had been remanded. On Monday, his third day in detention, the boy told his adoptive mother that he owed $165 to the court. The woman, who lived on a small pension, had $10. The street hustler had lately been trying to get out of "the life," which meant he had nothing at all. The boy's older brother had lost his job two weeks earlier. The biological mother supported seven people and made both house and car payments on the wages she earned as a hospital worker.

The family had no money, literally none. Two weeks before being sent to detention, the family had been unable to raise $1.50 to buy a subway token. The boy had jumped over a turnstile and into the arms of a policeman, who wrote out a ticket and sent the boy on his way.

The boy telephoned his adoptive mother on Tuesday, his fifth day of detention. He wept openly. He was in the third year of five years of probation, and his probation officer had apparently recommended to the court, based on the "fare-beat" incident, that he spend the rest of the time in prison. His aunt wept and raged against the world. She managed to say over the telephone that he had a court date set for the next morning.

I told the aunt that I would ask my son, James, who had been an Assistant District Attorney in Manhattan, what he thought would happen to the boy. When I gave her the news that he would probably be reprimanded by the judge, sentenced to time served, and sent home, she seemed relieved.

At the end of the day on Tuesday, the Legal Aid attorney informed the court that he had a conflict and asked that the case be set over until Friday. The judge agreed; the boy stayed in the open cell in the basement of the courthouse. His mothers, real and adopted, descended into panic; they were sure he would be sent to prison, and they were worldly enough to know what two or three years in a state prison would do to a young boy. Panic mixed with rage: How could this have happened to the boy who spoke to hundreds at Kingdom Hall when he was only six years old?

On Friday morning, the boy was reprimanded by the judge and sentenced to time served, exactly as predicted. The force of prison, however, had been implanted in the family. The aunt could no longer trust her adopted son; she feared his friends, she worried him, she hounded him, demanding to know every move he made, every person he saw.

Once prison enters a family, the entire family feels the force of it.[33] And the force never abates. Most poor people have no experience with prison, which is why I have not included it among the more usual forces in the surround; but a tendency to imprison people for long periods for non-violent crimes, mainly involving drugs, has begun to change that pattern. The number of young men, most of them black or Latino, now serving time or on parole or probation describes an epidemic. As of now, it is an epidemic of punishment rather than crime. But the force of prison on the prisoner's family may change the character of the epidemic, for prison is a force that creates crime as well as poverty.[34]

By contrast, public welfare, which draws constant attacks from conservative officeholders and aspirants on the grounds that it creates crime and perpetuates poverty, exerts no force against the poor, unless it is misadministered or does not provide sufficient amounts of money.

Only then does welfare become a force. Unfortunately, welfare workers frequently mistreat their clients, making a system intended to alleviate the forces that press on the poor into yet another force in the surround. But the administration of the system should not be confused with its intent. Welfare, properly administered and adequately funded, should be helpful to the poor, especially in times of crisis. Ideally, it would be part of a comprehensive system to give the poor the tools to learn reflection and politics and enter the world of citizens, where they could earn an adequate living without depending on the state.

Instead, it has become one of the key points in every racist argument.

---

[33] See Chapter IV for the experiences of Margarette Williams and her family.

[34] Because the Clemente Course was also offered in the Bedford Hills Correctional Institution, I spent quite a lot of time in the maximum-security prison for women, mainly teaching moral philosophy, which hardly qualifies me as an expert on the prison system. But one need not be an expert to notice that prison is the modern poorhouse.

Rich people rarely go to prison, unless they commit famous crimes or steal billions. Poor people can spend a week in jail for beating a $1.50 subway fare. Blacks and Latinos get longer sentences than whites for the same crimes. In fact, the entire system is patently unfair, from mandatory sentencing to parole boards motivated more by political considerations than judgment of the hazard to society of releasing prisoners.

Some people should be sent to prison and some should stay in prison for a long time, but the number of people in prison in America and the duration of their sentences makes no sense at all. Prison should be used as a last resort, not as a first choice.

Black women and their children, more than any other group, have become associated with the failure of the welfare system. There may actually be some truth in that argument, but the failure belongs to the system, not to the objects of it. One of the classic mistakes of the system came to light during a conversation with a young woman and her father on the Lyndale Plantation near Egremont, Mississipi.[35]

They had recently moved into better housing from one of the places in the row of shacks down near the ditch. The new house belonged to the lady of the plantation, they said, and she allowed the Lewis family to live there rent-free, because whenever Mrs. Lewis wasn't out chopping cotton she worked in the plantation lady's house.

Barbara Newell, Mrs. Lewis's twenty-nine-year-old daughter, lolled in an easy chair near the front door of the house. "Momma chops all day," she said. "Chops the vines and milkweed. Chop with the hoe . . . but Johnson grass, they spray it." While she spoke, she wound herself around the arm and the back of the chair, smiling, half clothed in a white T-shirt so big that the neck opening reached halfway down her side, exposing her shoulder and the narrow white strap of her brassiere. With every sentence, she rearranged herself in the chair, a barefoot woman, wearing shorts, smoothly muscled, perfectly formed, as naturally seductive as a cat.

She worked when she could, chopping cotton all through the summer, working the margin when the picking machines went through the fields, jumping into the box that held the cotton spewing out of the machine, packing the edges, working ten to fourteen hours a day at minimum wage during the picking season, then back to the welfare rolls and taking care of this house while her mother took care of the plantation house.

Sixteen people lived in the Lewis house, distributed over three bedrooms, in bunk beds, couches in the living room, cots in the dining area. Barbara Newell kept the house in order, sparse and airy in the summer heat, cool and yet light. She had three children and no man, no house, no job. In the lazy heat of the day I think she was half dreaming, talking easily, taking turns with her father, describing the racism of the Delta, her sense that it had never changed, nothing had changed; this was a plantation, cotton

---

[35] Egremont, a very small town, is just south of Rolling Fork on the edge of the Delta National Forest in Sharkey-Issaquena County. The hyphenated county results from the unification of two extremely poor, partially depopulated counties. Great numbers of black families, driven off the land in the area by the advent of mechanization, moved north. The heaviest migration came after the war, in the 1950's. At one stage 2,200 blacks moved into Chicago every week. Between 1940 and 1970, 5 million blacks moved north.

grew in rows neater than nature, stretching as far as the forest on the east and all the way to the great mound that held the river on the west. She packed the corners of cotton modules and hoed milkweed and vines, and now she was dreaming. "I never been to New York."

"Chicago?"

"No."

"Memphis."

She nodded.

I do not quite know what happened then, but the face of the cat in the chair turned wise, and she and her father began a long dialogue about injustice: White men got better pay than blacks for the same work. Whites got the best jobs. "Some whites is prejudiced. Quite a few of em. These folks right here, they still playin the same thing." She said, "Seem like the welfare don't want you to do better for yourself, be proud. If they find out that I was choppin, they cut your check, cut your AFDC and the stamps. If they see you tryin to do good for yourself, they shouldn't cut your stamps. They just want you to depend on welfare."

Then her father started to talk about the plantation system. "Somebody tell the Man, you lose your job, your house, everything, be out in the street."

They took turns speaking: He had done construction work, then come back to the plantation. She had never lived anywhere else. The little fantasy of escape that had made her kittenish in the chair vanished. She sat forward, sharp-eyed, considering, speaking in little bursts. He prowled the kitchen area, a big man, stone-heavy, limping slightly. His heart had begun to fail; the weakness had dimmed his voice to a whisper.

"I guess they scared," she said of the men on the plantation.

He turned at her, the only sudden move he had made all afternoon. I thought it might be anger, but something else had happened. Lewis and his daughter looked at each other with the most intent expressions of surprise. They fell into silence, they did not move, they looked at each other, almost as if they had just met again after a long separation. It took a moment or two for me to catch up with them, to understand the epiphany: The welfare system was merely a continuation of plantation life by another means.

Of course, it was true. They had suddenly come upon the reason why so many blacks had been caught up in the welfare system when the machines drove them off the plantations. There had been no intervention (to borrow a term from the psychologists). With no preparation for the move from the farm to the city, the millions had simply been shifted by society to another plantation. Welfare workers had quickly adapted to plantation ways, turning the system from its original intention into a terrible force that battered, threatened, demanded, and punished instead of nurturing, protecting, teaching, and thus preparing the poor first to move into the political world of free men and then to move up into the ranks of the comfortable majority.

The dialogue of the Lewis house revealed the antinomy of American social policy: There was nothing wrong with the concept of public welfare; it simply hadn't been tried.

I HAVE NO DOUBT THAT OTHER FORCES press on the poor, forces that did not appear during the years of cobbling together this book. Can clothing be a force? Or religion? The culture of force takes up the next chapter here.

Even if some force or forces have been overlooked, it would seem difficult to deny, given the evidence, that the multigenerational poor live within a surround of forces, a situation in which political life may be all but impossible for most people—a fragmenting, panicking situation that requires acts of constant courage and character merely to survive, and something like a miracle to escape.

X.

The Best and the Brightest Redux

Ther life of the poor in the United States has been described up to this point as a series of oppositions: Absolute/Relative; Temporary/Enduring; Winning/Losing; Inclusive (power)/Exclusive (force). All of these lead up to the Public/Private opposition, which has not yet been explored.

There is also an opposition concerning the causes of poverty, but this is not so much in the lives of the poor as in the minds of the people who observe them. Some of the observers think poverty has external (structural) causes and others believe the cause is internal; that is, within the poor themselves. This difference is sometimes thought of as part of the general left-liberal-progressive/right-conservative-reactionary opposition. It is not.

Connections can be made, but the internal/external opposition does not grow out of the political and economic beliefs that separate left and right in America. It comes instead from a moralistic view of work that goes back to Richard Baxter and the rise of capitalism. In this view of work versus idleness, Karl Marx and Adam Smith sleep together chastely in the same bed.

The clearest distinction between internal and external views of the causes of poverty occurs in the comparison of the views prevalent in the Roosevelt administration and the underclass theory. The Roosevelt

Democrats (not to be confused with the current Clinton Democrats) believed that poverty had external causes, and attempted to change the economic structure of the country to eliminate those aspects that caused poverty. In other words, they said that the poor lost because the game was unfair. The theory of the internal cause of poverty, currently popular with both Republicans and Clinton Democrats, holds that the moral and intellectual failings of the poor cause them to live in poverty. In this view, the game is fair, but the poor are not the moral equals of the rich. Surprisingly, it would be erroneous and unfair to attribute this moralistic view entirely to the conservatives, because they were not alone at the genesis of it.

Contemporary moralizing about the poor exhibits its ecumenical character most clearly in the concept of the underclass and its antecedent, the culture of poverty. A concise definition of the concept appeared in the publisher's flap copy (presumably approved by the author) of *The Underclass:*

> They are the underclass: the people who prey on our communities committing the senseless, heinous murders, rapes and muggings that haunt the news every day; the thieves who break into our homes night after night; the hard-core unemployed; the hustlers of the underground economy—the peddlers of loot, the "gentlemen of leisure," the prostitutes, the drug pushers; the passive poor who are unable to cope in the workaday world; the single mothers living chronically on welfare; the strung-out junkies and the aimless juvenile delinquents; the deranged vagrants and the homeless and helpless shopping-bag ladies. These new millions . . . account for a disproportionate amount of the street crime, long-term welfare dependency, chronic unemployment and antisocial behavior in America today.

With the acknowledged assistance of Mitchell Sviridoff and Robert Schrank of the Ford Foundation, and the editorial assistance of William Whitworth and William Shawn at *The New Yorker* and Jason Epstein and Erroll McDonald of Random House, Ken Auletta wrote the book that almost merited the introduction above.

Credit (or blame) for the concept of the underclass went almost entirely to Auletta. *Time* got a little of the honor for using the word as its cover line. Herbert Gans and a few other careful writers identify Gunnar Myrdal as the inventor of the word, but not the concept as we now generally understand it. Journalists, writers, political figures, practically everyone took it up. No other term seemed so apt, said so much, had such resonance with readers and listeners. I used it, and my guess is that most of the people reading this book have used the word at one time or another.

This action of the liberals against the poor bears a marked resemblance to those whom David Halberstam characterized with deadly irony as "the best and the brightest" during the Vietnam War. The men in the Kennedy-Johnson and Nixon administrations, especially those who advised both Kennedy and Johnson on the war, were thought at the time to be among the finest young students of government policy. Moreover, the high moral character of these men was a given; it was assumed that their devotion to justice and their love of country directed them to public service.

Similarly, the men who devised the theories leading to the concept of the underclass, those who publicized it, and continue to prosecute it, were presumed to be of high moral character and devoted to justice.[1] In both cases, the later stages were taken over by people whose motives were less clear: the Nixon administration for Vietnam, and the Charles Murray, Thomas Sowell, Newt Gingrich crowd for the underclass.

Whether the Bundy brothers, Walt Rostow, Robert Macnamara, and company were brighter or morally superior to Oscar Lewis, Ken Auletta, Mickey Kaus, and the entire War on Poverty is not at issue. In both instances the road to hell was paved with pretty good intentions. The Vietnam War led to millions of dead and wounded and the destruction of much of the national fabric of the United States. The underclass concept bears at least some, if not much, of the responsibility for the great number of long-term poor and prisoners in America.

The Vietnam War, in retrospect, was born of the marriage of racism and moral machismo; *The War Against the Poor,* as Herbert Gans called it, came out of a similar union. The notion of the poor as the gook, the other, something less than human, available to be talked about, done to, experimented with, lay at the bottom of both actions. In Vietnam the enemy was not white and in America the enemy is not thought to be white.[2]

Before condemning these men of pretty good intentions, however, the question has to be asked: Would it have been better to do nothing? Remain quiet? What is the greater danger: Doing something or doing nothing? Until some bold revisionist comes along, the case of the Vietnam War seems clear: It would have been better if the United States had not intervened in support of a corrupt, unpopular government. The case of the underclass does not offer the same clarity, for it was built on ideas that go back at least as far as Karl Marx, who described the *Lumpenproletariat* as "scum," "leavings," "the refuse of all classes." He filled his version of the

---

[1] No women played important roles in either the Vietnam War or the concept of the underclass and the theories surrounding it.

[2] This may be one of the early stages of converting poverty into a race or caste. The poor, of course, are mostly white, but the underclass is perceived as black or Latino even when its members are white.

underclass with people who ran whorehouses, confidence men, beggars, and for some strange reason, organ grinders.

When the phrase "the undeserving poor" is substituted for the underclass, following the critical notions of Christopher Jencks and Michael B. Katz, it recalls the early origin of this concept of poverty in Herbert Spencer and Social Darwinism.[3] But it stands in sharp contrast to what might be described as the Jesus view (to distinguish the biblical Jesus from the current Christian right). To Jesus, and to the Hebrews who followed the prescription for mercy in the Old Testament and left the corners of the field to the indigent, the poor were not undeserving. On the contrary, one might interpret the words and acts of Jesus to mean that the poor were more deserving than the affluent.

The Jesus view never held sway in the United States. The earliest American notions of charity and then welfare were based on the distinction between deserving and undeserving poor. A widow was deserving, but a woman who had a child out of wedlock was not. The point of distinguishing the two classes of poor, as Katz makes so clear, has to do with moral judgment rather than need. The children of the unmarried woman and those of the widow require the same number of calories every day, and both need shoes and shelter, but only the widow and her children deserve help.

This idea of undeserving innocents still figures very strongly in American attitudes toward the poor: Legislators in several states want to punish single mothers on welfare by refusing to increase their grants if they have more children. In August 1996, both houses of Congress passed, and President Clinton signed, a welfare reform bill that effectively ends grants to poor women with children after a short time, although states and other jurisdictions may find ways to extend this period. The policy seems to present a moral dilemma. Which is the greater sin, to cause the suffering of innocents or to have children out of wedlock? If the reason for opposing out-of-wedlock births is that the children will suffer (and not that their mothers will have a hot time in bed), then the elimination of benefits for the newly born violates the law of the excluded middle; that is, the suffering of the children cannot be both not good and good.[4]

---

[3] See Jencks, *Rethinking Social Policy* (Cambridge, MA: Harvard University Press, 1992); and Katz, *The Undeserving Poor* (New York: Pantheon, 1989).

[4] The 1996 Welfare Reform Bill also ends SSI (disability) payments for many people, including children; reduces food stamp stipends; and cuts virtually all assistance to legal immigrants.

At this writing, President Clinton has pledged to restore some cuts and the Republican-dominated Congress has vowed to keep the cuts. The president's effort to restore some cuts may simply be a strategic feint to placate those people in his party who still hold to the Jesus view of poverty.

The reasoning or emotion behind this attitude toward poor children is difficult to understand. Martin Luther practically invented the idea of welfare. Even Herbert Spencer said that charity was good, if only for the improvement of the character of the charitable. Nevertheless, the idea of punishment, including the deprivation of children, has become the linchpin of many new proposals for dealing with the poor. There can be little doubt that it was the motive behind the Welfare Reform Bill of 1996 in which Mr. Clinton and his Republican allies in his effort to "end welfare as we know it" set about punishing the poor for what has become the sin of being poor.

Could it be that something in the Reformation led to this view of poverty? That somewhere in the sudden worldliness of the birth of capitalism, with its emphasis on time as God's own and the waste of time as an affront to God, the Western world lost sight of the blessedness of the meek? Martin Luther may have begun a welfare program, but Protestant clergy did not wash the feet of the poor. God was served in many ways, but poverty was not one of them. The notion that trade and moneymaking was sinful disappeared. Was it then that the idea of poverty as sin was born?

If so, it was to meld perfectly in the fledgling United States with the idea that blacks were not quite human.[5] And although the sinful nature of poverty faded from the forefront of the national consciousness for a long time, especially during the Great Depression, it arose again with the concept of an underclass, black even when it was not black, and sinful by definition.

The contemporary version of the sinfulness of the poor, which is at the heart of the internal view of the cause of poverty, did not arise directly from the Reformation. It grew partly out of Daniel Patrick Moynihan's 1965 *Report on the Negro Family,* in which he argued that it was the growth of single-parent black families that caused black poverty, and a Jewish socialist's observations of the Latin American and Latino poor in Mexico, Cuba, and New York City.

Oscar Lewis was a serious-minded, industrious anthropologist at the University of Illinois who had produced an interesting book about poor people living in a Mexican village, when he published *Five Families* (1959), which carried the subtitle, *Mexican Case Studies in the Culture of Poverty.* It took place in a *vecindad* (something between a neighborhood and an apartment house) in Mexico City, and was to be followed by a book about one of the families, *The Children of Sanchez (1961).*

---

[5] In 1996, Albert Petersen of Belle Glade, Florida, told me that whites in Belle Glade had said it was "a sin to be born black."

The phrase "culture of poverty" and the idea of people living in a distinct culture everywhere in the world—one that came about as people moved from "primitive" to "impoverished" conditions—caught the attention of the press. In the Introduction to *La Vida: A Puerto Rican Family in the Culture of Poverty—San Juan and New York,* published in 1966, Lewis complained of the lack of attention his idea had received in the academic world and of the misuse of it in the popular press. He made specific mention of Michael Harrington, who, he said, used it "in a much broader and somewhat less technical sense than I had intended."

Nevertheless, Harrington wrote in the *New York Times Book Review* that "*La Vida* is unquestionably one of the most important books published in the United States this year. . . ." The book was an almost unqualified hit in the reviewing media. Years later, criticism of the culture of poverty has become something of an art form among liberal sociologists.

Michael B. Katz found no less than eleven flaws in Oscar Lewis's theory.[6] The first flaw he noted was the most serious: Lewis did not provide a definition of culture. Since more than fifty different definitions of culture have been used by anthropologists, Lewis left his readers confused by the term. He further confused the issue by saying, "While the term 'subculture of poverty' is technically more accurate, I have used 'culture of poverty' as a shorter form."

It would be presumptuous to provide a definition of culture for Oscar Lewis, but there are several characteristics of culture that ought to be considered when thinking about a "culture of poverty." First, in the anthropological sense of the word, culture is usually thought of as the pattern of life in its totality: both thought and action, language, family, customs, etc. Second, culture is transmitted from one generation to the next. Lewis had no doubt about that. He wrote, "By the time slum children are age six or seven, they have usually absorbed the basic values and attitudes of their subculture and are not psychologically geared to take full advantage of changing conditions or increased opportunities that may occur in their lifetime."

In other words, the culture of poverty, like any other culture, was likely to endure. For that subgroup of poor people whom he identified as living in a culture of poverty, there was little or no hope. Poverty produced the culture of poverty, which in turn produced poverty, which produced the culture of poverty. Katz said the argument was "tautological," and that may be true, but cultures do tend to perpetuate themselves.

Unfortunately, even cultural relativists can find little to admire in the

---

[6] See *The Undeserving Poor.*

values Lewis attributed to those who live in the culture of poverty. It was a "present-oriented" culture of ignorance, violence, sloth, fatalism, irresponsible sexual couplings, drugs, theft, disloyalty, and extentended families without clear responsibility for child rearing. The culture produced little wealth and got little in return. If people who lived in the culture of poverty protested that they had other values, Lewis had an answer for that, too:

"[They] are aware of middle-class values, talk about them and even claim some of them as their own, but on the whole they do not live by them. Thus, it is important to distinguish between what they say and what they do."[7]

By claiming a distinct culture for the multigenerational poor, Lewis separated them from the rest of us as surely as Margaret Mead separated her Samoans from us or Lévi-Strauss distinguished his Boróros from Belgians. Until Lewis published his work on the culture of poverty, the poor had always been the poor among us. He defined them out of our world, our culture. We no longer caused their poverty; they did it to themselves. It was their culture.

Lewis, who was a socialist and an admirer of Castro's Cuban revolution, must have realized that he had painted himself into a political corner, for he tempered his exile of the poor by claiming that "the culture of poverty [has] a high potential for protest and for being used in political movements aimed against the existing social order." Marx would not have agreed.

The Kennedy and Johnson administrations, interested and apparently motivated by Harrington's "walking tour of poverty" and his "misuse" of Lewis's concept of the culture of poverty, set out to deal with the problem. Lewis and Harrington had given them a view of the causes of poverty as internal, and that was how they dealt with it. As Lyndon Johnson's War on Poverty was gearing up in 1964, Christopher Jencks, writing in *The New Republic,* saw it as "fundamentally conservative." Jencks knew what the government meant when it concentrated its efforts on "education, training, and character building." In his view, the government assumed "that the poor are poor not because the economy is mismanaged but because the poor themselves have something wrong with them."[8]

During the same period, the Voting Rights Act and other measures to guarantee the civil rights of minorities opened the gates of the black and to a lesser extent Latino ghettos and allowed great numbers of people to escape from segregation and poverty. Looking back, it was civil rights legislation

---

[7] See Oscar Lewis, *La Vida* (New York: Random House, 1996), pp. xlv, xlvi.
[8] Quoted in Marvin E. Gettlemen and David Mermelstein, *The Great Society Reader* (New York: Random House, 1967), p. 197.

rather than Great Society programs that produced the new world of economically comfortable blacks and Latinos. The nation—particularly in the South—had been building an educated, politically and socially sophisticated cadre, mainly around the black churches, since Reconstruction. They did not need the Great Society, there was nothing "wrong" with them. The moment the gates of the ghetto opened, allowing them physically and economically out into the general society, they were gone.

Lyndon Johnson put the Great Society into the hands of Sargent Shriver, and gave him instructions to have the program up and running in a great hurry. What he failed to give Shriver was enough money to make a difference. To make the program seem larger than it really was, Shriver had the appropriations for all of the programs put under the Office of Economic Opportunity (OEO). "The total appropriation for the first year of the OEO was three-quarters of a billion dollars, less than 10 per cent of the annual cost of the war in Vietnam."[9]

Costs for the War on Poverty added up to about two-tenths of 1 percent of the gross national product, which was not exactly an all-out war in economic terms. Moreover, it had detractors right from the start. Nathan Glazer, a man in whom any form of social justice produces an allergic reaction, wrote in the *New York Times Magazine* (Feb. 27, 1966) that community action programs were a nation funding "guerrilla warfare" against itself. His ideas were later adopted by Ronald Reagan via Edwin Meese as a reason to dismantle federal Legal Services programs.[10]

Underfunded and beleaguered from the start, the War on Poverty remained as much a sales pitch as a set of social programs. LBJ's salesmen had four markets, the rich and the poor, the left and the right, and they sold them all the same product: helplessness, weakness (economic and moral), and the general incapacity of the poor. It satisfied the liberals at the time and flowed smoothly into later, openly conservative views, such as those of Edward C. Banfield and Charles Murray.

Tally's Corner, by Elliot Liebow, published in 1967, claimed no moral stance, but showed a group of poor black men as morally deficient, with no work ethic and some criminal tendencies.[11] At the time, it was hailed as brilliant ethnography, but no one realized that Liebow had made a major con-

---

[9] Ibid., p. 173.

[10] Personal interview with Meese while he served then Governor Ronald Reagan as a legal adviser. Sitting in a tiny office in the basement of the Governor's Mansion in Sacramento, Meese quoted Glazer's article against dissent. Later, he told me he thought the court system, especially the Supreme Court, ought to be abolished and such decisions given into the hands of the legislature.

[11] (Boston: Little, Brown, 1967).

tribution to the view of poverty that *Time* and Auletta were soon to codify.

Liebow's work also meshed with the idea of a culture of poverty and some of the notions about a ghetto that would soon be forthcoming from William Julius Wilson. Wilson differed from Oscar Lewis on the character of a ghetto. Lewis argued for an appreciation of ghetto life as heterogeneous, despite his notion of a culture of poverty. Wilson disputed the idea of a culture of poverty, replacing it with a "ghetto culture." In effect, Wilson made the culture of poverty black.

The problem with the notion of a black ghetto culture is that it consigns everyone in the ghetto to poverty, joblessness, asocial values, etc. But that has not been the case in the United States, as Wilson said. Harlem before integration produced the Harlem Renaissance. In fact, the contribution by ghetto blacks to the general culture, both high and low, of the United States is so great that one might reasonably argue the case for something like cultural imperialism spreading out of the black ghetto into the rest of society.

The culture of poverty found a new kind of support in 1974 from Edward Banfield. In *The Unheavenly City Revisited,* he accused the poor of "an outlook and style of life which is radically present-oriented and which therefore attaches no value to work, sacrifice, self-improvement or service to family, friends or community." The view of the poor brought to the fore by Lewis and Harrington and Liebow and Sargent Shriver and the War on Poverty had found its way across the aisle to Glazer and Moynihan, and all the way over to Banfield.[12]

For the next ten years the ideas about the poor that came initially from Moynihan, Lewis, Harrington, and the War on Poverty moved into the conservative camp, where the moral view of poverty, especially black and Latino poverty, took hold. The idea of the "welfare queen"—a woman who lived in luxury on the grant paid to her and her children—became a popular target for political figures as widely separated on other issues as New York's Mayor Edward I. Koch and President Ronald Reagan. Koch expressed shock and outrage upon finding that a woman on welfare had a color television set and *Horrors!* a video cassette player.

It did not occur to Koch or the reporters who repeated his tale that it was economically efficient for a woman and five children to rent a videotape of a movie instead of going to a theater. At 1996 New York prices, a woman

---

[12] Banfield, *The Unheavenly City Revisited* (Boston: Little, Brown, 1974), p. 235.

Daniel Patrick Moynihan was elected to the U.S. Senate as a Democrat from New York, but he would have been counted among the conservatives during the Nixon administration. One of the curiosities of the shift to the right in American politics, Senator Moynihan has become, without any major change in his own opinions, one of the liberal voices of the nineties.

and four children, two of whom pay full price and the others half, would pay $4 for a videotape rental and a couple of bags of homemade popcorn, compared to $36 plus the price of popcorn to see the movie in a theater. At that rate, a serviceable video cassette player would pay for itself in three or four evenings. Women who live on Aid to Families with Dependent Children have no choice but to think that way; prudence really is a part of the culture of poverty.

In the moralistic view of poverty, however, ownership of a video cassette machine implied laziness, misuse of public monies, and a general lack of character. Moreover, it was a clear sign of the injustice of transfer payments: The government was taking from the industrious to give to the indolent! Ronald Reagan used similar examples when he was governor of California, presidential candidate, and President of the United States. For Reagan, the idea of the poor as morally deficient provided a rationale for the redistribution of America's wealth away from the poor. It did not matter to the marketing of his policies that the people in the middle suffered as much or more than the poor in this redistribution; the moral unworthiness of the poor was a powerful incentive.

The country accepted Reagan's redistribution scheme and the vast increase in the national debt that accompanied it. A moralistic fervor came over much of America, along with a revival of religious fundamentalism. The waste of time by the poor corroborated the idea of the waste of money on the poor. The idea of the internal cause of poverty was firmly entrenched in the mind of the American public; all it lacked was codification and a name for the turpitude of the poor. It was time for the underclass.

Auletta, along with *Time*, supplied the word and the description. Auletta codified the underclass, dividing it into four parts: passive, hostile, hustlers, and traumatized. No one asked whether hustlers were hostile or the traumatized were passive. It was tabloid sociology, but Auletta had delivered exactly what the market wanted: a basis for dismantling whatever was left of the social programs that had been swept into the category called the War on Poverty.

He got some help from Nicholas Lemann in an article on the underclass in *The Atlantic* in which Lemann claimed that the underclass was made up largely of poor blacks who had come up from the South. According to Michael B. Katz and others, Lemann was not quite correct about the persistence of poverty. In fact, he was off by one-hundred eighty degrees; recent black migrants from the South were doing better on average than blacks who had been born in the North. In their view, Lemann had added another misperception to the stereotype. My own view is that there are many instances to support both Lemann's and Katz's arguments. The important point is that plantation life had simply ended and no effort had been made to bring the plantation families into the public, political life. Welfare took on the role and the character of plantation life.

If the notion of the underclass grew out of the work of men of pretty good intentions, Auletta made it clear in 1984 that he would no longer be counted among such men. He joined Nathan Glazer in praise of a new book about the poor: Charles Murray's *Losing Ground*.

In *Losing Ground,* Murray begins by describing the situation of the poor in 1950. He quotes a *Harper's* piece by Robert L. Heilbroner, in which the Harvard economist described the problem of poverty in America. Thirty percent of the population was poor, according to Heilbroner. Murray puts the actual number of poor people at 45 million, works out the total costs for all entitlement programs, including Social Security, AFDC, and unemployment insurance, and says that it came to an annual expenditure of $250 dollars per poor person (in 1980 dollars). Murray then jumps to 1968, when the unemployment rate was 3.6 percent, which was considered full employment. He points out that inflation had averaged only 1.6 percent during the preceding nine years, but that the country had suffered the terrible riots of 1968, and was, as he put it, "hysterical," demanding the creation of 2 million new jobs.

Murray next looks at the poverty statistics for the period 1968–80. In 1968, he says, the poverty rate was 13 percent. In 1980, it was still 13 percent, yet during the preceding "12 years, our expenditures on social welfare quadrupled."

He sums up the change from 1950 to 1980: "Overall, civilian social welfare costs increased by twenty times from 1950 to 1980, in constant dollars. During the same period, the United States population increased by half."[13]

The statistics were hardly necessary. In the first chapter of the book, Murray made his point: There are the poor and the undeserving poor, and the burden of the rich has always been to judge these wretches, to decide which are the "involuntary" poor and which are "taking advantage of the community's generosity." Murray must have been overjoyed at reading Auletta's book, for Auletta had relieved much of the moral problem of judging the poor, condemning them to a special, despicable class of persons. Murray was empowered to made the next move. He found the reason behind the degenerate character of the poor: welfare!

Step by step, from the misguided and misunderstood theories of Oscar Lewis, through the unfortunate view of poverty Michael Harrington drew out of Lewis's work, to the underlying message of the War on Poverty, to the market-driven response of Auletta, a new case for the moral superiori-

[13] Charles Murray, *Losing Ground* (New York: Basic Books, 1984), p. 14.

ty of the rich came together. Murray relieved his fellow judges of any future guilt for the suffering of the poor by arguing that the more help the poor received, the more despicable they became.

Murray's arguments were based largely on statistics. If he wanted to know anything about poor individuals, he could always refer to the pimps, prostitutes, criminals, cheats, and drug addicts presented by Lewis, Liebow, and Auletta. Underlying Murray's views in this book, we have since learned, was the conviction that the native intelligence of blacks is inferior to that of whites. But that was to come later.

In 1987, long before Murray's race theories were published, William Julius Wilson put forward the idea of *The Truly Disadvantaged*. He had first spoken of an underclass in *The Declining Significance of Race* in 1980, defining it as "the very bottom of the economic hierarchy . . . not only includ(ing) those lower-class workers whose income falls below the poverty level but also the more or less permanent welfare recipients, the long-term unemployed, and those who have dropped out of the labor market." He went on to describe the adult males with no fixed addresses and the female-headed households in his version of the underclass.[14] But the most important point about his definition is that it is non-threatening, a class of people who suffer rather than a despicable class. The shift from moral turpitude to suffering is no small distinction.

By the time he wrote his second book, Wilson had rethought his definition of the underclass, essentially including the same threatening elements that had been part of the conservative definitions of Auletta, et al. He began the book by arguing with his liberal colleagues about the underclass, accusing them of (1) avoidance of unflattering or stigmatizing behavior; (2) refusal even to use the term; (3) emphasis on evidence that denies its existence; and (4) blaming it all on racism. On the other hand, he said the conservative argument "represents little more than the application of the late Oscar Lewis's culture-of-poverty arguments to the ghetto underclass."[15]

---

[14] W. J. Wison, *The Declining Significance of Race* (Chicago: University of Chicago Press, 1980), p. 156.

[15] W. J. Wilson, *The Truly Disadvantaged* (Chicago: University of Chicago Press, 1987), pp. 3–19. Wilson's arguments about racism are hard to follow. He says that racism is not the cause of poverty, but then he produces a view of poverty as a black ghetto problem.

One of his arguments against racism as the cause of poverty is that black employers are as unlikely as whites to hire people from the black ghettos. But what if white employers as well as blacks were unlikely to hire people from the white ghettos? The question, of course, is absurd: There are no white ghettos comparable to those in which blacks or Latinos live in the United States. Racism is not the sole cause of poverty, but it is one of the most effective of the forces that surround the poor.

In 1990, speaking as president of the American Sociological Association, Wilson changed his mind again. He no longer favored the use of the term or the concept "underclass." By 1995, he had moved away from the cultural aspects of the truly disadvantaged, by whom he meant inner-city blacks, to the problem of structural unemployment, not only in America but in the world. The idea of an external cause of poverty had not been heard for decades outside of a few left-liberal journals and an occasional book. If it was to regain currency, Wilson was an ideal champion. He had shown himself a thoughtful, serious man, and he certainly had the academic credentials.

In *When Work Disappears* (1996), the book that Wilson had worked on with a large research staff in Chicago, he pointed to the Works Progress Administration (WPA) of Franklin Delano Roosevelt as a solution to poverty. Unfortunately, the WPA did not end the Great Depression, although it did provide work and income for many people. Wilson failed to recognize, however, that poverty during the Great Depression was understood as absolute: Roosevelt gave the poor to understand that the entire nation was suffering. At the end of the century, poverty in America is more relative than at any other time in recent history. Moreover, the emphasis on marketing required now to keep the economy afloat exerts enormous force on the poor, such that paying wages below the poverty level today and during the Great Depression will not have the same effect. The manipulation of desire and the allure of the world as constructed by salespeople heightens the sense of lack among the poor. The shame of not having goods—a problem for those in the economic middle—is a terrible chronic pain for the poor: To apply the rules of 1936 to 1996 is anachronistic.

Unlike advocates of workfare, however, Wilson sees the unemployment problem as largely structural, although his work still leaves the impression of poverty as a black, urban problem. Wilson apparently arrived at that conclusion a priori or he would not have limited his study to minority neighborhoods in Chicago. By doing so he could not help but contribute to the theory of an internal cause, an underclass or "culture of poverty," even though he had finally come down against both of these notions.

Michael B. Katz published his answer to the idea of an internal cause of poverty in 1989. Three years later, in what had begun to seem like a debate between internal and external views, Mickey Kaus made the case for the conservatives once again in *The End of Equality*. Kaus was not satisfied with anecdotal information about the underclass; he had numbers. Quoting a 1986 estimate by the economist Kip Viscusi, Kaus said that 25 percent of the money earned by young ghetto men comes from crime.

Kaus did not say how a ghetto was defined or who lived in ghettos, but it was easy enough to divine what he meant: blacks. To get himself off the racist hook, he added a curious comment about the number: "That's less than many stereotypes would have it."

In a book based on secondary and tertiary sources, Kaus finally comes to the kind of Draconian solution available only to people who do not know whom they are talking about: An end to all welfare payments and ". . . an offer of employment for every American citizen over eighteen who wants it, in a useful public job at a wage slightly below the minimum wage for private sector work."

It is an offer worth considering. If a man with a wife and two children needs $15,600 a year (1996) to equal the federal poverty level (figure almost half again that much in New York, San Francisco, Boston, and so on) and Kaus thinks he should be *entitled* to about $4 an hour for his labor, give or take a few cents, what Kaus is actually saying is that the family is entitled *only* to a little more than half of the federal poverty level, which is one third of what it would take to live at the same level in New York or San Francisco.[16] He tries to sell the idea by saying that additional money would be supplied by the government "to ensure that every American who works full-time has enough money to raise a normal-sized family with dignity, out of poverty." Then he explains what would happen to people who do not accept the jobs offered to them: "—you don't get paid. Simple."

Kaus offers no definition of a "normal-sized" family and he does not say what he means by dignity. He does not even take full credit for the idea, reminding the reader that Senator Russell Long of Louisiana and "straitlaced Republican economist Arthur Burns" put forward similar proposals in the past.

If living above the real poverty line defined a life of dignity, at least in economic terms, the government would have to supplement a minimum-wage job in New York City with over a thousand dollars a month, which is probably not what Kaus had in mind.

But it isn't the money, Kaus avers. "You're offering work itself." And should those people whom he wants to have the moral pleasure of "work itself" not accept jobs at starvation wages —although with some undetermined government supplement—and actually come close to starving, Kaus leaves the burden of keeping them and their children alive to "charitable organizations."[17]

---

[16] In 1996, it took $7.80 an hour to meet the federal poverty level. Add 50 percent for the cost of living in New York, San Francisco, etc., and the rate comes to $11.70 an hour. I am not accounting for either earned income credits or payroll taxes. The poverty level will, of course, have been adjusted upward by the time this book is published.

[17] See Mickey Kaus, *The End of Equality* (New York: Basic Books, 1992), pp. 125–128.

The whole idea would be easy to dismiss as mere foolishness, if it were not for the fact that governors and legislators around the country hold similar views, some of them learned perhaps from Kaus.

Another conservative view followed in 1994 from Thomas Sowell: *Race and Culture*. His ideas, which had been published before and were well known, had been neatly summed up and opposed to liberal views by Christopher Jencks in 1992 in *Rethinking Social Policy*, but it is worth reprising Sowell's ideas here, because they have been used so often to oppose affirmative action programs.[18]

Sowell says that victims of racial discrimination often end up richer than those who discriminated against them. He cites Jews, Irish, and Asians as examples, merely repeating the error Glazer and Moynihan made in their first version of *Beyond the Melting Pot* (1963) by applying the behavior of other groups, who suffered less discrimination and had a different history, to blacks, Latinos, and poor whites from Appalachia, as well as parts of Eastern Europe and Italy.

Then he argues that discrimination is too expensive for a capitalist economy—a theory that does not quite correlate with the economic history of the United States in this hemisphere or South Africa on that continent or Japan in the Pacific, all countries that became wealthy while discriminating against minorities.

Finally, he claims that government efforts to eliminate discrimination do more harm than good, because they do not help the truly poor blacks, only the members of the middle class. And here history would seem to support his view, at least in part. Government efforts, of course, helped many poor blacks to move up into higher economic brackets, but the very poor have been left out.

To conclude from this that government actions cannot help is not correct, for it is but one of several possible conclusions that can be reached based on the evidence. A more likely reason for the failure of government to help the very poor is the paucity of effort, beginning with the minuscule amount of money that has been put against the problem.

Some of the arguments in Sowell's *Race and Culture* verge on the ridiculous. The real thesis of the book is that ethnic stereotyping is correct: Jews are in the rag trade, Chinese are shopkeepers, Italians are fishermen, Scots are doctors. He does not have the stereotypes quite right, in the way that people who come to a language late in life get the clichés wrong, but he does his best with a dangerous idea. Culture persists, according to Sowell, no matter what the material conditions.

---

[18] See Thomas Sowell, *Race and Culture* (New York: Basic Books, 1994).

Sowell's theory, which argues that the economic life of people of the same culture would be roughly similar, cannot account for the 13 percent of Jewish families in New York who live at or below 150 percent of the federal poverty line when Jews as a group have a very high average household income. Nor would it account for the high economic status of Irish Catholics on average, but the great disparity between the richest and poorest quintiles among them. In fact, his theory would have some difficulty accommodating the existence of Thomas Sowell, an American of African descent, when African Americans have a high percentage of their number living in poverty.[19]

On the other hand, Sowell offers some astonishing insights. On slavery, for example, he has discovered that people who were freed before the Civil War did better than those who were enslaved.

In 1994, Charles Murray of the American Enterprise Institute and Richard J. Herrnstein, a member of the faculty of Harvard University until his death, published an 845-page racist tract, *The Bell Curve*. Preceding the publication of the book, Murray appeared on the cover of the *New York Times Magazine*. His work was greeted with a grand symposium in *The New Republic*, beginning on page 9 and ending on page 37. The *New York Times Book Review* gave it 2 and 2/3 pages, leavening it slightly by including two other books in the review. In the *New York Review of Books*, Charles Lane, using some material unearthed by Michael Lind, connected Murray and Herrnstein's research to *The Mankind Quarterly*, which Lane characterized as "a notorious journal of 'racial history' founded, and funded, by men who believe in the genetic superiority of the white race." Lane counted seventeen references in Bell and Herrnstein's bibliography to people with connections to the quarterly. In all, he noted, their work was cited more than ninety times in *The Bell Curve*.

Debate over Murray's theories went on for months while the book remained on best-seller lists everywhere. With the publication of *The Bell*

---

[19] Jencks uses statistics gathered by the National Opinion Research Center showing that over the period 1972–89, English-speaking Mexicans and Puerto Ricans had lower household incomes than African Americans. By 1995, the percentage of Latinos living in poverty was higher than that of blacks, according to the Census Bureau, but immigration may account for some of the problem of low income among Latinos.

The statistical difference between blacks and Latinos, is complicated by two factors: Some blacks are also Latinos, and within both the Latino communities and the general society light-skinned Latinos generally do better economically than Latinos with more African or Indian features, carrying on a pattern of unfairness set by the Spaniards in the sixteenth century.

In general, it appears that the Latino community, like the black community, is splitting into distinct socioeconomic groups, with those who have developed a political life as a way out of the surround of force managing to break even or win at the game of modern society.

Curve, Murray had at last given the underclass theory a scientific basis: Blacks were simply inferior. Where Sowell's cultural arguments against affirmative action had not convinced, Murray's "scientific" argument did. There is no way to know what went on in the minds of legislators and university trustees in California and other states, but it seems reasonable to think that Murray's rewriting of what had been a commonly accepted view among civilized persons of the equality of all human beings had its effect.

The philosophical implications of Murray's thesis cannot be overestimated. For example, if blacks are not equal to whites, do they or should they have the same rights, according to natural law? Or if blacks have one of the highest percentages of poor people of any large defined group, is it not simply a result of their natural endowments or lack thereof, and therefore beyond remedy?[20] Or if there are fewer blacks in universities, can it be that nature rather than society has done the discriminating and that nature cannot be overturned by legislation, including affirmative action? Or if a third of young black men have some involvement with the prison system, can it be that nature rather than society has chosen this disaster for them, and there is no remedy for it but to build more prisons and incarcerate more young black men? And what of Jurgen Habermas's "ideal speech situation"? Should blacks be allowed to participate, if they are inferior? After all, Habermas calls for equal power among the participants.

Similar implications may hold for Latinos, according to Murray and Herrnstein, although they readily admit that language problems may affect measures of Latino IQ. "With that in mind," they wrote, "it may be said that their test results generally fall about half to one standard deviation below the national mean."[21]

As many readers noted, Murray and Herrnstein have a very difficult scientific problem when it comes to defining race. Lani Guinier, the woman so badly treated by the Clinton administration when conservatives objected to her appointment to a job in the Justice Department, offers a good example of the futility of a work like *The Bell Curve.* Ms. Guinier's father, she said, was African-American; her mother was Jewish. Is Ms. Guinier white, black, Jewish? According to Murray and Herrnstein, European Jews have IQs almost one full standard deviation above the mean, while blacks

---

[20] See chapter 14 of *The Bell Curve* (New York: The Free Press, 1994) for confirmation of Murray's interest in these aspects of behavior. He demonstrates the effects of his thesis by showing that people of higher IQ are less often poor, less often imprisoned, and so on. "Controlling for IQ cuts the poverty differential by 77 percent for blacks and 74 percent for Latinos" (p. 326). "Controlling for IQ cuts the black-white difference in incarceration by almost three-quarters," (p. 338).

[21] Ibid., p. 275. On a normal Bell Curve distribution, one standard deviation below the mean is at the 16th percentile. Two standard deviations below the mean is at the 2nd percentile.

fall below the mean. Would that make Ms. Guinier, on average, average? Given her academic credentials, Jewish genes must be dominant.

David Unger, a bright young translator and literary critic, is a European Jew, born and raised in Central America. Is he a Jew or a Latino? What shall we expect from the children of marriages between black Americans and Vietnamese?

For the last year or so I have been working with a group of prisoners in a maximum-security prison. My teaching assistant there is a person with fair skin and some African ancestry; black or white? In prison, but with an exceptionally high IQ.

The Murray-Herrnstein thesis does not seem useful or even credible in such cases. There would be something verging on the comic about their idea were it not that it can be used as validation for the existence of an underclass, a genetics of poverty, if you will, and an attack on the universality of natural rights. Like nothing else, Murray's tainted research points to an internal cause of poverty. And despite its flaws, it has, so far, been able to outshout solid evidence to the contrary.

For example, when researchers for the federal Centers for Disease Control and Prevention and Emory University reported on mild mental retardation and poverty, hardly anyone noticed the contention of the author of the paper, Dr. Carolyn Drews, that the study "knocked down arguments that race plays a bigger role than preventable socioeconomic problems in intelligence." About 400 words were devoted to the topic on page A17 of the *New York Times* on March 31, 1995. Following its policy of seeking balance in such stories, the *Times* also mentioned *The Bell Curve* and its argument.

In the end, the men of pretty good intentions, despite the work of such people as Carolyn Drews, have won out, if only for the moment. The idea of an internal cause of poverty is now widely accepted in America. Irresponsible schemes, like that of Mickey Kaus, have captured the imagination of lawmakers in the post-Reagan era. The notion of an underclass is firmly established in the American consciousness. In 1996, after Congress passed the Welfare Reform Bill completely eliminating such "entitlements" as Aid to Families with Dependent Children, Mickey Kaus published an Op-Ed piece in the *New York Times* (Aug. 9) in which he argued that the bill "spells the end of Gingrichism" and will therefore "set the stage for a revival of liberalism and . . . public faith in government." He went on to describe the reaction of E. J. Dionne in *The Washington Post* ("The bill simply says, we give up") as "absurd."

On the question of social justice the battle between the liberals, as exemplified by Dionne, and the reactionaries, like Kaus, has not been so clear for a very long time.

Herbert Gans may have overstated somewhat the dangers of labeling per se, but his idea deserves more attention than it has received so far. The problem of definition by the other cannot be discounted. Among the forces that complete the surround in which the poor live and die in America, none injures them more than the diptych of distorting mirrors; one fashioned by men of pretty good intentions, the other by the coldly conservative, including those who believe in the genetic injustices of the Creator.

In a time when campuses are turned into riot and presidents of universities are brought down by a word or phrase considered dangerous to the sensibilities of any group of persons, such news must be considered devastating. To be an underclass, of insufficient intelligence, morally corrupt, an unwanted breeder of unwanted children, born to lose in the game of America, cannot be an easy burden. Yet the poor have learned well; they have located the problem in themselves, becoming the truest believers in the concept of an underclass. They say it again and again, like a mantra: "I'm shit, I'm a piece of shit." And worse: "I'm nothin. I ain't shit!"

It took a long time, for the word came by indirection and implication, in codes and misunderstandings. But that is how the news got to the poor that they were not beautiful and that God did not love them.

XI.

The Fallacy of Work

B Y NOON, ONE OF MY HANDS was beginning to bleed where the skin had been rubbed off the little pad of flesh on the palm just below the forefinger. Some of the other men, those who had not been warned, were already smoking dope or taking long draughts of wine to cover the pain. I had not come to that point yet. I was young and I had a pair of rough gray leather gloves to keep the ropes from cutting into my flesh. A joint smoked at noon got me to the two-thirty break, and another joint got me through to the end of the day.

We were paid daily, $8.40 gross, for going down to the third sub-basement of Union Station to drag sacks of mail across a wooden platform to the proper cart, then to push, throw, kick, or drop the sacks over the edge of the platform onto the cart. The only way to drag them was by the loose end of the rope used to tie the tops of the sacks closed, and the heavier the sack, the more deeply the ropes cut into our hands. The worst day was Thursday, when sacks of *Life* magazine were dumped down the chute to us. The sacks weighed sixty pounds, and there were hundreds of them.

In the time I worked there, I seldom saw the same man two days in a row. We rarely spoke. I learned only one man's full name; for most of us not even a nickname was said. The foreman spoke to us by pointing or by description: "You! With the fireman's gloves," or: "You! With the specs."

The character of most of the men was easily observed. You could smell the drunks, the potheads had a touch of style, and the real addicts were usually too sickly or malnourished to get through the day. The unidentifiable men, according to my only acquaintance, were either ex-cons or just unlucky. His advice was to stay away from the unlucky ones. "They'll bring you down," he said.

In all, we were probably the most unsavory group of workingmen in Chicago: stinking and grumbling, shuffling across the floor worn smooth and shining by the canvas sacks; blacks, the dourest Mexicans I ever saw, and a lot of bedraggled whites, mostly Eastern European by the look and sound of them. If the men had any feeling for each other, it was hatred: the drunks hated the junkies, the blacks hated the whites, the whites hated the blacks, everyone hated the Mexicans; the young hated the old, the old hated the young; there were even open animosities between the short and the tall, the fat and the lean.

When the men brushed against each other as they dragged the sacks across the platform, they glowered, grunted, "Watchit" or "Lookout," but never did I hear a man say, "Excuse me," or "Pardon me."

The work was probably not as difficult as chopping cotton or shoveling coal, and it was less demanding physically, but it was more lonely, silent, and without a common enemy to unite us.

Work is not life, I learned on that platform, nor does it structure a life or set it in time and place. If we replace the word "work" with the more accurate name for most kinds of work, "labor," some of the false promise of work disappears. Work is not a home for most people in America, it is merely labor—often repetitive, rarely interesting, sometimes dangerous, usually not well paid.

My coworkers in the third sub-basement could not build their lives around work; instead, they worried and schemed about avoiding it. Work for them existed on a level comparable to ingestion and excretion. Unlike happiness or even virtue, such activities belonged as well to animals and even vegetables as to humans. Work life bore no relation to human life. As a solution to the moral problems of the wretched men in the third sub-basement, it failed.

Even so, common sense would argue that work provides a defense against hunger; after all, what is the purpose of work, if not to supply the basic needs of life . . . and perhaps a little more? Virtually every person, left or right, who makes policy for the poor takes the position a priori that work is what is needed. Work has become the common-sense solution to the problem of poverty in America.

Work! The word has a good, solid, Old English sound. It is as blunt as the Protestant Ethic, as stern as a strap, as good as gruel on an icy morning. Work! Verb or noun, it grunts the old values, before Marx and FDR, before babies having babies and rock 'n' roll. Work is what good people do. And its opposite is sin: Sloth! Idle hands. . . . Welfare queens.

Work is not only good for the pocketbook, it soothes the soul and brings order to the mind. "Work itself," said Mickey Kaus, not money, but work itself will cure the poor of their moral ailments and rid the nation of the welfare system. Work itself, the slogan of the Protestant Ethic, has caught the imagination of Americans. Everyone in power in America has heard the message. The President of the United States wanted to "end welfare as we know it." The chain gang, that sermon in the southern sun, has come back.[1] The governor of Wisconsin has experimented with forcing people to work by making the alternative unbearable; other governors have similar plans. Workfare is a national craze, like the mambo or the macarena. At the end of the twentieth century, work is the popular response of God and man to both the bleating and the rage of the poor.

But what of the Weedens? By working nights on a gambling boat anchored off Greenville, Mississippi, he earns a little over the minimum wage. She works, too. And they have devised a schedule that spares them the cost of child care. How is it that they have been so badly beaten in the game of American life? What moral flaw has thrown them into the surround of force?

Work does not guarantee the Weedens even a steady diet of rice and beans augmented with pork fat and bread. The problem for them, like most of the working poor, is that there are many hungers. After the Weedens pool their wages, they simply do not have enough to live on. Take the rent, the electric bill, the child support payment, the mandatory school uniforms, gasoline, shoes, soap, toothpaste, medicine, socks, and underwear out of Robert and Barbara Weeden's $1,100 monthly net income, and what is left for food? A hundred dollars a week to feed six people? They have never had that much.[2]

---

[1] Alabama, the first state to use the chain gang again, stopped the practice in June, 1996.

[2] Their annual net income of $13,200 (their earnings minus Social Security, Workmens Comprehensive Insurance, child support, etc.) left the Weedens well below the federal poverty line, which was $15,600 for a family of four in 1996. The increase in the minimum wage passed in 1966 would not be sufficient to bring the Weedens out of poverty.

A response to this problem of the working poor has begun on the local level. In Baltimore, Milwaukee, Santa Clara County in California, and other local jurisdictions, a "living-wage movement" has led to raised minimum wages for a small number of employees of city or county contractors to $6 an hour and up, according to the New York Times (April 9, 1996). In most

A budget so divided makes the final hunger a controlling force, not only on the day when the last item in the pantry has been eaten, but on all the other days leading up to the crisis. A budget attempts to reduce the pain by spreading it out over all the days. In that way, hunger takes only a little from the plate every day, but hunger takes it every day, even the day when the restaurant or the clothing factory or the fish-processing plant or the lady of the house passes out the checks.

The work ethic belongs in the realm of theory; it proposes that the world conform to an abstraction: work for its own sake. The theoreticians of the work ethic claim this abstraction has divine inspiration and high moral purpose, but in reality it is a strategy for playing the game of modern society. Whatever its genesis, moral or economic, the work ethic is intended to modify the behavior of those who have fallen from equality and to increase the gap between winners and losers.

In order to put the theory of the work ethic into practice, its champions have been forced by the secular nature of America at the end of the century to abandon much of the argument of divine inspiration that was so useful in earlier centuries, and turn instead to self-interest and common sense. The common-sense argument for work is that it will provide an adequate economic and social life for a person and his or her family. But in many cases it does not.

Since the theory of the work ethic has such currency again in America, especially as a cure-all for the problems of the poor, it is imperative that the social, economic, and moral character of work be considered from the point of view of the poor rather than from the God's eye-view of the makers of theory. It may be that "work itself" does not solve the problem of poverty when the rules of the game are so well known as in contemporary America. Work itself may not offer a way out of the surround or the means to survive within it. Perhaps the poor are unable to work or do not know how to work; life in the surround may teach habits of reaction to force that put the political world of work beyond the reach of the poor.

Economic questions about work are not new. Karl Marx wrote about the value of labor and who got to enjoy it, and labor unions organized workers by teaching politics and economics to people whose jobs were still conducted according to the ancient rule of capitalism, which was to pay the

---

instances, so far, the minimums apply only to direct contractors, not to their suppliers. In one city the minimums are in effect only for contractors to the school district.

The living-wage movement was spurred by the Industrial Areas Foundation (IAF) and churches affiliated with it. The IAF, begun by Saul Alinsky, is a politically liberal, often socially conservative, organization, operating in both urban and rural areas throughout the United States.

workers only as much as was necessary to keep them alive so they could continue to work.

Marx's labor theory of value does not explain much in a world of global outsourcing of labor and other kinds of international competition, but the effect of unions on the lives of working people may be an important clue to the failure of work itself to solve the problems of poverty. A union is first a political, then an economic organization; without its political basis, a union could not conduct collective bargaining. Although it is almost always an economic issue that opens people to the process of political organizing, collective bargaining cannot begin without a collective.

The lives of the working poor raise several questions about the work ethic in contemporary America: Who is served by the work ethic? Does work performed for other people, even if the work is not done alone, constitute a political life? Or is work, in the case of the poor, those at the bottom of the dual labor market, another force in the enclosing surround? Current theories of the value of "work itself" impose work on the poor; these theories assume that the imposition of work will be an act of force, necessary for an unruly mob of poor people. Can people who already live according to the rules of force accept work under such conditions as anything other than more force, adding to a vicious circle—force, reaction, force, reaction, force—in which the moral character of satisfying work can have no role?

The rest of this chapter, until the very end, takes place within the surround of force, among people who work. At the end, it should be possible to see how work and the work ethic fit into the structure of the lives of the poor, using the resulting concept not as theory but as another piece of the real world.

1. Christian Friends

Sleeping Arrangements:

She waited for him. He would come for her, she knew, but she did not know when. At night, she lay on the old brown couch beside the front door, with two tire irons beside her, tucked into the narrowness, or clasped to her bosom. She kept the gun in her bedroom, where the girls would not find it.

She did not sleep easily. She woke up often, her arms flailing, the tire irons in her hands. She had nightmares, chainsaw dreams.

The House:

The moment she saw the wreckage of the house, she started making plans. It was the worst house on the street in the worst part of Sand Springs. Weeds had grown chest-high in the yards front and back, the windows were all broken or missing, the front steps had rotted out, the roof leaked. And inside it was worse. The appliances were gone or destroyed, some of the doors had been torn off the hinges and taken away, the thin layer of carpeting in the front room was black with filth, and what little paint was left on the walls was coming off in chips and cracks and curls.

She told the landlord she wanted to "rent to own." He agreed to let her stay all summer without paying rent, then in October to begin paying $150 a month for the next twenty-two years. For $39,600, the house would be hers.

Toni Sherred began working on the house the day she moved in. By late summer she had repaired the roof and all the windows but one. The frame was missing from that one, and she did not know how to fix it. She taped and tacked a piece of thick plastic over the hole. The rug had been a problem, too. She had shampooed it twice, and it was just beginning to show the color under the blackness—brown. Or was it maroon? After the next cleaning, she would know.

She bought the living-room and bedroom furniture at junk shops, and she stole a kitchen stove.

When winter came to the weary suburb of Tulsa, she and the girls would be warm and dry.

A Telephone Call:

It had come the day before, in the evening, after she got off work at the supermarket. "Toni?"

He identified himself as one of her husband's friends. "He owes six thousand dollars," the caller said, "maybe eight thousand. He run the bill up in a month. There's seven guys out to kill him.

"Toni, you better watch out for your car because he'll probably steal it. His truck's been stole.

"You better watch the guys that's after him, because they'll break down the door to come in and see if he's there, because they think he's stayin at your house."

What Her Mother Said:

"I wish you had been an abortion," she often said to Toni, but never to the younger girls. She did not blame her marriage to a poor, drunken, abusive truck driver on them.

Aunt Jane:

She comforted her favorite niece with cocaine. At the age of thirty-three, when she had a good job and a profitable business dealing drugs, Aunt Jane put a four ten shotgun in her mouth and pulled the trigger.

"All I got left is a headstone," Toni said.

The Grand Farm and the Pig Farm:

Before Toni was born, in a vague place, far from Oologah, where a few hundred people lived beside the lake, her grandparents had owned a great farm, which made them very rich. Toni had never seen the farm, for her grandparents were old when she was born, but she had constructed it very carefully in her mind, making fields of words and cash crops as indestructible as dreams.

Her parents had left Oologah, Oklahoma, for a pig farm in Wyoming, but it bore no resemblance to the grand farm her grandparents had owned. Her parents did not get rich; the pig farm did not even produce enough money for them to live on.

When Toni stayed with them, she worked as a cashier to help pay the bills at the pig farm. They always asked her for money; she thought of them that way, demanding money from her, wanting her only when she could give them money.

Jack Dallas Sherred:

He could be so sweet! Smooth-talking, dark, and crazy, with a cross tattooed over his heart. He was in the Tulsa County Jail when she met him. She agreed to speak to him, she said to the friend who made the introductions over the telephone, because "I like to meet people. I am a jolly person."

After their first conversation, he telephoned her every day. Three months later, she went to visit him. "It was love at first sight," she said.

For his twenty-first birthday, she spent $500 to send him Levis and shoes and shirts and biker's gloves and cards and lots of little things, intimate things that might one day become the memories of which lasting connections are made.

When he got out of jail, he did not telephone her.

Romance:

She languished until she found him. And then she implored him. She made him gifts of things, she made him the gift of herself. He took what she gave him.

Killing:

"You gotta do something. If he kills me, I'm the one that's innocent. If I kill him, I'm the one that's gonna go to jail."

The Girls:

In Oologah, between Aunt Jane's suicide and the telephone call to Dallas, she gave birth to her first child, who came into the world to be blue-eyed, clean of limb, blond, pretty, slim, and deaf. After Tanya, she had two children by Dallas. Jesse, whose head was surrounded by thick curls of dark brown hair, and little Jennette, who was darker than the other girls and not yet pretty. Tanya had entered the age of neatness, Jesse had taken to flirtation and touching, and Jennette rolled in dirt and waddled in conformance to the impediment of a diaper.

Toni believed that Tanya had saved her from cocaine, then Jesse had saved her from alcohol, and finally, Jennette, born when the vices had been shed, became her greatest supporter. "I am thankful to Dallas," she said, "for the two beautiful girls that me an him had together and makin me finally admit my daughter is deaf, because I was in a denial stage, but he got me out of it."

The Good Woman:

She cooked three meals a day so that he would not have to take sandwiches to his job. When he came home at night, she had his bathwater running.

She scrubbed him from head to toe and rubbed him dry and massaged him; she did whatever he desired, because he was her husband.

Beatings:

Her father beat her, the men she knew before she met Dallas beat her; she said she thought it was the way of the world of men and women.

Dallas beat her eight times in one week. He strangled her until she lost consciousness. After she gave birth to her last child, when she still felt the staples inside her, he came home drunk and raging, and put a chainsaw to her throat. While the older girls watched, he started up the motor. She thinks he would have killed her if the chain had not snapped.

Despite the beatings, she stayed with him. When he was sober, he was good to her, dark and a little crazy, but smooth and terrifying.

Whenever she found work, he came around the office or the store and harassed her. He believed she had affairs with her bosses. She smiled too much, she talked too much, she was too much the jolly person. He made scenes, threats; she lost the jobs.

One night, at the beginning of summer, he turned on Tanya. He beat her, and then he picked her up and threw her against a wall. That was the end. Toni threw him out, and to keep him out she got a restraining order. A Legal Services lawyer took her case; she had found an ally.

Then the telephone calls began. He was shooting cocaine and crank (amphetamines), and he said he was coming to kill her. She called her ally at Legal Services, she called the police. There was nothing to do but wait.

He had killed before, when he was still a juvenile. When he threatened her, she did not doubt him.

Chelsea:

Because of him, she had run away to the pig farm her parents had bought in Wyoming. And she came back because of him, because he said he would go up to Wyoming and burn down the pig farm if she did not come home.

She went first to Chelsea, near Oologah Lake and the coal patch, in the midst of the hills where she had smoked marijuana and snorted cocaine, where she was happiest being close to water, under the stars.

She would have stayed there, but she could not find work, and she was not the kind of person who went on welfare. She had good friends in Chelsea, Christian friends. They even co-signed a loan for her.

Rick:

He went to her house to claim a stove he said she had stolen from him. They came to see it as a misunderstanding, something comic in her difficult life. Rick was a Christian, hardworking, twenty years old, and he wanted to take charge of her life. The second time they met, he carried flowers in his hand. She wept, for no one had ever brought her flowers before.

Evening:

It began with pizza, 7-Up, and albums filled with photographs. Toni, Tanya, and I sat on the couch, eating and looking at the pictures. Jesse stood in front of us, teasing, rolling on the floor, the middle child, a demanding coquette— funny, barefoot, with dimpled cheeks and thick curls.

Tanya turned the pages of the album until she came to a picture of Dallas. He wore no shirt, displaying a thin, flatly muscular torso, with two blue lines in the shape of a cross tattooed above his left nipple. He had drunken eyes, red-rimmed and narrowed, and he wore a strange smile, cruel and yet disinterested, like bitterness.

A noise came from Tanya, a deaf child's attempt at speech. She pointed to the picture and made the sound again. "Dallas?" I asked, as if she could hear.

She slapped the picture with her open hand, then again. Then she growled, as if to say hatred, upset the album onto the floor, and ran away into the bedroom.

Jennette, the baby, fell down on the floor, screaming.

It took a long time for Toni to arrange the household again, coaxing Tanya back from the bedroom, signing furiously to her, picking up the baby, touching Jesse's back, her halo of curls. A radio played somewhere in the house. We seated ourselves in order on the couch again. She opened the album to her wedding pictures. "I wore blue jeans," she said, "to show that I didn't want to get married. His mom and dad made us get married. We had been living together four years. They made me get married, because they're the rulers of you. But I wore blue jeans."

We heard a knock at the door. Her eyes narrowed. She put the album from her. The tire irons leaned against the wall, between the end of the couch and the door. She stepped in front of the girls, shielding them from the door. The tire irons were close at hand.

"It's Rick," he said through the door.

A sturdy young man came in, short and thick like Toni, but quicker, aggressive, taking short steps with his arms held wide in a wrestler's walk. He greeted everyone, declined a slice of pizza, and went through the kitchen, into the backyard. We heard the engine of the "weed-eater" start up.

We had started to look at the album again when we heard a horn blowing outside. Toni recognized the sound. Her Christian friends had arrived from Chelsea in their red pickup truck. A fat blond woman in a housedress and her husband—a tall, thin man, with long, greasy hair and eyeglasses—got out of the cab. He wore red shorts and a yellow muscle shirt. Three children, a boy and a girl about eight or nine years old, and another, younger boy, climbed down from the bed of the truck.

They clambered up onto the square block of cement where Toni and I stood. The woman, whose skin was extremely fair, almost translucent, moved up close to Toni. "I have something to talk to you about," she said. "The loan company called me and they're going to sue on that loan we co-signed for."

"I made the last payment," Toni said. "I went to the Post Office and had them trace the letter. It cost twenty-six dollars to put a tracer on it. I sent them the money order from Pick n' Go. Fifty, ten. It was my fourth payment or my third. I forgot now. It must have been the fourth. Let's see. I got that loan in May. Yes, it was May, because it was Jesse's birthday the day before. So, I paid in June, July, August. It must have been the fourth payment, because this is August and I made it last month."

The people she called her Christian friends moved inside the house. The fat blond woman pressed Toni to find the receipt. Toni went into the kitchen and came out with a big cardboard folder full of papers and began looking through it.

The children of the Christian friends ran through the house, shouting, whirling around the adults, using them as pylons. The oldest boy threw Tanya to the floor. When she tried to speak to him in her incomprehensible voice, he and his sister laughed and taunted her. Jesse ran from room to room shouting. The baby lay crying in a corner. Toni searched through some papers stacked in a cupboard near the couch.

A tall, slim blond girl came in without knocking. She looked like a large version of Tanya, and she, too, was deaf. She tried signing to the Christian woman, who showed no interest. She signed to Tanya, who had gotten up off the floor. Then she spoke to anyone who could hear, talking in the voice of the deaf, explaining with painful effort that she had smashed up her brand-new truck that afternoon, careened off the road into a ditch.

The children ran screaming from room to room. The Christian man and his wife told Toni she had to find the receipt for the payment. They pushed her out of the way and looked for it themselves, pulling papers out of cabinets and drawers, dumping the contents of Toni's purse onto a table, fishing through the spilled contents.

Rick came in carrying a plate of spaghetti and sat in a reclining chair that rested on the floor, its mechanism lost with age or torn away. He folded himself almost double to accommodate his body to the low seat.

The Christian man complained of having no work, his wife said she had been an abused child, and all the while they searched through Toni's house, wilder than thieves. "Where is the receipt? Where is that receipt?" The Christian man said he hoped to be put on at the General Motors plant, not for the money, but to get health insurance and retirement.

Rick got up out of the chair, unfolding his legs and torso. "I must have left the receipt at the Post Office," Toni pleaded. The search went on. The deaf woman said the repairs to her truck would cost $2,060. The Christian boy ran after Tanya and socked her in the face.

Toni said again, now with tears running down her face, that she had probably left the receipt at the Post Office. Rick announced that everyone had to leave; Toni needed rest, she had to go to work in the morning. He gave the order a second time, barking, in a sergeant's voice. Toni gathered up the children and fled to the bedroom.

Rick shut the door and locked it. The house grew quiet; now he was in charge.

2. A Bird in My Hand

On a winter night at the El Paso Evening School the light of the long blue-white fluorescent bulbs entombs the men and women who study there. The weight of the light crushes conversation. There is no laughter in the evening school.

At the break between the hours the students stand outside in the cold, under the starless sky, smoking cigarettes, shivering, more silent than the night.

A boy, nineteen; a girl, seventeen; a woman of thirty. Mothers, fathers, daughters, and sons. Almost all are Latinos—Chicanos, Tejanos, Mejicanos. High school, from seven to eleven in the evening, night after night, for as long as it takes to get a diploma; semesters, years under the weight of the lights.

Some who study there are sure to finish; more are at risk. Of those at risk, one woman, just eighteen years old, came to a small office to talk with me. We sat on metal chairs with plastic seats, facing each other, forced together by the clutter of the office.

In a denim jacket and pants, Norteño style, she had a certain sturdiness, a deception told by the fabric and the cut of the clothes. She had a tiny voice, like a cricket song.

When she was fourteen, she met a boy who made her pregnant and went away. Then she found a job at Burger King, where she met another boy, this one of seventeen, who said he loved her and loved her child. They could not afford even the smallest apartment together, she and her child, and the boy who loved them. They lived at home—she with her parents, he with his. They were married. She gave birth to his child, a girl. Then there were two girls, one more beautiful than the other.

She and the boy loved the girls, but to care for them, they had to work. Every morning, they met at Burger King. She awakened before six to get the children ready for day care. Then she went to work. In the afternoon, when the children were returned from day care, a woman came to the house and stayed with them until she came home from work.

She washed and cooked and cleaned and cared for the children until it was time to go to school. Her mother helped when she could, but she was a sickly woman who worked long hours. It was almost midnight when the girl in blue jeans got home again. She studied for a while, went to sleep, and awakened before six to prepare the children for the day-care van. Then to Burger King and home and school and home to sleep for a few hours before the morning began again in darkness.

Her head and hands trembled. Below her eyes the skin had lost its elasticity. Puffs of darkness lay on her cheekbones. She appeared to have no other flesh beneath her skin, only bone and the gristle that had become her metaphor.

No one knew how long she would last at the school.

When our conversation was over, she put her hand in mine to say good-bye. Her hand had volume but no weight. It was as if I held a tiny bird.

3. Perversity's Children

Something went awry in the moral world of Okeechobee, Florida. It often involves incest, which the residents speak about openly and apparently without shame or even discomfort. Everyone who has lived or worked around Okeechobee knows of this curious flaw, but no one even hazards a guess about what caused it: the heat or isolation, fruit rotting in the sun, the methane stench of the dairy farms, patternless migrations. It cannot be that aberrant people are drawn to Okeechobee as if it were a homeland for deviants, nor can the behavior be attributed to racism or some other form of oppression, for the people in whom the most basic moral sense appears to be missing are white, Christian, and working.

They follow the economic rule of work, which is that work at less than a living wage will not extricate the poor, like Toni Sherred, from the surround of force, and at the same time their deviant behavior denies the long-standing moral rule of the work ethic—ethic meaning habit, as in Aristotle's *Nicomachean Ethics,* which argued that good habits were the way to the *summum bonum.*

At twenty-three, Michele Hoanshalt has entered the last phase of her flower. She will always have the palest eyes, the blue of noon, and her nose will never lose its fraulein's point. She looks a country beauty, a cherub grown up to be a dairy maid, but after a moment or two, something else about her face makes itself known, something subtle, not immediately comprehensible, merely discomfiting, like a chair that rests unevenly on the floor: Her face is asymmetrical. The arrangement of the eyes, the point of the nose, the tiny pucker of the lips, everything is out of kilter by a millimeter or two, as if the sculptor had labored and brought forth a flaw from the stone.

She describes herself as a woman who can go to bars and drink until she cannot remember where she is, the descendant of long lines of alcoholics on both sides. For at least two generations, as many as she knew on her mother's side, they were all the children of single parents, women who learned during World War II how to live without men, and divorced them when they came home after the war. Her father grew up in foster homes. And everyone worked; they always worked, from the time they were children, unless they were laid off or old or on their way to another town.

The Hoanshalts moved south in steps. First, to Virginia, where her father worked in a shipyard and her mother worked at Pizza Hut. Then to South Carolina to live in a trailer, on to Fort Pierce in Florida, and finally to Okeechobee, where he worked in air conditioning and she rose to be the manager of a small office. Everyone in the family works. The Craigs, who have been in Florida and South Georgia for generations, also work. Michele described the moral and economic trajectories of the families:

Me and my dad are closer than me and my mom, even though my mom tells me things she shouldn't, like she was havin an affair at one time. How I found out was I was at Wal-Mart. Me and my mom were shoppin, and I was in the eleventh grade, and this man come up behind her and grabbed her by her waist and hugged her from behind. And she sort of jumped. And

I know the look on my mom's face. I wasn't naive then. I knew about sex, about guys and stuff. She goes, "This is my daughter, Michele." She's never introduced me as "her daughter Michele." It's always, This is Michele or something. To let him know, cool it. She goes, "Here, go get what you need. Pay for your stuff, and go out to the van and wait for me."

I waited, like twenty minutes in the van, and here she comes pullin up in the parkin lot with him, and I was like, "He's only a friend?" and she says, "Yeah."

Well, about a month later, she tells me, and starts bringin me over there when she goes, which really upsets my dad when he found out, cause I went and told my dad.

We had a lot of hard times at the house after that. I tried to commit suicide and I ended up in the hospital for about a week. I didn't want to die, though. I just wanted to escape, leave for a while.

In December of eighty-nine I turned eighteen, and in January I met a guy that my parents don't like. They did at first, but now they don't. I moved out in January, and I moved in with him. We've been together about five years. We don't live together. We did for the first three years. Two years after we were livin together, I got pregnant and had a child.

He's always doin somethin wrong, causing a ruckus, so he got in trouble, violation of probation or something. He went to jail. They took him to Georgia. That's where he's from. And he served his time out there, like a year. I moved in with my parents when he went to jail, and I've been with my parents ever since.

I have a two-year-old little girl, Heather. She looks like her daddy, blond hair, blue eyes, very pretty, very smart, very spoiled. My mom and dad, they spoil her pretty much.

Being a single mother, it sucks. It does. It really does. It's hard, because I only make like a hundred bucks a week here and it seems like I'm here day in and day out every day. I just got a raise. I was here for three months and I got a raise to four fifty.[3] I was making minimum wage, four twenty-five. So I make four fifty an hour here and a third of it goes to my mom, another third of it goes to day care. By the time I pay my bills I have twenty bucks left for the week, so it's like I work all week for twenty dollars. It's kind of depressing, but I have to pay my bills. Eventually one day I'll make more money, hopefully.

When I started, we worked anywhere from twenty to twenty-five hours a week. Now that season's in, I work anywhere from twenty-five to forty. This week I have thirty-seven hours in, and it's the first time I have almost

[3] The conversations took place before the increase in the minimum wage in 1996.

a forty-hour week. But it's better than no job at all. I started workin when I was sixteen and I've been workin ever since.

Who would ever thought that I did crack? I was on it for like four months. I wasn't one of the ones that did it every night or every day. I'd do it every weekend for about a couple months. And then a month later I got to where I'd do it every single day.

When Dale went to prison in Georgia I was real depressed and lonely and all that kind of stuff, so I started datin his cousin TJ. It ain't one of the Craigs. It's a different family. I was smokin pot with him and stuff, and that's how I got on it, from it bein in the pot. Then about two weeks later he said, "Let's do some of this, this is what you been smokin. That's why you like this weed so much."

So, I did it and then I started doin it more and more. And then one day I got up to get ready to go to work and I was shakin real bad and Heather was lookin at me, and she was, like, Mommy, what's wrong with you? And from then on, I've never touched it. I've never been around it.

I didn't know the first couple of times that I was doin crack. I knew it tasted different. It's a different, unique taste. It didn't taste like cocaine, because I've tried that once and I didn't like it at all. I guess because I'm overweight or whatever, and my heart started beatin real fast, plus what I heard in school about it can kill you.

Dale, my boyfriend, he gets like fifty (dollars) a day. That's not much really. He don't work for like a company. He works for a person that owns their own business and they just do jobs here and there in town. He makes a couple hundred dollars some weeks, but most of it goes to his probation.*

He roommates with a friend of his. We're trying to get our own place, but money's real tight right now, we haven't been able to. We got a car, but I haven't got insurance or nothin on it yet, so I can't drive it, because I have to take my little girl in it, and if somethin happens and us not being insured, I don't want nothin to happen.

We argue. Dale says terrible things sometimes, you know, like, "I'm just gon leave, forget all this, f... it! I'm goin back home." And I cry. Or he gets mad at me, and he says, "Shut up, you fat bitch!"

I love him. He had a rough life, really bad, rough life. He was sexually molested. His mother was an alcoholic. She was a single mother. He was doin drugs, hard drugs, at the age of six and seven, and his mother had him out on the street doin things he shouldn't have been doin, sellin drugs, sellin himself, from what I understand.

Dale's mother has eleven children and Dale's the youngest. I don't know

---

* She probably means restitution.

if you've ever heard of the Craigs, that was their last name. They're not a well to like people around here. There's incest, molestation, rape, murder, all that stuff in that family. They grew up on dairies, they was all dairy people. That's why my mom thinks he's like them, but he's not. He has an alcohol problem, but he don't molest anybody or rape anybody. But his mom, she comes from that family, she's a Craig. And I guess that's why all that stuff happened in his family with him.

He was molested when he was six by a man. His mother's brother's child, which was his cousin. He was molested by him. He was gay. This guy molested him and told him he was gay and had Dale believin that. When you're six years old or seven years old, you don't know, you don't know what the difference is, or what's what, so he had Dale believin that until one day Dale was about ten or eleven and Dale was sittin there thinkin, and he's like, "I don't like this. I don't enjoy this." He never had actual sex with him or anything like that. He just had, I don't whatcha call it, oral sex. He'd always do it to him, oral sex with him. And he'd always tell Dale manipulative things, like, "I'm pregnant with your baby. You have to feed the baby."

And his brother, the guy that did this to him, his brother raped his sister and killed her. This was out on Butler's Dairy. These are all the Craigs. They're a really weird family.

I lived with the Craigs when I met Dale. I lived with them for three or four months. It was a totally different type of living than I have ever lived. I've lived, you know, where you don't have money and food isn't the best, but we still have it, but over there people . . . it's nothin to them to sit there and talk about sex in front of a two- or three-year-old little child or have sex in front of a two- or three-year-old little child. The way they talk! They all sleep together! I wasn't raised that way. I was raised it was wrong to do that stuff, and they weren't. It's always been that way for them. They marry each other and all kinds of stuff.

The Lord, sometimes I wonder if there's one really up there. So many bad things happen to too many innocent people. Too many innocent children. Things happen to children that shouldn't happen, like molesting or murdered or killed. I don't understand it. If He's so powerful, why's He lettin this happen?

4. On the Old Plantation

Ike Lane's house in Egremont, Mississippi, sits on the side of a stream into which he dumps raw sewage. When the rains come and the stream runs fast, it drives the sewage downstream, away from his house, but it has been a dry summer. The beans are wilting all around the Delta, the farmers are waiting for rain, and the stream has slowed to a trickle. If it does not rain soon, the untreated sewage from the seventeen people who live in the wooden shell of a house at the end of the gravel road will begin to slow the stream even more, and there will be bad days, evil days until the rains come.

The seventeen people sleep in all the rooms of the house. Ike sits in his chair to the side of the door and looks out the window. The gas heater, cold now in August, sits beside him. The light cords, bulbs attached to long red rubber lines, waterproof lines, the only kind that can be used under the leaking roof, provide some light after dusk. There are no lamps, no over-head lights, just the red rubber industrial cords looped around hooks and hung on the wall outside the kitchen.

Unmade beds occupy every corner of every room. Ike sits on the only exception, his chair beside the window. Everything else becomes a bed.

The girls have been sent home from the first day of school for wearing scanty halter tops, failing to meet the dress code. They sit on one of the beds watching television. The picture on the television set, provided by a cable system, could not be better. It is even better, they say, than the pic-ture that comes in from the satellite dish outside the house.

On the wall above the television set, all the bills and important papers have been carefully arranged in a slotted wooden holder. The girls can easily put their hands on the bills due when the next check comes: The satellite dish costs $49 a month and the cable costs $36. How the salesman convinced them to rent the satellite dish when they had cable service is not open for dis-cussion; the importance of television has been long established in the Lane family.

Ike Lane wears a straw hat with a green cellophane piece in the front of the brim. The green cellophane has come loose on one side, and the hat is dusty and torn here and there, but it is an unusual hat, a treasured hat in this routine world of denim and worn plaids and work shirts.

He wears sandals with no socks. His toenails have grown long and very thick, as strong as talons. Ike aches. His hair has turned gray and he has let the whiskers of age grow on his face for several days now in the terrible heat, the morbid heat of deep summer, the heat so bad they have stopped chopping cotton, waiting for clouds and cooler weather. He smokes and spits and beats the children and grandchildren to keep order in the crowd-ed house when night comes.

He was born in Macomb City, near the Louisiana line. "That's where folks fight and kill and hurt each other every night," he said. "That's the reason I left there. That's a wild place. All through the week they was hurtin, cuttin, shootin, killin one another, and I just didn't want to be in it. I had a aunt live up here on the next place. She got burnt up in a trailer. Caught afire one night, nobody home but her. And that was about the onliest relations I had up here."

He stayed on the plantation and married and worked and raised children, and worked harder and faster and smarter than anybody else who picked cotton by hand, or later, when the machines came in, by cotton-picking machine.

After nearly fifty years on the plantation, he blacked out one day while trying to repair the cotton-picker, and retired to disability. "When I first started here," he said, "they paid a dollar and a half a day, and they raised that up to two dollars a day. Then they said a good worker, the best worker, they was gon give him six dollars a day. An the one that didn't work too good got five dollars a day. I was paid eight dollars a day in 1990, that's all. Whoever picked more cotton on the machine, they were gonna give him one dollar more. So they would buy your lunch and dinner and supper, too, because we picked till nine o'clock at night. I got nine dollars."

Ike, whose real name is Irving, had sixteen children, but most of them have moved south to New Orleans. He stays at home, on plantation land, in this wreck of a house, caring for his grandchildren and great-grandchildren. His children have asked him to come to New Orleans to live with them, but he says, "New Orleans too rough for me. If you can make it, and walk the streets, somebody'll take it."

He plans to stay in Egremont in this house with the leaking roof, with the wind in the winter and the heat in the summer. "They give this house to me, long as I live," he said, "Mister Bob Moses did. Mister Ricky Lee is the boss on the place now." He pays no rent, but the rest of the houses on the row leading from the road to the stream have been abandoned.

"Everybody in this county know me," he said. "They call me Ike, but my name is Irving. The guys they think they bad come up, say, 'Ike, Ike.'

"I say, 'What?'

"They say, 'I need a dollar.'

"I say, 'You know what? I won't give you a dollar, but I beat you till you holler.'"

His reputation in the white world means more to Ike: "They told me in the courthouse (They had my son's trial up there), they say, 'Mister Lane, you the best colored man in this country.' Say, 'We all love you.' I say, 'I love y'all.

"I don't be havin money, but they's a nice white man I used to work for—I thanks him every day and the good Lord—Mister Jimmy Walker, he's a real nice white man. He's known me all my life and he tells me, 'Ike, I never heard nothin bad about you. If you need help some way or somehow, let me know.' I say, 'Yes, sir, I thank you.' I used to cut his yard and keep it clean til my hands foul up on me. And he say, 'Ike, don't worry about tryin to keep the yard clean for me. I see you can't hardly walk or use your hands.' He done me more good than the white man I worked for all these years."

When he needed a substantial amount of money, the whites who loved him did not provide it. "I got some money from a place up here you call Tower Loan," he said, "borrowed it for me an my daughter-in-law. My daughter-in-law got the money an she left here. That put all the bill on me. Last month I had to pay two hundred dollars. That hurt me, cause that was big as I had right there. Then they was gon take my TV, my car, my refrigerator, and everything in the house, cause I missed one month payment.

"I had to go to the doctor, cause I had the pain in my hand, an I had to pay them two hundred dollars for a shot right there.

"Car and TV paid for. Had to get a refrigerator.

"I told them I didn't have the money.

"Said, 'Mister Lane, we gon give you till tomorrow to pay us or resess you car (I said my car ain't in it), your refrigerator, and every TV in the house.'

"I said, 'Y'all do me that dirty and I tole you I'm gon pay you next month.'

"'I got to have my money, Mister Lane, or we gon take it.'

"I said, 'I don't know whether you is or not. I try to be nice to every-body, but now, you know you're doin me wrong. I ain't never owed a per-son, didn't pay em. You can't trust me till the next month, if God let me live?'

"'No, we got to have it right now.'"

He gave them the money. In the end, he always gives what the whites demand. His grandchildren say he is a mean man, one who "tears them up," and he does not deny that he uses a switch to keep peace in the house. His grandchildren know the whites have sent their children to private schools, they do not hesitate to speak of the affront they feel when a white store clerk uses the common white gesture of letting the change drop into a black person's hand to avoid touching black skin. The civil rights move-ment means nothing to them; they do not recognize its history or see its effect. They have never heard of Thurgood Marshall, they think the NAACP is a white man's organization. Ike does not instruct them; his life was about work, not politics.

At the end of his working life, when he survives on disability payments and whatever his grandchildren can collect in welfare, he still thinks about his good habits, by which he means that he does not drink anything stronger than Coca-Cola and he never displeases the white man. He worked because it was God's will for man to work; he was the best worker. He sits beside the window and considers the heat and the possibility of rain. He does not reflect upon his life—certainly not in the presence of the children—but when he gazes out on the dying grass, the fields of somber summer earth beyond the stream, his eyes narrow. Perhaps it is only the afternoon sun that causes him to narrow his eyes, and not the thought of his son who went to prison and his daughters who ran away and left their babies with him in the last inhabitable house beside the foulest stream in Sharkey-Issaquena County, Mississippi.

5. The Baccer Knife

The vertical boards of the building had long ago turned gray and spindly; they leaked, like an old man's body.

In the yard between the outhouse and the abandoned store, amid great trees and a dog too mean to let run free of its tether, Jerry Parker pointed to the south, "A ole man tole me once that if the thunder comes from thar, the rain will be light. But if thunder comes from over thar, northwest, the rain will be heavy for a long time." The clouds formed a solid, silvery darkness to the northwest, over the Cumberland Gap. Thunder came, then the rains. We had to go inside.

It was not what he wanted.

What is the word for feeling another man's shame? Or the word for the disappearance of shame, which does not happen among normal people?

Strips of flypaper hung from the ceiling, so covered with dead flies there was no room for another death. Flies walked along the older girl's arm; she did not appear to notice them. In the soaked summer air she covered herself with a thin blanket to keep the flies away. A fly walked on her face. She smoked a cigarette, for the pleasure of it and to turn the flies away.

If there was no shame, but I shared his shame, what had happened between him and me? And why did Mary, who had been deafened by the noise of a machine in a factory, ask her daughter to look under the bed, where she kept her treasured collection of never-released Elvis tapes in its original red velvet case, and bring them out for me to see? "Momma don't play these tapes," Kim, the older daughter, said.

They were the only treasure of the family. "That collection cost seventy dollars," he said. "We don't play those tapes."

When you sit in a house, any house, with people you like, the house becomes comfortable, I thought. Did I mean to think that I had become comfortable with the people or comfortable with shame? In the presence of shame? What is the word for not being ashamed to be comfortable in the presence of another man's shame?

The old tobacco knife lay on the low table. A cloth without color, torn at all the edges, covered the table, hung down at the sides, almost touched the small rug marked with strips of black electrical tape. A word is not a picture. The knife of tobacco is a piece of steel bent at right angles in three directions to fit the shape of a stick, nailed solid to the stick to make a knife more like an ax. The steel had rusted, the handle had been covered with black electrical tape, a piece of the wood had fallen away near the blade. An old tobacco knife is a picture of work. It is said, "Baccer nyfe."

A picture cannot be romantic; it will not stop speaking until someone turns it face-down or puts it out with the trash. Even then, it lacks only a listener.

In Lamont, Mississippi, a child, who looked like me at eleven years and loved Mister William Shakespeare as I had then, raised the question of the efficacy of language in comparison to a face or the floods of memory; but there were no memories in Tennessee. Unless cigarette smoke is a memory.

Work.

He was a picture of work.

Earlier in the day, he and I had been talking; we had just come back down the mile of dirt road leading to the well where he picked up fresh water for cooking and drinking. A man drove up in a new sedan. He asked Jerry if he would be willing to work for a few hours hanging tobacco. "Six dollars an hour," Jerry said.

"I'll pay you seven."

When the man brought him back at dusk, Jerry's shirt was open to the waist and his great chest and belly still shone with sweat. No one but Jerry could have hung tobacco that evening, lifting the damp sticks loaded with leaves, placing them on drying racks high above the floor of the barn. The sticks weighed thirty-five pounds when they were dry; damp they weighed half again as much, or more. He stood on a narrow beam, forty feet above the ground, and lifted the sticks, like a mule, like a machine. He came home laughing, with the money still in his hand, and rubbed his sweaty belly as if to thank it for his strength.

He was a picture of work. If nouns are names, the name of work is Jerry Parker.

The tree frogs made a din before the rain.

He had a tic. Every few moments he drew his lips back from his teeth like an animal snarling; it was exactly the facial movement employed by actors to distinguish between Dr. Jekyll and Mr. Hyde. In a man so large, the tic was terrifying.

According to Miss Anne Cabbage, Jerry Parker was the biggest, strongest, most cross-eyed child she ever taught at the Lone Mountain School. He fought with everyone, including the school principal, who on one occasion would have bludgeoned Jerry with a baseball bat had Miss Cabbage not come between them.

Kim Parker, at fifteen, was suspended from high school for twenty-five days during the last school year, all but five of the days as punishment for fighting. "I get in fights every day," she said, "knock down, drag out, blood! I got in a fight with a girl and broke her nose." She broke another girl's arm, cracked yet another girl's ribs.

She smiled, a delicate version of her father's oval face, some trace of dime-store darkness painted on her eyelids, long, light brown hair turned into strings by the dampness and the rain. Her mother and father have the same small nose, with little round nostrils; the noses are repeated in the girls.

Amy, ten years old, eats more than anyone else in the house and remains thin. She tried to light a wet cigarette with the triangular flame from the Zippo lighter that had been on the table next to the tobacco knife. Her father laughed: "You can't fire up wet tobacco."

"I been smokin for three years," Amy answered.

"Well, I been smokin for twenty-five years, so I know somethin about it," he said, arguing as if they were equals.

She has been coughing for more than two years, a deep cough, full of phlegm. It shakes her body and doubles her over. In that position, she flaps her arms, like a chicken attempting to fly. The picture is comic, but the cough is not.

What is said does not matter to Mary Parker; she cannot hear the telephone or the honk of a horn. What does she make of her husband's tic?

Water for washing and bathing collects in rain barrels at the corners of the building. Three old white round washing machines, each with a top wringer, stand in the kitchen. With no running water, it takes three tubs to do the wash.

He praises Mary's cooking, but in the evening the children go next door to Noah's Cedar Fork Store to buy onion sandwiches with mayonnaise on white bread.

When Jerry worked at the Black Diamond trailer truck factory, he worked so hard and so well that the company used its insurance to have a surgeon set his eyes straight in his head. The factory closed.

He set pipe in Knoxville, but it took more than a fourth of his minimum wages to pay the cost of an eighty-six mile round trip in his 1968 Dodge truck.

He found one minimum-wage job after another, never anything permanent. "I'll say times is harder now than they were during the Depression. You see people standin on the side of the road with a sign sayin, '*I'll work for somethin to eat.*' "

"I tried farmin," Jerry said, "but there ain't no money to be made in farmin. Believe me, I know. I farmed on one man's place fore I moved here. I got tired o puttin fifteen acres of baccer up to git five. One man can't do it. It was supposed to be me, him, and another man, but the other man's feet was tore up so he couldn't walk, and the man that owned the farm, he wasn't gon do no work; he didn't have to. When he come in, he'd turn on the TV and watch soap operas.

"I done fifteen acres. That's the reason I ain't there now. Had to use a hand spray to spray it with, a back spray. And I begged him, me and that other guy both begged him to git a boom spray.

"I was growin that five acres on the halfs, so I had to do all that labor to git my baccer put up.

"On a good crop o baccer you could git three thousand dollars a acre, about that. But I didn't git fifteen thousand dollars; I had to split that five acres, so I only got two and a half acres. He helped to pay to cut it, but I had to pay him back. Me an her [Mary] come out with about six thousand for the whole year. That's hard to live on with two kids. Plus I was livin on his farm an we was paying a hundred and twenty-five dollars a month rent, which we shouldn't even have been payin.

"I hauled water from the spring with his tractor, but he complained that I was usin too much fuel to haul the water, so he limited the amount we could haul."

Mary and the girls listened. They had set the tobacco plants in the ground, sitting side by side, one working with her left hand, the other with her right as they were pulled over the acres. The landlord paid them $40 dollars for their week of setting tobacco, and deducted the cost of their labor from their share of the proceeds when they settled up at the end of the season.

This house rented for $50 a month, and this landlord, Gordon Buis, who lived across the road, refused to let them draw water from his well. And when the Parkers would not work without wages to spray his thistles, he told them he would not fix the roof.

As the rain came down, they set out pots to collect the water that leaked through the roof. In one corner of the bedroom the rainwater came in with such force that Mary had considered making it into a shower stall. It would be better than the pan baths, she said, in the longest paragraph I ever heard her utter.

No place in the house was safe from water, although there was no water in the house. They kept their treasures—tapes and albums filled with photographs—in metal boxes wrapped in plastic under the bed.

We talked late into the night, until the rain stopped and the tree frogs began again. The shame of the poor is unutterable.

Jerry Parker stopped going to church a long time ago after the preacher "got me off to myself and said there ain't no sense in me comin back, cuz there was no hope for me. An I told him there was as much hope for me as there was for him. It was because I didn't have as much money as other people."

Of the forms of shame, the least common is juridical and the most distressing is social. Can a man so alone know shame? What is it that he cannot say but which I say with him?

Jerry despairs of honesty in the county. "Money talks and bullshit walks," he says. He believes that the sheriff tried to cover up a murder by claiming a man was shot in the back of the head by a dog. He bares his teeth in the snarling tic. Or could it be some unutterable pain?

During my last week in Claiborne County, I chanced to ask Kim and Amy about the movies. They had never been to a movie theater. "It costs too much," Amy said. "Tapes is better." The next afternoon I drove them up to Middlesboro, Kentucky, to a shopping mall that included a four-screen moviehouse. Amy wore a cowboy hat I had given her, twisting the brim so that she appeared to be an urchin one moment, a fashion model the next, and a farmworker the moment after that. She had put on lipstick for the occasion.

Kim was more dignified. She turned away from Amy's antic performances, paying attention only when the coughing shook the Coca-Cola and popcorn out of the containers in Amy's hands. A group of high school students from Claiborne County passed by on their way into one of the theaters in the complex. Amy said they were stuck up. "Bitch," she called after them. Kim looked away.

The theater was very large and nearly empty. The size of the screen intimidated the children, who insisted that we sit in the last row, close to the door. After a while, the house lights went down and the huge, empty room before us went black. No curtain rose in slow foldings, no tiny points of incandescence imitated stars in the ceiling, as in the movie palaces of old. Life, light, and sound stopped. Unseen, unknown, we waited in darkness. Then, without warning, there was an explosion of brass and brilliance—the movies—and I heard Kim exclaim, "God-a-mighty!"

6. Monsa and the Preacher

The subject for the past few days in the offices of the African American Contractors Association on the second floor of a formerly handsome building on the losing edge of downtown Oakland had been work. Monsa Nitoto had contracted to paint a large church with a crew of unemployed black men, and now that the job was completed, a dispute had erupted over the payment.

For several weeks Monsa stayed with his crew, buying the paint as they needed it, urging them on to complete the job. He put off the negotiation until the end. The dispute was over this: The preacher had given him an ancient set of plans to use in estimating the job. Seven thousand square feet of surface to be painted did not appear in the plans.

"I underbid the job," Monsa said.

"Negotiate," I said. We had talked often about the problem of force in the lives of the poor. He had a bad temper, and it had gotten him into trouble many times. There were rumors about him. He had to go underground after an enemy told the police Monsa had bought a .45 caliber pistol and was planning to kill the governor. He had put women on the street, been "in the life." He still wore thin-soled, reddish-brown shoes with pointed toes, the mark of a man "in the life."

He sat at the small desk he shared with Tilynne, the receptionist-typist. He overflowed the chair, his hands were too big for the keys of the old Apple computer. Although we had not seen each other for a while, he offered no greeting. Instead, he showed a deep scowl.

"Negotiate," I said.

"He don't want to negotiate."

"Get a lawyer, tell him you'll get a lawyer."

"I'm thirty-two hundred dollars short."

"The church owes it to you."

"Yeah, but the preacher don want to pay it."

"You worked for it."

"He ain't payin."

"Negotiate."

"Can't."

"You can always negotiate."

He took off his tiny African hat and wiped his face with it. For a moment, we stared at each other, then he grabbed my arm, pulled me close to him, and said, half whispering, half shouting, "The preacher put a gun to my head and told me he was going to blow my fucking brains out."

"Praise the Lord!"

He pushed me away, scowling, and then he laughed. He had been a Black Panther, he had been "in the life," he had bought buildings and run beautiful women, and squandered it all, and started again, and watched his fortunes fall again. He laughed. No irony was ever lost on him.

Monsa had lived all his life in the surround of force. He remembered the death of his father, a small California town, the sixties, the irony of work as well as life. He maneuvered now between worlds, and it was the world of work that most often disappointed him. At $5 or $6 or $7 an hour, the wages could not support the habit of work.

Children need shoes and doctors and the ability now and then to satisfy the insistence of the salespeople who control their dreams. And everyone must eat. Some way must also be found to combat the loneliness of life within the surround of force, to ease the panic that makes society impossible. Work itself cannot solve such problems; at less than a living wage, work is no antidote to force, it is merely force in the form most useful to those with power.

Work itself has no moral influence. Acquiescence to superior force is not what Aristotle meant by a good habit; ethics does not mean defeat.

The problem with work, as viewed by the world of thoughtful people, comes as much in the definition of the word as in the set of tasks itself. Work has come to mean, even to those with the best intentions and the largest, most competent staffs of researchers and analysts, work like the work they do. It follows logically to them that such work will produce lives like the lives they live. But there is no reason to expect that life within a surround of force will ever be like that of the world of the university or the foundation.

Those who want to solve the problem of poverty through work will have to take a different view of the lives of the poor—black, white, brown, and Asian—if they want to "end welfare as we know it." Work must, of course, be the greatest part of the antidote to poverty, but work within the surround of poverty is disorderly. The force of such work produces force in response, increasing the panic of the poor within the surround; the worker is not rebellious, merely unruly. The result of the panic cannot be moral, for the frame of mind of morality begins from temperance and panic is not a temperate state.

This does not mean that poverty is permanent, as in a culture of poverty. The role of force in the life of the poor points to a different antidote—one that includes work, but is not so limited or so wishful on the surface and exploitive at the core as "work itself." The poor do not suffer from sloth or indolence, but from force. If the antidote to force can be found, work will follow, if there is work to be done.

XII.

Citizenship by Exclusion

*Hence it is evident that the state is a
creation of nature, and that man is by
nature a political animal. And he who
by nature and not by mere accident is
without a state, is either a bad man or
above humanity; he is like the
"Tribeless, lawless, hearthless one"
whom Homer denounces—the natural
outcast is forthwith a lover of war; he
may be compared to an isolated piece at
draughts.*

— ARISTOTLE,
Politics, Bk. I

SHORTLY AFTER THE WATTS RIOT in 1965, an old friend
and I visited the Los Angeles headquarters of H. Rap Brown, a young black
radical who had made a reputation as a speaker and community organizer.
While my friend conducted his business, I waited outside on the sidewalk,
leaning up against the building, chatting with some of the men who milled
around the headquarters, passing time, waiting for something to happen.
The subject was the riot.

There was some rueful laughter, but the mood was mainly one of regret.
So much had been destroyed, burned, smashed, looted, washed down into

a muck of glass and ashes, and so little had been won. "Why?" I asked the men who stood outside the headquarters with me, waiting, knowing that it could begin again. The afternoon was strange, cloudy, at the end of summer; the light was the color of ashes.

Regret speaks in shrugs, but it does not break a person's back, like remorse. Regret was in the air; it colored the light. This man's house had burned, that man had been arrested, booked, and turned back to the street.

No one could answer my question, no one knew why he had rioted, no one spoke of pent-up anger or a divided America; neither hunger nor hatred merited their attention. Marcuse was not there to advise them.[1] Watts had burned, and they had to live in the remains.

"Why didn't you burn down Beverly Hills?" I asked.

A young man dressed in autumn clothes, the colors muted by the light, put his face up close to mine, showing me his teeth, in anger or a grin. "You know how far it is from Watts to Beverly Hills?" he asked. And added, "We ain't got no fucking cars, you know."

He stepped away, hands on hips, head cocked to one side, making a burlesque of examining me. "To get to Beverly Hills on the bus take three transfers, one hour and twenty-five minutes, if you make connections. Man, how you gon keep your rage up through three transfers?"

For many years I thought it was mother wit I had heard that afternoon. It seemed so logical and funny, segregation's story defused in humor, blacks using methods Freud had told us belonged to Jews, the revolution lost in the grotesqueries of the Los Angeles transit system. It had not seemed likely then, thirty years closer to the juridical betrayal of the *Dred Scott* decision, that the view of Chief Justice Taney of the U.S. Supreme Court still held, and the rioters of Watts were not citizens.

1

The Watts Riot was the first of a series of explosions of the poor in the last third of the century—Chicago, Detroit, Atlanta. At first, most of the rioters were black, but as the century neared its end, a different pattern emerged: In the riots that broke out in response to the verdict in the trial of the white police officers who beat Rodney King, as many as half or even more of the rioters were not black. Most of the others were Latinos, but

---

[1] Herbert Marcuse, the Marxist philosopher and writer, who taught in the California state university system. His work was popular among young radicals at the time.

apparently some whites and Asians also participated in the burning and looting. The riots spread out of south-central Los Angeles County into the heavily Latino sections of the central city and on to the less affluent commercial streets in Hollywood. What had appeared at first to be a pattern of rioting based on race had changed into the rioting of poor people of many races—mostly blacks and Latinos, still almost exclusively non-white, but no longer defined by African origins and a history of American enslavement.

This time the wealthier sections of the county of Los Angeles were not out of reach of the rioters. It was not necessary to "keep your rage up through three transfers," but the destruction was still confined mainly to the neighborhoods where the rioters lived and often worked.

In all the writing and talking that followed the riots, very little was made of the location of the looting and burning, and it was only months later that the media recognized the multi-racial makeup of the rioters. The destruction of their own neighborhoods by the rioters, now the non-white poor, had in the past been attributed to rage, shrugged off as striking out at the things closest to hand. But this matter of destroying their own place, in large ways or small, has been an aspect of the behavior of the poor in America for a long time.

Whether the poor actually destroy neighborhoods or are prohibited from living in anything but run-down areas is one of those chicken or egg arguments, answered only by stipulating that the poor generally move into neighborhoods that have been abandoned by richer people, and then make them worse. This kind of behavior has been ascribed to a culture of poverty. If that were so, however, it would be among the few human cultures, if not the only one, that purposefully destroys its immediate surroundings.[2]

A culture of self-destruction does not fit with any known patterns of human behavior, and if such a culture did exist, it would be very short-lived. The obvious fact of culture is that it arises to preserve the species rather than to destroy it. Cultures have to do with continuity, as we know from the monuments and other records left behind by cultures that died out as a result of war or climatic change. The idea of a culture of poverty devoted to the destruction of its habitat and eventually of itself is every bit as crazy as it sounds. The riots must have some other explanation.

Had the rioters been citizens of the place in which they lived, their

---

[2] Ecologists will be quick to point out that humans have been destroying the land, sea, and air around them since the demise of Neolithic societies and their cultural view of living in harmony with nature. The ecologists are correct, but I am speaking here of knowing destruction, a form of war on one's own place and kind.

interest would have been in the preservation of the place rather than the destruction of it. Citizens have always been the defenders of the polis, the nation, the state. The tie of the citizen to place was one of the ways in which Solon's reforms constructed the Athenian polis: They broke down the power of the clans, redirecting it to the geographically defined *demes*, setting the stage for the political reforms of Cleisthenes.

The defense of the polis as the responsibility of the citizen goes back to the arguments of Archidamus and the Funeral Oration of Pericles, spoken over the graves of the first Athenians who fell in the Peloponnesian War. According to Thucydides, Pericles said:

> . . . there is justice in the claim that steadfastness in his country's battles should be as a cloak to cover a man's other imperfections; since the good action has blotted out the bad, and his merit as a citizen more than out-weighed his demerits as an individual. But none of these allowed either wealth with its prospect of future enjoyment to unnerve his spirit, or poverty with its hope of a day of freedom and riches to tempt him to shrink from danger. No, holding that vengeance upon their enemies was more to be desired than any personal blessings, and reckoning this to be the most glorious of hazards, they joyfully determined to accept the risk. . . . So died these men as became Athenians.[3]

All through history the character of the citizen has been loyalty to the polis. The Greek word for citizen comes from *polis;* the Latin word for citizen, *civis*, joins with the word for home to work its way through the French *cité* to become our English word "city." The city is home, home is the city. When the citizen destroys the city, it can only be madness or some strategy to save the polis in time of war, as in the destruction of foodstuffs and shelter to make it impossible for an invader to live off the land.

A person who abandons the polis by leaving it or turning against it cannot be a citizen. That person is excluded from citizenship, made a part of the vast world outside the polis, an internal or external exile; in the Athenian view, like a dead person. When the poor riot in the streets or in other ways destroy the places in which they live and work, it is not an act of madness, but a result of their exclusion from citizenship, which means they have no place, no home.

---

[3] *The Complete Writings of Thucydides,* trans. R. Crawley (New York: The Modern Library, 1934), pp. 106–107.

In the United States, we say that a citizen is a person who was born here or born overseas to parents who were U.S. citizens. We also accept small numbers of people into citizenship every year by asking them to swear loyalty to the state, to obey its laws, and so on. Because the Constitution describes rights in terms of persons rather than citizens, the citizen has little more than the non-citizen in that way, except the right to vote. And even that distinction has been eliminated in some jurisdictions, where non-citizens may vote in local elections.

Citizenship no longer follows the rigid rules of ancient Greece, where women and slaves and foreigners were not citizens, and prior to Solon's reforms, only landholding citizens could vote. At the founding of the United States, citizenship rules, in the sense of how widely citizenship was to be conferred, followed closely on the Athenian model before Solon. Only very slowly did the Roman view, based on the Stoic notion of the brotherhood of all men, come into favor, expanding the category of citizen. Even so, the *Dred Scott* decision held, in 1857, that people of African descent were not citizens; women's suffrage came only in this century; and the poll tax, which effectively limited voting rights to property owners, was not completely abolished until the second half of this century. Through one means or another, the poor have been excluded from full citizenship for most of the history of the United States.[4]

---

[4] Garry Wills drew a distinction between ancient and American views of rights and the state in *Inventing America,* (New York: Doubleday, 1978):

> In classical and mediaeval thought, the "rights" of the individual were not a topic of conventional discourse; there, the citizen did not rule but was ruled. Of course every man had certain things owed to him by divine and human law—his *dike* or *jus*. But these were not pregovernmental "rights" in the modern sense. They could not be. A man received political status by initiation into a tribe or people, by vows to a liege lord or suzerain. These gave each member privileges *of the body*.
>
> The idea of an original "rule" over oneself, partly surrendered to another power (aliened), arose as a corollary to fully articulated social-contract theory in the seventeenth century. (pp. 214–215)

Whether or not citizens have rights under the social contract to equal nutrition, housing, education, health care, and so on is the critical political question in the United States. It is also the critical moral question, for the moral stance of the founders was deeply influenced by the seventeenth-century Scottish philosher Francis Hutcheson's notion of moral goodness as the promotion of the happiness of others.

The only way in which a state founded on a social contract, which assumes the right to the decent minimums of life required for the "pursuit of happiness," can avoid the contractual question of large-scale multigenerational poverty is by removing the poor from consideration as citizens. Of course, even this maneuver cannot release the state from its moral obligations to human beings within its boundaries, unless they are declared enemies of the state.

Voting rights issues still come before the courts. Joaquin G. Avila, formerly President and general counsel of the Mexican-American Legal Defense and Education Fund, tried a voting rights case before the U.S. Supreme Court in 1996. Nevertheless, the legal prohibition from citizenship has largely disappeared for native-born Americans. How, then, is it possible to argue that the rioters of Los Angeles and Chicago and millions of other poor people in the United States are not citizens?

Why does contemporary America have more fiercely exclusionary economic criteria than ancient Athens, where Pericles said poverty was no bar to citizenship? He sought a kind of equal opportunity of service to the polis, quite different from the equal opportunity to make money that we fight for in the United States. But his ambition for the Athenians stands to reason, for they revered political and cultural life, and he wished the citizens nothing more than to enjoy their citizenship, in the public life:

> If we look to the laws, they afford equal justice to all in their private differences; if to social standing, advancement in public life falls to reputation for capacity, class considerations not being allowed to interfere with merit; nor again does poverty bar the way if a man is able to serve the state, he is not hindered by the obscurity of his condition.[5]

There is some truth in what Pericles said about the condition of Athenian citizens, but a closer look at the reality of citizenship in Athens, where it began, and in the United States, where it enjoyed a rebirth at the end of the eighteenth century, will show that even in Athens, where no more than forty thousand men enjoyed the possibilities of citizenship, there were few citizens.

Citizens are not merely residents; Pericles very pointedly asked more than mere residency of citizens. Those who were not legally excluded had to pass through another set of exclusionary tests. "Our public men," he said,

> have, besides politics, their private affairs to attend to, and our ordinary citizens, though occupied with the pursuits of industry, are still fair judges of public matters; for, unlike any other nation, regarding him who takes no part in these duties not as unambitious but as useless, we Athenians are able to judge at all events if we cannot originate, and instead of looking on discussion as a stumbling-block in the way of

---

[5] Thucydides, *The Complete Works*, p. 104.

action, we think it an indispensable preliminary to any wise action at all. Again, in our enterprises we present the singular spectacle of daring and deliberation, each carried to its highest point, and both united in the same persons; although usually decision is the fruit of ignorance, hesitation of reflexion.[6]

Idios and *koinos*, private and public, set up another binary system. Citizenship excluded private persons, for even "ordinary citizens" were "fair judges of public matters. . . ." Those who lived a private life were excluded, for they were passive persons, the subjects of the citizenry. The process of exclusion defined the circle in which legitimate power was held. To open this circle to men other than aristocrats, Pericles began the system of payment for public service. His goal was to give the values of the aristocrats, by whom he meant the public men, to the rest of the citizenry.

Although it may be anachronistic to ascribe modern political and social sensibilities to such an act, it seems likely that he wanted the poor among the citizenry to understand themselves as citizens, which meant living the public life, the *vita activa*. For citizens did not truly feel loyal to the clan or *phratry*, but to the *vita activa,* which was the life of action, the Athens that existed in the doing of politics or philosophy or the making of art. There was little else to attract them. Fecundity and ease could not have been the allure of the polis; Athens itself was merely another city in a poor country, where the land was worn out. Herodotus said that Greece and poverty had always been bedfellows. Homer thought Ithaca was "a rugged place."

The wonder of the polis, as Protagoras and Socrates and the great discussants knew, lay in dialogue, the active life, which was always a public life, for the obvious reason that men who talk to themselves are more often loony than wise. Political life was the real life of the polis; there was no other worth considering. But political life in Athens had certain requirements, among them leisure.

In considering this aspect of political life, it is important again to avoid anachronism. "Leisure" did not hold the same meaning for the ancient Greeks that it does for us. There were no labor-saving devices; slaves, women, most of the alien residents, the metics, and the poor among the citizenry worked long, exhausting hours, leaving little, if any, time to rest their bones, let alone to enjoy what Aristotle called the *summum bonum,* the contemplative life. Even in the democracy, politics, the *vita activa,* belonged to those with the leisure to live it.

Solon and after him Pericles attempted to draw those citizens who had

---

[6] Ibid., p. 105.

no leisure out of the isolation of tedious labor into the public life. In that way, the Athenians attempted to solve the political problem of the game of modern society in which the losers are not citizens. The primary act was payment for service in the legislature, leisure provided by the state, the active life subsidized, citizenship granted to the citizens.

The freedom of Athenian citizens was entirely public; it differentiated them from the excluded, especially the slaves, who (except for those who toiled in the mines) looked very much like the citizens. In fact, the Athenians were criticized by other states because it was difficult to tell, by their dress and demeanor, the less affluent citizens from the slaves.

In contemporary America, no such confusion exists. The discerning can easily separate the rich from the poor, and no one is more discerning than the poor themselves. The poor understand that they have been excluded from the circle of power; that is, from citizenship. They cannot deceive themselves about who operates the government, for they are administered to by the government. Nothing indicates this more clearly than the language of the allies of the poor, the people who speak constantly of "empowering" their clients.

The deceit that resides in the word "empower" has yet to be discovered by most poor people; to them, the thought of being empowered carries some hope. In practice, however, "empowerment" has come to mean learning to deal with power, much like the psychotherapeutic concept of "adjustment."

Critics of the philosophy of adjustment have often asked why one should adjust to a bad life. Empowerment deserves similar scrutiny. When women are empowered to deal with the welfare department, they learn to accommodate their behavior to the rules, however arcane and unfair, of the system. Power, on the other hand, means taking control of the welfare department through legitimate means. Empowerment grows out of the passive role of the non-citizen, the one who has accepted exclusion from the circle of power. Power results from the *vita activa,* the citizen's public life; power *is* the *vita activa.* There can be no legitimate power except in the doing; it cannot, as Hannah Arendt said, be stored up. Power dies the moment action ceases.

However, this action of a citizen must fall within the agreed-upon limits of the circle of power; political life is not anomic. When the residents of Watts or Detroit riot in their own neighborhoods, it is because they are not citizens of Watts or Detroit or the United States of America. There is no polis they can call their own; they have been excluded and dishonored, condemned to privacy. In the private panic of the surround, people become enemies of each other, even of themselves. Of all the effects of living in a surround of force, the most profound is the isolation of people, one from the other, the absolute prohibition of power. Cicero's idea of men being "born for each other" has no place inside the surround, where men are set against each other. Politics for the poor is difficult. Citizenship, the *vita activa,* is virtually impossible.

2

If the chief reward of the public life is inclusion in the circle of legitimate power, a secondary, but not inconsiderable, reward comes in the honor of citizenship. We can read it in the speech of Archidamus and again in the words of Pericles. "Honor" held one meaning for Sparta, where it was opposed to shame, and another for Athens, where it meant devotion to the polis life. In Rome, Cicero declared honor was the citizen's reward. In each instance, honor required citizenship, inclusion in the Greek polis or the Roman state.

There were no levels of citizenship, but there were levels of honor. Greece and Rome were modern societies, constantly sorting the winners and losers. Everyone entered contests: playwrights, javelin throwers, philosophers, and boxers. Playwrights who were enormously successful, like Sophocles, were elevated to the highest positions. Roman honors included elevation to the position of Caesar.

The *vita activa,* worldly, public, yet reflective, produced citizens who were both artists and military leaders, poets and senators, philosophers and consuls.[7] Honors often came in more than one field of endeavor to those who were included in the circle of power.

In the United States, some groups of the excluded have managed to live the *vita activa* by creating a virtual polis, making citizens of themselves, collecting honors, living a public life, while holding no power in the general society. These citizens of the virtual polis, some of them poor by economic measures, have been able to escape the panic and isolation of the surround of force, even though they live partly within it.

Inside the virtual polis, it has been possible for those who were excluded from the actual polis to live a political life. The best known virtual polis in America was, until it was disrupted by racial integration in the 1960s, the sphere of influence of the black churches, particularly in the South. Within the virtual polis centered on the church, southern blacks were able to live in virtual, if not actual, autonomy. Honors were accorded the citi-

---

[7] In the *Nicomachean Ethics,* Artistotle's notion of the highest form of the *vita activa* is the *vita contemplativa,* which is arrived at through action.

zens who served the polis best in social, political, artistic, and economic functions.

A less successful virtual polis existed in the hills of Appalachia—one so separated from the larger state that many members of the virtual polis did not ever in all their lives mingle with the citizens of the larger state, the one from which they were effectively excluded.

Latinos, Jews, Swedes, Chinese, Japanese, and a host of religions, from the Mormons to sects having only a few members, constructed the same kind of virtual state in which their members could live the political life. Although the virtual polis began with poor people in almost every instance, the citizens did not remain in that condition for long. The rule of the political life, reflection instead of reaction, power instead of force, leads to success in many areas of life, including economics.

Blacks, who suffered the greatest force and were the poorest, having come up from slavery, built businesses, colleges, and professional schools. An aristocracy of the educated, most of them teachers, grew up in the South. Like Pericles, these aristocrats attempted to spread the values of the aristocracy to all the citizens, and many were successful at their work.

When the civil rights laws of the 1960s opened the doors of the virtual polis onto the wider horizons of the entire nation, those who had practiced the public life within the virtual polis rushed out into the real state prepared to be citizens, and were immediately successful. Teachers in segregated schools, graduates of segregated colleges, practically everyone connected to the black churches, and the owners of funeral homes and other businesses that the whites left to the blacks suddenly leaped into the economic mainstream. But more important, their children and grandchildren quickly became government employees, corporate managers, and entrepreneurs.

The practice of creating a virtual polis continues among many excluded groups. Among Latinos, Asians, some recent Russian immigrants, and others, such devices for the creation and maintenance of the virtual polis as bilingualism are being used to good effect. More than anything else, even more than skin color, language enables the creation of a separate state, although it is only a state of mind. A distinct language, along with other cultural attributes, enhances the autonomous character of the virtual polis. A body that governs itself in Farsi, Hindustani, Russian, one Chinese dialect or another, or Spanish, can be more easily self-governing than one that speaks English, for the simple reason that its speakers can be public persons within their own community even though limited to private life in the actual polis.

In time, members of the virtual polis, prepared by virtual citizenship to live the *vita activa,* use their political skills to move into the actual polis, where they quickly find themselves at ease and able to negotiate their way past the surround of force.

Sometimes the virtual polis pleases everyone who observes it. Many people who are not African-American make donations to the United Negro College Fund; no one can fail to be charmed by a first-rate bilingual education class in Miami or San Francisco; and the style and sound of the black churches have been widely noted as one of the glories of American culture. But it is not quite the same when one hears Louis Farrakhan ranting his anti-white, anti-Semitic, anti-American line, or when a Muslim religious leader urges his followers to blow up the World Trade Center, or radical right-wing groups destroy a federal building in Oklahoma or declare themselves a separate nation-state in Montana.

The distinction between autonomy and anomie applies to the virtual polis as well as to the general society. Anomie is never a training ground for politics; it is a prescription for tragedy.

XIII.

The Loneliness of the Apolitical World

In isolation, never power—only force.
— H A N N A H   A R E N D T

1. The Cave of the Poets

ON THE EAST SIDE of Mount Franklin, almost a thousand feet up the steepening slope, hidden by mesquite and boulders and a strange hump in the stony surface of the mountain, there is a shallow cave known to no one but the poets.

They have painted the walls of the cave with graffiti, signs of the conversation of the cave, reminders first of the death of Darline Gonzales, who was killed in a nightclub shooting, and then of the death of them all. "It's weird that two weeks before it happened we were with her, talking with her, and all of a sudden she's gone. The bullet came through the wall and got her in the spinal cord. She was killed instantly," said Marta, the poet of the tiny voice, the hint of Asia, the Filipino father.

Then Monica, whom the others call Moca, took the newspaper clipping from her wallet. "I would see her different places and stuff. I would call her. I knew her from basketball. There was a lot of people that knew her more."

The girl died in December, when she was thirteen years old. The poet said a rosary for her and went to her funeral.

"When I saw her in the casket," Moca said, "it was shocking, because she was dead.

"My brother suffocated. I remember, he had a little casket, but I was too young to understand. But Darline, she was so beautiful, so innocent. I wrote a poem for her. It's called, 'Why?' In my room it's on the wall."

Marta said, "I want to be a mortician. I like to be secluded. I'm good with people, but I get tired of them, so I'll be able to talk to the dead. I get a little bit closer to the dead. I like morbidity, how many different ways people could die." She spoke in the flat, quick voice of the dead as she imagined them, describing a boy who was on the telephone outside the QuickieMart: "And they shot him because his brother was in a gang. And he laid there twenty minutes before they found him. And he was very calm, and he probably was reviewing. It was eleven-thirty, and he died at two-thirty A.M."

"I think it might happen to me," Moca said. "It wouldn't hurt me, but it might hurt someone who loved me, if anyone loved me."

All afternoon the poets had been talking of death and Morrissey. In the middle of the longest hot spell in memory—twenty-three days of temperatures above a hundred degrees—when the old begin to die even in the shade of the ancient adobe houses near the river, the poets made their metaphysical conversation: Moca, Marta, and Jesse, three children sorted out into loneliness and drugs, learning to take comfort in the welcome of aberration.

Of the three poets, Marta, at fourteen, looks the oldest, although she is the youngest. Tiny, very delicate, Mexican and Filipino. She wears her hair cut short, drawn down into a sleek ducktail in the back. A stainless-steel semicircle, like a ring, pierces her upper lip. She cannot remember where she lost the little ball that keeps the metal from slipping out or hooking into her flesh. As she speaks or eats, even in repose, she toys with the piece of steel, adjusting it, fondling it, drawing attention to her mouth, the thin lips, tiny teeth like baby teeth. She has a series of sinuous gestures that belong to an older woman, a world-weary woman, the woman who appears in her eyes. At fourteen, Marta buys cigarettes and liquor, crosses the border at night into Mexico to dance until morning, slips into gay bars, where she attracts men and women—the men who think of her as a boy, the women who want her as a woman. She laughs; they buy her drinks. The gay women teach her, she said.

Although Marta and Jesse have known each other for a long time and Moca and Jesse have known each other for less than a year, the most intense communication in the cave happens when Jesse and Moca begin to tell each other their fears. "When I talk with Jesse," she said, "it's like heart to heart, you know."

And he continued, "We tell everyone else, 'You can't even understand it, you know. One day, Moca and I were ridin around, you know, and I got scared. It's like the world, we're just a little dot in the universe. Let's say it was like El Paso was like a big black sheet and we're a little white spot. And it's like we're there. We're alive in there. We're just in there, you know. It scares you, cause you don't know what's out there."

Moca added, "How do you know that she's not an alien? That he's not an alien?"

They do not often go to her house, where her stepfather stands outside, working on a neighbor's driveway, stripped to the waist, a big man with a pale, puffy face, like a busted-up middleweight gone to fat; and her mother sits at a table in the main room, a dark place in contrast to the ferocious desert sun, and slowly adds up the green and white slips on which she wrote out the dinner checks of the night before. Moca and Mrs. Silva have developed a routine: Mrs. Silva does not hurry; her daughter does not interrupt her counting. Mrs. Silva sits in silhouette against the white light of the afternoon and tells of the pride she feels because of Moca's refusal to use drugs. It is impossible to tell whether she is dissembling or unaware. She glances up at her daughter, but seems to choose not to see her. The girl presented herself in a dark red T-shirt shirt and very large blue jeans. For shoes she wore cheap black sneakers, with the laces left untied. Her hair had been cut short, exactly like a boy's haircut. There was nothing stylishly exaggerated and feminine about it; she had a boy's haircut.Had she been a boy, she might have been twelve years old, a beautiful child, with the whitest teeth and brown skin, a cherub on the verge of adolescence.

The surprise of Moca is in her room. When Jesse and I visited with her there, the bed was made, the Morrissey posters on the walls were neatly arranged, the clothes were hung neatly in the closet. Nothing in the room was out of place but Moca.

A few months earlier, when she had just turned fifteen, Moca tried to kill herself in this room, in this half-empty, fried summer house without a telephone, where the ceiling fan turns slowly over the child's bed and the small, high windows along one wall have a prison caste. "I took aspirin, a lot of pills," she said. "I didn't do it because I wanted to die. I just wanted to be noticed, I just wanted to be sick. And I tried to overdose with drugs, like smoke a lot of weed, do as many lines as I can, get plastered, drink as much as I can. But now that I see, you know, I'll wait for death. I'll wait for death to come to me instead of me going to it."

The cocaine comes from her sister's boyfriend, a dealer who supplies schoolchildren, members of the girls' basketball team. Moca said it was not at all like the movies. When she didn't sell all the cocaine, he didn't threaten her, he told her to keep whatever she did not sell.

She stood in the center of the room, looked around at the posters, a newspaper clipping in which her mother was identified as the waitress serving two neighborhood people, the order of the wall, and sighed. "I wake up every morning and I think, like, Darline's not here."

A long silence followed while she studied another newspaper clipping, one about Darline. "You kill my brother and I kill your brother," she said. "It's like that. Pain to me is our society. I think there is sometimes days when just the sights of people make me sick. On those days I see everybody and they're all doing the same thing, not being different, not being themselves, and it's very depressing, because they're afraid to come and speak of the truth, of the sorrow and pain that hides behind them. Ever since I met Jesse, I haven't been afraid to like tell him what I think. There's times when I think how it would be to be like gay and stuff, and I go, 'I wonder how it would be and stuff, if I would turn out like that, and well, that's the way I am, you know.' I tried out for the football team in school.

"People may call me a lowlife, okay. This one guy, he said straight out, okay, 'You're gonna be a lowlife when you grow up.' I look at him, I go, 'How do you know? Can you predict the future? Do you have a scholarship in predicting the future? You don't know that. You don't know if I'm gonna quit [school] or not.'

"Words, I think words can hurt you more than fists and a kick, you know.

"I told my mom that I used to sell drugs: acid, marijuana, and cocaine." Marta was her best customer.

In Marta's house, a few blocks away, her sister and a boyfriend sat on the couch in the cramped living room, watching television through the afternoon. Down the narrow hall that bisected the rest of the house, someone was bathing; Marta ran ahead to shut the door. She lived in an amateur's construction, a tiny room without a window or a closet, airless, like a cell made for punishment. Marta had painted her room black; all the walls and the ceiling, too. Then she filled the walls with photographs and album covers, posters, a portrait that failed in its attempt to resemble her.

When she tried to kill herself on the first day of school, she did not do it in the black room, but at a friend's house. "I took Nyquil; these huge bottles of Tylenol, I took half a bottle. I took Seldene. It was all because of my mom. We got in a big fight. She made me real sad and depressed. I got real mad and I got out knives and I cut my wrist. I went to a friend's house and right there I just fell, and he saw all my blood and everything, and his mom took me to a hospital. My liver was damaged. If I wouldn't have got there for about fifteen minutes, I would of died.

"I was just lying there, and I was thinking, I'm not afraid of it."

She worries more about Jesse: "What if he's in his room, and he's lying there dead? What if he got a bad hit of acid and he's dead?"

Marta has begun to separate from the other poets. In the gay bar, where she goes with Moca, the men approach her first, turning away when they realize she is female. A gay woman has become her confidante. She and Marta go on long drives together in the woman's convertible. According to Marta, the woman has become the teacher of the girl and the girl has become the teacher of the woman.

When they do not go to the cave, the poets go to Jesse's room. He lives in a tiny cubicle atop a mother-in-law apartment. No one sees the poets there, no one hears them. They enter the cubicle from a narrow spiral staircase. Jesse leads. He is a very thin boy, pale in a sallow way. He has a long Spanish face, like that of his grandfather on his mother's side; the distance between his nose and his upper lip will be so great as he grows older that Jesse, like his grandfather, will be unable to solve the problem of that great space with a mustache.

Jesse spends many hours in the room, often late into the night, listening to music, sitting before his curiously bubbling lamp, perched on a high stool, bent over a cube of wood, something like a desk or worktable, writing his thoughts in a notebook, drawing out his dreams in psychedelic fashion, thinking. If thinking seems too grand a word to use for a thin boy with the beginnings of a mustache and a few hairs on his chin, it is only partly so, for Jesse's nightmares are cousins to thinking. He lives in the place between thoughts and dreams.

With black construction paper and thumbtacks, Jesse has made a checkerboard of one wall of his room. He sleeps on a tiny bed beside the only window, using a shade to keep the room dark, black. It is his dreaming place, his talking place; in this room Jesse and Moca spend their afternoons, evenings, talking, talking late into the night. Their conversation sounds like love, but it is complicated in that Moca says she does not like sex and she thinks that love is the greatest pain.

As the sincerity of the poets becomes clear, it seems out of character for Jesse to have been expelled from school after a security guard caught him with a large amount of marijuana. He is fifteen years old, timid in the world, exiled from the life of his peers. The thought of leaving his room frightens him. "You can't go out at night," he said, "because you got to be watching your back."

He sat hunched over the box that served as a desk, while the girls lolled on his bed. The window shade swayed in the breeze, confusing the light on the checkerboard wall. The poets spoke of death; they recited poems.

Unknown Feelings
As I walked outside the reality of the world I lit a cigarette, and then

came a song that spoke of depression. As I was listening to it I broke down in tears! I really thought I was happy, but I came to think that my life hasn't been as beautiful as the sky above us! We dream of peace on this earth, but in reality it's just a fantasy! Sometimes I wish I was never born, because the sights of this crummy world is very sickening to me and others; we push ourselves to succeed in this world and people that are uglier than you and push further and get nowhere! Love peace and harmony very very nice, but maybe in the next world, if there is one! Is there really hope for a next world? If there is, these unknown feelings will stay shut behind a door until this world goes into total kaus [sic] like the first one! So wake up when it's not just a fantasy!
—Monica

A CRY
The streets are silent
All night long
You hear a cry
A cry for help
A cry that says death

Finding a loved one on the floor
Looking at the wrists
Looking at all the blood
Not knowing what to do
Not able to do anything

As the loved one lies on the floor
HELPLESS
—Marta

"The last time we went up to the cave, we went up there to get stoned," Monica said. "We were in the cave and we just started sparking it up. And I don't know, we just started talking about stuff, taking pictures, posing. We just started: How did this get here? Is there really a God? Is there really a devil? Were we really for real here or is it just a dream?"

"A big dream that we all don't know," Jesse said. "Maybe we'll wake up millions of years later. I think it's a story."

Monica said, "I think death is in a way . . . it's beautiful, because there's no more pain, you don't have to put up with problems. You're free, your soul is set free. Dying is the end of earth, when your spirit's like free."

"Like life to me is like a straight line," Jesse said. "People are like slaves, following. I want to be on the edge." He turned his thoughts to the government, how it wants to get rid of them, and the girls agreed. They believe the government will employ diseases to do it.

"We think government wants to control the kids," Monica said. "Like they wanted to stop the smoking, and what's the difference? There's pollution in the air and we're all gonna die from it anyway."

Then Jesse recited part of a poem he had written at two-thirty in the morning:

Every night I dream a little boy named Atlantis
standing before a big,
strange window of the palace.
It seemed that everything he loved most was dying.
He could do nothing about it.
Beyond him lay his father,
the Emperor, in the last hours of life.

He dreamed about a place
where no madness would be.
He dreamed about a place
where there was no anger
or madness, violence or even killing.
He dreamed of Atlantis.
He would describe Atlantis
as a beautiful jewel.

That's where I would like to go
in the last hours of my life.
Cashmeres, goats, top wool.
For me, I like to dance in a soft light, sax,
in the place where there would be nothing but peace and love
and we could walk,
be wild,
walk free whenever,
wherever I want to.

I want dreams,
dream lives.
Trees, flowers must now replace madness.
I must go again in one unique hour,
in the last seconds of life.

All through that afternoon we sat in Jesse's aerie. It was the best place to talk, although the shade flapped and the light was unreliable. Toward the end of the afternoon, Jesse told his revelation, and for a moment I thought it was genius:

"The dark to me," he said, "is it like light to you? The color green to you, like a tree is green—you might see it purple; who's gonna know that? I don't know what's your mind doing, like other people's. We could be seeing different stuff."

Had he discovered Plato's problem of other men's minds? He could not have read the *Theaetetus*; I was sure he did not know Wittgenstein or Strawson or Ayer or Moore or any of the other contemporary philosophers who had struggled with this question of private language, this grand modern skepticism.

Then Moca said, "If you really think about it, it's true. He could think this is black, I could think this is gray."

And Jesse added, "It has nothing to do with being color-blind, either."

With no transition that I could discern, Moca turned the conversation back to death. I stopped listening. What had they said? It was not genius, Plato reborn, Wittgenstein in Texas. They were three children who met in this aerie or the cave. Secret places, secret thoughts. They did not raise questions of philosophy; they were poets, speaking of isolation, of aliens and the ultimate loneliness of incompatible minds.

2. Blues for Gurtha

In Dogpatch or on Catfish Row—the color of the residents makes no difference—the poor live in busy intimacy, ragged, often hungry, frequently illiterate, but never lonely, as if a ghetto was a great extended family. It is a useful myth in that it spares the rest of society the itch of conscience caused by the undue suffering of others. But it is a myth. The poor are not only isolated from the rest of society, as William Julius Wilson has said, they are isolated from each other as well. There are few, if any, neighborhoods among the poor; people live in rows, on blocks, in projects, but they do not live in association; they have no public life.

When the poets of the cave encountered three schoolmates near the foot of the mountain, the poets and the other children looked at each other suspiciously, barely civil, communicative enough only to compete, to engage in their version of the constant internecine warfare of the poor: Liars, lowlifes, glue-sniffers, they muttered after each other.

On the 300 block of Cleveland Street in Greenville, Mississipi, a row of strangers has grown up over the years. Mrs. Irene Guster lives in the best house on the block, a big place, full of children and grandchildren on a Saturday afternoon, rich in the smell of food cooking, with conversations carried on in every corner of every room.[1] Her husband, grown old and too ill to work, spends his days and evenings in a chair before the television set in the front room. The Gusters are the most successful family on Cleveland Street. Most of their children have completed college and hold advanced degrees. Irene Guster is a vehement woman, with Native American features and skin so smooth and beautifully red underlying the brown it appears almost unnatural, like some miraculous pancake makeup that can turn a great-grandmother's skin into the handsome perfection of middle age. She has a habit of tilting her head back and looking down her nose when she speaks.

Nothing infuriates Mrs. Guster more than her neighbors, particularly the woman in the broken-down old shotgun house next door, the woman who fights with men out in public, "that one!" She has nothing to do with "that one," never did, never would.

That one is Gurtha.

When I left Mrs. Guster's house, Gurtha was there next door, sitting on the little front porch beside the only window, talking to someone inside, someone hidden in the darkness of the house. We said good afternoon, and commented on the heat. She offered me a cold drink. I asked to come back another time.

She smiled, showing a great gap and two white teeth, like alabaster stanchions, hippopotamus teeth. I smiled in return. She had no self-consciousness about the missing teeth, and the gap did not affect her speech.

"Saturday?" I asked.

"Goin fishin. Sunday."

"After church?"

She laughed. "I'll be here." Gurtha looked country and talked city, Mississipi feet and northern diction. She used the full range of her voice when she spoke; in a single sentence she could drop from a girlish squeal to the blues.

"Chicago?"

"Uh-huh."

"South Side?"

"Wabash and Thirty-Eight. Was it Thirty-Eighth? Yes, it was. We lived up over a liquor store. At night, I used to look out the window at the fancy

---

[1] Portions of a conversation with Mrs. Guster appear in Chapter XV.

men and their ladies. Oh, there was excitement on the street."

"Did you know the Zebra Lounge over on Forty-First? I saw Billie Holiday there the last time she worked in Chicago."

"I might have been there once or twice."

"The High Hat, the Beehive, the Pershing. . . ."

"I sang a little, you know, with one of B. B. King's bands."

After the exchange of credentials, I told her what I was doing, that I wanted to talk with her for the book. "Oh, Earl," she said, "you've made my day." Before I left she gave me her telephone number and a warning: The man she lived with was very jealous. And then she laughed again, showing pretty eyes and a sassy turn of her head. I stood on the porch for a moment, captured by the gesture, as she had intended. Her figure was gone, her feet were bare; her hair was half straightened, chopped off at the temples, but she had been something in her time, one time, not so long ago, and it had remained in her eyes and the insinuating lilt of her voice.

"You sure you wouldn't like a cold drink? Sonny won't be home for a little while." She smiled again, toothless and fetching. She made anachronisms: the warning had been her cosmetic, the only perfume, the prettiest dress she could afford.

On Sunday she had prepared for a visit, dressed in a yellow tanktop and a loose skirt. And shoes. When she smiled, the gap was still there, and it surprised me, I don't know why. Perhaps I had imagined her with teeth, believing the anachronism she had created on the porch. She put out a bowl of watermelon chunks, covered with a striped yellow towel to keep the flies away. And next to it a pitcher of Kool-Aid, iced down against the summer heat.

How had she arrived at that place? She had taken the train in the wrong direction: no one goes from Chicago to the Delta.

Sonny was there on Sunday, a fair-skinned man, skinny as a bedslat, with deep vertical creases in his cheeks, the Delta version of a Kentucky mountain man. It was two o'clock; he had not shaved or tied his shoes, and he was drunk. But not as drunk as his fat-faced pal, Willie, who slumped in a chair and drank beer and mumbled so incoherently that no one bothered to respond to his noises.

Gurtha had a history on Cleveland Street and a history in Chicago and another on a farm and in a restaurant, and a separate history about the time she got in with "some wrong people" and ended up doing "something" to support her children. "Mama will always make do. Chop cotton for her babies, if she have to." She slurred words, turned southern, spoke Delta as if it were a foreign language, the old country language, forgotten in America.

It was the loneliness of Chicago that drove her south, she said, home, back where her cousins lived, where her grandmother was born. What she loved about the South was the way the people spoke to each other on the street. "Good morning, Miz Morris, and how are you today?"

How could I tell her that I knew she was lying? Hadn't she seen me on the street before? How many white men wearing poplin suits had parked a rented Buick and walked down Cleveland Street? Was she so distant from her own world that she did not realize I knew her neighbors and how none of them had anything to do with each other, much less with Gurtha?

"It's just nice here," she said. "That's why I stay."

On Cleveland Street, everyone knew. Five years earlier, Gurtha Morris had moved in with the man who lived in the second house down from the Guster place. It was just as small and twice as run-down as the one she lived in with Sonny. She had not lived there long when it happened: Her man went to work one morning, she got a look at Sonny, liked what she saw, and moved.

The men came very close to killing each other over her; the memory of it brings a little shiver of delight from Gurtha. But the rage has left them; they have become almost cordial in the last year or two. Sonny mumbles at the recounting of the story. Gurtha rolls over him, full of tales, on stage.

She cannot say what she sees in Sonny, except that he works hard at setting tiles. "He's got all plastic parts inside," she said. "That's how come he's on Social Security, but he works hard." In return, Gurtha cooks and cares for "My Moms," which is the name she uses for Sonny's aunt, the motionless old woman who lies in the bed beside the window. "We would leave this place," Gurtha said, "move on out, but My Moms loves to lay by that window. That's her window. She was good to Sonny; she raised him."

Gurtha married three times. She was pregnant at fourteen, married and a mother at fifteen, in 1951. She and her first husband had six children before they split up. A second marriage lasted only a week. "You know how black men are," she said, as if to explain. "He needed my six kids for his income tax. Got back thirty-four dollars and twenty cents, and that was all he gave me when he left."

After the third husband, she came south. For a little while she was a sky-rocket in Greenville, a woman who had sung with B. B. King come back to the South to the site of the great annual blues festival. She was the ebullient part owner and chief cook of a restaurant, the proprietor of a store, suddenly broke, in debt, chopping cotton between ventures. Then she fell in with "the wrong people." I did not ask the details: When a woman says *the wrong people,* it is an old song.

In the end, she came to Cleveland Street to stay with the dullard who lived in the shotgun house next door. Sonny was her last adventure. He knows something about her the others could not fathom; now and then he looks up out of his drunkenness and his eyes are narrow, mean, when they focus on Gurtha. Every year he promises to marry her at the end of summer, in September, and every year he changes his mind. He can turn nasty when he drinks, she said, but a woman who has had three husbands and six children and spent more than a little time with "the wrong people" can take care of herself.

According to Gurtha, the story her neighbors tell is true. She and Sonny had been fighting, hitting each other, cursing, raising hell. Gurtha chased him from the house out into the middle of the street, battering him with a two-by-four. Sonny fell down, and Gurtha jumped on him. She was sitting astride Sonny in the middle of the street, beating him with the two-by-four when the police came by. They took Gurtha to jail and kept her there for two days before they let her go home to Sonny.

After that, the neighbors did not speak to her, even to say, "Good morning, Miz Morris, and how are you today?" Her world narrowed to Sonny and the old woman who lay beside the window that had been propped open with a broken broomstick. Gurtha turned to memories, Chicago photographs, black and white, cracked, ragged at the edges—one of a little girl in a formal pose, and others of high times. In one picture, taken in 1967, a group of plump men in suits, wearing fedoras and mustaches, one of them looking very much like Fats Waller, stand with several overdressed women. Under the names of the people in the picture the photographer has signed his own name and the words "were the picture taken."

Ina Lance, who lives in a tiny structure behind her mother's house a few doors down from Gurtha and Sonny, does not know Gurtha or care to. Ina Lance lives apart from her mother, who enjoys the comforts of the other big house on the block. In the daughter's room there are two chairs and a bed. Everything is neat, the bed dressed in a striped comforter and decorated with pillows. Her sense of style dominates the room; it is girlish, slightly offputting in a woman of fifty-three. But there are only two chairs, and as Thoreau said, it requires three for society.

Like Gurtha, Ina Lance lives very much in other times, but the wrong kind of people played no part in her life. She speaks of the tragedy of her marriage, a fire in which her husband was burned and their child died. The marriage could not survive the tragedy, she said, although they tried.

She knows the street, what had been a neighborhood, the history of it. History shows in her face, in the felicitous combination of Choctaw and African features, the wedding of the genes in cheekbones and skin. The other side of history, the old black/white relations, resides in her, too. She has at the surface of her memory the story of a young black woman and a white plantation owner. When the woman refused to sleep with him, the white man tied her to the back of a wagon, and dragged her down the road and through the fields until she was dead. Ina Lance said her mother was a child when it happened, but that she saw it all.

Ina Lance and her mother have lived on Cleveland Street for more than forty years, since the blacks owned their own homes on Cleveland Street, before the old people went north and their children rented the family homes out to strangers, before the paint peeled off the wood and the gardens went to ruin and the grass died. Forty years ago little girls wore starched dresses to school on weekdays and their very best to church on Sunday, and all the little girls, like Ina, knew the names of all the people who lived in the nice houses, large and small, on that eminently respectable block of Cleveland Street.

It was a very long time ago, when the people went to Chicago, long before they began to come back from the North, bearing crack cocaine and loneliness.

Everyone on Cleveland Street is homeless now, even the Gusters and Ina Lance and her mother. These people of the vestigial community know the details of the history of the last half of the century, and they have begun to develop a theory. "We have freedom now," they say, "but freedom for what?" Integration drove a hard bargain; the people learned to vote just as they lost their sense of home, and with it all they had learned of politics.

In Mississippi, it was the whites who took away the politics of the poor, lovingly, with great subtlety, but as surely as if they had continued to do it with the whip and the hanging tree. Integration, as Dr. Goldie Wells said, had cost the blacks the life of black community. It had left the churches bereft of members. The private, church-sponsored academies, like the one she had reopened in Lexington in 1995, had closed. The blacks who were prepared for integration separated from the poor, moving into a clearly defined purgatory between the black and white worlds. The public world of the segregated collapsed.

It is not a pleasant thought for a white who supported integration to hear, but one hears it again and again: Integration, demanded by blacks and implemented by whites, had a devastating effect on the black poor in Mississippi. For the poor, the villain was justice—not true justice, as integration should have been, but justice misguided, misinterpreted, misused. The grandest line of modern tragedy, the one Aristotle might have appreciated most, expresses just such a murderous perversity: "I kissed thee 'ere I killed thee. . . ."

Until the last half of this century, the poor, like the people on Cleveland Street or in the cave of the poets, had been separated from the rest of society, but not from each other. Dogpatch and Catfish Row, like most myths, had some grounding in reality. The society portrayed in the myth was pre-modern, made of people who were more or less equal, maintained in their equality by the ritualistic life of Dogpatch or Catfish Row. The characters in *The Grapes of Wrath* fit into a similar pattern: Within the community of migrants, there was equality, ritualized in the act of migration.[2] Isolated as groups, they maintained a political life, joining unions, supporting various reform candidates, and so on. Even blacks and Latinos, although far fewer in number than the poor whites and suffering from much more virulent prejudice, were able to live a nascent political life within their own communities.

Political loneliness has two sources: hatred of others, who are not good enough to be friends or allies, and hatred of oneself, who is not good enough to have friends or allies. On Cleveland Street, Mrs. Guster represented one view, and Gurtha, whose mother told her almost from infancy that she was "bad," represented the other. The same loneliness of the poor occurs in Chicago and Oakland, Belle Glade and the new Jewish ghettos of New York. Of the hundreds of people I listened to over the years of writing this book, only a few had a sense of community. All the rest lived in caves, feared aliens from outer space or across the borders of race or culture, and depended for any help at all on family or prying, mean-spirited minions of a reluctant government.

Much of the hatred of oneself and others is connected with migration. A snaggle-toothed woman with two children in Oklahoma had been moving steadily westward over a dozen years, abused by her parents in North Carolina, beaten by a husband in Ohio, deprived of her front teeth by a boyfriend's fist in Kansas, come to Oklahoma to live with her sister who carried a shotgun over the back window of her pickup truck. The snaggle-toothed woman, who was part Cherokee, had a vague sense of another Cherokee migration, more painful than hers, but she did not know when, nor did she know the details; it had happened before, at some time before. At the end of the century, she lived among strangers in Oklahoma, as her kin had done before her. She feared her neighbors, whom she knew as thieves, drunks, and drug addicts, and fought the government for sustenance.

The trend away from community has found its way into the language in this century. At one time the phrase "kith and kin" referred to two distinct

---

[2] The political naivete of Steinbeck's novel is not widely recognized. His white migrants displaced the Mexican-American laborers who had worked the farms in California, cutting their incomes, putting many of them out of work, and eventually supporting the government when it deported huge numbers of American citizens of Mexican descent for the avowed purpose of giving their jobs to the white migrants.

groups: "kin" referred to blood relations; "kith" first meant knowledge, then the rules of behavior, the place of residence, and then for the longest time it described one's friends, acquaintances, neighbors, and countrymen. But "kith" has lost its meaning now, becoming nothing more than a synonym for "kin." The phrase "kith and kin," which once described a person's world in its social and political entirety, has become a common example of pleonasm, the useless repetition of words.

Perhaps the loss of meaning of a single word cannot describe the end of political life, but there is some history to be considered: It was the great reform of Cleisthenes that separated kith from kin in ancient Athens, ending the role of kinship alliances in the ruling of the polis and replacing them with the new power of the *deme*, the kith of Athens.

While the notion of kith has fled from every economic level, the loss has been most devastating to the poor, for "kith" had meaning beyond mere locality, it included behavior and knowledge, the common world of political animals, the public world. Among kin, one set of rules existed, dominated by culture; among one's kith, another set of rules existed, influenced by culture but not dominated by it. The world of kith could include people from distant places, other cultures, come together to live in the brilliant place between the chaos of absolute liberty and the rigid order of intransigent culture—the political world. The rich of the modern world transformed their kith into an economic polis, politics of the pocketbook, the suburb, exurb, management, unions, ownership. The poor were left with loneliness and kin.

XIV.

Across Cultures

IN AMERICA THE WAR of cultures did not begin in earnest until the middle of the twentieth century. There had always been wars between the dominant culture and the others, but cultural differences had been no more than an excuse to take another person's land, force people into slavery, replace slavery with cheap labor; it had been a reason to despise the poor and so to make the use of them more comfortable for the rich. Culture itself had been of little interest; the framers of the Constitution had not even bothered to make English the official language of the new country. They were concerned with politics. The United States of America was the most political creation in the history of states: There were no economists, few churchmen, and not a single anthropologist present at its birth.

No culture but Western culture was in the minds of the colonists, and for all but a few of the very rich there was precious little of that.[1] As for blacks and Native Americans, they were thought of more as members of a different species than people of other cultures.

Questions of culture did not even arise with the emancipation of blacks;

---

[1] Ethnocentrism was not, as some have argued, a European invention. Most of the cultures native to the Americas named themselves "the People," as if no others could even be described as human beings. The practice was not limited to any language group—the Siouan-speaking Lakota of the Great Plains as well as the Ute-Aztecan speakers of the Southwest gave themselves such names. We know them, of course, by the names given them by their adversaries. The Lakotas, Dakotas, and Nakotas are known to us as "Sioux," a word their neighbors to the east used for them; it means snake or enemy. Similarly, the word "Apache" or "Apache de Nabajo," used to describe the Diné of Arizona and New Mexico by the Pueblos to the east and south of them, meant enemy, while the word the Apaches, including the Navaho branch, used for themselves, "Diné," means the People.

it was assumed that blacks would choose to become like their former masters. Otherwise, white citizens of the time reasoned, why would they want to be freed? At the time of emancipation, Native Americans were still a military problem; the whites, with the help of many black troops, were interested in eliminating them by any means possible—slaughter, disease, starvation, alcohol, or schoolbooks and beans—the choice, such as it was, belonged to the Indians. In that case, as with blacks, culture was not an issue, for the whites placed no value at all on their cultures. The sentiment was returned by Native Americans who had to pay attention to the military prowess of the Europeans, but had no regard at all for their culture. The natives thought of the invaders as avaricious individualists who smelled bad; the word for a white in the Lakota language, for example, meant greedy (literally, he-who-eats-the-fat).

During the great waves of immigration at the end of the nineteenth century and the beginning of the twentieth, culture did not become a major issue because it was assumed that immigrants would first adapt to the established culture, then adopt it. And for the most part, the immigrants did just that. They settled in the ghettos of the great cities, and worked their way out. Some Germans had their own schools for a time, as did some Jews, Chinese, Swedes, and so on, but immigration had been a way to come to America, not to retain old country values. For these people there was one culture, American culture; they jumped into the melting pot, and were glad to be there.

The melting pot did not welcome everyone, however; blacks, Latinos, Native Americans, a good number of Southeast Asians, some Southern Italians and Eastern Europeans, and others, did not fit comfortably into the pot. The discomfort of these people, many of them non-white, led to the view that it was not merely the prejudice of the dominant culture but their lack of love and understanding of their own cultures that caused their suffering.[2] Multiculturalism was born as a response to the purported problem. Americans began to dress themselves in masks of lost cultures, a papier-mâché of inconceivable values, irretrievable times; they did not learn their antecedents, they attempted to become their antecedents.

An undisciplined discipline was invented: Multiculturalism, which should have been taught by historians and anthropologists, became the province of multiculturalists. Each culture thought itself superior to all the others. "Black is beautiful" soon came to mean black is most beautiful. At

---

[2] This lack of appreciation of their own cultures is blamed entirely on the dominant culture, the historical process of assimilation, the demand of the dominant culture for conformity, and so on. The argument is well known. The question here is not about the value of cultures, since a pluralistic view is assumed all through this book, but about the effect of culture on poverty in the United States.

the same time, Oscar Lewis's "culture of poverty" was revised by Ken Auletta to mean the "underclass," which was exclusively brown and black. The lines were drawn.

The battle was joined on one side by such social and political conservatives as the late Allan Bloom, who wrote a prissy diatribe, *The Closing of the American Mind,* in which he said, "Culture is a cave," referring to Plato's Allegory of the Cave.[3] Bloom's ethnocentrism was so all-consuming that he considered Western civilization beyond mere culture as it was lived by all other peoples. On the other side, Orlando Patterson wrote *Freedom*[4] in which he redefined the word into a "triad" of personal, sovereignal, and civic freedoms, giving the West credit for the invention of personal freedom, although only as a response to slavery, and showing that other cultures did not need the West's notion of personal freedom because they offered their people sovereignal and civic freedom.[5]

---

[3] (New York: Simon & Schuster, 1987). Bloom's idea of "culture as a cave" implies the existence of an excluded middle. He claims a place for philosophy outside the cave. But philosophy was a part of Athenian culture, so it must have been both within Bloom's cave of culture and outside it.

[4] (New York: Basic Books, 1991). Patterson and Bloom both offer views of the ancient world to explain the contemporary world. Patterson's concept of a chordal triad of freedom may not survive the test of time, and a few of his ideas fail my admittedly Western idea of the test of reason, but there can be little doubt that slavery played an important role in permitting, if not causing, the Athenian democracy, the practice of philosophy, and so on. If nothing else, slavery gave the Athenians the leisure Aristotle said was absolutely vital to the practice of politics.

Bloom, who translated *The Republic,* seems not to have read it. He credits Plato with what he was not (an advocate of the liberal arts, which include the humanities) and neglects Plato's antidemocratic views. But the worst part of Bloom's work is that his Greeks are all dead, even in their own time. The intellectual excitement that is the true enduring gift of Greece appears nowhere in Bloom's work. He apparently did not understand the role of Protagoras, for neither Protagoras nor the Sophists even merit listing in the index of his book. It is difficult to imagine a man who spent much of his life with the classics, even teaching dialectic as method, yet did not understand that the glory of unjust, imperfect, reflective, disputatious, democratic Greece was not the answers but the questions.

[5] Patterson, Freedom:

I have suggested that freedom as a value was generated by, and socially constructed out of, the interaction among master, slave, and native nonslaves. Elsewhere, I have demonstrated that slavery was a nearly universal institution. It should follow that the value of freedom was constructed everywhere. Yet, we know that this was not so. Indeed, one of the major objectives of this work is to show that freedom was a peculiarly Western value and ideal. How is the discrepancy explained?

Simply, by noting that while the idea of freedom was certainly engendered wherever slavery existed, it never came to term. . . . Resisting the promotion of freedom as value was the natural thing to do for most human societies. . . . What is unusual is the institutionalization and idealization of this value, given its degraded, servile source. It is the ancient West that needs explanation. Because we are of the West and share its central value, we have turned the history of human societies around, and ethnocentrically assumed that it is the rest of humankind, in its failure to embrace freedom, that needs explaining. (p. 20)

At one time the structure of this book was based on culture. It was divided into sections describing the existence of multigenerational poverty separately among African Americans, Latinos, Europeans, Asians, and Native Americans.[6] I had theorized that each culture produced a different response to force, conforming to the rule of the war of cultures, which is that America has no common culture, but a collection of mutually exclusive cultures, each of which determines other aspects of life for those born into that culture. Even the politics of the book could be argued according to the rules of the war of cultures, using as a basis both Herder's idea of a culture as a person's one and only home and Hegel's belief that "Freedom is to be at home."

The trouble with trying to make a structure out of what already exists, however, is that the collection of bric-à-brac we call the world does not always lend itself to the expectations the writer brings with him to his labors. The idea that poverty is generated by culture would not even make a wall; no matter how the pieces were twisted and turned, the structure would not stand. But another structure, unlike culture, asserted itself.

Listening to the poor, taking what they said and showed as the only world to be considered, led to the understanding that culture affected American economic life, but did not alone determine it. A taste for certain foods, a set of gestures, choices of clothing, child-rearing practices, skin color, even language could not overcome the fact of living within a surround of force in a society so determinedly political that it subsumed everything else under the idea of legitimate power.

It might be argued that those who came from or ally themselves with a non-Western culture do not participate in the exercise of legitimate power because the idea is too foreign to them, but the nature of immigration is the search for a new social contract, inclusion, citizenship. Immigration is perhaps the only possible revolution in the twentieth century. And for those who were born in the United States, the idea of legitimate power is home.[7]

The American state, for all its flaws, permits and even encourages diversity of opinion and the possibility of legitimate power for people descended

[6] In the war of cultures in the United States, cultures are often conflated into larger categories identified as races. Of course, Latinos "may be of any race," which is the most obvious breakdown of the racial categories.

In April 1996, *Harper's* magazine published a conversation in which I served as moderator while Professors Cornel West of Harvard and Jorge Klor de Alva of U.C. Berkeley discussed the question of race. Both men said race was "a social construct," but West was unwilling to give up the idea of race, while Klor de Alva argued that it was an unreasonable and damaging concept and should be gotten rid of as soon as possible.

[7] Compare this to Herder's notion of a culture as a person's one and only home.

from any and all cultures; it offers a home in politics to all of its citizens. Politics is transcendent in America. In every descendant culture it determines who will long suffer poverty and who will not.[8] Any American, any person, may be strengthened by taking pride and pleasure in the knowledge of the culture of his forebears, but an old culture cannot make a new life.

Culture plays a powerful role in the lives of each of the families chronicled in the rest of this chapter, and each family is descended from a different culture. They have only three attributes in common: All of them live in the United States; all of them are poor; and none of them has discovered how to live the political life at any level of social organization, from the family to the polis. Reflective thinking plays little or no role in the lives of these families, although several of them have had a political moment or at the very least, a moment of false politics. Yet there is no American descendant culture I know of that prohibits reflection. And there is a simple proof of political thinking by most people in every culture in the United States: They are not poor.

1. El Baz

Two weeks before the great Lubavitcher Rebbe Menachem Schneerson was left unconscious and near death by a massive stroke, he was visited by a short, thick man with a putty nose, a Kabbalist who was born on an American Air Force base in Casablanca. Photographs were made of the meeting. In one of them, the Rebbe, whom his followers worshipped as the Messiah, faced the Kabbalist from Casablanca: They looked into each other's eyes; the snap brims of their black fedoras nearly touched; their long white beards hung from their cheeks and chins like ethereal medallions of wisdom. There was a preternatural electricity in the air. The photographs, developed some days later, were brilliant with color: the flesh of the faces was of an extraordinary pinkness, as if the men glowed with thought or intensity or something more, piety, even holiness.

---

[8] I have used the adjective "descendant" to describe cultural groups within the United States because there are few, if any, unbroken cultures. Every group has been affected greatly by the dominant culture as well as by other descendant cultures. I have eaten tacos with Chinese Americans and joined a group of Mexican Americans for lunch in a Japanese restaurant. An Irish American recently sent me a note in which he used the Yiddish word *gelt*. America is not a melting pot, but neither is it Paris, Bombay, or Tenochtitlán. Contemporary cultures cannot be transplanted whole to new nations and Neolithic cultures cannot survive unchanged when the chiefs operate casinos and preach computer literacy to the young braves.

A moment after the photographs were taken, El Baz, the Kabbalist, leaned forward until his nose nearly touched that of the great Rebbe, and whispered, "In two weeks, Rebbe, you will be struck down by sickness. It has been revealed to me. Blessed be His Name. I see it in your eyes."

Who is El Baz? American, North African, French, Israeli? He speaks Hebrew, Arabic, French, Spanish, English, and a little Russian to please his wife. He walks on crutches. "I am a sick man," he said, "sick. The operation on my leg took eight hours. Also I have pancreatitis, my cholesterol over five hundred, triglycerides more than thirty-four hundred. Sick. Sick man."

And then he said he was strong. He raised his arm and made a fist. "Strong," he said, showing me his fist, threatening.

I did not know what to believe about him, and I was not alone in this. Whoever knew El Baz did not know him. The man who brought him donations of food, the social worker who had known him for five years, believed the cupboards and the refrigerator in the house were full to overflowing. But who would dare to ask? "Strong," El Baz said, and showed his fist.

He had been in Israel at one time, but it was not clear about when or for how long. His children, he said, were American citizens, born in America. But El Baz?

The Intifada had driven him out of Israel, he claimed, and then he railed against the Israeli government which had accused him of child abuse, threatened to take his children from him, cut off all state aid. "The Intifada," he said; "I was afraid for my children."

The aspects of El Baz are so powerful and so concentrated they strike all at once, overwhelming whoever encounters him. His head is completely bald beneath the yarmulke, not shaved, but hairless and freckled. He has light eyes, blue-green-brown, multicolored, changeable, like cat's eyes. He cannot be more than five feet tall, perhaps less, and his beard is very long, becoming wispy near the tip, where he has combed it into a point. He wears white shirts, very fresh, crisp, but he centers himself in his hands, which are short and thick, with black hair growing on the backs of his fingers and hands and up his forearms, which protrude from under the doubled-back shirtcuffs like two powerful pistons.

El Baz lives in a synagogue; that is, he lives in a basement apartment below a house in Borough Park, Brooklyn, that has been converted into a synagogue. When I first saw him, he was seated on a narrow bed which was covered with a black and white striped cloth. A small couch of dark red sculpted velvet had been placed at a right angle to the bed, and between the two, serving both, was a large ivory-colored coffee table, oval-shaped and incised with blue curlicues. He keeps a few of his books behind him on a shelf, but not the precious ones. They are somewhere in the back rooms of the apartment, hidden from thieves and other strangers.

"I am the only poor Jew in New York," said El Baz. "All the others live in houses worth two or three hundred thousand dollars, but they put them in the name of their wives or other relatives so they can collect welfare. In this building I cannot get a rent receipt because my landlord pays taxes for a synagogue instead of an apartment building. Would he give me a receipt? Evidence of his illegal activity?

"If I cannot get a rent receipt, how can I get welfare, even for my children?"

He said he could not work, because he could not stand.

What work could he do?

Computers, he said. He could build them, repair them, do whatever was needed for them.

Must you stand to do such work?

"I need a lawyer."

The social worker who had brought food to El Baz gave him the name of a lawyer. El Baz telephoned. After a few moments of mild conversation, he shouted into the telephone, "If you're such a good lawyer, why can't you take my case?"

The social worker cautioned him to behave in a more rational way, to suppress his rage.

El Baz smiled into the telephone. He listened for a moment, then ended the conversation by wishing the lawyer well.

When he hung up, we asked why he had treated a good man, one who was willing to help others pro bono, so rudely.

"He told me it was good question," El Baz said, but then he went on: The lawyer was weak, the social worker was weak, his Russian wife was weak because she could not ask for food or money. He, El Baz, was strong, he could ask for food, demand food.

The social worker said he could not go on bringing food to El Baz, subsidizing his rent. It had been five years since El Baz had worked at a job. "You must find work," the social worker said.

El Baz changed the subject. He smiled, his voice softened. He turned away from the social worker to focus on me, speaking of Kabbala, of miraculous cures he had effected. Once a man had flown him down to Florida to help his son, who was dying, in desperate need of a heart transplant. El Baz cured the boy. "I tell doctor, take tubes from throat, not need machine. And doctor takes away tube. Boy lives. Heart is good. You do not believe? Ask doctor. I give you number. Ask doctor."

He went on, telling of other cures, of great powers, of the people who come to see him. "Give me money, but is not business. Kabbala is not business."

We talked about the Kabbala, of which I knew nothing, except that it involved numerology. He showed me his books, he invited me to come back, to talk, to learn. The social worker said we could not wait, we must go. After we left the apartment, the social worker said he could not put up with El Baz much longer. I nodded, listening politely, but I had the impression that the social worker had been saying this for a long time, for years. It was an endless contest, in which El Baz was armed with crutches and the social worker was crippled by compassion.

Some months later, I spoke again with El Baz. He did not discuss his health; instead, he inquired about mine: heart? sugar? In Kabbala there are answers.

I thought of the photograph of the Grand Rebbe and El Baz, what the mystical diagnostician had said. I remembered his oldest son, skulking through the apartment, a thin boy, tall and blond, a Russian face and a spine bent at the shoulders and again at the neck, like a twig that could not bear the force of. . . . And I was afraid.

"Let me call you," he said. "You live in Brooklyn? Spell for me your name."

"Yes, yes, I'll call you," I lied, for I knew I would never see him again, never speak to him, never give him the spelling of my name, the date of my birth, whatever he needed to delve into me through his velvet-bound books. Of course, I think about him now and then: the brilliantly shined black shoes, the putty nose, the black hair on his fingers. But I comfort myself with the belief that he does not think about me. I am too distant for war, and he does not do politics. Anyway, if he is such a good Kabbalist, how come he doesn't know how to spell my name?

2. Yapos Sopay

Once, in all the long history of the Washingtons of Oakland, California, a member of the family entered the public life. I first met them during that political instant in a meeting room in downtown Oakland, and I was to see them often over the years, to learn from the Washingtons that politics and culture are separate countries. Although it was Yapos whom I met first, whose political awareness interested me, promising to upset the thesis of this book or at least to offer a heuristic exception, I think it best to begin three-quarters of a century ago on a cotton farm in Alabama.

The best place to talk to Annie Washington is in her car. The car is always parked in the same place, under the fig tree, the one tall tree on 91st Street, in the only shady spot in the great flat ghetto that runs from the Oakland Hills to San Francisco Bay. Every afternoon when the sun heats up, Mrs. Washington goes out to sit in the car and take the air. She walks down the cement steps of her house, careful to stay on the part covered with outdoor carpeting, going slowly on ancient arthritic bones—step and rest, step and rest—hanging on, the knee joints almost gone. Then she waddles down the walk to the curb, a woman of eighty, built on the square, peering out through ornate eyeglasses at the unfamiliar world of the street she has lived on for the last fifty-five years.

She opens the door to her big, old American car, eases herself into the driver's seat, touches the leather, the smooth maroon luxury of the car, remembering how it had been. Then she closes the door and turns on the radio, adjusts the rearview mirror and the side mirror to give herself the best view of her neighbors, and smiles, satisfied.

Her grandson, who belongs to the Hip Hop Nation, has a commercial view of Mrs. Washington's custom. "It's her trademark," he says, as if it were something salable or a passport to fame to sit in an old maroon car under a fig tree to take the air on 91st Street. One dreams, the other remembers; in the present, the neighborhood children have exploded firecrackers on the roof of her car and the people next door are selling crack cocaine in the front yard.

Annie Washington is a big woman, and wide, but hardly taller than a child. She is almost always dressed in a white blouse, which gives her the air of a nurse or a nurse's aide, someone professional but not businesslike. She laughs easily, striving to keep hidden the place where her teeth are missing. She speaks with a heavy accent of Alabama, although she has been in Oakland for fifty-five years.

When she speaks of her husband and their courtship, she giggles, like a girl again; the memory comes over her, as if she had been transported, "Well, I used to live in the country country. I grew up on a farm. My father owned his home. It was a big farm. We used to have to chop cotton and pick cotton and all that kind of stuff. Cows and hogs and chickens and turkeys and all of that stuff. Yeah, he had a big place. Boy, was it hot! But when it get hot, I'd take off and go slip off and go home to de house. They'd miss me, didn't know I was goin out of that sun. Yeah, they did. Yes, indeed, I come from a long way down there.

"My mother and father raised me to be a Christian, goin to church all the time and treat people nice. I liked the way they raised me up. I didn't like it then. Because I thought they was too strict. They didn't let me go places. I wanted to go to parties. And we had to be home before the sun go down. You better not let the sun catch you down before you get home or you'll get a spankin. They spank you, I mean, you get a whippin."

The romance in Annie Washington's life began when she was very young, a schoolgirl allowed to go up to Birmingham. "We met at a picnic. You know how you have em. Well, I was so glad to meet somebody. Oh, yeah, it was fine. So he come over and he wanted to buy soda waters for me. We spent a few hours. Then it was gettin late. We had to go home. So from there, me and my husband, we courted for around six years, off and on, cause he was goin to high school."

The Washingtons married and moved to Birmingham. When the war came, he went. She stayed home, putting as much as she could of his allot-ment checks into the bank. When he returned, they bought a house of their own: "It wasn't expensive, but I saved up the money. We didn't have to pay much then to get a down payment for a home there. It was a new house, too.

"My husband used to sell ice. He used to work for a company. He learned the route, then he bought one of those, I forgot, but it was a Army truck with the big wheels, set up high. He learned the route, so he took the customer from who he was workin for, and was sellin on his own.

"This was a vacant lot when I moved here in 1950 from Birmingham, Alabama. My husband came here. I came with him. He was havin it hard back there. Well, he heard about how good it was right here in California, so he migrated right on out here. On Greyhound bus. It was a long trip, oooh, but I was young then. He found somethin. First, he worked in a foundry, A & B Foundry, out on San Leandro.

"It was nice when we was livin here. All the people what used to live here, they passed on. I had a friend lived in the house where the bricks at, right there, she was a Filipino. She died, though. She was eighty-some years old. All these people round here. My friend used to live there, she don't no more. All them across the corner. We knowed everybody on down this cor-ner. It built up a lot since I been here.

"Everybody here worked, they had a job. They was all mixed up, cause when we started to buyin down here, most of em, they left out. White peo-ple used to live there.

"It didn't make me mad when the whites left, cause they were nice peo-ple, you know. They was movin up in the hills, so we moved on up in the hills, too. (Laughs) Yeah, everywhere they moved, we moved on up in the hills."

She pauses for a moment, as if to turn a page in her memory. "Well, it was kind of rough. I raised my kids and four grand-kids. I had Matthew ever since he was nine years old. He graduated from Skyline, so his sister graduated from Castlemont. (She in the house.) And the baby girl, she graduated.

"[The neighborhood now is] much different. It's rough. I have to stay in the house most of the time. I've seen the neighbors what sell drugs. In this block. Right on the left side, right here. In the next house. I'm tellin you. I just look for the man to run through my house. They sell it through my driveway. I've seen it right up in the house there. They don't care. They must be sellin all the time, because the people be runnin after them.

"It started to changing the last nine years. It started to change and change. You know, when I first moved here, the neighbors, we'll have more fun, talk to each other and talkin over the fence and visit my friends used to live right there.

"I used to be a Avon lady. All around in the neighborhood. I stopped, because it be too rough. I couldn't be goin out there now, knockin on these people's doors. They were nice then, but it got to changin, you run up on crazy people. They'd let me come in and order whole bunch of Avon and wouldn't get it. I'd run there five or six times tryin to catch em. They'd tell me, come a certain time, but you knows peoples. I had some good customers, and I just stopped sellin when it got like that.

"I don't feel like doin it now. People's got guns now, cause I hear em shootin em all the time. Sometimes I think I should [keep a gun].[9] Never been robbed . . . Knock on the wood. I been lucky myself.

"My two sons is passed away. My oldest son, he was in Chicago. Somebody robbed him, and killed him, that's how he got killed. Went in his house and rob him and kill him. Yeah. My other son, he got sick, he had diabetes, like his father had, and heart trouble.

"I have one daughter workin, she works. Matthew's mother don't work. She don't do nothing. She stay here with me, though. She kind of ill mentally. She all right, though, but she stay here with me, sometimes. Sometimes she gone. I don't know where Matthew's father at. Matthew's been sayin he was gon find him, but he hasn't been able to find him yet."

On another day, when her grandson and I were taking his son, Jazz, back to his mother, Mrs. Washington recalled the world again, but without the blinding comforts of nostalgia.

"Every year different people move in and out. Every year, the peoples change. The neighbors never get together. We used to get together. The lady used to live right there, she was nice. We were nice to everybody. We would talk. Wasn't no fighting goin on and no jealousy or nothing.

[9] She keeps a loaded shotgun in the house.

"They're tryin to run me out this neighborhood. And you know, this world, you have to be so careful, because if you don't, they will shoot your head off in a minute. You can't go roun runnin your mouth. You know the drug dealers, they don't want you to talk about them and tell the police on them. And so, that's why I said the neighbors not like they used to be, because if you had a neighbor then and you talked to em about it, they won't get back and spill it out, but the neighbors now, they patronize the drug dealer. They want it, and you can't say nothing to them about it. Or you find yourself out of a house and home.

"The young people around here, they don't work. Them people over there, I ain't never knowed none of em to work. And she got the two houses right there. They ain't never worked. Let's see, like my daughter worked and the peoples in that house right there and that house right there, the Mexican live right there and the Mexican over there, they work. But that's it. Everybody else, AFDC and they sellin the drugs.

"When I come here, everybody worked, everybody round here worked. Yeah, they did. Everybody was gettin up early in the mornin and goin to work. I really don't know when it stopped, but it been stopped for a while.

"The world is generally unfair here. You know, most of the people, we have to stick to each other kind of, because now, Mexicans, they don't want to mix with us. We don want to mix with them, so it jes a problem."

At first, her tale of the neighborhood sounds like an old woman's lament, cranky and unreliable, but when we put our heads together to watch the action in the rearview mirror, we saw money and drugs exchanged as easily and openly as if it was a matter of radishes or fish. And when the Mexican family across the street looked at the round black face in which the girl of Alabama still lived, like a ghost of youth, they turned away without a word.

If ever 91st Street had been something like a community, such politics had died. The trees were a sign; in fifty-five years a forest might have grown. Instead, there was only the fig tree in front of the Washington house and a series of saplings dying in the sun.

She turned her thoughts to Matthew—Yapos Sopay was a name she never said. "I hope Matthew do good. Matthew smart. He's helped me around here, too. You know, I lost my son. And he was the onlyiest one around here to help me out. But Matthew got to work. Matthew got to get up, try to make hisself good.

"Matt like to write music. Matt's good at that. Matt used to model for Sears, Roebuck when he was six or seven years old. When he was sixteen years old, Matt had him a job working out in San Leandro. He worked. Matt had some good jobs. He used to be a guard.

"His momma was good with them kids. She married, but she and her husband didn't get along. Like me, if things get rough, I kept on, but young people they don't want to stick with nobody if they don't want to be nice to em. They want to get out. You know, sometimes you get a husband and he ain't no husband to you."

And then with a howl of laughter, "My husband and me, we get in scrambles sometimes. I'm tellin you."

She shrugs. Matthew and his sister were coming down the stairs, carrying the baby. "You know, I was up in my fifties when I took them kids, but I didn't take em to keep, because I thought they mother and father get back together, but they never did, so I got stuck with em. So the last one, she's seventeen, so I'm tell her, she got to be on her own, but as long as they around me, I say, 'You all don't stay out here late at night. It's not safe now, because I be up there worryin about it.' So they doin all right."

She looked away for a long time. She knew the summation was not quite correct, but she did not want to say more.

I thought of how the laughter faded when she spoke of her son who was murdered in Chicago. She said it was a robber who killed him; Yapos says it was his friend. She has one daughter who works and one, Yapos's mother, who is, as she says, the victim of mental problems.

Yapos's mother has been described in various ways, as a drug abuser, a loose woman, and most recently as a schizophrenic, a person who does not live in a world in common. And Matthew himself, how much does his grandmother know of him? Or wish to know? What does she think about her great-grandson, Jazz, who lies in his crib, with great staring eyes and tiny hands, at ten months still not much bigger than a newborn, sucking mush, and faintly weeping.

I do not know why Matthew came to the conference where I met him. The meeting, held in conjunction with WEAP (Women's Economic Agenda Project), was devoted to helping the families of men held in California prisons. Two speakers had come up from Los Angeles, old-time radicals, a gigantic black man and a Mexican-American woman who transformed herself with makeup and eyeshadow from the weary woman who had driven up the Interstate into a vibrant revolutionary. They spoke well, without much cant, of the difficulties poor people and prisoners faced in California. The black man talked about his years in the prison system. He answered questions for the mother of a boy in California's special maximum-security prison at Pelican Bay. The Latina talked more about poor people. They had no plan, no answers beyond anger. Before they took questions, they collected a few dollars to help defray the cost of their trip.

The audience was respectful, black and white, with a few schoolteachers sprinkled among the mothers and wives of the prisoners. In the center of the third row of folding chairs, a young man and woman sat together. Now and then they whispered to each other, putting their heads together, her short-cropped natural and his dredlocks. I could not see their faces, but the set of their shoulders, the attentiveness and whispering, separated them from the troubled women and worn-out Berkeley radicals who filled the rest of the chairs.

When the question and answer period began, conducted by the gigantic ex-convict, the young man and woman attacked the premise of his speech and his work, demanding to know why people of color were always associated with violence, why poor people and prisons were always "put into the same bag."

The ex-convict glowered at them. Neither the young man nor the young woman next to him was intimidated. They turned to the audience, competing with the ex-convict for eye contact, as they made their case against the "stereotyping" of the people. In the end, the ex-convict won, as moderators always win, by cutting off the comments of his antagonists.

I crept up through the seats to where the two young people sat, asking if I could meet with them later. The young man wrote his name and three telephone numbers in my notebook: Yapos Sopay. "This is where I stay. This is where my son stays. And this is my friend's house."

We arranged to meet at a record store off Telegraph Avenue in Berkeley. He was late, and he came bursting in, talking, touching the CDs, eyeing the charts, examining every display, every advertisement, offering comments on records and persons as if he were the King of Hip-Hop or at the very least the Michelin Guide to Rap. Short, stocky, dressed in saggies half again his size, his short dredlocks bouncing with every gesture, he addressed the world with large black eyes, at once omniscient and full of pain, as if to say he was some sort of an orphaned genius.

On the street, on the way to a café on Telegraph Avenue where the young woman was to meet us, he knew every third or fourth person we passed. One had seen him act as master of ceremonies at a dance, another had known him in school, a third had met him at a party. Depending upon how well they knew him, they asked about his music or his child. They touched him, they shook his hand. He laughed, he strutted, the pain went out of his eyes. Young African Prophet of Soul, Yapos, and backwards, Sopay.

"Oh, man, I saw your books in Cody's, a big stack of em. Cool."

"Steal one."

And then two more people came by to speak to him. "This is my man,

Earl Shorris; he's a writer," Yapos said by way of introduction or explanation. And we went on.

The café was one of those grim, barnlike places at the dying end of Telegraph. We bought coffee and soft drinks and went upstairs. No one had cleared the tables since breakfast that morning or dinner the night before. The young woman was there. She carried a sheaf of papers, including a letter of protest attacking the Reverend Jesse Jackson as a sellout to the establishment. The letter, almost in the form of a poster, was clear, well-written, and the arguments were not entirely without merit. They planned to distribute the letter during Jackson's forthcoming visit to Berkeley.

We talked for several hours. Yapos and the young woman had theories about everything. He was twenty-two and she was nineteen; the sense of omniscience I had seen in his eyes was in keeping with his years. I liked them, the aspect of them that came to the café: He wanted to be a hip-hop star, she wanted to be an actress; they cared about politics and poverty; they had ideas; they hated racism, but it had not infected them. They were well-mannered and well-spoken. When they could not wait to make their ideas known, they talked over each other, on occasion rising out of their chairs with the excitement of their views.

I never saw her again; she went east, or was it south to Los Angeles? Yapos disappeared for a while, and then one day he telephoned, asking if I could meet him at a house on 91st Street. I picked him up there, and we drove back toward downtown Oakland to the studio Trixie Garcia had rented in a warehouse district. It was the first time we talked about hip-hop music. Trixie was there, a chunky girl in shorts, a painter with little training and no talent that I could see in the huge canvases hung on the walls and stacked in the corners of the warehouse room. Other people drifted in and out: Jamal, her former boyfriend; CharleZ Lyle, Yapos's collaborator and close friend; and Tim Taylor, who preferred the stage name FuryUs Styles.

Taylor, who had his small daughter with him, offered his views on hip-hop: "I think everybody has been in a broken home, I think everybody has been in that situation where they had to eat breakfast for dinner. You do what you can with what you got. If you got a twelve hundred and a four-track, you make the beat."

He lolled on a couch, as we all did, while a daytime talk show played on a small television set without an aerial, fading in and out, sometimes made of ghosts or scrambled into patterns far more interesting than the program. As the afternoon wore on, they changed the station again and again, mostly to find cartoons.

"You got the misogynous lyrics," Tim said, "it's just like misogyny in the home. If I see pops beatin on moms, it must be right for me to beat up on my girlfriend. If I see my homey shootin that fool over stupidshit [one word], why not grab a gat and blast somebody and get some money? Especially if it's all about CREAM [Cash Rules Everything Around Me]?"

Then he leaned forward, interested in his own thoughts, defensive in a different way: "There's just got to be a balance. Everything has got to be a balance between order and chaos. There's always got to be a balance, so that's where hip-hop comes in. Hip-hop is that balance."

When I asked him the origins of his idea, he said, "Order and chaos is something I deal with. It isn't something I think about a lot—it just came into my head. It's like battle rap."

The conversation soon turned to shootings. Yapos said he had seen someone get shot. CharleZ joined in the description of shootings, especially at YWCA dances. Tim said, "It's not a thing that I want recognition because I pack. I haven't expended none of these bullets on a person." Then he described going down to the bay and shooting holes in a boat. The conversation stayed on packing for a long time. Each of them remembered being robbed at gunpoint. Tim said he had been robbed three times. He wondered if he would use the gun if he was robbed again.

That afternoon passed. Others followed. Tim never appeared again, but CharleZ was often there, and of course Trixie. At times, when Yapos and CharleZ and I were out somewhere alone without Trixie, they talked about her, the money her father, Jerry Garcia, had put into a trust fund for her. She would not stay in Oakland for very long, they knew. Jamal had been with her, now he wasn't. She could be difficult, they said, but they liked her.

A few weeks later, Yapos and I drove to a cul-de-sac in Berkeley, parked, and went up the steps to a small bungalow. No one was home. Yapos walked around to the side of the house, looking for a way in, but he could not find one. We went back to the car, moved it into the shade, and waited. There was a small park in the center of the cul-de-sac. All the houses around it were of similar size and quality, bungalows with big front porches and lawns that sloped down toward the sidewalk.

We waited for a long time, but no one appeared at the house.

The next time we went to the house, Yapos said, "I want you to meet my son Jazz." This time there was someone home. Yapos said the woman who answered the door was the mother of his child. The young woman surprised me. I had expected someone vivacious, like the girl who had come to the meeting and the café with him. Instead, the woman who came to the door was very slim, a pale brown woman, elegant in form, like a sculpture by Modigliani or something fashioned by Picasso after he had seen the works of West Africa.

As it turned out, Rose was the daughter of a man from Benin who met a girl from Detroit while they were both students at a school in Perugia, Italy. Rose has never seen her father, for when the school year in Perugia ended, he went home to Benin and the woman who carried his child went home to America and gave birth to Rose.

In photographs Rose looks so much like her mother that it is easy to mistake them one for the other. It is as if Rose had no father; there is no sign of her father in her face or even in the slim, slightly elongated lip of her Picasso mouth.

Rose did not laugh easily, nor did her child ever laugh or even smile. Jazz was seven months old then, a baby born prematurely, kept in the hospital for weeks, finally growing, but tiny. She gave Jazz to me to hold. When I touched him, he grasped my finger. His hands were still tiny, smaller than the hands of my own children when they were newborn.

Rose and Yapos explained why he had been born prematurely. Rose and her mother had been in a Burger King restaurant when Rose was late in her pregnancy. "My mother got in a argument with a woman over a napkin," Rose said. "Then the woman started fighting with her. When they were fighting, the woman's boyfriend came over to help her fight with my mom. The man punched me in the stomach. I was almost nine months pregnant. I went into shock. The restaurant didn't call the police or try to stop the fight. The police came with the ambulance. They put me in the hospital and tried to keep the baby from coming. He came two days later. My delivery took twenty minutes."

The baby was tiny. Although Rose had completed training as a nurse's aid, she could not follow the vague instructions given by the hospital. She went there expecting to take the baby home, but they did not allow him to leave. She went often. Then one day, without notice, they told her to take him home.

She found a place in a home for unwed mothers. A church group put four young women together in the single-family house on the circular street in Berkeley. Rose said that when the four young women moved into the house it was very sudden, coming just after the previous owners moved out without notice. The neighbors came by to see what was going on, thinking to protect the property of the former owner. After they met the four young mothers, all the neighbors on the round street wrote their names and telephone numbers on a sheet of paper and gave it to the young women, saying that they should telephone if they need anything. Rose said it was just like *Leave It to Beaver.* She had never seen anything like it before.

She and Yapos compared his neighborhood on 91st Street to the round street. On 91st Street, he said, "people were suspicious of each other." He referred to a hip-hop song, "Snake Eyes," by the Professor, in which the

Professor talked at length about the people in the neighborhood who were all out for themselves, who couldn't be trusted, who might stab you in the back at any time.

Rose and Yapos agreed that this was the key difference between a poor neighborhood and a middle-class neighborhood. Yapos said, "In my neighborhood, nobody wants to get got; you never know when a eighty-year-old grandma will meet you at the door with a shotgun in her hand." He and Rose agreed that "when you don't have food in the house, you have to just look after your own needs; you can't be worried about anyone else."

They make a curious couple. Rose has only tasted liquor twice in her life; she has never used dope. Yapos said he smokes marijuana on a regular basis. Rose said Yapos was not a bad father, better than most. She spoke a lot about bad fathers, those who had children by different women within a two- or three-month period.

Yapos said he was waiting to see what kind of settlement Rose would get from her lawsuit against Burger King. He expected they would get a place and live together after the money came in. Rose planned to go to Detroit.

Among the many problems Yapos and Rose cannot resolve, none looms so large as her mother. Yapos said he does not like her because she treats Rose "like a slave," constantly ordering her to perform inconsequential tasks. As an example, he said that Rose's mother might call her in from another room to demand that she change the station on the television set.

When I met Rose's mother a few months later, I found her a hard-eyed woman, penniless and angry, imperious. She said she had left Detroit because she was Roman Catholic and people in Detroit were uncomfortable with a black woman who is Roman Catholic. She said it was better in Oakland. Although she drove one of the most battered old sedans—a Pontiac, I think—that I had ever seen on the road, she offered to give me a lift to wherever I was going.

She and Yapos glowered at each other. They talked about where Rose was going to live when her time in the home for unwed mothers was up. Rose's mother said she had a place. Her plans did not include Yapos. She and Rose were going to move into her place and wait until they got the money from the Burger King suit. She would know how to take care of things, the mother said; Rose would not.

I never saw Rose without Jazz, although I often saw the child when he was alone with his father. One day, when we were driving in the car, Yapos sat in the front passenger seat with Jazz in his arms. CharleZ sat in the back. Suddenly, I heard a terrible conk. Yapos had banged the child's head against the window. I could not imagine how it happened. There had been no sudden stop, we were not going around a curve. When I asked what had happened, Yapos became very upset: "Why do you want to know? Didn't you see? I don't want to think about it. It was a accident!" Since I was driving, I had not seen exactly what happened, but CharleZ had, and he was visibly upset.

When we went to restaurants, Rose chewed pieces of food, then took the chewed gruel out of her mouth with her forefinger and put it on her baby's tongue. It was an ancient method; I thought of Benin. She corresponded with her father, writing to him regularly in French. Had he told her how to feed the child?

She had great difficulty getting Jazz to sleep. She fed him and changed his diaper, rubbed his irritations with K-Y Jelly, then stood with him held tightly in her arms, dancing with him, gracefully, in a rhythm I did not recognize, dancing and dancing. She wore blue jeans and she was very fair, but when she held her son and danced with him across the polished wood floor of the nearly bare living room of the house on the round street, it was clear that she wished to be her father's daughter, the girl of Benin.

Jazz lay quietly in her arms for a while, through the chorus of a song she hummed to him, and then he cried. To quiet his crying she shook him, gently at first, so that there was not much difference between the dance and the shaking, and then harder and harder, until her whole body convulsed with every spasm, and his head banged against the limits of his spine. She shook him and shook him, no longer dancing, standing with her bare feet planted on the wooden floor, shaking the child until the lids closed over his staring eyes and he was still.

Rose and Matthew had known each other for a long time before their affair began. He said she was unlike other women, but he never said he loved her. He had dreams for Jazz, claiming that he would be "like a friend to him," but when the conversation came around to marrying Rose, he said, "I don't want to be tied down to her. I want to have experience with other women."

One day, in a Mexican restaurant about a mile from Annie Washington's house, Rose spoke about her son, who lay squirming in her arms, spitting out his pacifier every time she put it in his mouth. "I remember when his mouth was too small to hold his pacifier," she said. Then she passed him across the table to me, asking if I wanted to hold him. He felt cool to the touch and his skin was very dry. He would not drink anything but water. Rose said he liked beans. I mashed up a few *frijoles de la olla* and put them on the end of my finger to feed him, for there was no spoon small enough to fit into his mouth. He did not eat much, but he grasped my finger in his tiny hand and held on as tightly as he could.

Rose and Matthew disagreed over the roles of men and women. She was something of a feminist, and he could bring himself only so far as to say that in some instances rappers were wrong to call women "bitches and hos." In the park outside the house where Rose lived, he recited, as best he could remember it, a freestyle rap he had done at a party a few weeks earlier:

> *I appear with a crash,*
> *Slashin, bashin;*
> *MCs is the greater.*
> *I'm servin mad niggers*
> *Like a waiter.*
> *My stroke is so hard*
> *I leave the girl's ass achin.*
> *I'm exploitin cunts*
> *Like the system does homo sapiens.*

She had no comment about the freestyle verse, other than to nod in agreement about his memory of it.

After that, I did not see Yapos or his grandma for most of a year. I remembered to send her a birthday present on January 26, which was her eightieth birthday, a little thing to put on her mantelpiece where she kept the crockery she had collected over the years.

When I saw Yapos again, he had grown a beard and gained weight. Nothing had happened in his life other than the beard and Rose's move back to Detroit with the baby. He did not know when, if ever, she planned to come back to California, and he had no plans to go to Detroit. His grandmother and Rose's mother had been fighting in telephone conversations; his own mother continued to live in a tiny basement apartment under Annie Washington's house. He had not yet secured a record contract. His grandmother was pressing him to get a job.

He and Jamal and CharleZ got an apartment of their own near downtown Oakland after Trixie Garcia gave up her studio and moved back to San Francisco. They paid the rent and the utility bills for a few months, and then moved out. An acquaintance of theirs, the only person in their circle with money, other than Trixie, killed himself. He was the son of a highly placed black executive. They said the boy's father had given him a good car, spending money, recording equipment; they could not understand why he had killed himself.

The last time I saw Matthew, his beard and dredlocks were gone. An ordinary man came down the stairs of his grandma's house, still wearing saggies, but without the air of rebellion I had seen in the meeting in downtown Oakland or in the café on Telegraph Avenue. It took a long time before we were comfortable with each other again. We asked the kinds of questions we had never needed before, a dialogue of strangers: How much did this car cost? Are you going to school?

We went far from 91st Street, south, down a long boulevard to a suburban shopping area, where Matt knew a restaurant that served limitless portions of chicken fingers, coleslaw, and fried potatoes. He had a job again, working nights as a security guard. CharleZ worked in the same place but on a different shift. They did not see each other often, not often enough to make new hip-hop tracks. Matthew had to be content trying to sell the old ones.

Rose was still in Detroit. Matthew's mother was still in the basement. He had been robbed again, for the third time. "It was some kids, sixteen years old. If they didn't have a gun, I would have slapped the shit out of them." He smiled, the old, confident smile, the look of intelligence again. "It won't happen no more."

After lunch, we went out to the car. He looked around carefully, then reached inside his saggies and withdrew a small, squared-off automatic pistol. He removed the clip, and passed the weapon to me. The dead, concentrated weight of an automatic weapon, even a small one, is always a surprise. I held the gun for a moment or two, then gave it back to him. He said it was a light weapon, without much stopping power, but he had bought hollow-nose bullets to compensate for the low velocity and light weight of the slugs.

"For God's sake," I said, "you don't want to shoot somebody with one of those. There's a reason why they're illegal."

He smiled, and slipped the pistol back into his saggies. After lunch I dropped him off about half a block from a house halfway up into the Oakland Hills. "I don't know how they would act to a white guy. It's a drug house; they use a lot of drugs."

We said good-bye. Before he left, I reminded him of a little speech he had made to me once about Us and Them.

America's not glorious at all, and us poor people who are livin here like Third World countries, our standard of living is really low, and there needs to be somethin done about this government. People need to know that we're all in the same boat and that it's Us versus Them, and Them is the ruling class. Them is not white, Them is not Jew, Them is not French, Them is not African. Them is the people with all of the resources and all of the capital and the land and the money and the guns, who run everyone else. That's who Them is!

He offered no response. In the rearview mirror I could see the drug house, the people sitting on the steps, young men with nothing else to do in the middle of the day, waiting for him. "Remember me to your grandma," I said, "and to Rose." He nodded, but he was not listening. His head was turned away, his eye was on the drug house, and he was uncomfortable; he could not be seen with me any more.

3. Sapulpa

Just east of the Sapulpa turnoff on the Oklahoma toll road, going back toward Tulsa, a small community, no more than a village, sits in seclusion, isolated from the rest of the world. The one entrance to the village, the street that turns down past the big lot that sells used school buses, is unknown even to people who live in Sapulpa. The village church has no ties outside East Sapulpa. There are no stores, there is no town; people who live in the village drive to Sapulpa for whatever they need.

The culture of East Sapulpa is as limited as that of an out-of-the-way island. It is rich in resentments and xenophobia, tense, rooted, with no interest in change. There are no strangers and no neighbors in East Sapulpa. Everyone is white and Protestant; nevertheless, people watch each other. Even the dogs watch, growling from behind chain-link fences and signs that say: BEWARE OF DOG or: BAD DOG. Although some families have been there for generations and most remember the tornado that touched down at the junction of Hill and Andrew streets and skipped over to Main and Hill and then tore down 12th, there is no community in the village. It is a series of isolations, one nesting within the next; the individualism of the prairie carried to its lonely end.

Beverly Cross lives in a house on 12th Street. She rents the house from her son-in-law, who lives next door with Beverly's only child, a girl of twenty-one, Loy, and their two daughters. Since it is a matter of family, the chain-link fence surrounds both houses, linking them together more firmly than blood.

Beverly is forty years old, an Oklahoma woman, slim, with long brown hair and light blue, startling eyes. Her nose is slightly too long, and her face is just a little heavy now at the jawline and too square at the cheekbones, fleshy, but her figure is still good. She wears tight cutoff jeans to show the flatness of her belly.

On a Friday afternoon when the green corner of Oklahoma was hot and still steaming from the rainstorm of the night before, Beverly and Loy stood outside in the sun, waiting for a visit from Loy's sister-in-law. One baby was with them; the older one was in the house.

Gnats, flies, butterflies, and bees drifted on the air. The street was quiet. The baby complained a little, threw a stone to the ground. A tiny black dog sneaked out under the gate in the fence. Beverly called it back with a whistle. The dog obeyed. A butterfly passed in the air. All was calm on 12th Street.

Loy, the young woman with the Cherokee features, said that the houses were given to them by her father-in-law. His wife, from whom he was long divorced, had lived in the bigger house, the brown wood house, when she came home late one night from a bar and was murdered by a man who followed her home. Loy said, "The man stabbed her, then he tried to crush her head under the water tank."

After that, the ex-husband grieved; he did not want to come to East Sapulpa again. He gave the house to his son.

Beverly married early, at eighteen, to a half Cherokee man. He fathered Loy, but the marriage lasted only eight months. "He was an Indian and he drank," she said. "I couldn't put up with it."

She married again, this time to a man with two children, a girl of seven and a boy of nine. The boy stole, she said; he shoplifted. The girl was crazy about money, she talked constantly about money. "Nothing ever worked out with them," Beverly said. Her husband was hard on the boy. He beat him. He had beaten their mother. Only the girl was spared.

Beverly divorced the second husband, too. She has no contact with him, but she stays in contact with her stepchildren. Her stepson went to prison for the first time when he was sixteen years old, for stealing and fleeing the police, running through roadblocks in a terrifying chase. He has been out of jail for only thirty days in the last six years. She writes to him, but she does not see him often. Her accomplishment with him, she said, is that he has earned a GED while in prison. She has no further ambitions for him. He will not be home soon.

Her stepdaughter, she said, will soon be in prison too. Beverly co-signed a loan for her stepdaughter once, when the girl wanted to buy a car. She bought a pretty one, a new one, but she did not make the payments, not even one. It angers Beverly: "She ruined my credit. I don't have no credit now."

The girl is on parole for passing bad checks. The only work she can seem to get is at night, dancing naked in a club in Tulsa. Beverly shook her head: The girl will be in prison too, and soon, she is sure of it.

Loy is her dream child, her real child. Loy had been a model, had been taken all the way to Oklahoma City to model, starting when she was in the ninth grade. "She could have been a real professional model, if she hadn't of got married. But I love these kids. The little one's dark like her father.

The older one's more fair. I keep asking her when is she going to give me a white grandchild." She laughed. "Loy knows I don't mean nothing by that. I'm just a person who speaks my mind."

At the end of the block, in a white frame house, an oblong box, perhaps six hundred square feet inside, behind the broken screen, in darkened rooms with soft-drink bottles on the tables and empty cups still standing at one in the afternoon, in the living room dominated by the great square of the console model television set, Myrenda Marie Carlock lives with her stepmother. They have just come home from town, scattering the chickens as they drive the truck up beside the back door to the house. They had been to town to find out why their water was shut off. On the way home, they bought a pizza.

Myrenda—whose name was made up from Myrna and Linda, her mother's and grandmother's names—is seventeen years old and married to a man who is serving three prison sentences concurrently (eight years served out in three), has a son by a first wife, a disputed child by another woman, and has never had a steady job.

She met her husband when she was still in school. He had a motorcycle, a small one, not something massive, like a Harley, she said, and he gave her a ride on it. She had always liked motorcycles, which is why she started talking to him. "He's a good talker," Myrenda said. The first time they met after the motorcycle ride, they just talked and talked. She liked talking to him. As it turned out, the motorcycle wasn't his, and he was on parole for "bad checks, burglary, and theft," none of which he told her about. Nor did he tell her about his first wife and son.

She connects her difficulties to school, the people she met there. She did not like the blacks and Indians she met in school; she kept to her own kind, she said. Her memories of school betoken loneliness, the life of a big girl, fat-backed and bovine, like the grassfeeders that had been hunted there.

Myrenda has been living with her stepmother since she was seventeen months old, when her real mother abandoned her and her brother, on the doorstep of Myrenda's paternal grandmother—a blind woman who was unable to care for herself, let alone two tiny children abandoned somewhere in the darkness of her life.

Myrenda's brother found his way to a cousin's house, who came and rescued Myrenda from the blind woman. She said it was not good for her, being abandoned by her mother. She did not learn to walk until she was more than two years old and she did not speak until her fourth year.

She has grown into a big woman, heavy with child, a girl, according to the ultrasound, Breanna Marie, due in a month. Myrenda's face has turned brutish in pregnancy, fat, so that all the little scars of childhood are stretched into shallow craters. Her hair is light brown and her eyebrows are heavy. She toys nervously with her hair as she speaks, twirling the strands around thick fingers. When she was living with her husband, he called her names, she said, he called her terrible things, names she would not repeat.

In the few months before he went to prison, he did not work; neither did she. He smoked marijuana and drank and said terrible things about his seventeen-year-old wife who was beginning to grow fat with child and to sleep, some days until eleven, some days past noon. Myrenda still doesn't work, although she would like to have some spending money. She gets Title 19 coverage for her pregnancy, although she had an infection that cost her $120. "A hundred and twenty bucks isn't much, but when you don't have it. . . ." She gets food stamps, but she has no pocket money, absolutely nothing except what her stepmother and father give her, and "they don't have much." She said, "After the baby is born, I'll get AFDC."

"My mom don't do nothing now." "She's been married six times. The only one I remember, he was a real bad drug addict. My own dad was an alcoholic. I remember him and my stepmother fighting all the time. Once he gave me a bloody nose.

"When he was drinking we got in a car wreck once. My brother and me were sitting in the front, but we climbed over to the back. I told him he was going too fast. He hit a telephone pole and smashed in the passenger side of the car, so it was right up next to him. If we'd of still been sittin there, we would of been killed. My brother broke out the back window with a flashlight. That's how we got out. They had to cut my dad out of the car.

"My brother won't work. He lives with my mom. She keeps him in cigarettes, does everything for him. He's nineteen and he's going to be a daddy now. But he won't work, he just gets messed up on drugs, crack, crank [methamphetamine], and marijuana. He just started having seizures. He takes medicine for them and he can't drive for a year. He hopes he'll be on disability all his life. That's all he wants to do.

"I don't go to church, but my husband used to go to church sometimes before he went to jail. His parents, they go to church all the time, every chance they get, to the church right here nearby, every Sunday and every Wednesday night."

She looked around her for a moment, as if she could find the future in the chickens or the cat that had crawled under her car. Suddenly, she brightened. "The one thing about my daughter, Breanna Marie," she said, "when she grows up and goes to school, I don't want her to go to no public school."

4. Ameer

Culture, politics, and poverty do not exist entirely separately in America: Poverty occurs almost exclusively in the absence of politics, which must be considered a relation. Cultural politics, in the sense of black power, Chicano power, and so on, have become widespread during the last third of the century. And something more like culture than politics, which I call "false politics," can come to what appears to be political life when the practitioners operate in secret, unconnected to public life.

At an individual level, false politics, by which I mean a system of control that gives the appearance of politics without permitting people to govern themselves, also exhibits many of the characteristics of culture. It grows out of poverty, but it is not a culture of poverty; false politics is a misstep, tragic in the way the Nation of Islam has become another tragic experience for blacks in America, disastrous in the way the white militias have led to disaster for isolated whites across the country. False politics begins from the highest plane, promising a democratic struggle for justice, and falls into the mire, delivering rage and the continuation of poverty under a veil of fascist or totalitarian rhetoric. False politics makes great demands upon its followers: They may not reflect on their beliefs or acts; they must agree to obey.

I first learned of the possibility of false politics at an individual level from Ameer Abdul Aboulima, a black Egyptian, who sowed the revolution among poor blacks in Oakland, California. Ameer was a burly giant, more than six feet tall, heavily muscled, with the sloping shoulders of an executioner, the kind who did his work with an ax. He had a deep voice and he used it along with his great bulk to push other men aside, threatening them with his presence.

I do not know how old he was, perhaps forty or fifty; the edges of his beard had turned white and he had no hair on the shiny, bullet-shaped top of his head. He always wore a starched white shirt, dark trousers, and new, brilliantly shined black wingtip shoes. His face had a deceptive sweetness—round cheeks, a gentle mouth, the melted eyes of the Middle East. He looked like a great brown cherub, but there was nothing cherubic in his demeanor. No matter what the subject or the circumstance, he maintained a high state of choler. He said his anger came from the difficult life of his people, Black Egyptians, a minority who could not find a home among other Egyptians. As a result, Ameer spent his time among blacks, allying himself with the pan-Africanists.

African Americans were tolerant of him, listening to his booming rhetoric with great patience, but when he was not in the room, they said of him, "He's po like me, just hustlin, lookin for some way to get along." Their view seemed unlikely, given the timbre of his voice and the shine of his shoes.

Once, after a meeting of pan-Africanists, when everyone was standing in the hallway waiting for the elevator, Ameer erupted into a sudden rage, shouting in a voice so loud and pitched so low that those close to him could feel the rumble of it: "I'm through talking. It's time to start taking people out. Jews, niggers, whites, I don't care. Whoever gets in our way! And when I take them out, I'm going to take out their wives and their children and their mothers; I'm going to take them all out. I'm tired of talking. I'm sick of talking. It's time to start taking people out. That's the only way we going to get anything done."

The other men who had been in the meeting listened politely, but when the elevator arrived, they turned away, leaving Ameer and me to stand in silence, looking at each other, until the elevator had made its round trip to the ground floor and back, and we were able to descend and go our separate ways.

Wherever I went that year, Ameer seemed to be there, lecturing every black person he met, man or woman, on the revolution. He informed them of the methods of the CIA, the FBI, and the Mossad. The word "conspiracy" was always on his mind. The conspirators were the capitalists, the whites, the Jews, other blacks. His anger was enormous: it filled up rooms, forced out other ideas, other feelings. Wherever he was, conversation turned into speechmaking, and it was always the same, time to "begin taking people out." He made no apologies for his views. He said he was a Marxist-Leninist, a follower of Malcolm X, a true revolutionary, and killing was on his mind.

One afternoon near the end of summer, after a conversation with three ex-convicts in an outdoor space in one of the large public buildings in downtown Oakland, Ameer and I were the last two people left. While I had been talking with two of the ex-convicts, Ameer had drawn the third man away to lecture to him on Marxism. I had heard his voice somewhere off in the background, the rumbling revolutionary counterpoint to whatever else was said: "Time to start taking people out, brother," he had told the ex-con. "The man leaves you no choice. It's time, brother." He had made no converts that afternoon, but he had not been totally unsuccessful. I had offered to buy him a cup of coffee, and he had ordered a meal to go with it. He was grateful, not for the food, but for having "got over" on me. The sense of victory he exhibited over cadging a meal surprised me; there was something not quite revolutionary about it. We talked for a few minutes while he finished his food. "Those boys are naive," he said; "they don't know nothing about politics."

I nodded, not wanting to provoke the litany. He asked if I was going back to the building where we often met. I said I was going to San Francisco.

"Can you drop me off in Berkeley? I'm staying in the flats."

The revolution was not on his mind that afternoon. After he pushed the seat back to permit himself to fit into the car, he rolled the window down and put his face into the wind. The sun was hot, but the air off the bay was cool. It was a perfect afternoon. We had gone no more than half a mile up San Pablo Avenue when he said, "Can you give me five bucks?"

At the next stoplight I reached into my pocket, found some bills, and gave him what he had asked for. "To make the revolution," I said.

It was the first time I had seen him laugh.

"I need a job," he said. And then, as we drove up the avenue, he explained that he could not get "clearance" for a job because he could not get bonding, and he could not be bonded because he had served eight and a half years of a ten- to twenty-year sentence in New York for bank robbery.

"I can drive trucks," he said, "but a man has to own a rig, and it costs thirty-five thousand dollars. Where can I get thirty-five thousand dollars? Who would give that kind of money to a bank robber?"

He talked about prison, recalling the day the warden had called him into his office to give Ameer the papers finalizing his divorce. He spoke bitterly of his wife. "I knew she would find someone else," he said. "I gave her the money. I knew she would spend some of the money, but I hoped she would wait for me." He was quiet for a while, looking at cars on the street as we passed them. Perhaps he was thinking of what he could have done with the money.

"You know how I got caught?" he said. "That dumb nigger, that stupid nigger. I told him to lay low. Don't show the money around, don't buy a car. Lay low. The next thing you know, that stupid nigger bought himself a purple Cadillac and he's driving down the street in Queens with a white woman sitting next to him in his purple Cadillac. Stupid motherfucker—stupid, stupid, stupid. I told him to lay low. Police arrest him, and he gives me up right away; they don't even have to beat on him.

"Naturally, I planned everything. It was my idea, my plans, everything. They give me the long sentence because I was the organizer."

He said his only real interest in life was to find the man who had given him up to the police, and kill him.

"Ameer, that's no way to make the revolution."

"Fuck the revolution! I get my hands on that stupid motherfuckin nigger, I'm gonna take him out."

We had come to the area where he was living. The conversation stopped while we negotiated a series of turns down one-way streets into the flats. He lived with six other men in a run-down house. When we arrived, three of them were out in the street in front of the house trying to install a sound system in an old Chevy Camaro. They drank beer as they worked, two black men, one of them very fair, and a Latino. Ameer did not speak to them or even nod to them, although they noted our arrival, commenting to each other quietly about it.

When Ameer got out of the car he began talking about the Fundamentalist Christians, who "control forty-five percent, maybe forty-eight percent of the vote."

I reminded him that Trotsky had said Fundamentalists were the easiest to convert to Marxism-Leninism.

"It can't happen that way in modern times," he said, speaking loudly enough to be heard by the men who worked on the Camaro, "not with Billy Graham."

Then he leaned into the car and said almost in a whisper, "Can we meet somewhere tomorrow? Can I telephone you? I need to talk. I'm with these stupid niggers and their rock 'n' roll music, I can't even read in the house."

The mendicant eyes of the Middle East do not bespeak politics. In the crowded, ramshackle house, all the men, including the false revolutionary, Ameer Abdul Aboulima of Queens, New York, lived private lives.

Part Two

Public Life

XV.

Political Inventions

WITHIN THE WORLD OF relative poverty, which comprises most of the nations of the earth, and especially the United States, neither nature nor culture keeps people poor. In the modern world, it is never easy to escape from poverty and never impossible. The problem, of course, is that the nature of the modern world is as nearly intractable as the nature of the sub-Saharan desert. Modern society is built upon the concept of inequality, and even though inequality does not require that anyone be poor, in the sense of suffering physical want, it has always worked out that way.

In contemporary America, the poor must overcome the panicked reaction of people who live in a surround of force in order to escape from poverty; that is, they must learn to think reflectively and act politically. Tens of millions of people have done so. Since the early part of the nineteenth century, social mobility has been the hallmark of American society. Toqueville foresaw the great leveling of America into a single class, a single culture, a desperately powerful majority. Blacks, Latinos, and Native Americans did not have a place in this great, overbearing majority, but for everyone else an almost primitive equality seemed possible.

NEW AMERICAN BLUES

The early years of the twentieth century saw a new kind of social mobility as the waves of immigrants came, but their change in status, from poor Polish or Southern Italian greenhorn to middle-class white was not cultural or even economical at its core. The successful immigrants were the beneficiaries of a political epiphany. To emigrate was to revolt against the past and to immigrate was to strike a new social contract that permitted, among other things, inclusion in the circle of power. The dames of Fifth Avenue, Back Bay, and Newport may not have invited the Irish and the Italians and the Jews into any parts of their lives other than the kitchens and the countinghouses, but they did permit them into their political parties.

Three-quarters of a century later, in Texas, Willie Velasquez founded the Southwest Voter Registration and Education Program.[1] His grasp of the issues of immigration and poverty was extraordinary. During the height of the Brown Beret radical movement, Velasquez often invited the radicals to barbecues in the backyard of his house, where he advised them to put aside their copies of Marx and Mao and read Aristotle. It was, as I have noted elsewhere, his attempt to make Mexicans into ancient Athenians or Englishmen, not culturally—Velasquez was pleased to be Chicano—but politically. He had learned how immigrants succeeded and what had to take place before the poor could bring themselves up out of poverty.

Velasquez was not the only leader of poor people to register voters. At about the time he first became a political activist, voter registration drives among poor blacks, especially in the South, were recruiting tens of thousands of people in every state. Not every person who registered voters shared Velasquez's sophistication. Fannie Lou Hamer and the Mississippi Freedom Democratic Party had a somewhat less philosophical approach, which in no way detracts from her courage or goodwill or her role in history, but may have contributed to the failure of some registered voters to become political persons.[2] The Reverend Martin Luther King, Jr., preached a far more political view, although he couched his politics in a code of ethics grounded in the teachings of the church.

The wisdom of Dr. King in connecting politics to the black church simply cannot be overestimated. Unlike the whites who controlled the War on

---

[1] More about the late Willie Velasquez, the Mexican-American Legal Defense and Education Fund lawyer Joaquin G. Avila, and Vilma Martinez, then executive director of MALDEF, can be found in *Latinos: A Biography of the People*. Velasquez's understanding of immigration, poverty, the inclusive aspect of political power, and the origins of political thinking were an important influence on this book.

[2] See Chapter IV, the Wilson Family, for an example of people who were mobilized, but not politicized.

Poverty, Dr. King knew something about the behavior of black people in circumstances that permitted, even in a limited way, reflective thinking and the *vita activa*. After all, he was himself the beneficiary of this limited public life. He did not understand black people, or any poor people for that matter, as deficient. To Dr. King it was the larger society, not the poor, who were at fault. Perhaps that is what so interested J. Edgar Hoover.

The Reverend Martin Luther King understood full well that when poor people, including blacks, were able to evade the panic of the surround of force, they could think reflectively, behave politically, and succeed economically, even in the face of racism. He knew, too, that the only place where autonomy could be practiced by the poor was the church, for whites did not attend black churches, enabling the blacks to manage their own affairs, to establish circles of power within the world permitted them. The development of the black leadership, I believe, grows directly out of the syncretism of Dr. King's movement.

On the other hand, poor whites, like Jerry Parker and his family in eastern Tennessee,[3] were often unwelcome in churches, although the exclusion was politically less important because the white churches were not separated from the general life of the city in the same way as the black churches; autonomy could not be enjoyed in the same way, for the circles of power in the white community overlapped. Dr. King was surely aware of this aspect of the lives of poor whites, for the oppressed are invariably the best students of the character of the oppressor. And he put his knowledge to use. Whether it was for moral or political reasons or a felicitous combination of both, Dr. King made a church of his movement, granting a sense of autonomy to the poor within the confines of his Southern *Christian* organization that would not have been possible in a purely secular organization. The inclusion of the white poor culminated in the Poor People's March on Washington, and died with the murder of Martin Luther King and the ensuing separation of the races.

Since the death of Dr. King and the dual effects of the dispiriting attitude of the "culture of poverty" theorists in the War on Poverty and the dismantling of many federal programs to assist the poor, the problem of relative poverty in the United States has consistenly worsened. Changes in federal programs to assist the poor, proposed by the Congress and approved by President Clinton in 1996, will make life more difficult for millions of Americans, many of them children, in the future.

Even so, people continue to move out of poverty. The reasons for this movement, particularly off the welfare rolls, have been quantified a thou-

---

[3] See Chapter XI.

sand times over. Single mothers on welfare get married, and live better, at least for a while. People find jobs that pay enough money to move them out of the federally defined slough of poverty. Unfortunately, the number of people moving out of poverty between 1967 and 1979 was 35.5 percent, but the number who moved out between 1980 and 1991 was only 30.4 percent, a decline of 14.3 percent in the rate of moving up. Meanwhile, the increase in the number of people moving down into poverty rose from 6.2 percent to 8.5 percent in the same periods, an increase of 37.1 percent in the rate of fall. There can be no doubt that getting out of poverty has become more difficult, while the slide into poverty has become far easier.

Looking at poverty by race confuses the issue even further. Far more black single mothers work than either whites or Latinas, but fewer blacks live in complete families, although the number of white single mothers is increasing far more rapidly than the number of blacks.[4] The racial breakout of single mothers indicates that a new kind of family unit is being defined by the American culture: it includes a mother and children, but no father. Black women, perhaps because they have more experience with the new family unit, appear to be adapting better to the circumstance.

Government policies, however, fail to recognize the new cultural definition of the family, and continue to punish these families, particularly the children, when a more rational view would attempt to adjust the government to this increasing number of its constituents, enabling the number of people who move out of poverty to increase while at the same time slowing the rate of fall into poverty.

The punishing character of government and society makes it far more difficult for people to follow what appears to be the path out of long-term

---

[4] The increase in the number of children born out of wedlock may be deceptive, since it is almost always expressed as a percentage of all children born during the specified period. If the total number of births falls, largely because married couples are having fewer children, while the number of births among unmarried women remains stable, it will appear that the number of out-of-wedlock births has risen.

Nevertheless, the single-parent family has become a part of modern American society, regardless of the economic condition of the parent, and should be considered a legitimate family, with the efforts of the general society revised to support the new family rather than wounding it with specious arguments about illegitimacy and lack of family values. Such arguments and the policies that flow from them cannot help but wound great numbers of American families economically as well as morally.

The consistent attacks on single parents, all but a tiny percentage of whom are women, by people who support "family values" may be the cruelest irony of our time. The idea, consistent among social conservatives over generations, that a widow with children is a family while an unmarried woman with children is not, makes clear the sexual origin of the problem that leads social conservatives to hurt those they claim to love. The problem for thoughtful people, those who value the family in all of its expressions, is how to teach ethics to social conservatives.

poverty, but still not impossible. This path, curiously enough, follows the rules Tolstoy set for happy and unhappy families. While families in poverty seem to be apolitical each in their individual ways, those that escape are much more alike: political. Moreover, they become political in similar ways.

The role of the family in the establishment of a political life continues to follow a pattern established during the very invention of politics. The barrier to political life in that time came in the extended family, which Fustel de Coulanges defined as people who had a common ancestor; followed by the *phratry*, in which one extended family joined with another that followed the same god; and finally, the tribe, which was made up of several phratrys.[5] Among the differences between these familial groupings and the geographically defined *demes*, according to Fustel, was the capacity of the deme to participate in change, "to be flexible and variable"; that is, to govern itself rather than to be governed by the absolutism of religion and ritual. Autonomy was not only uncommon in the extended family; it was expressly forbidden. Members of the extended family could not worship strange gods or disobey the rulings of the patriarch.

Extended families in the ancient city were based on ancestor worship (a practice that operates in a more subtle way in extended families today), and though there may be economic aspects to kinship structures, there is nothing political about them: they are not flexible or variable; a cousin cannot become a brother and an uncle cannot become a sister-in-law. Kinship rules have always been stable, more than stable, immutable: incest, for both genetic and economic reasons, is taboo, everyone must marry out; on the other hand, in many societies a man with a wife and children is obliged to marry the widow of a dead brother to maintain the stability of the extended family.[6]

Within the nuclear family, however, relations change constantly. The unit forms out of the union of a man and woman; the birth of a child revises the unit; the departure of either the male or female adult revises the unit again, as does the birth of more children. Perhaps even more importantly, the unit is constantly revised by the change in status of the children, from infant to adult, and all the stages along the way. Kinship rules, such as the prohibition against incest, apply within the nuclear unit, but the general stability of the extended family cannot apply to the dynamic nuclear family. The nuclear family changes, and in worldly ways, chooses its alliances

---

[5] See Fustel de Coulanges, *The Ancient City* (New York: Doubleday Anchor, 1955).
[6] This was a custom among the Lakota of the Great Plains, who accepted polygamy in that situation, but it also happened in my wife's family, where a widower married his brother's widow.

outside the unit. In the extended family, alliances are defined by the rules of kinship.

Extended families can, of course, include many nuclear families. The distinction I want to make—one that has been drawn many times before—is between the nuclear family and the family that functions only in its extended form. It is these two kinds of families that can be likened to the distinction Fustel made between the forms of organization in his Ancient City.

Given its propensity for change, the nuclear family adapts much more easily to political life. One of the expectations of the nuclear family is that the children will achieve a certain degree of autonomy as part of the process of maturation. In the extended family, however, the relationships remain the same throughout the lifetime of all the members, with the exception of the new patriarch, who inherits the position according to the rules of kinship rather than through the free choosing of the members of the extended family.

In the United States, as many anthropologists and sociologists, including Oscar Lewis, have noted, the long-term poor tend to live in extended families—an arrangement which I believe affords them a certain amount of stability but inhibits political life. Within the nuclear family, however, which is naturally unstable, the flexibility and variability that Fustel related to the establishment of political life happens quite easily.

Of the many instances of families moving out of poverty, almost every one I encountered followed the same pattern of flexibility within the nuclear family and distance or even separation from the extended family. This may be construed to mean that the separated unit was forced to be autonomous without the economic and emotional support of the extended family, but I do not think so. The details of the rise from poverty indicate otherwise. In fact, in the case of the Kinslers of Sneedville, Tennessee, the nuclear family took a direction opposite to that of the extended family. A similar situation occurs within the gang, which functions like an extended family rather than a political unit. In El Paso, Texas, Chendo Montes and his family live in a middle ground at the edge of Los Blue Diamonds.

The rise from poverty of eight different families, in places as diverse as Sneedville, Manhattan, Dallas, and the Mississippi Delta, follows. Although instances of the rise out of poverty of nuclear families are common and similar, I do not know of a single instance of the rise of an entire extended family, with the exception of immigrants, from poverty to a more comfortable and secure economic situation; nor do I know of an instance where an entire extended family of poor people began to think reflectively and to live a political life.[7]

---

[7] Such occurrences among extended families are not impossible, although they are not likely.

1. The Kinsler Clan

Fox

In the middle of the nineteenth century, three brothers came from Germany to Hancock County, Tennessee. Soon afterward one went off to fight in the Civil War and was killed, or at any rate disappeared and was never heard from again. The remaining brothers became the patriarchs of an extended family, which divided into two distinct groups, the Panther Creek branch and the Fox branch, named after the areas near Sneedville where the brothers settled. Exactly how the branches developed economically and socially is not known, but at some time during the Great Depression the trajectories separated.

The best, perhaps the only way to begin to understand the family is from the sanctuary of the front porch of Ruth and Wayland Kinsler's house on Panther Creek Road. The house, encircled by a small farm, looks across the road to a rounded old Appalachian mountain, too steep for cattle or corn, but rich in white oaks and pines, hickory, walnut, and some of the best cedarwood in the world. Just beyond the porch, under the walnut tree, a coon dog, a mountain prize, sleeps in the shade.

At seventy, Ruth Kinsler wears her hair parted in the middle and gathered and tied on either side just below her ears. It is an ancient style, in keeping with her strong cheekbones and the long brown overblouse and trousers she wears. Her nose is short, narrow, and slightly hooked, a Cherokee feature to match the subtle darkness in her skin. But her eyes are blue.

Wayland Kinsler, nearing eighty, sits unmoving in the comfort of his rocker, taciturn, like old hardwood dressed in denim overalls. When he speaks, the words come out as a whisper of age.

Shelby, his daughter, sits opposite him, a pretty woman in her mid-fifties, but weakened by congestive heart failure and terrible battles with

---

This book is based on conversations with about eight hundred people, perhaps a few more, even as many as a thousand (I am not a statistician and keep no such records, as anyone who has read this far will no doubt have discovered), which is a small sample of all the poor families in America.

During the 1960s, when the civil rights movement opened the doors of the ghetto for many black families, the economic status of these families changed. But to say that these families were poor and apolitical prior to the civil rights movement would be incorrect, a misunderstanding of the autonomous aspects of black community life prior to integration.

arthritis, which she pronounces with an extra syllable, in the accent of the mountains. Shelby has divorced three husbands. "The first two abused me physically," she said, "and the third one abused me mentally."

One of her husbands threatened to kill Shelby and her child with a .38 caliber pistol. "He was drunk and wild," she said. "I had a twenty-two." She aimed at her husband and fired. The bullet hit him in the trigger finger. But the old ammunition had so little force the tiny slug fell out of his finger. Even so, it stopped the fight and gained her a reputation as "Pistol Packin' Mama."

She laughed at the story. "I'm not by nature a violent person," she said, "but I started to imagine a bullet hole in the center of my husband's forehead. That's when I knew I had to leave him or kill him." Once she left, he paid no child support, and she had to apply for AFDC. Shelby could not work, because she could not find anyone to care for her children. Her mother worked full time as a nurse's aid and there was no day care available in the county.

The conversation strayed to a dozen subjects: fried poke, which Ruth prepared in the spring when the pokeberry stalks were young and tender. Pokeberry wine, ginseng. How the names of Ruth's forebears were confusing, because they were mainly Cherokee and Melungeon, and those that were illegitimate carried their mother's names. Cornbread, tenths of tobacco. But it always came back to abuse.

"Here, in poor counties, there's so much abuse. I don't know whether the men feel small. I'm trying to get this in perspective. Men here have to be in complete control. We have been taught women were not worth anything."

Ruth agreed. "I never did feel self-worthy much. Here, male is the dominating figure. About two-thirds is abusive. But my husband's not gon boss me around. He never did and never will."

Shelby said she talked about abuse with her women friends. They all tried to perform their duties, "cook the meals on time. But we're abused."

Wayland listened quietly to the conversation. His wife had worked from the time the children were young. They were comfortable now because of her; they could afford a real coon dog, one worth a lot of money, because of her.

"My dad wasn't abusive," Ruth said. "My mom would stand up to him." Later, it would become clear that her mother had been a rebel of sorts; "devil-may-care" was Ruth's only description of her.

Then Shelby talked about the role of women at home in Hancock County.[8] "Women could not talk at home at the dinner table," she said,

---

[8] Hancock County is not only one of the poorest counties in the United States, it had one of the

"but the men and boys could." Her mother nodded: It had been that way in her time, too. Shelby said her own troubles had grown out of what she had learned at home. Solemnly, without anger, but with something more like puzzlement, she looked over at her father, a man now concerned with his eyedrops and pills, too old to farm, reduced to whittling and waiting, and blamed him for teaching her to expect abuse.

He said nothing. Hardwood, a man like the trees that grew on the mountain across the road from his farm. His wife ordered him about now: "Wayland, cut one of them pokeberries."

The house reflected her tastes entirely: Cherokee, with bedspreads she crocheted in the unique knot she called "the Cherokee stitch." There was no sign of him in the house. He leased out the tenths of tobacco beside the house, unable to do the work any more. The women picked the beans.

"We've all been raised poor," Ruth said. "It's always been hard, but we were happy. I never did think I was smart. I was intelligent, but I never did think I was smart. Dad wouldn't let me go past eighth grade. So when I had Shelby, I was sixteen. And then her sister who was born with a scar on her face and had to have fifteen surgeries. I just thought when I got them through high school, I'd go get my GED. Then I went to beauty school, but I didn't like fixin people's hair. That didn't satisfy me, so I went to work for the health department. When I quit that, I went to work at the hospital as a nurse's aid.

"When I was a little girl, I wanted to be a nurse. I used to look at pictures in magazines, but Dad didn't want me to, so when my girls got grown-up, I was determined. When you got the love of God in your heart and you know he don't like lazy people, you've got to be determined. I was determined to be somethin. I'm not sayin I went to church all those years, but it had to be my love for Him, my love for people."

A refrain emerged: "You've got to love yourself and you've got to love the people."

Something outward had happened in Ruth's life. She had become a public person in a place more private than perhaps any other section of the country, a county where people said, "Don't go up to that house. If

---

lowest literacy rates. A survey done by then U.S. Representative Jim Cooper's office in 1987 claimed 71 percent of the adult population was functionally illiterate. Through the efforts of Cooper and others, illiteracy has declined in the county since then, and along with it, the poverty rate, which stood at 40 percent.

Although there is very little work available in the county, officials there estimated that in 1994 more than nine hundred people left the town of Sneedville (the county seat) every day to work in Morristown or Tazewell, in adjoining counties.

they see a stranger, they'll shoot you." Again and again she spoke of loving the people.

It could not have been party politics that interested her. She said she had stopped voting long ago, after she discovered that politicians lied. "It would be a sin to vote for a person who lied," she said.

Perhaps it had been her mother, the woman who had dared to talk back to her husband. "My mother was just devil-may-care," she said. "She would leave me just nine years old to take care of four kids and one of em had spinal meningitis, was crippled. When she would leave and go off to her sisters, I would lock the door. My mom, she couldn't have been afraid to leave me alone with those kids—and we had a wood stove then."

"Love the people." Begin with the siblings. Dream of being a nurse. Perhaps it had begun there. Ruth Kinsler said she hated violence, could not even kill a chicken. Or had it been the opposition learned from her mother? More than half a century later, those were the salients of her life: love and opposition. The nuclear family had broken away from the ethos of the extended family; it had been variable, capable of change. But it had not survived the next generation.

Shelby sat on the porch. Her father sat a few feet away. Across the length of the porch, seated in a swing, one leg tucked under her, Ruth Kinsler contemplated the making of herself, how she had come up out of poverty, and why her daughter lived up the road in a small house near the Virginia border and collected welfare. A light rain, more like mist, began to fall. The coon dog got up from its place under the walnut tree, stretched, and came up onto the porch. Wayland had forgotten his eyedrops. There was a flutter of activity, and the afternoon settled in.

Panther Creek

In front of the barbershop on the shady side of the street in Sneedville two of the Panther Creek Kinslers, Milford and Paul, stood. They did not stand together, as if they were speaking. They simply stood, in silence, five or six feet apart. Neither man leaned against the wall. They just stood, and smoked, and Paul spat. Milford stood shyly. His arms were thin and white, although he wore a short-sleeved shirt. Milford's head was strangely large on his skinny neck. He wore a billed cap at least two sizes too large. The overall impression was of a pale and aged hydrocephalic.

Paul looked like a wild man. He wore no hat. His hair was full and long, dark brown going gray. His face was partly covered with a thin beard that grew in wild patches of white, dark brown, and red. His teeth were rotted, tobacco-stained, crushed into a gapped mess in the center of his small mouth. He spat every few minutes, letting the spittle dribble out of his mouth onto the sidewalk, as if he had too little energy to get the bubbly saliva any further.

His gray shirt was filthy at the shoulders, brown with earth or merely filth, as if he had used his shoulders as a place to wipe his hands. The long sleeves were buttonless at the cuff, hanging open, revealing one dark brown powerful hand and one useless claw. It was an unexpected facade for an honorable man.

Milford has been on SSI since he had a heart attack many years ago. He said the attack left him unconscious for three weeks. Milford has not worked since.

Paul has also been "drawing" for many years. He said that he and his sister fell out of a second-story window when he was six months old. His head hit a rock and was split open, causing him to lose part of the control of his left arm. From time to time he has worked. He drove a truck for a while, until he got into a terrible accident.

Milford and Paul are known in the community and to each other as Poz and Hergel, although they could not explain how Milford became Poz or Paul turned into Hergel. "There's fifteen of us all together," Hergel said, speaking in the deep mumble of a man who had lived alone in a hollow for many years. "Nine still living. Some lives in Roseville, some lives here in the county, some lives in Kingsport. Far as I know, they's all a-drawin.

"My daddy was a preacher. He preached right on up over there."

Long silences stopped the flow of his sentences. He did not seem to be thinking between sentences so much as waiting, just waiting. Waiting. "And when we was boys and he laid into you, when he was done you knowed you got a whippin."

Silence. Waiting.

"He was preachin before I was born."

Silence. Waiting. The expense of time was his extravagance.

"He whipped us all. It's changed now. People ain't allowed to whip young uns now. They protest to the welfare. Report you. Back then, wasn't nothin like that."

An expense of time.

"He preached and farmed, grew a little tobacco.

"His brothers and sisters quarreled all the time. He had some evil as a hornet. They was hateful."

Hergel did not say what the rest of the family knew, what Ruth and Shelby told. He did not say that his father had let the children come close to starving, that he beat his wife, Minnie, and sent her out along the roads in winter to pick up firewood.

Milford sank down into a squat, folding himself up like a beggar in

Bombay. He had tattoos on the fingers of both hands, blue letters written in rows along the first and second joints. One said: LOVE LBN and the other, LUC ILLE. She is his first cousin. He said they got drunk one night and were thrown into jail together. Poz was twenty-eight years old then. He had a tattoo artist write the words and initials on his fingers. They are the only words he can read.

When Lucille's family moved to Indiana, he moved up there, too. "Lucille's sister got burnt up," he said, "got drunk and burnt herself up in the house."

Unlike his brother, he speaks quickly, but in an almost inaudible whisper, as if everything he told should be kept secret.

Did he love Lucille?

He shook his head.

What happened to her?

He got to his feet, not speaking any more. Upright, he looked like a stick figure. He stood there for a long time, unmoving except to smoke one cigarette after another. When a woman passed by, he and Hergel called out to her, leering, rolling their eyes and pursing their lips obscenely. The woman hurried on past them, looking straight ahead. As soon as she had passed, the Kinslers returned to waiting and smoking. They made no comment about the woman or the speed with which she passed them.

Neither Poz nor Hergel has ever been married. Hergel now lives as his father and grandfather did before him. He does not own a car. He walks eight miles to and from town. He does not have a farm, but he has a garden in which he grows vegetables, a little corn, and a little tobacco. He said it would cost $921 to buy the tub, toilet, sink, and pipes he needs to bring water and plumbing into his house. He plans to do the work himself, but he knows that he is unlikely ever to have $921.

The only member of their branch of the family who has been married and still lives in Sneedville is Sam Kinsler, who ran for office on the Republican ticket in the last county election. Sambo, as he is known, was the butt of a joke. The Republicans put his name on the ballot without his permission. When he found out about it, he tried to withdraw, but it was too late. They had put him up against Jack Stapleton, the county clerk and probably the most popular public official in the county. Sam Kinsler knew it was a joke, but he did not know what to do about it. He was more used to drinking and fighting than politics.

In his most recent fight, Sam, who is as old and scrawny as Poz, was beaten up by four young men, including his own nephew. He said they knocked him down eighteen times and broke his ribs before he quit. If he had not had so many heart attacks, he swore, he would have continued fighting.

Sam and Poz live on large doses of Valium, prescribed for them by a doctor. They are sly men, who beat the system by hunting for cans and scrap metal. One afternoon, up on the hill in the housing project where Poz lives in a one-bedroom apartment and tries to grow tobacco in the patch of ground in front of his place, he and Sam and another man unloaded a pile of scrap wood and metal from the back of a pickup truck. They spread the wood out on the lawn in front of the housing project office and began ripping the metal loose from the wood with their bare hands. It came away grudgingly, long pieces of aluminum full of nails, screeching as the men tore it loose with their fingers. They squatted and bent and knelt over the boards and the metal, contorted like the pieces of aluminum as they sought better angles to approach their salvage work.

At the end of the afternoon of work on the scrap, which they had taken from a demolition project, they tossed all of their work into the back of the pickup and headed off to the scrap-metal yard. Before they left, Poz went into his house and brought out a plastic garbage sack that he had filled with cans picked out of trash barrels in town. Together with the aluminum salvage the scrap would bring enough money to buy a couple of gallons of gas, a pack of cigarettes and a few pills, Poz said.

Hergel was there, but he did not participate in the salvage work. He was different from the other Panther Creek Kinslers. Where they were sly, he was forthright. "It's all you kin do to git by. The big man that's got it don't want to turn it loose. We just barely livin to tell the truth about it; all poor people's doin. Every time somebody tries to do somethin bout it, them what's got knocks em in the head. They don't want poor people to git hold of nothin."

His grasp of local economics was surprising. He said that landowners in Sneedville refused to sell property at any price, because they were also the owners of the stores and shops and rental property, and they did not want competition coming to town, raising wages and lowering prices. He named the people in power; he was not afraid of them. As he talked on, speaking in knowledgeable detail about the business of the town, his voice rose from the incomprehensible rumble in his chest. He said the words clearly and with the inflections of a man for whom the public world was no longer unimaginable.

Perhaps the story about Hergel, the one told by both branches of the Kinsler clan, might be true. When he was forty-five years old, at about the time of the big truck accident, there was a loose woman in town, blond and perfumed, a tramp, some people said. And she became pregnant. When she was asked who fathered the child, she pointed to Hergel. Of course, everyone in Sneedville knew it wasn't Hergel Kinsler; most people doubted he had ever been to bed with the woman. But when the baby was born, a girl,

Hergel agreed to give the child his name. He also agreed to give the girl's mother a share of his pension to support the child. The woman, who left the county long ago, has no cause for complaint. Every month, with the precision of the bureaucracy that mails the SSI check to him, Hergel sends his support to the child. When he received $446, he sent $223, exactly half.

He has not seen the mother or the girl for a very long time. The only contact he has with them is the cashing of the money orders, which also happens with the precision of the bureaucracy that sends the checks to him.

2. Hopson's Choice

Politics in Claiborne County, Tennessee, comes down to two people these days. Bill D. Hurst, who has run the county with a big, grasping, iron fist for many years, and Dr. Joyce Hopson, a young woman who has taught school, managed the local Democratic Party, worked for former Tennessee Congressman Jim Cooper in Washington and in his district, and sat on virtually every public oversight committee and board of directors in the county. They are wary friends, as people in electoral politics must be. In conversation, Hurst does not say much about Hopson, although Hopson speaks respectfully both publicly and privately about him. Hurst talks slowly at the end of his career, a shrewd old salesman protecting his territory. By contrast, Hopson is young, blond, pretty, slim going on thin, and probably the second- or third-fastest-talking person in eastern Tennessee.

I met Dr. Hopson through John Cooper, who managed his brother Jim's U.S. Senate campaign. It was a hopeless year for Democrats, especially in the South. Jim Cooper's Republican opponent was a slick, engaging movie actor/lawyer named Fred Thompson, and Cooper, a Rhodes Scholar and son of a former governor of the state, had all the ease and charm of reinforced concrete. Hopson remained loyal and enthusiastic until the end, but by midsummer everyone knew Cooper had lost.

As we drove from place to place around the Appalachian counties, we talked about problems of poverty and illiteracy there. It had not occurred to me that the Hopsons had been poor, for Joyce and her brothers had all done well, and her mother ran a successful business providing oxygen to people who suffered from asthma, emphysema, and other respiratory problems. She and her mother lived in handsome new two-story houses outside Tazewell, and when I had dinner with the Hopsons, I found them charming, educated, and generous.

We were driving along one of the narrow mountain roads used by coal trucks near Clairfield when Joyce told me that she and her father had been in a head-on collision with a coal truck. He had been killed, and she had been severely injured. Only after many operations and a long course of physical therapy had she been able to walk again. I admired her courage at being able to drive the same roads, and said no more about it.

Once or twice, she exhibited what seemed like an almost preternatural understanding of the lives of the Appalachian poor, but I attributed it to her years of teaching grammar school in the Lone Mountain area. When I asked her how she knew so much about being poor, she said flatly that the Hopsons had been very poor, desperately poor, with nothing but a piece of steep Appalachian land and a couple of cows to keep them alive.

She described the organization of the family. With so little to live on, and so much hardscrabble work just to get enough out of the place to feed them, they met to discuss the apportioning of tasks. Each one had his own work, for which he or she was responsible. Each one knew the value of his contribution within the overall family situation. They formed a miniature polis inside the household. Goals were established, work was done. No one in the Hopson household at that time had ever heard of Athens, let alone Pericles, but they had organized the household as Pericles had said Athenians lived; they governed themselves, they obeyed the laws they made.

The astonishing thing about the Hopsons was not the success of Joyce, but the ability of the family to offer success to each other, and not only to the children but back to the mother, who went to school, studied nursing, and eventually became the family entrepreneur.

3. Red Beans and Rice

She preferred to call herself Reka, which had very little relation to her name, and if that is her preference, Reka it must be. She used that name with clients and with the soup kitchens and food pantries she sent them to. After a short time at the Food & Hunger Hotline, Reka became the manager of the heart of the agency's activities: She was responsible for the small group of women who listened to the problems of New York's hungry and sent them to soup kitchens, if they were homeless; or food pantries, if they had a place to store and cook the cheese and grains and canned goods the pantries offered.

Reka was as smart as a cat. She knew everything about poverty in New York City. She could tell from a thirty-second telephone interview who was lying and who was hungry, who had a man at home who demanded that she get free food from a pantry and who had hungry kids. She could predict how many people on Social Security would find their mailboxes broken open and their checks stolen at the beginning of the month. Reka knew.

And if her supervisee at the next desk raised too much hell with people on food stamps and AFDC for managing badly and running out of food at the end of the month, Reka knew how to calm her without creating a war. She could negotiate anything, largely because she knew all the answers. Her head contained everything from recipes to subway maps to a great file of "regulars"—people who could not find a way to supplement the pittance paid by AFDC or SSI by working "off the books," and had to get free food somewhere during the last few days before the check came.

When I asked her how she knew so much, she said, "We was poor," using the rare grammatical error to underline her knowledge of the life.

As with everything else, Reka knew exactly when and how her family stopped being poor. It happened while they were still living in the projects. Her mother decided one day that the children were old enough to understand a proposition she put before them. She explained that she did not want them to live all their lives in the projects, but that it was impossible for them to move into an apartment unless they had enough money to pay the first and last month's rent and another month's rent as a security deposit. To do that, she explained, they would have to change their habits, save their money. They agreed: For two years they would eat nothing but red beans and rice, and at the end of that time they would move out of the projects.

Two years later, Reka's family moved into an apartment of their own; they were out of the projects. They had discovered a way to make their own lives by making their own rules. No one asked them to eat red beans and rice for two years. The idea was their own, the commitment was their own, and the results were their reward. They had learned to live in a way unlike that of the other people in the projects: They got out, they were free, autonomous.

4. Chendo

The only poor people's organizations of any consequence in the United States are gangs, which some people believe are nascent political organizations, assertions of power rather than force. According to this romantic view, the killings, drug dealing, and other criminal activities common to gangs grow out of the conflict between the gang, which represents the oppressed, and the larger society, which oppresses all people of color and all poor people, causing them to form gangs as a kind of advance guard of the proletarian revolution.

In my experience, which I grant is very limited, gangs are not political or pre-political organizations, nor do they even serve as instruments of legitimate power, as in the use of outside chiefs by the Pueblos.[9] Gangs model themselves on the extended family, following similarly rigid rules. Like the extended family, the gang does not permit autonomy, which it regards as nothing other than rebellion, the first step toward betrayal.

Gangs, like extended families, define themselves by exclusion, expelling autonomous members. Instead of saying, We don't talk to him or her, or, We don't have anything to do with that branch of the family, the gang may choose to punish autonomy with a beating prior to exile. In extreme situations, the punishment for challenging the rules of the gang may be death.

Many gangsters live and die as gang members, progressing from termite to gangster to veteran, succumbing to murder, prison, drug addiction, or the diseases of old age without ever leaving the extended family. For a person to remain close to the gang, within gang territory, and yet to think reflectively, to embark on a political life, requires extraordinary force of will. But it happens. In such instances, a struggle ensues between the newly political person and the extended family or gang over the question of the public life. The political man tries to change the inherently conservative gang into a flexible, variable, autonomous organization, and the gang resists. Many former gangsters have come to the political life, generally at the level of the nuclear family, but I do not know of a single instance in which one of these men has been able to convert the clan to the *deme*, thus to match even in miniature the accomplishments of Solon or Cleisthenes. Yet they continue to arise.

One such man is Ochendo "Chendo" Montes of Los Blue Diamonds in the Salazar Projects in El Paso, Texas. He is married now, the father of four: a girl of six; a boy, Matthew, three; and newborn twins, who suffered from apnea and had to be constantly monitored to be certain they did not sud-

---

[9] I have some acquaintance with several gangs in the Aliso-Pico section of the east side of Los Angeles, mainly through Father Gregory Boyle of the Dolores Mission there. In Chicago, I know the BGs very slightly through Rita Ashford, the mother and surrogate mother of gang members and, like Father Boyle, a person who tries to prevent internecine warfare in the gang world as well as to mediate between the gang members and an equally violent police force.

In El Paso, Texas, I have known the Flaming Angels and Los Blue Diamonds since 1989, although I have not spent enough time with them to consider myself expert in the rites and rituals of gang life. There are many experts, however, among them Father Boyle, Ms. Ashford, and in El Paso, Eusebio "Chevo" Quiroga and Ochendo "Chendo" Montes, all of whom I know, like, and admire. Before Greg Boyle, my old friend Harold J. Rahm, S.J., author of *Padre in the Alley,* a book about his experiences at the Guadalupe Youth Center in El Paso, was as close to the gangs as anyone I know of.

denly stop breathing. Chendo's wife, Juanita, is a huge woman who stands on enormous thighs, like one of the great Aztec statues in the Museum of Anthropology and History in Mexico City. She pulls her hair straight up and ties it into a knot on the top of her head, drawing the corners of her eyes upward, adding to the appearance of an ancient Aztec.

Her husband is a hero among gangsters—the bravest, toughest, most loyal of all the gangsters in the history of The Flaming Angels or Los Blue Diamonds. From the time he was a boy, Chendo was wild, with an uncontrollable temper. In an attempt to curb his temper, his mother once chained him to a heavy bed. For four days Chendo lived at the end of a long chain, able to go only as far as the bathroom. When his mother finally relented and unchained him, Chendo climbed out the window and went back to fighting in the streets.

The years of fighting have battered his face, swelling and scarring it so that he looks like a welterweight club fighter at the end of his career. He sees the world through very thick lenses. The eye doctors have told him that he will go blind from the damage caused by the chains and fists and bricks and baseball bats. Like most other gang bangers, Chendo has night sweats. He relives the beatings, he said, but not the victories. In 1995, Chendo came upon a man beating up a young boy with a baseball bat. When he stepped in to stop the fight, the man hit him in the face with the bat and broke Chendo's jaw.

Perhaps Chendo does not represent gangsters accurately. Perhaps he has suffered too much, learned too much. He is thirty-four years old, a former VISTA volunteer, the conscience of the gang rather than its war leader. No one pays him now, as VISTA did, but he continues to work with the gangsters. As part of his effort, Chendo holds open house. Gangsters, community members of the board of directors of the Salazar Projects, friends, minor political figures all pass through his house in the course of a day or a week.

Chendo and Juanita, whose family fights have achieved the status of legend in the projects, cannot agree on his relation to the gang. Like many women on AFDC, Juanita has used her welfare money as a college scholarship; she has become an accountant. She can envision their escape from the projects: she has friends who have gotten out, away from the gangsters and the Housing Authority. She thinks Chendo is still too close to the gang, that his efforts to change it keep him in it. Juanita does not want the gangsters in her house, around her children, especially the boy. She knows the rules of the extended family, the conservatism of the gang; she knows the gang will take her children, but she does not know how, even though it happens in her own living room, while she sits on the couch in front of the window and a videotape of a violent black exploitation movie plays yet again on the television set.

Javier, the crazy coke addict, comes to Chendo's house. I saw him one brilliant winter afternoon through the door of the apartment, following the tortilla seller down the street, copying his chant, creating an insane echo, a voice twice as loud as that of the peddler, wild, frightening the peddler, who called out to him timidly, "Thank you, thank you." And Javier shouted again, "*Tortillas!*" And the peddler thanked him again in a little minuet of the lion and the lamb.

A moment later, Javier came trotting across the street to Chendo's house. His shirt was unbuttoned, hanging loose; his chest was bare. He jumped in through the door, a fair-skinned man with curly, light brown hair, talking rapidly in a mix of Spanish and English: The housing police were looking for him, there were warrants out for him, had we seen the housing? Which one?

When Chendo's son, Matthew, heard Javier's voice, he came running, throwing himself into Javier's arms. Javier immediately started to agitate the boy, teasing him, tickling him, turning him round and round until the tension of the game contorted his features and the boy screamed with excitement. Chendo and Juanita watched, saying nothing.

Javier tired of the game after a while and allowed the child to slip away, out of his grasp. Matthew ran upstairs to the room he shared with his sister, and came down with a plastic baseball bat and ball. Javier took the bat from him and began teaching him how to use it as a weapon, showing him how to wield it, where to hit someone to do the most damage. To Javier and to the child as well, the bat has nothing to do with the ball; it is only a weapon, an instrument of force.

Although it was not apparent to Chendo or Juanita, Javier was teaching the boy the culture of the gang, where sport is not under consideration. An occasional gangster may participate in sports, but there are no gang tournaments or leagues. Sport is a pre-political activity; the players can make some of their own rules, but they must obey the rules they make. For example, a baseball game may involve as few as two or even one person on a side or as many as ten or more, but the players may not deliberately hit each other with a bat. Gangs do not compete through games, for every gangster knows Javier's lesson of the rule of force: The bat has nothing to do with the ball.

Chendo Montes came to politics through the lesson of defeat. He saw the *tecatos* (drug addicts) move into the projects and then he saw the way the Colombian drug dealers across the border in Ciudad Juárez dealt with members of the El Paso gangs. He tells stories of torture, a naked man whose flesh had been burned and torn away crawling through the streets of Juárez, brothers dying in their attempts to avenge each other. Caught between the extremes of love and force, his children and the drug dealers, he came to reflect on his life, to move to a place between the changing political life of his nuclear family and the dire conservatism of the extended family.

The lure of the gang made no sense to me until I was invited to a party for Los Blue Diamonds and their predecessors, The Flaming Angels. The party was held in the last house at the end of a street, high up on the slope of Mount Franklin. A hundred cars, perhaps more, had been parked in rows of five or six deep, and more were coming when I arrived. I parked at the bottom of the hill, at the cross street, so I could leave without having to wait for others to move their cars.

The entire gang had come to the party. The veterans brought their wives and children; the younger members walked through the crowd, drinking beer, talking, eating, looking for something to do. A disc jockey alternated with a rock band. An inflatable rubber castle, fifteen feet high and twenty-five feet across, stood next to the entrance to the grounds of the house. Children crawled through it at every level. Dozens of couples danced in front of the disc jockey, lighted in greens and purples and spots of orange. It was a nightmare of pleasures, louder than trains at full roar, packed with elbows and running children. Big Pepe sat with his wife, who drank beer while she nursed their son. "Eighteen months old and he's already kicking ass," Big Pepe said.

I moved on. Pee Wee found me and asked if I wanted to meet some of the *veteranos*. I agreed to follow him, for Pee Wee was the only one of Los Blue Diamonds who made me uncomfortable. At thirteen, a little boy, with tiny features, dressed according to his mother's tastes, Pee Wee had already made his reputation: He was the shooter. Everyone treated him with great deference, even Chendo, who said of him, "He has balls. He'll pick up a brick or . . . whatever he has to do."

We went through the crowd to meet some of the veterans, the men who had started the gang shortly after the projects were built. If war broke out between gangs, a big war, Chendo said, the veterans would come back. I wondered if it would be so. They did not look like the Marines. One was a fat man dressed in a sleeveless undershirt and striped shorts that could have been pajamas or even underwear. Another, a tall man, dressed like a cowboy in a Mexican movie, with long sideburns and a big hat, lamented the fact that he had never finished school. "Now, I go to school every day, all my life," he said. "I am the janitor."

The veterans tried to stay off by themselves, for they looked out of place among the children and families. The wives of the veterans were all inside the house, cooking, setting out great trays of food, playing with the children who came into the dining room and the kitchen.

Abel, whom I had known since he was a high school student, and his brother, Eddie, appeared. Over the years Abel had grown sour. One of his brothers had been murdered, Abel's ambitions had all been thwarted. He had become overly neat, tense; he chewed on his own teeth. "It's getting late," Eddie said. "There's going to be a fight."

"Why?" I asked. "Who's going to fight?"

"I don't know," he said, "but there's always a big fight. When there's a party, there's a big fight."

Abel was drunk, stumbling, rolling against the shoulders and backs of the crowd. "Give me a hundred dollars," he said to me.

"No."

"I'll pay you back, man. Don't be a *pinche gabacho,* give me a hundred dollars. I need it. These guys are going to get me if I don't give them a hundred dollars."

"When?"

"Right now."

"No."

"I thought I told you I need it now."

Sapo suddenly stepped between us, skinny, ugly, the boy named Toad, who could slither like a snake. "What chu doing, man?" Sapo was a shooter, like Pee Wee, but older; he had to be more careful, he could be sentenced to hard time. Nevertheless, Abel backed away.

The party got louder. Tiny girls no more than five or six years old, dressed like their mothers, rouged and spangled, danced in the center of the crowd, creating open spaces around themselves, exaggerating the hip movements and leerings of the dance. A shoving match broke out, raised the temperature of the party for a moment, then faded as the contestants were absorbed into the crowd.

The moon came up, and with it the wind. The noise of the party was echoed by the mountain. It grew cold. The inflated castle sprang a leak; one corner softened and sagged; it looked as if it might collapse. Honkings came from the mass of parked cars. Miguel, who said his uncle owned the house, walked among the partygoers speaking of drugs and money, the greatness of the gang.

It was the end of the evening for me. I stopped to say good-bye and to exchange the complicated handshake with some of Los Blue Diamonds on my way out to the street. When I had passed the band and the dancers and the sagging castle, I found myself surrounded by four of the younger members of the gang, the fighters.

"We'll go with you to your car," Sapo said.

I protested that it was not necessary; I was quite capable of making my own way to the foot of the hill where my car sat on the corner. They explained that we were in territory that belonged to a rival gang. There had been beatings, a shooting. The other gang often waited across the road in the darkness to catch one of The Flaming Angels or Los Blue Diamonds by himself, to "hit him with a bat or shoot him in the ass." That was why all of the cars were crowded together at the end of the street near the mountain.

Four of us walked down the hill together—Sapo, Abel, the Pee Wee, and me. The Pee Wee touched the pocket of his jacket, Sapo patted his pants pocket, Abel smiled icily. They were all armed: Sapo and the Pee Wee on either side of me, and Abel walking behind, the oldest one, the man in charge. I looked back at him once, but he did not see me. His eyes were focused far ahead of us, at the cross street and beyond.

For the first time, I understood the essence of the gang, why Chendo could not change them. My embarrassment disappeared. I was happy to be among them, surrounded by people who were willing to kill or die, if not for me, for glory, but willing, and willing now, in the moment, without reflection.

5. Two Families in the Senator's House

If Johnnie Walls, Jr., does not become the governor of Mississippi or one of its U.S. senators, it will be proof of the two-edged sword of integration: on one side an illusion of integration, as state senator Walls says, enabling successful blacks to assimilate, but not to integrate their own culture with that of the whites; and on the other side continuing to weaken the black community by destroying its stores and schools and general sense of pride in self and community. Johnnie Walls has already made quite a lot of progress on the road to high office. He is a state senator, the chairman of the Mississippi State Democratic Party, and the lead partner in a successful and very profitable law firm.

Should nothing more happen in the political carer of Senator Walls or Chairman Walls or Johnnie Walls, Esquire, his life would still appear to be more than tolerable. He lives in a grand old house, made beautiful and modern under his wife's direction and filled with laughter and children. If the senator's life sounds like a fairy tale, it has some of those aspects, although a lawyer's life is never without one gut-wrenching problem or another, and a black man, even one so successful and famous as Johnnie Walls, cannot be completely at his ease in Mississippi. The senator is filled with memories. He recalls the white judge who could not believe Walls was a lawyer. "We've never had a colored lawyer in this county," the judge told Walls, and asked where the young man went to law school. When Walls replied that he had graduated from Ole Miss, the judge asked to see his diploma.

That was a long time ago, in the beginning of the senator's career. He laughs at the experience now, but he cannot yet laugh at the experiences of racism. He still tends to do his business quickly in a store, never picking up anything he does not intend to buy, following the lesson his father taught him when the senator was a child. And it was only recently that he dared look at a white woman in a bathing suit; he remembered his father's advice about where not to look when he passed the white swimming pool. In the same context he remembered the night his father gathered the family around the pot-bellied stove in the three-room house outside Clarksdale, and read aloud the entire *Life* magazine article about the murder of the Till boy there in Mississippi.

In the journey from a shotgun house where his parents, a grandmother, and eleven children lived in the "front room, the middle room, and the kitchen," the Walls family followed the pattern of politicization at the nuclear family level, with a few exceptions. One of the children became an All-American basketball player and Johnnie, the oldest, was a star at football. Unlike some of the others in the black area on the edge of Clarksdale, the Walls family had a business. The senator's father earned a living providing transportation for migrant workers. He was away from home for long periods, working in Florida or going up north with his crew, leaving his wife to raise the children in his absence. Money was always short; sometimes three months went by before he could send anything home.

While Mrs. Walls occasionally resorted to the willow switch to maintain order in the household, her general method was to establish a balance between order and liberty, with emphasis on the value of order. "She would not tolerate fighting or arguing," the senator said. "She told us, 'You boys and girls, you're all you have. You have to look out for each other while your father's off workin. Brothers and sisters shouldn't fight each other. Older ones are supposed to look after the younger ones.'"

As in the Hopson family, each child was assigned the tasks appropriate to his or her age. Johnnie Walls might be assigned the dishwashing one day, bedmaking the next, tending to the cow the next. He said he changed the diapers of every one of his ten brothers and sisters, including the big, tall one who became the All-American. As soon as they were old enough, all the children chopped cotton, bringing home to their mother the $3 they were paid at the end of the day.

With eleven children in a three-room house, there were plenty of disputes, but the method for settling them followed the rules of order rather than force. They were encouraged to bring their cases before Mrs. Walls, and "she would hear them out, and decide who was right."

All eleven of the Walls children did not succeed in life, according to the senator. "The first five of us went to college," he said. "After we got into the seventies, it started dropping off. There was less opposition; you didn't have to struggle as hard. The whole idea was different. There was less achievement toward the end. One or two of us faltered."

He does not, of course, favor a return to segregation, yet he cannot help but note the weakening of the black community that came with the end of outright oppression. Like many black leaders in the Delta, Johnnie Walls understands that the political family, the talking, negotiating unit, public by choice or necessity within its own boundaries, got up out of poverty as soon as it was possible, even before it was possible. But he also understands that autonomy means first the ability to govern oneself as an entity, and that the rule holds today as in ancient Athens. The problem is how to produce the autonomy of opposition in a war with subtle enemies.

This effect of opposition and order in creating the political life of the poor was demonstrated again one evening by a visitor to the senator's house.

Two of the best known women in the Delta town of Greenville came to Johnnie Wall's house that evening. Both had been schoolteachers when schoolteachers were the black elite in the Delta, and both had retired, with some relief, after desegregation had brought about the flight of white children to private academies and the replacement of many black public school teachers with whites. It was yet another way that whites had turned desegregation to their advantage; neither the black students nor the teachers had been protected from what had turned out to be the destruction of their political and economic world.

Thelma Giles, a slim, delicate woman, starched and cool despite the Delta summer, who spoke in saddening detail about the ravages of desegregation in the school where she had taught third grade, walked quietly and shyly through the house. Ms. Giles, as everyone, including her peers, addresses her, displayed reserve to match the senator's ebullience and used her perfect diction to equal his charm. It was the quietest of confrontations, a matter of styles, but difficult, for the styles were also the substance, presenting a choice between two goods in a difficult world.

A second rendezvous between the generations came to overshadow it. The other teacher, Mrs. Barbara Bacon-Quinn, had been raised in the big house that now belonged to Senator Walls. Until that night, she had not been inside the house for many years. Two generations of owners had occupied the house between her tenure and that of the senator. The house had never fallen into disrepair, but it had become antiquated over nearly half a century. The senator's wife, who had a gift for architecture and decoration, had rejuvenated the old house, modernizing it, and then furnishing it with antiques.

Over the course of many years, a long career, Mrs. Bacon-Quinn had become distinguished among clubwomen and schoolteachers in Mississippi. She lived in a spacious ranch house on a cul-de-sac in an affluent suburb north of Greenville. Although she was twice widowed, she had surrounded herself with children and grandchildren, all the woes and satisfactions of generations, and she passed through the life of the town in her silk summer dresses, with hats to match, at her ease inside the Cadillac, where the temperature was maintained in all seasons at the same comfortable mark.

She wore eyeglasses and jewels, and she liked the look of gold against her skin. Dressed casually, to supervise the gardeners at her house, she was a vigorous, good-looking woman, but in silk and pearls she was lost to overstatement, like some well-formed plants that lose their symmetry in bloom.

The senator, who was not exactly houseproud but somewhere in the very narrow space between vanity and irony, guided Mrs. Bacon-Quinn, Ms. Giles, Frank Clarke, and me through the house. That is, he began the tour of the house. Before we had gone through more than one or two rooms, Mrs. Bacon-Quinn had abandoned her silky natterings and taken over the tour. As we went from room to room, she remembered her childhood, the woman who had run the house, "Germans," she said, and recited all that they had owned—the land, the crops, and the warehouses down near the river.

She lost control of the tour for a moment in the upstairs master bedroom and Jacuzzi across the hall. The senator made a joke about the rooms, saying that the house he had lived in as a boy in Clarksdale had not been as large as the bedroom and bath of this house. We all laughed, and followed Senator Walls back down to the first floor.

"And this was the music room," Mrs. Bacon-Quinn said. "The piano was right there. Oh, how I hated to practice! Had to practice every afternoon. And then the piano teacher came every week; she was so strict!"

In the next room, which was dominated by a gigantic television screen, she said, "This was where we had the Christmas tree, right there, in that corner. It was always such a big tree, right up to the ceiling."

Finally, the tour moved into the dining room, where we all stood around the table, which sat sixteen in comfort. Mrs. Bacon-Quinn pointed to the single chair at the end of the table. "Is there still a buzzer in the floor beside that chair?" she asked.

"No," the senator said. "We had the floors refinished, and didn't see a buzzer."

"It was right there, under the rug," Mrs. Bacon-Quinn said, pointing to the spot. "She would *mash* that button, and it rang in the kitchen for my mother to come and bring more food to the table."

The room fell silent for a moment. The American troubles hung in the air: black/white, rich/poor, politics/loneliness, class/race, the role of class/the end of class, and now the attempt to build classes again within the races. No one spoke. Then Mrs. Bacon-Quinn, in summer silk with matching hat, resumed her nattering. She had shown the anger that drove her success, the politicizing anger, and chosen to put it away again, beside that of her host, in a far closet, in the house of oppositions.

6. Ms. Ebron's Meeting

When Jackie Ebron was fourteen years old, living in a project in New York City, her parents split up. There were seven children, and according to Mrs. Ebron, their father left them with close to nothing. Their situation was desperate. They were poor and black, and they had no extended family they could go to for help. To deal with the problem, Mrs. Ebron called a meeting of the newly fatherless family. She gathered all the children around the dining table and made a presentation of their situation. She showed them their economic balance sheet, income and expenses, and invited them to participate in the affairs of the family; that is, with their father gone, to begin governing themselves.

Although there was never enough money, all seven children completed school and are well along in their careers in business or the professions. Jackie Ebron became a social worker at the Metropolitan Council on Jewish Poverty, where she has run the emergency assistance program for many years.

She is a bustling New York woman, with the competent eyes one hopes for in a person who deals with desperate situations. After we talked for a while about her situation compared to that of the clients she worked with, she said that her mother's decision to form a little community in their household had been a deep influence in the lives of the children. When I asked if she thought her mother had made the family political, in the Periclean sense of politics at all levels, she considered the idea for a while, then she smiled. "Yes, you could say that. Yes."

7. Dallas

Of all the people who came out of poverty through the political life, none illustrates the process more clearly than Frances Rizo. Anyone who watched the television soap opera *Dallas* would find Mrs. Rizo a familiar face, for she had a small but continuing part in the serial, playing, as Mexican-American actors are fated to do, the maid. But that came in middle age for her, after she had married and divorced, and all but completed raising her family. Within a few years after the television serial ended, Mrs. Rizo could look at her children and say that one was a social worker, another was a lieutenant in Army intelligence, a third was at West Point, and her daughter, who had two children, was attending college. She was anxious to tell what had happened to her, to explain why she was no longer poor.

"When I met the father of my children," she said, "he had been in Gatesville reform school for stealing. He was almost four years older than me. He was tough, he was mean. The first time I remember seeing him, he was in a fight at H. L. Green's store. He was supposed to be from Ledbetter, from West Dallas, but he was talking to the guys from El Barrio.

"He was *güero.*[10] I guess the Jimmy Dean syndrome, the Marlon Brando type, the nonconformist is what attracted me to him, and the fact that all the guys respected him.

"I was the first person on my mother's side of the family to get to high school, so I was allowed to go out and date a little.

"So I started dating, and the man never let me loose after that. I said my mother didn't like him, she wouldn't sign the papers for us to get married, so he said, 'I'm not gonna take you home, and she'll sign the papers.' So he didn't take me home, and she signed the papers, and three weeks later we were married.

"I was fifteen, and I was working. I wanted to get my GED. I wanted to continue going to school. In 1966, we both took the GED test, with no preparation, and both passed. I then enrolled in a secretarial school, and I was working forty hours a week.

"He became an officer in the local union and became a union organizer for the carpenters' union. He was wearing suits and boots. His life changed because of the stature he was carrying, but as you know, the unions are probably the most racist institutions in this country; he couldn't get ahead. Then he started drinking.

"My husband was extremely possessive and jealous. I was very friendly. I was trying to get everybody to like me. He decided it was flirting. He intimidated me to the point that I started looking down at the sidewalk when we went out. He was a big-time womanizer, plus he was abusive, so I left him.

"I got involved in PTA, and I would go down to City Council to demand

---

[10] Of fair complexion, often with light-colored hair.

that they fix our neighborhood. This was during the Chicano movement, the civil rights movement. I was an activist. I don't believe I was ever a radical, but a lot of other people thought I was. I supported Cesar Chavez and the United Farmworkers.

"I got a scholarship to go to El Centro College. Then I transferred to SMU. We were only getting by. We only had one bathroom for five people. We even had an order in which we used the bathroom. We had so little money, I would go to the grocery store and buy only the things that were on my list that was on the menu plan for the week. The menu plan was on the refrigerator, so everybody knew what the thing in the cupboard or in the refrigerator was intended for. My income was between ten and fifteen thousand, depending on whether I was going to school full time or part time.

"In our family everybody had input, everybody had part of the decision-making process, but when we got to where we wanted something we couldn't afford or something illogical, I could step in with my authority.

"All the children had to carry their own load. The boys learned early how to wash their own clothes. We had a family conference when the kids started fudging on the chores. I asked them for a solution. We used to change assignments every day, but then we turned to having the same assignment all week long. When I had a problem I couldn't solve, generally with money, I would sit down with the kids and explain it, and they would come up with a solution. We called it 'our little democracy.'"

The pattern of the escape from multigenerational or long-term poverty repeats itself with little variation. The histories of the Ebrons, Hopsons, and Rizos are practically indistinguishable. Ruth Kinsler spoke of loving the people and Sam Kinsler spoke of being knocked down eighteen times in a fight with four young men, including his own nephew. Reka and her family, like the others, avoided the envy that drives people away from politics into anomie.

Mrs. Irene Guster of Greenville, Mississippi, who grew up picking cotton on a plantation and now lives in a fine house, with generations of successful children around her, thought for a very long time before she could say exactly what had changed in her family, how they had learned something that brought them up out of poverty. She did not minimize the fact that she had been born under the yoke of servitude almost indistinguishable from slavery. She gave much credit to the church and the study of the Bible, which had made a cultured woman of her and professionals and intellectuals of her seven children; but when she thought about the difference between her family and so many others, she recalled a lesson her father had taught his children.

He sat under a tree with his six children gathered around him and taught them a lesson with a piece of string and six sticks. He tied the string around the sticks and showed the children how the six together could stand. He demonstrated the strength of them. Then he untied the sticks, and let them fall.

It was not a lesson in family, she said, for people are born into a family. It was his lesson in how to live. Politics.

His lesson did not raise the pay they collected for chopping cotton. The earth still steamed in August when little Irene Guster and her brothers and sisters bent to their work. People still fell breathless in the fields.

The surround of force existed for those who got out of poverty just as it did for those who remained behind, but they overcame the panic that limits the surrounded to a desperate life of reaction. In all those who moved out of poverty, not just the few people whose lives are described here, but in the Bradley family in Mississippi and the Gutiérrez family in East Los Angeles and the Harvin family of north-central Florida, there is also a sense of creative opposition, a positive response to the surround of force, which bears more relation to the development of freedom in opposition to fate than to the concept of class struggle.

When nuclear families move out of poverty, and they do so one-at-a-time, not as part of extended families or clans, the first step is always the end of isolation not from the wider world but from the nuclear family itself. The members of the nuclear unit begin to understand their survival and success as the survival and success of the unit, but they do not do this according to ritual or even culture. The first norm they learn is the norm of the unit, and they establish this miniature polis consciously; they understand that they are each other's "hostages to fortune." The screaming silence of private life comes to a close, the endless dialogue begins, they are reborn for each other, and within the tiny polis the surround of force is broken.

XVI.

A Prison Epiphany

"Slaves," so ran a Greek proverb,
"have no leisure"—
it was a definition.
— BERNARD KNOX

I N RETROSPECT, IT SHOULD HAVE been no surprise that the idea came from a woman who had been in a maximum-security prison for more than eight years, because prison lies at the extreme end of the continuum of society, where a cold-eyed view of all the rest of the world may come more readily, if the prisoner can see at all. Prison shares very little with what the prisoners call "the free world," for the first rule of prison life is the denial of autonomy. That is the function of the rolls of razor wire, the guard towers, the weapons aimed at the prisoners, the cell doors, the constant searches and counts, and the punishments: isolation, transfer, and withdrawal of the few amenities permitted prisoners. Prison is worse than slavery in many respects, worse than long-term relative poverty in others.[1]

What better place than prison to think about how to avoid poverty or escape from it? Inside those prisons still concerned with rehabilitation as well as punishment, the staff[2] and the prisoners attempt to use the

---

[1] For a detailed comparison of slavery and life among the poor, see Appendix B.
[2] Psychologists, social workers, teachers, and medical practitioners, as distinct from the guards.

metaphor of the prison to understand the real world. Much of this is futile stuff, amateur psychotherapy, a way to pass the time without having to break rocks or wash dishes, but some programs work.

At the Bedford Hills Correctional Facility, the maximum-security prison and intake and processing center about fifty miles north of New York City, the Family Violence Program, designed largely by Sharon Smolick and managed now by Roberta Falk and Terri McNair, encourages prisoners to explore damaging aspects of family life through the invention of revealing dramas.

These dramas show that those who live within a surround of force either sink into passivity or react to force with force. Nothing of the ideas of Sartre and Fanon, in which man recreates himself through violence, succeeds, according to the dramas; man cannot recreate himself that way. The practice of viewing the world through the clarifying filter of these dramas has taught some of the women in the program to use a cold eye to view other situations. And no one has learned it better than Viniece Walker.[3]

She came to Bedford when she was nineteen years old, a high school dropout who read at the level of a college sophomore, a graduate of crack houses, the streets of Harlem, and a long alliance with a brutal man.[4] On the surface, Viniece has remained as tough as she had been on the streets of Harlem. She speaks bluntly, and even though the AIDS infection has progressed during her time in prison, she still swaggers as she walks down the long prison corridors. While in Bedford Hills, she completed her high school requirements and pursued a college degree, with a concentration in philosophy. She became a counselor to women with a history of family violence and a comforter of other women who suffered the debility and certain fate of AIDS.

Only the deaths of other women cause her to stumble in the midst of her swaggering step, to spend days alone with the remorse that drives her to seek redemption. She goes through life as if she had been imagined by Dostoyevsky, but even more complex than his fictions, alive, a person, fair-skinned and freckled, and in prison. It was she who responded to the sudden question, Why do you think people are poor?

We had never met before. The conversation around us focused on the abuse of women. Niecie's eyes were perfectly opaque, hostile, prison eyes. Her mouth was set in the beginning of a sneer.

"You got to begin with the children," she said, speaking rapidly, clip-

[3] Viniece "Niecie" Walker and I have known each other for several years. We started out as acquaintances, then became allies, and finally friends.

[4] It is considered bad form in prison to discuss a person's crime. I will follow that rule here.

ping out the street sounds, southern sounds, as they came into her speech, in the way Norman Mailer bowdlerizes his own speech by editing out the Yiddish past.

She paused long enough to let the change of direction take effect, then resumed the rapid, rhythmless speech. "You've got to teach the moral life of downtown to the children. And the way you do that, Earl, is by taking them downtown to plays, museums, concerts, lectures, where they can learn the moral life of downtown."

I smiled at her, misunderstanding, thinking I was indulging her. "And then they won't be poor anymore."

She read every nuance of my response, and answered angrily, "And they won't be poor *no more.*"

"What you mean is . . ."

"What I mean is what I said, a moral alternative to the street."

She did not speak of jobs or money, not then or ever during the years we have talked about poverty in America. From her vantage within the prison, a place in which spies and informers rob people of their very thoughts, putting them, as Tacitus said, into a life worse than slavery, she had discovered something about reality. And it was not an aberration, something grown up in Harlem and nurtured in the bitter soil of prison. She did not speak of God or church or the bosom of family. She had a cold eye. In a glance, passing, like the horseman of the Yeats poem, she saw what others had said, and went on.

Of all those I had listened to, the poor and yesterday's poor as well, none had spoken of jobs or money. They thanked God, but they did so rich or poor, the poor more than the formerly poor, because their fear was greater. No one spoke of God the employment agent or God the paymaster. They thanked God, but not for the business of life.

It was not release from poverty that interested Niecie; she had been in prison long enough to know that release had nothing to do with autonomy: A prisoner cannot release herself, she can only be released from prison. The moral life does not consist in being acted upon, but in acting. Autonomous persons act.

But what of politics? Had she skipped a step or failed to take a step?

"The moral life of downtown?" What kind of moral life does music teach?

How can a museum push poverty away? Who can dress in statues or eat the past?

The answer was politics, not "the moral life of downtown." Only politics could overcome the tutelage of force. But to enter the public world, to practice the political life, the poor had first to learn to reflect. That was what she meant by "the moral life of downtown." She did not know downtown, she could not even imagine the moral life of Wall Street or Fifth Avenue. She lived in prison, in a cloud of Dostoyevskian remorse, amid dreams of redemption. The moral life was the political life in her mind; she did not make the error of divorcing ethics from politics. Niecie had simply said, in a kind of shorthand, that no one could step out of the surround of force directly into the public world.

There are many paths out of poverty. Those who know poverty least concentrate on jobs and money, as if poverty was merely quantitative and labor was God's own panacea. The formerly poor, and those who live in the distance of metaphor, know that the game of the modern world can be overcome; that politics, unlike economics or the strutting of status, is not a contest but a public accomplishment of power.[5]

No one can release the poor from poverty, no one can accomplish power for them. Efforts to mobilize the poor, as exemplified in the history of the National Welfare Rights Organization, have always failed. In 1971, Frances Fox Piven and Richard Cloward, in *Regulating the Poor,* described the movement as "burgeoning." Six years later, in *Poor People's Movements,* they tried to explain why the mobilization had failed.[6] It did not occur to them that they, the political people, had attempted to release the poor from poverty.

In her answer to the question about poverty, Niecie had assumed that the poor could not be mobilized or otherwise released from poverty. She knew they would have to act as autonomous persons; what she meant by "the moral life of downtown" was something that had happened to her. She did not describe what had happened; perhaps she was not even entirely aware of it. But she knew that because of her education a radical transformation had occurred: She had discovered the extent of her own humanness.

---

[5] This kind of change has happened before. Josiah Ober described one instance in *Mass and Elite in Democratic Athens* (Princeton, N.J.: Princeton University Press, 1989): "The bonds of mutual interdependence between citizens were now based on an assumption of political equality. This assumption tended to weaken the old bonds of deference which had been based on class and status inequality, because the new ties cut across the horizontal strata of birth and wealth." Ober went on to compare many of the aspects of this kind of decision making in ancient Greece after Cleisthenes instituted the system of *demes* to that of Massachusetts towns at the end of the seventeenth century (pp. 70–71).

Resistance to the change in Greek social and political organization was apparently minimal. In the United States, where the rules of the game have become a bulwark against the leveling character of fairness, such change would most likely encounter strong resistance.

[6] *Poor People's Movements* (New York: Pantheon, 1978). The extent of the failure of the organization they founded with George Wiley was described by Michael Harrington, who wrote that Wiley was able to enroll only 22,000 people out of a potential membership of "around 9 million."

The radical solution to the plight of the poor did not await them on the right, with its plan of deprivation and coercion; the poor knew full well that jobs and money were ancillary aspects of getting out of poverty, outcomes rather than process. And the other side had no solution to offer at all; liberals and leftists simply stood by, tongue-tied and bankrupt, remembering Roosevelt and relying on the sputter of compassion in the twilight hours of Daniel Patrick Moynihan, while more people descended into poverty, and the lives of the poor, especially the children, worsened year after year.

Niecie Walker had followed the same path that led to the invention of politics in ancient Greece. She had learned to reflect. In further conversation it became clear that when she spoke of "the moral life of downtown," she meant the humanities, which had been the source of reflection for the secular world since the Greeks first stepped back from nature to experience wonder at what they beheld.

If the political life was the way out of poverty, the humanities provided an entrance to reflection and the political life: the poor did not need anyone to release them; an escape route existed. But to open this avenue to reflection and politics, a major distinction between the preparation for life of the rich and poor has to be eliminated. The game of modern society, as it has been practiced in America since the founding, will have to be reinvented, with a new set of rules promoting fairness and a commitment to the dialogue of equals. To do so will require revisions and reforms not only in the lives of the poor but in the entire society.

XVII.

Radical Humanism

Man is the measure of all things.
— P R O T A G O R A S

Wildflower

THE WOMAN SAT HUNCHED over a metal and wood veneer table in the intake section of the clinic. It was the beginning of winter in New York, the season of darkening days and influenza. She wore two knit caps, one atop the other, both of them pulled down over her temples. Her body was thin, curled like a bent wire inside her pale, almost white raincoat. She wore the coat buttoned to her chin and belted tightly at the waist, even though she was indoors in a heated room. Her name was Silveria, which means "of the woods," like a wildflower.

In profile, she appeared to be drawn down, curled over her woes. All the forms of her were curled in the same way, as if she had been painted by an artist overly concerned with repetitions. Even her hands were curled, half-closed, resting tensely upon the table.

The girls, her daughters, were also bent over the table. They had not curled up like their mother, but their eyes were downcast, and their elegant, equine faces were impassive. The mother and the girls sat alone, shut off from the rest of the room. The psychologist in charge of the session whispered that they lived in a shelter for battered women and they were very depressed.

During the intake session the woman and her daughters said little. They filled out the forms provided to them by the psychologist. The mother did not remove her coat or her caps. The faces of the girls remained stony, a practiced gray.

When some workmen came to repair a wall in the intake room, the session was moved into another, smaller room. The mother, who had curled up in the new place to fill out the intake forms, wanted to know the meaning of a word as it was used in one of the questions and how it could apply to a person's mental state.

I responded as best I could. She accepted the answer and went on filling out the form. The girls finished their forms first, and sat still and silent in their chairs, gray stone horses. I asked one of the girls if she went to school.

She said she was a high school student, but that she was not happy in her school.

"Are you a good student?"

"Yes, I get only A's."

"And what is your favorite subject?"

"I like to read books."

"Do you have a favorite author?" I asked.

"Yes, Gabriel García Márquez."

We began to talk about García Márquez, about this story and that. About *One Hundred Years of Solitude,* which we spoke of as *Cien Años de Soledad.* In a matter of moments, the two girls and I were in deep discussion about our favorite Latin American writers. Then the mother joined in. "Neruda," the girls said. The mother reminded us of the value of the Cuban, Carpentier. Did I know that it was Carpentier who had first written of a rain of butterflies? I asked if they knew the Dominican poet, Chiqui Vicioso.

We talked about the Mexicans: Carlos Fuentes and Sor Juana. Octavio Paz was still too difficult for the girls. They were interested in Elena Poniatowska, but they had not read her. They did not like Isabel Allende very much.

The mother uncurled, opening like a fern. The equine girls laughed. They told their favorite stories from literature, they talked about the Cuban movies made from the García Márquez stories: *The Handsomest Drowned Man in the World, Innocent Erendira, A Very Old Gentleman with Some Enormous Wings.*

Soon, the young psychologist joined in. One of the girls recited a poem she had written. Everyone in the room listened. The mother told a joke, pausing twice in the middle to cough. A Puerto Rican woman on the other side of the small room told the names of her favorite stories. Before long, the curled-up woman and her equine daughters and all the other people in the room, including the psychologist and the writer, had created a public world. The room of depression became a community of equals. The battered woman, who had no work, no place to call home but a secret shelter far from any place she had ever known, shared in the power of the public place. She removed her caps and let her hair fall loose, and when she smiled everyone could see that she was the source of the elegance of her daughters.

1

There are many routes to the political life, but it is a long journey up from loneliness, and very difficult, perhaps the most radical act in human history. Nothing quite compares to it. To expect the multigenerational poor, who live within the surround of force, in panic, to accomplish so radical a dream would seem to demand too much of them. But it happens. Human beings recreate themselves; by one method or another, by instinct or instruction, they prepare themselves for politics.

These are some of the ways in which the long-term poor become political:

1. Immigration can lead people into politics, if they understand the process. However, for those who feel unwelcome in the new country, as they did not feel at home in the old country, immigration is often not a way of recreating themselves, but only the transporting of their loneliness and suffering from one place to another. Immigration, of course, is not an option for people born in the United States.

2. Doing politics can make people political, but only when they *choose* to do politics; when people are mobilized, as so often happens to the poor, they do not experience autonomy. Choosing to do politics occurs when people join together in the public world to fend off criminals or protect their environment. The Mothers of East L.A. is an example of this learning of politics through doing politics.

The organizations that follow Saul Alinsky's methods have staked out a middle ground between mobilization and autonomous politics. Most of the organizations are church-based and all engage in political education and politics at the neighborhood level and community level on up through city and state politics. There is, however, a question about the autonomy of the organizations, whether the people choose politics or acquiesce to mobilization. They belong to a larger structure and follow guidelines written many years ago by Alinsky. The executive director, appointed by a regional authority, holds sway over the local group.

3. Unions and other forms of cooperative endeavor, from tenant organi-

zations to sweat equity housing to the PTA, bring people into the public world and in many instances enable them to do politics. Even corrupt unions may do this for their members, because of the sense of autonomy of the union. Unions fail to bring people into the public world when the membership does not understand what they are doing; that is, when union membership is like mobilization.

Historically, progressive labor organizations have used education, including literature, history, politics, and economics, to bring their members to politics. Corrupt unions do not usually make such efforts.

4. Some churches create a public world for their members. The church itself may be an autonomous or semi-autonomous organization in which politics and worship support each other, but the most important function of the church in making the poor political grows out of the teaching of the humanities.

Black churches in the South have had this effect. Through the charismatic movement and practices brought to the United States by priests who had worked in the *comunidades de base* in Latin America, the Roman Catholic Church is attempting to change its practices to accommodate this need for the parishoners to practice exegesis by reading directly from Scripture and to organize more along the lines of small Protestant churches.

Some churches hold the practice of politicizing their members as a goal nearly equal to that of believing in the tenets of the religion. The small church in Sun River Terrace, Illinois, a black community near Kankakee, has taken the creation of a public life for its members as a vital part of its work. Among those who preach to the membership, which includes some ex-convicts and recovering addicts, is Robert Ervin, a former Chicago police officer. Ervin understands the dual function of the church, and preaches accordingly.

5. Families devise strategies for survival that require a public life within the family unit that then extends to the larger community. In many instances these strategies are worked out in conjunction with church or legal rights organizations.

The surprise comes in the similarity of the method, which has continued over centuries and across cultures: Human beings become political by cultivating their inborn humanity. They follow the pattern established at the beginning. They embrace the humanities in one way or another; most often religion leads to reflection, but the law or organizational theory or political philosophy can have the same effect. They must do so, however, with little help from those who claim to care either for the poor or for the humanities.

To call for the study of the humanities now as an answer to the problem of poverty in the United States contravenes the views of both the left and the right. The left has abandoned the study of the humanities as the cultural imperialism of dead white European males, giving it over to the conservatives, who have claimed it as their own. In fact, the humanities should belong to the left, for the study of the humanities by large numbers of people, especially the poor, is in itself a redistribution of the wealth. The right, on the other hand, has had no use for the living humanities since Plato banned poets from *The Republic*.

Objection by the left to the study of the humanities can be dealt with quickly: The division should come between market-driven culture and the humanities, not between the beauty of an Asian poem and a European poem. When Petrarch called for a return to the classics, meaning the work of Greece and Rome, he knew no other. His notion of civic humanism would not include the study of bricklaying or popular culture now as it did not then. Nor would the humanities comprise the manufacture, programming, or repair of computers. But I think Petrarch would make world literature his text and find art influenced by Africa, Asia, and the Americas as interesting as the sculptures of Greece or the architecture of Rome. History, of course, has no limits and logic no substitute. The answers arrived at by philosophers differ from time to time and place to place, but the questions, as Kant set them out, have always been the same: What can I know? How shall I live? What may I hope? And what is man?

The humanities will always be heavily influenced by the work of the dead white men of Europe, for they have been history's troublemakers, the fomenters of revolutions and inventions, the impetus of change, the implacable enemies of the silence in which humanity perishes. No other great body of work invites criticism or denies loneliness to the same extent, and no other body of work in all the history of the world led to politics, with its still astonishing notion of autonomy. The left abandons the humanities at its peril, for without the humanities for a gadfly, the left sits idly, contented by memories of distant thoughts and small victories, and dies.

Conservatism presents a more complex problem, because conservatives have attempted to seize the university, especially those aspects of education dealing with Western civilization, as their own. The most widely read exponent of this view, the late Allan Bloom, a member of the Committee on Social Thought at the University of Chicago, advised readers of his *Closing of the American Mind* of the kind of students included in his "sample" (his quote marks):

It consists of thousands of students of comparatively high intelligence, materially and spiritually free to do pretty much what they want with the few years of college they are privileged to have—in short, the kind of young persons who populate the twenty or thirty best universities.

There are other kinds of students whom circumstances of one sort or another prevent from having the freedom required to pursue a liberal education. They have their own needs and may very well have different characters from those I describe here.

Lest there be any mistake about those he considers proper students of the liberal arts, Bloom quotes himself from an unidentified source in 1965:

I am referring to . . . those to whom a liberal education is primarily directed and who are the objects of a training which presupposes the best possible material. These young people have never experienced the anxieties about simple physical well-being that their parents experienced during the depression. They have been raised in comfort and with the expectation of ever increasing comfort.

To Professor Bloom, "these students are a kind of democratic version of an aristocracy." And these are the only students he deems fit for a liberal education.[1]

---

[1] *The Closing of the American Mind* (New York: Simon & Schuster, 1987), pp. 22, 49. Professor Bloom and I both came under the influence of the University of Chicago during the Hutchins era when students in The College were required to take fourteen courses, each of a year's duration. The curriculum, based largely on the Great Books, allowed for only two elective courses, generally in the fourth year. Some of the students entered The College after two years of high school by taking a long and quite rigorous entrance examination, made longer and far more rigorous for those who applied for scholarships.

The Hutchins Plan, as it was known, was flawed, but it was in my opinion the best education available in America. Some years later, after he had left the university, I talked with Hutchins about it. He spoke matter-of-factly about his years at Chicago, wondering aloud, in the chill, ironic fashion he reserved for people he did not know well, especially former students, why anyone would be interested in his experiment.

I do not know how Hutchins would have responded to Bloom's book. I suspect that parts of it would have made him laugh, but that Bloom's antipathy to freedom and fairness would have disgusted him. Perhaps not. When I met Hutchins, he was already exhausted, a *Wunderkind* in late middle age. He had been both more forgiving and sharper in his youth.

Bloom does not mention Hutchins or the Hutchins Plan in his book, although he does talk about the university during the 1950s, which leads me to think that we may have read Plato for the first time in the same surroundings, two bright young Jews, confounded and excited by the same lectures, the same examinations.

My interest in Professor Bloom's personal life does not go beyond this coincidence. To avoid the temptation to argue *ad hominem,* I have refrained from learning any more about him, other than the facts that he never married and taught at Cornell as well as Chicago. Our divergence on the value of the humanities and the importance of freedom may have personal or intellectual sources or both. For my part, the experience of The College of the University of Chicago was difficult and formative. I still have the newspaper clipping headlined, "Boy, 13, Wins Scholarship to U. of Chicago." The humanities helped to raise me; Plato also had his chance at parenting.

As he goes on, however, it becomes more and more difficult to associate Bloom's ideas with an education in the humanities. He cites Plato's *Republic* as the great work on education, taking comfort in Plato's antidemocratic sorting, which underlies Bloom's own ideas about society and the university. He begins with a *fundamentalist* reading of the Allegory of the Cave, writing of Plato's intent: "Nature should be the standard by which we judge our own lives and the lives of peoples. That is why philosophy, not anthropology or history, is the most important human science."[2]

Bloom has put his foot down: Man is not the measure of all things! With a couple of sentences, he dismisses Protagoras and the Sophists.[3] They will never merit mention in his book on education. Unlike Plato or Aristophanes, Bloom doesn't even bother to have some fun with his opponents. He goes glumly about his business of saving democracy from itself, with elitism for his sword and tradition his shield.

For Bloom, the fundamentalist, the idea of man as the measure of all things leads to relativism, and nothing else. He will take nothing from it in the way of praise for the works of man, including politics and the humanities, for Plato has said no to Protagoras. When the Sophist says that the discussion of poetry is the most important part of a man's education, the fundamentalist cannot even hear him, for Plato has banned the poets from his ideal republic. The idea of Protagoras as a teacher of the humanities, using critique as an avenue to the consideration of ethical questions, including politics, must be rejected by the fundamentalist, because Plato has labeled the poets subversive.[4]

All of this may have something to do with the idea of radical humanism as an answer to long-term poverty: a rebellion against the politics of Plato's *Republic*, the sense of one's own insignificance beside the Great Books, nostalgia, etc. I would like to think not. Leo Strauss led Professor Bloom to the right, the world led me to the left; it is as clear as that.

[2] Ibid., p. 38. My choice of the word "fundamentalist" is used here with only a little irony. Bloom claims in the preface to his version of *The Republic* to have done a perfectly literal translation. He devotes the rest of the preface to an attempt to bury the lively, readable Cornford translation under pages of scorn and abuse.

[3] A distinction should be drawn between sophistry and the Sophists. Plato, who was a rival of the Sophists, used them as foils in several of his dialogues, and he did it so effectively that we now understand "sophistry" to mean a false or misleading argument, deceit.

His caricature of sophistic argument comes close to what we now understand as subtlely deceptive selling or advertising; that is, it appears to be true, but isn't. Protagoras was reputed to have been able to argue either side of a question (probably in the practice of *eristic,* a form of debate), like a modern salesman, who can champion one product or its competitor, or a political consultant, who can work for George Bush in one election and Bill Clinton the next.

[4] Bloom's insistence upon students who were born to the comforts of wealth may have some relation to Plato's arguments against poets. Bloom, like Plato, is interested in happiness and not in

Protagoras confirms the assertion that he intends to teach the art of politics and to make men good citizens—an intention one would expect the right, with all their professed patriotism, to cherish, but it is not so. Protagoras is a subversive among the good citizens of Plato's idea of a republic, a democrat; he was chosen by Pericles to help write the constitution for a state based on the idea of participation by autonomous persons. The connection between this first critic and professor of the humanities and the codification of democracy makes clear that the Greeks understood the relation of critical thinking inspired by the humanities and the ongoing dialogue of which political power is made.

On the other hand, Plato, the arch conservative, and Bloom, his fundamentalist follower, have opted for the state as "the man writ large," an immutable organization prescribed by nature, and ruled by a philosopher-king. Poetry will confuse this perfect state, corrupt it. The study of the humanities makes poor men disputatious, unruly, a sickness in the state. The nightmare on the right is today, as it has always been, the humanity of the poor. They "have their own needs," according to Bloom and the fundamentalists, which are not the same as the needs of those who "have been raised in comfort."

The conservatives permit the humanities only under special terms, on the recommendation of Plato. Certain things must not be permitted, especially for the poor who do not know better (by virtue of their poverty perhaps?) than to think they can also live the public life, outside the domination of violent necessity.

Allan Bloom has identified a view of literature, philosophy, history, and

---

catastrophes or suffering. His view of the rock 'n' roll sixties is Plato's view in Book IX of *The Republic* of the man who is commanded by the lowest part of the psyche.

Stripped of its references to the world of philosophers after Plato, Bloom's book is a repetition of Plato's exposition of the "long-standing quarrel between poetry and philosophy," and might be summed up by these lines, from Book X, ". . . when you encounter admirers of Homer who say that this poet is the tutor of Greece, that to study him is to refine human conduct and culture, and that we should order our entire lives in accordance with his precepts, you must welcome them and love them as people who are doing the best they can. You can certainly agree that Homer is the greatest of poets and first among tragedians. But you must hold firm to the position that our city will admit no poetry except hymns to the gods and fair words about good men. Once entry is permitted to the honey-tongued Muse, whether in lyric or epic form, pleasure and pain will become kings of the city, law will be displaced, and so will that governing reason which time and opinion have approved"—trans. Richard W. Sterling and William C. Scott (New York: W. W. Norton, 1985). Francis Cornford ends the paragraph in a more straightforward political fashion: ". . . pleasure and pain will usurp the sovereignty of law and of the principles always recognized by common consent as the best."

Thomas Gould has devoted an interesting and enlightening book to *The Ancient Quarrel Between Poetry and Philosophy* (Princeton, N.J.: Princeton University Press, 1990).

art which is to him the canon. Like Plato in Book III of *The Republic,* he will permit the citizens to read only those works he deems good for them. Furthermore, the canon is not just the work, but the official, acceptable interpretation of the work. Therein lies the greatest distinction between the liberals and the fundamentalists: The humanities, as Protagoras taught, live; the dialogue never ends, the works never die. Like Socrates, who objected to the death of dialogue caused by writing, Protagoras chooses the life-giving character of the changing world. His humanities are the preparation for politics.

It is not merely the reaction to slavery, but the struggle against fate that gives rise to the idea of freedom.[5] The essence of tragedy comes of man's will to be free, independent of his fate, whether it is determined by gods or government. That is the great lesson of the humanities and the reason why Plato found the humanities intolerable in his state.

Following Plato, the right has laid claim to education, while opposing the very idea of the humanities. In his detestation of Cornford's sense of the living humanities, Bloom sets down the canon of the right: No word will be changed, no debate permitted. For him, no one could have been more in error than Socrates: Everything should be written, cast in stone; the humanities must die. But the world has not yet come to an end; the problem for the rich remains how to keep the world from changing, while the poor must find a way to reverse the damage. That is the argument between Protagoras and Plato, between the humanities and the sepulchral business the conservatives would use as a replacement, between inclusion and exclusion, power and force, democracy and our last breath.

2

The living humanities still have the same possibilities that produced the marvel of politics in Athens, only now in a radical way as an instrument of justice for the poor. Unfortunately, we have been so conditioned to understand the humanities as the province of the rich that the idea of teaching the humanities to the poor seems preposterous, a prisoner's fantasy, a joke told by Aristophanes.

The next chapter describes a small experiment in pedagogy, but there was an experiment with a far larger sample in the black communities of the

---

[5] Compare this idea of George Steiner and others to Orlando Patterson's views in Appendix B.

American South. The political life and the rise from poverty of Americans descended from slaves was engendered by the study of the humanities. Even before manumission, the study of the humanities went on in the slave quarters. There was one text, but there were many different courses, ontology, ethics, literature, rhetoric, and epistemology among them. The text, of course, was the King James Version of the Bible.[6]

Despite the horrors of life after Africa, including a broken culture and generations of chattel slavery, the blacks developed communities and practiced politics. As Dr. Goldie Wells and others remembered, the black churches revered reading, loved the language and the cadences of their text, put their text to music and sang it (imagine the consternation of Plato!), and discussed every chapter, every verse in church meetings and at home. Black preachers delivered sermons that were more often than not exercises in exegesis. With nothing more than the King James Bible and the powers of the human mind, the descendants of slaves reinvented themselves through the humanities, preparing themselves for the political life.

A political world populated by people of African descent, educated to autonomy through the humanities, grew up under the low ceiling of white hegemony. Not all blacks found a home in the humanities and not all of those who did became educated to politics. The surround of force in which blacks were forced to live made the leisure to learn the humanities all but impossible, yet the study went on.

As I said earlier, Dr. Martin Luther King, Jr., recognized this connection of church and politics and used it to focus his movement, but the church he brought to politics was the church of the humanities, the education for politics. The movement headed by Dr. King did not mobilize people without politicizing them; he took people prepared by the humanities and gave them focus for their politics. The sense of autonomy or the possibility of autonomy, of choosing to begin, was already there: the evidence is in the art produced by people of African ancestry and in the profusion of different denominations in the black religious world. These students of the humanities were not of one mind; there was no true canon but dialogue; they were alive, and human.

The civil rights movement was not the idea of whites; the blacks already

---

[6] It is important here to draw a distinction between superstition and religion. Millennialists and premillennialists, all those who know with certainty what is to come, practice superstition. Superstition cannot be questioned; shamans, *santeros*, faith healers, snake handlers, swamis, and religious revivalists do not debate cures or causes with their patients. Superstition belongs to the explained world of the Neolithic mind. It is literal, fixed; if the circle is broken and the world changes, everything falls apart. But in the collapse of superstition, politics and freedom become possible.

lived in the public sphere in their own communities. The movement came out of generations of the study of the humanities in the only form available to blacks—the King James Bible. No one gave the blacks their civil rights. They took them. The humanities prepared them for politics, which cannot be separated from autonomy. The great division now in the black community, as in the rest of America, is between those who live the reflective, political life and those who cannot escape the surround of force.

3

Blacks differed from most Americans in that slavery barred them from the immigrant experience, which has been the primary education for politics over the last two hundred years. Immigrants, who came largely for economic reasons, did not understand freedom in contrast to slavery but as the alternative to fate, which had been the condition of their lives. They did not study the humanities, but in the overcoming of their fate or at least in the expectation of it, they became the material of the humanities; they undertook to live the political life in many instances without even knowing what it was. They experienced democracy without experiencing its underpinning in the humanities, which is what Tocqueville saw when he visited America in the nineteenth century. Market democracy, that is, democracy in its unreflective form, grew out of this.

The immigrants, who learned politics as an enduring struggle against fate, saw the alternative to politics not as tyranny or silence but as the lack of things. The public life of the West Side of Chicago during the Depression was based on felt hunger and unrecognized autonomy. Nevertheless, the immigrants formed a polis and produced a life of inclusion rather than force. They had the comfort of power, which enabled them to survive the irony of coming to America to escape hunger and finding it again in the streets of Chicago.

Immigration still teaches politics, when immigrants can expect inclusion in the circle of power, if not immediately, then in the next generation. But the exclusion of immigrants from the possibility of power leaves them permanently in the surround of force, with no alternatives. These immigrants without politics fall into the category of the poor; all the rest have committed themselves to the struggle against fate. The action of the humanities takes place within them, as it always has.

This is not to suggest some irremediable difference in the character of blacks and whites, but to describe at least one more common path to the political life. The end is always fragile, no matter how one comes to it. The political life has always been beset by enemies: those that Plato and Aristotle imagined, and more. Sophrosyne has a brief season, and then something less human, sameness or rage, attempts to take its place.

4

Although the idea of the humanities as the original precursor to politics rarely meets with objection, very little has been written specifically about the process, mainly because, as M. I. Finley said, the Greeks had no theory of politics.[7] Bernard Knox assures us that it happened, but he does not describe the process. Cynthia Farrar, who wrote about "Athenian political theory," places the origin of politics in reflection, but for her, tragic drama provided a concrete example of the theory and "promoted exploration of the questions raised by . . . democratic politics. . . ."[8]

Farrar sees the sense of autonomy in Greece arising from the ability of men to separate themselves from the control of the gods, to take personal responsibility for their actions. Homer may have provided another impetus to political thinking, surely to reflection, in his portrayal of the battle for Troy. Never before had there been an "objective" telling of a story, until Homer gave his readers the chance to consider two sides of an argument. Before that, the point of view had always rested with the storyteller.

After Homer, the listener or reader had to consider more than one possibility, which may be as good a definition as any of the practice of reflection. The audience for *Antigone* could debate forever the political implications of the play. The only certainty one could take away from it was that Creon and Antigone could not do politics; each held on to a single idea, preferring death or destruction to mediation. With the prize-winning play of Sophocles to inspire them, ordinary people reflected on the polarities of social life: order and liberty. They invented politics, they took control of themselves.

This self-control, or *sophrosyne*, was also a synonym for politics. Thucydides used the word to mean a "moderate form of government." Violent behavior, like that of the suitors in Aeschylus' *The Suppliants*, transgressed the idea of sophrosyne.

---

[7] He suggests, in *Democracy Ancient and Modern,* that Protagoras may have had such a theory, which led Plato to spend so much time and effort mocking him. But it is only speculation; Finley concedes that no concrete evidence has survived (p. 28).

[8] Farrar, *The Origins of Democratic Thinking,* p. 30.

There may have been many instances when the humanities, reflection, and politics united in a single concept, but none contains them all so well as sophrosyne, which denoted the temper of the world of public persons. In the idea of sophrosyne, the history of politics can be traced from its inception in the distancing of men from fate to the implementation of autonomy. Sophrosyne contains the road traversed by the humanities, the calm, contemplative path through the undeniable oppositions of human life; it is a defense against force, a definition of power, humanness.

5

The case for the humanities as a radical antidote to long-term poverty rests finally on the question of who is born human and to what extent a person is capable of enjoying his or her humanity. Pericles faced the question as it applied to the citizens of Athens, and he responded that all citizens were capable of noble deeds, "nor does poverty bar the way; if a man is able to serve the state, he is not hindered by the obscurity of his condition."

Elitism in the United States, in this manifestation the withholding of excellent education from the poor, as suggested by Allan Bloom, has its analogue in the Greek view of slaves. Aristotle thought they were slaves by nature; the education of them for politics was therefore out of consideration. Bloom, Charles Murray, et al. take this view toward the poor, particularly blacks and Latinos.

There is, however, no reason to think the multigenerational poor any less capable than the rich of the study of the humanities. The a priori assertions of the elitists have been accepted without ever being put to the test. On their advice the poor have been denied access to the humanities, and therefore to one path to politics. The evidence, however, points to the unfairness of the elitist position. Even within the surround of force that existed under chattel slavery and the systematic oppression that followed on it, American blacks found a way to study the humanities, develop a political life, and burst out of their bonds in a noble movement for civil rights. Through the humanities, they had become more human than their oppressors.

Before he was murdered, Dr. King sought to extend this state of enhanced humanness to the poor of all races. Though we cannot know whether his national pulpit could have replaced generations of exegesis and art, it is undeniable that the humanities, presented in the full flower of freedom, can be as effective for the poor as for the rich. Neither wealth nor poverty bar the way to enjoying a more human life; the economic situation of the student is irrelevant. Sentience and intelligence are all that matter.

The rightists are not fools in the defense of their own interests, however; they take Plato's warning with utmost seriousness. And from their point of view rightly so, for the study of the humanities is a radical act on the part of the poor, almost certain to educate them to the political life and catapult them into the public world, where power resides.

Reflection and the publicking of life benefit the poor more than the rich, because the winners in the game and even those in the middle have other means to power: They are included at birth, the favored of the game, without the tutelage of force to impede them.

The radicalism of the humanities in America is the denial of this essential distinction between rich and poor: the birthright of power. Once this happens, freedom is possible in the minds of the poor, and Plato's republic falls before the onslaught of poets, the parents of politics.

Those who appreciate ancient history understand the radical character of the humanities, for they know that politics did not begin in a perfect world, but in a society even more flawed than ours—one that embraced slavery, denied the rights of women, accepted a form of homosexuality that verged on pedophilia, and endured the intrigues and corruption of its leaders. The genius of that society originated in man's recreation of himself through the recognition of his humanness in the expression of it by art, literature, rhetoric, philosophy, and the unique notion of freedom. At that moment, the isolation of the private life ended, and politics began.

Why not let it happen again now? Why should the poor be excluded, made to live out their lives in a surround of force? Robert Maynard Hutchins and Viniece Walker have the same prescription for America: radical humanism. As Hutchins said, "The best education for the best is the best education for all."

XVIII.

The Clemente Experiment

After the final no there comes a yes
And on that yes the future world depends.
No was the night. Yes is this present sun.

. . .

It can never be satisfied, the mind, never.
— W A L L A C E   S T E V E N S ,
"The Well Dressed Man with a Beard"

1

BY SPRING OF 1995 the comforts of bricolage had come to an end; I could no longer make an homage to the happenstance world, and rest. A theory had appeared, and the mere suggestion of a theory implies a will to change the world. At the same time a theory demands some form of proof or else it will have no weight, and float away on the next hypothetical breeze. Among the inescapable questions posed by the theory were these:

A. Can a method be found and institutionalized to help poor people become political?

B. Will the humanities lead poor people to reflection, which is a necessary stage on the way to political life?

C. If the first two questions can be answered with a yes, does it strongly suggest that the long-term poor are human, equal, and capable, and imply that there is neither an underclass nor a culture of poverty?

D. Since there are other ways for poor people to become political, is teaching the humanities a relatively effective and efficient way to bring the poor to the public world? Or would teaching the humanities merely repeat something learned long ago in a psychological experiment: If we pay attention to people, they will behave differently?

M Y MENTORS—Petrarch, Hutchins, and Viniece Walker—could not help. Two were dead and the third was in prison. The choice was to find some way to test the theory or simply to assert it, as Allan Bloom had done with the idea that the poor were unfit for a liberal education.

There was a third option. Claim that the journey from slavery to the civil rights movement proves the case, and go on from there. The proof is a good one, but anything connected to race in America invites argument.

A study of students who came from poverty, entered prestigious universities, and succeeded in the world would leave two unanswered questions: Did they study the humanities? And were they exceptions to the rule? To the first, few universities offer an education in the humanities and few students choose such an education when it is available.[1] To the second, such students were by definition exceptional, and if the humanities affected only exceptional people, the elitist argument would be proved.

A search of existing data for the effect of the humanities on the poor was not possible, because the conservative argument against teaching the humanities to the poor had been put into practice with very close to complete effectiveness in the United States. The data would have to be generated from something new. Three things were required: students, faculty, and facilities. Quantitative measures would have to be developed, but with only a small sample, anecdotal information would also be useful.

Finally, the ethics of the experiment had to be considered. Experiments involving human beings usually find a moral stance in the notion of the greatest good for the greatest number: a hundred people get the pill that can save their lives and a hundred get a placebo. The test works perfectly: a hundred live and a hundred die. For an experiment in the humanities no such choice was necessary: the control group was vast, and growing. This

---

[1] The Great Books curriculum at St. John's is perhaps the only exception, although a core curriculum has become more important at many universities during this decade.

experiment could follow a different rule: First, do no harm. Using that rule, the experiment would not have a "sink or swim" character; it could aim to keep as many afloat as possible.

When the idea for an experimental course became clear in my mind, I discussed it with Dr. Jaime Inclán. If anyone was prepared by experience and character to consider such an idea, it was Dr. Inclán. He had no fear of new ideas about institutions; he had founded the Roberto Clemente Family Guidance Center to provide counseling to poor people, mainly Latinos, in their own language in their own community. His writings on psychotherapy were interesting, often daring. And behind the apple cheeks and the twinkling eyes, the sympathetic therapist's face, was a sharp, highly trained intellect. I had seen him at work among his peers; he did not hesitate to point out errors.

It was with some trepidation that I revealed the idea to him. We had talked often about questions of force and power, reflection versus reaction, the political life, but we had only touched on the idea of the humanities as a precursor to politics, mainly as it had affected the abused and depressed Silveria and her daughters (see Chapter XVII). He listened attentively, without comment, while I set out the theory of the humanities as an education for politics and my intention to test the thesis through an experimental course.

I said that I wanted to pattern much of the course around The College of the University of Chicago during the Hutchins era: Two sessions a week, each lasting ninety minutes; the Socratic method, with students seated around a boat-shaped table; one comprehensive exam at the end of the year; and a sense of freedom in a formal setting.

Only then did he respond. The healer's smile broke across his face: "I'll give you the walls!"

"We'll call it the Clemente Course in the Humanities."

"That's good," he said. "The people in the community will be comfortable with the name."

The walls would be the conference room of the Center. In place of the finely made boat-shaped table of a University of Chicago classroom we would have three metal tables and one wooden table placed end to end and surrounded by two different kinds of metal and fabric armchairs. In the back corner of the room, we would set out fresh coffee and cookies on a card table. The front wall was covered by a floor-to-ceiling blackboard, and from time to time we were to make use of every inch of it.

2

The Clemente Course lacked only students and teachers. With no funds and a budget that grew every time a new idea for the course crossed my mind, I would have to ask the faculty to donate their time and effort. Moreover, when Hutchins said, "The best education for the best is the best education for all," he meant it. He insisted that full professors teach discussion sections in The College. The Clemente Course had to follow the same pattern. It required a faculty with the knowledge and prestige students might encounter in their first year at Harvard, Yale, Princeton, or Chicago. Ideally, they would be people of some accomplishment.

I turned first to the novelist Charles Simmons. We had been friends for many years, and I knew him to be a man of goodwill and a true literary man. He had been assistant editor of the *New York Times Book Review,* taught at Columbia University, and written criticism, editorials, and stories, but I admired him most for his novels, especially *Wrinkles*, which I had turned to many times for the lucidity of the prose and the author's masterful engagement of life and mind.

"I'll teach poetry," he said. And then, without hesitation, not even a pause to indicate a new paragraph, "I'll begin with simple poems, Housman, and end with Latin poetry. We won't have a textbook; I'll teach exactly as I was taught by Raymond Weaver at Columbia. At the beginning of the class I'll give them a copy of a poem. We'll read it and discuss it."

Grace Glueck, whose art news and criticism has long been one of the cultural lights of the *New York Times* and the *New York Observer,* said, "Oh, my dear, I don't know if I'm up to it. I'll have to prepare. I'll get the slides from the Met—they have a wonderful collection, and you can borrow them, you know.

"And we'll have to make field trips to the museums. When I was a little girl. . . ." All this in Grace's Seven Sisters vowels and neatly formed consonants, stylish, charming, but never flighty. She was one of the women who had fought the management of the *New York Times* over the hiring and promotion of women reporters and editors, and won. The fashionable woman was also a woman of politics.

"Sir, I should be delighted," said Timothy Koranda in his orotund, slightly ironic manner. "Before devising a curriculum, however, we shall have to ascertain whether any of them have had logic before." It had been twenty years since Tim had published his journal articles on mathematical logic. After MIT, where he had done his graduate work in logic at the end of a joint program with Cornell, Tim had paused to become fluent in Chinese and earn an MBA before building a career as a speechwriter. He had traveled, as he might have put it, from logic to rhetoric, but logic had been his first love, and I think he was genuinely pleased at the thought of coming back to it.

Thomas Wallace, a historian by training and an editor by profession, taught the first few classes in American history, but then withdrew for personal reasons.[2] For my part, I began putting together a syllabus to teach moral philosophy. Some help in that endeavor would come later, from an unexpected source.

Since I was a naif in this endeavor, it did not immediately occur to me that recruiting students would present a problem. I did not even know how many students I needed. All I had were the criteria for selection:

Age: 18–35;

Household Income: Less than 150 percent of the federal poverty level (although this was to change slightly);

Educational level: Ability to read a tabloid newspaper;

Educational goals: An expression of intent to complete the course.

Dr. Inclán and I talked about where to find such students and how many we would need to form a class. He put together a group of people who worked with the poor and were interested in the possibilities of an experimental course in the humanities. A week later, the group met in the conference room at the Roberto Clemente Center. Of a dozen people he invited to the meeting, four showed up:

Lynette Lauretig, director of Educational Services at The Door, a large and extremely successful program that provided health care, counseling, instruction in English, GED preparation, painting and sculpture classes, even dinner and carfare to young people from around the city;

Saul Nieves, the community coordinator for U.S. Representative Nydia Velásquez, who also represented his wife, Susan Matloff, director of Youth Services at the Forest Hills Community House;

Rafael Pizarro, contract coordinator for Hospital Workers Local 1199; and Angel Roman, of the Grand Street Settlement House.

After I made a brief presentation, there was a silence that extended into two or three minutes as people drank coffee and considered the idea. I felt no enthusiasm in the room, no willingness. The silence went on. The presentation had been too brief, the idea of teaching the humanities at that level to people who lived in poverty was apparently too radical.

Before the course died in the silence, Rafael Pizarro spoke. "I know what the humanities can mean to a person," he began, leaning forward in his chair, his shoulders rolled forward, too, and his hands in motion, Nuyorican, a man

---

[2] It is not very courageous to attempt to assemble a faculty from one's friends, but I am lucky to have friends of such character and accomplishment.

sparring with the world. He told the story of the brothers Pizarro. They had been close, two boys growing up together in the barrios of New York. One, Rafael, had developed an interest in the humanities early in life. He loved opera, read Dante and Sophocles. His brother loved the "fast life" of the streets. One night, Rafael remembers, his brother telephoned to tell their mother that he had killed a man. "It was only a Cuban," the brother said.

Rafael's brother went to prison. Rafael went to Sarah Lawrence College. He concluded his story by saying that the only difference between him and his brother had been the humanities, and that was why the course made sense to him.

Pizarro's story transformed the meeting: The question of whether to hold such a course was behind us. The conversation turned immediately to the details. The hours changed, as did the schedule. Nieves was adamant about the need to offer college credit. Pizarro said that the humanities were reward enough, but he, too, believed that an offer of college credit would help to retain students.

The course had to provide bus and subway tokens, because fares ranged between $3 and $6 per class per student, and the students could not afford $60 or even $30 a month for transportation.[3] We had to offer dinner or a snack, because the classes were to be held from 6:00 to 7:30 P.M. And we needed a television camera and a camera operator to experiment with providing a mix of personal teaching and videotape to Viniece Walker and the other women who attended the course at Bedford Hills.

3

The first recruiting session came only a few days later. With the help of Nancy Mamis-King, executive director of the Bronx Neighborhood Youth and Family Services program, some prospective students were identified in the South Bronx. Through one of the programs she supervised, about twen-

---

[3] Some students needed both bus and subway tokens, because transfers from subway to ground transportation are generally not available in New York City and many people live too far from a subway station to walk, especially at night in winter. Three students did not live on a bus line, and traveled to the subway by jitney at a cost of $3 each way, a total cost of $9 for every class they attended.

During the first few classes, I stopped at a subway station and bought packets of tokens, doling them out very carefully to the students. After a while, I asked the students to sign up for as many tokens as they needed, and just take them out of the pile my wife Sylvia or I put on the table at the end of each class.

ty clients and their supervisors were assembled in a circle of chairs in a conference room. Everyone in the room was black or Latino, with the exception of one social worker and me.

After I explained the idea of the course, the white social worker was the first to ask a question: "Are you going to teach African history?"

"No. We'll be teaching a section on American history, based on documents, as I said. We want to teach the ideas of history so that . . ."

"You have to teach African history."

"This is America, so we'll teach American history. If we were in Africa, I would teach African history, and if we were in China, I would teach Chinese history."

"You're indoctrinating people in Western culture."

I tried to get beyond her. "We'll study African art," I said, "as it affects art in America. We'll study American history and literature; you can't do that without studying African-American culture, because culturally all Americans are black as well as white, Native American, Asian, and so on."

It was no use. The social worker convinced her clients that no education was better than an education in the humanities; not one of them applied for admission to the course.

Following my defeat by the white multiculturalist, I walked across Tremont Avenue to the Young Mothers Program, where I asked four of the women if they were interested in a course in the humanities. Two declined and two asked for application forms.

I was pleased to have two prospective students, but I did not know what to expect of them. Carmen Quiñones had not yet overcome her ten years in prison and there was still a question about her ability to control her addiction. Carmen had been on the street, slept in parks and shelters, and the state had taken her children from her. She said that her hatred of men had made her gay. I had never met such a tough-talking woman. On winter evenings she had walked to the bus with me, dressed in her black leather biker's jacket, fearless in the dark in the South Bronx. Yet she had the sweetest face, round and wide-eyed, a grown-up version of the face painted on dolls. Either she was mad—a disjunction of mind and body—or the little girl was still trying to figure out how to stay alive. I liked Carmen, but she would be a very difficult test for my thesis.

"If you'll fill out the application form," I told her, "I think you can do this work."

"Okay, Earl," she said, "I'll give it a try."

LYNETTE LAURETIG ARRANGED A MEETING with some of her staff at The Door. Celeste Gnutti, Candace Reyes D'Andrea, Mark

Schwartz, and I disagreed about the course and its contents. They thought it should be taught at a much lower level. We argued for nearly two hours. Although I could not change their views, they agreed to assemble a group of Door members who might be interested in the humanities.

A few days later, in the early evening, about twenty prospective students were scheduled to meet in a classroom at The Door. Most of them came late. Those who arrived first slumped in their chairs, staring at the floor or greeting me with sullen glances. A few ate candy or what appeared to be the remnants of a meal. The students were mostly black and Latino, one was Asian, a few were white, although all but one of the whites were immigrants who had severe problems with English. When I introduced myself, several of the students would not shake my hand, two or three refused even to look at me, one girl giggled, and the last person to volunteer his name, a young man dressed in a Tommy Hilfiger sweatshirt and wearing a cap turned sideways, drawled, "Henry Jones, but they call me Sleepy, because I got these sleepy eyes."

"In our class, we'll call you Mister Jones."

He smiled, and slid down in his chair so that his back was parallel to the floor. One eyelid remained closed to a slit, giving him the appearance of a drug addict or a drunk.

Before I finished attempting to shake hands with the prospective students, a waiflike Asian girl with her mouth half full of cake said, "Can we get on with it? I'm bored."

I could not imagine a better group. I liked them immediately.

Having failed in the South Bronx, I resolved to approach these prospective students differently. "You've been cheated," I said. "Rich people learn the humanities; you didn't. The humanities are a foundation for getting along in the world, for thinking, for learning to reflect on the world instead of just reacting to whatever force is turned against you. I think the humanities are one of the ways to become political, and I don't mean political in the sense of voting in an election, but political in the broad sense. The way Pericles, a man who lived in ancient Athens, used the word 'politics' to mean activity with other people at every level, from the family to the neighborhood to the broader community to the city/state in which he lived.

"Rich people know politics in that sense. They know how to negotiate instead of using force. They know how to use politics to get along, to get power. It doesn't mean rich people are good and poor people are bad. It simply means that rich people know a more effective method for living in this society.

"Do all rich people or people who are in the middle know the humanities? Not a chance. But some do. And it helps. It helps to live better and enjoy life more. Will the humanities make you rich? Yes, absolutely. But not in terms of money. In terms of life.

"Rich people learn the humanities in private schools and expensive universities. And that's one of the ways in which they learn the political life. At every level. I think that is the real difference between the Haves and Have-nots in this country. If you want real power, legitimate power, the kind that comes from the people and belongs to the people, you must understand politics; the humanities will help.

"Here's how it works. We'll pay your subway fare; take care of your children, if you have them; give you a snack or a sandwich; provide your books and any other materials you need. But we'll make you think harder, use your mind more fully than you ever have before. You'll have to read and think about the same kinds of ideas you would encounter in a first-year course at Harvard or Yale or Oxford.

"You'll have to come to class in the snow and the rain and the cold and the dark. No one will coddle you, no one will slow down for you. There will be tests to take, papers to write. And I can't promise you anything but a certificate of completion at the end of the course. I'll be talking to colleges about giving credit for the course, but I can't promise anything. If you come to the Clemente Course, you must do it because you want to study the humanities, because you want a certain kind of life, a richness of mind and spirit. That's all I offer you: philosophy, poetry, art history, logic, rhetoric, and American history.

"Your teachers will all be people of accomplishment in their own fields," I added, and spoke a little about each of them. "That's the course. October through May, with a two-week break at Christmas. Why are we doing it? This is a demonstration project. It is generally accepted in America that the liberal arts and the humanities in particular belong to the elite. I think you're the elite."

The young Asian woman said, "What are you getting out of this?"

"This is a demonstration project. I'm writing a book. This will be proof, I hope, of my idea about the humanities. Whether it succeeds or fails will be up to the teachers and you."

It worked. All but one of the prospective students applied for admission to the course.

I repeated the new presentation at the Grand Street Settlement House and at other places around the city. There were about fifty candidates for the thirty positions in the course. Personal interviews began in late September.

Meanwhile, almost all of my attempts to raise money had failed. Only Starling Lawrence, the AKC Foundation, Sophie MacArthur, and W. W.

Norton supported the experiment. We were far short of our budgeted expenses, but my wife Sylvia and I agreed that the cost was still very low, and we decided to go ahead.[4]

4

Of the fifty prospective students who showed up at the Clemente Center for personal interviews, a few were too rich (a postal supervisor's son; a fellow who claimed his father owned a factory in Nigeria that employed sixty people), and more than a few could not read. Two home-care workers from Local 1199 could not arrange their hours to enable them to take the course. Some of the applicants were too young: a thirteen-year-old, and two who had just turned sixteen.

Mrs. Medina, the woman with five children who had answered the door at the single-room occupancy hotel with a butcher knife in her hand, was the oldest person accepted into the course. Carmen Quiñones was the next eldest. Both were in their early thirties.

The interviews went on for days.

Abel Lomas shared an apartment and worked part-time wrapping packages at Macy's. His father had abandoned the family when Abel was born. His mother was murdered by his stepfather when Abel was thirteen years old. With no one to turn to and no place to stay, he lived on the streets, first in Florida, then back up to New York City. He used the tiny stipend from his mother's Social Security to keep himself alive.

All I knew about Abel came from a conversation held on the way uptown from the recruiting session at The Door. As I drove up Sixth Avenue from Canal Street, Abel talked about ethics. He had a street tough's delivery, spitting out his ideas in crudely formed sentences of four, five, eight words, strings of blunt declarations, with never a dependent clause to qualify his thoughts. He did not clear his throat with badinage, as timidity teaches us to do, nor did he waste his breath in tact. If it is true that the style is the man, I had never encountered a man like Abel.

"What do you think about drugs?" he asked, the blunt, strangely breathless delivery further coarsened by his Dominican accent. "My cousin is a dealer."

"I've seen a lot of people hurt by drugs."

"Your family has nothing to eat. You sell drugs. What's worse? Let your family starve. Or sell drugs?"

"Starvation and drug addiction are both bad, aren't they?"

"Yes," he said, not yeah or uh-huh, but a precise, almost formal "Yes."

---

[4] We cut the budget where we could. One of the cuts was a part-time administrator/bookkeeper, so we have only a vague idea of what it cost to hold the course.

"So it's a question of the worse of two evils? How shall we decide?"

The question came up near 34th Street, where Sixth Avenue remains a hellish place well into the night. Horns honked, people flooded into the street against the advice of the stoplight. Buses and trucks and taxicabs threatened their way from one lane to the next as the overcrowded avenue split into two even more overcrowded streets. When we were through Herald Square and making our way north again, I said, "There are a couple of ways to look at it. One comes from Immanuel Kant, who said that you should not do anything unless you want it to become a maxim for the general will; that is, unless you think it's what everybody should do. So Kant wouldn't agree to selling drugs or letting your family starve."

Again, he answered with a formal "Yes."

"There's another way to look at it, which is to ask, what is the greatest good for the greatest number? In this case, keeping your family from starvation, or keeping tens, perhaps hundreds of people from losing their lives to drugs. So which is the greatest good for the greatest number?"

"That's what I think," he said.

"What?"

"You shouldn't sell drugs. You can always get food to eat. Welfare. Something."

"You're a Kantian."

"Yes."

"You know who Kant is?"

"I think so."

We had arrived at 77th Street, where he got out to catch the subway before I turned east. I looked at him more carefully now as he opened the car door and the light came on. The almost military neatness of him struck me. He had the newly cropped hair of a cadet. His clothes were clean, without a wrinkle. He was an orphan, a street kid, an immaculate urchin. Within a few weeks he would be nineteen years old, the Social Security payments would end, and he would have to move into a shelter.

Some of those who came for interviews were too poor. I did not think that was possible when we began, and I would like not to believe it now, but it was true. There is a point at which the forces that surround the poor become insurmountable, when there is no time or energy left to be anything but poor. Lydia, who was twenty, marked by a strawberry patch the size of a hand on her face, lived in the back of the basement of a building in Brooklyn. She ate and slept there, in the same room, among sickly children and a hapless mother, living without daylight. And in the middle of the year they were evicted from that place, because they could not pay the rent, and they moved to even worse housing somewhere in the Bronx. She came to class only twice, both times with a small child who sat on her lap and ate cookies, but she telephoned now and then to speak of her woes, to ask if I could help her to find work, housing, help of any kind. But when I made suggestions, she could not act on them.

Near the end of the year, she appeared in the waiting room of the Clemente Center. She looked haggard, as if she had been ill. "I'm glad you came to class," I said.

"I can't stay."

"Do you need help? This is a family guidance center, you know."

"I lost some of the books and papers when we moved."

"I'll see if I can find another set for you."

"Can I have tokens? I don't have money to get home."

"We always give out tokens at the end of class."

"I can't stay," she said.

I gave her a handful of tokens.

She hefted the tokens in her palm, weighing them, counting the number by their weight. We looked at each other for a long time. I felt the winter of her loneliness.

"Do you live near any of the other students? Can they help you?"

"No," she said.

Over the days of interviewing, a class was slowly assembled. I could not then imagine who would last the year and who would not. One young woman submitted a neatly typed essay that said:

"I was homeless once, then I lived for some time in a shelter. Right now, I have got my own space granted by the Partnership for the Homeless.

My great-grandmother was very poor to the point that she could not afford to have running water into her place, nor electricity. She raised me partly. My grandmother was poor and could not make ends meet. My mother has been on public assistance with my brother.

Right now, I am living alone, with very limited means. Financially I am overwhelmed by debts. I can not afford all the food I need and all the supplies and books for the school. Even transportation can be an issue at some point. . . .

In the next-to-last paragraph she wrote: "A friend helped me work out this essay."

A brother and sister from Tashkent came to the little interviewing room. I had not planned to accept immigrants, for I thought immigration was a separate issue, but these were refugees; they had been driven out of their homes after the breakup of the Soviet Union. "We are Joosh peeple," the boy began. "When Musselmen. . . ." He and his sister had a tiny English vocabulary and an emerging sense of English syntax. When I asked questions, they spoke to each other in Russian, then one or the other tried to answer. As best I could understand, the Muslims had made life in Tashkent impossible for ethnic Russians and Jews. The brother and sister now lived with their parents in the farthest reaches of the borough of Queens, in some place far beyond the end of the subway line. Their parents were both ill, they had no money, and they had been refused admission by every college to which they had applied.

They gave their surnames as Iskhakov and Iskhakova, son and daughter, Russians, refugees, the new poor of New York City. I accepted them because I liked them and because I did not want the class to comprise only people of color; there would have been a misleading message in that. For the same reason I accepted a young Albanian who lived in a room without a telephone and survived by working part-time jobs making pizzas and washing dishes.

Laura,* the fourth white person who applied to the course, was a tall, slim girl with dyed blond hair and sickly pale skin. She wrote on her application, "I am nineteen years old. I'm originally from Dallas, Texas. I have spent the past five months in city shelters." She told me she had been abused by her father and stepmother and that she had run away from home to live with street people in Dallas. A girl she met there urged Laura to come up to New York, where they could live with the girl's mother.

It had not worked out. The girl's mother was schizophrenic, according to Laura, impossible to live with. Although she had no job and no money, Laura moved out. She went from shelter to shelter, finally ending up in a place in Harlem. The problem there was that when the police saw a young blond woman on the streets of Harlem at night, they assumed she was a "working girl," and arrested her.

"They took me to the station house and started slapping me around," Laura said, "so I hit them back. And they charged me with resisting arrest or something, and I have a fifty-dollar fine, and if I don't pay it, they're going to send me to Riker's Island. So if they don't send me to jail, I can come to the course."

"Will your shelter put up the money for the fine?"

"I don't think so," she said, her vowels growing broader, more southern. "I asked them, and they said no." Then, as an afterthought, "If I don't go to jail and come to the course, can I bring my friend?"

"If he applies and is accepted."

"Not he, my girlfriend."

"Same rules apply."

"You know how my stepmother and my father abused me? They went

---

* Not her real name.

into my room and took all my dolls and all my things off the wall, the pictures and everything, and all my pretty clothes . . . and burned them. That's when I left home."

I told her she would get a letter within ten days if she was accepted for the course. And I asked her to telephone me if she could not raise the money to pay the ticket. After she left, I went to Jaime Inclán's office to ask his opinion about Laura. After describing her and my doubts about the fine and the beating, I said, "I think she's going to make trouble. Or she's in trouble. Something's wrong. I don't know if I should accept her."

He said, "Earl, I think you are prejudiced against white people." We laughed. And of course I accepted her. She turned out to be smart, attentive, and gifted with a mordant sense of humor that all of the teachers and few of the students appreciated. For a long time I thought Jaime had been correct about Laura. Perhaps I was prejudiced against white people. I did not think so, but it was possible.

Hector Anderson, a tall, slim, supercooled fellow, with a pianist's slender fingers and a classic Brooklyn accent, said he had been to several high schools. "In my last semester I got a safety transfer," he said.

"What's that?" I asked.

"They gave me a safety transfer, because I got into a lot of fights."

"Did you win?"

He shook his head, "No, I lost, that's why they had to give me a transfer, for my safety." We had a great laugh together. He turned out to be one of the brightest students in the course. On the final exam he not only answered every question correctly, he wrote a charming parody of a Philip Larkin poem.

There were lies and confessions, crimes, pregnancies, and always loneliness. I argued with them about their possibilities, I sold them hope. They taught me to revise my definition of poverty. The federal guidelines were meaningless. People were poor who connected themselves to institutions that serve the poor: settlement houses, social welfare agencies, shelters, free clinics, gangs, minimum-wage jobs, drug programs, food pantries, soup kitchens. People are poor when they concede that they are poor, when there is no saving politics in their lives. That became the criterion for selection.

As I listened to them, I wondered what effect the course would have. They had no public life, no place; they lived within the surround of force, moving as fast as they could, without a moment to reflect. Why should they care about fourteenth century Italian painting or truth tables or the death of Socrates?

"I'm pregnant," one young woman said. "And I ain't getting no abortion. I don't believe in that's the right thing."

"Will your parents help you?"

"They are the lowest of the low, way down here, my parents. When I was sixteen, they sold me to a man to have a baby for him."

"What will you do?"

"I gotta move out. I'm sharing a space. I gotta get my own space."

She wept. And then as the pregnancy progressed, she learned to swagger, carrying a beeper and banging the heels of her heavy shoes on the classroom floor. She wore too much lipstick and she spoke of having to be "strapped" when she left the "L-E-S," the Lower East Side, where she lived. A few months into the year she could no longer tolerate the isolation. She disappeared, leaving word that she had gone "upstate."

5

Between the end of recruiting and the orientation session that would open the course, I made a visit to Bedford Hills to talk with Niecie Walker and to be certain everything was ready for the course to be held in the prison. Niecie and Sharon Smolick, who ran the Family Violence Program, and I met in a small office.

It was hot, and the drive up from the city had been unpleasant. I did not yet know Niecie very well. She did not trust me, and I did not know what to make of her. While we talked, she held a huge white pill in her hand. "For AIDS," she said.

"Are you sick?"

"My T-cell count is down. But that's neither here nor there. Tell me about the course, Earl. What are you going to teach?"

"Moral philosophy."

"And what does that include?"

She had turned the visit into an interrogation. I did not mind. At the end of the conversation I would be going out into "the free world"; if she wanted it to be an interrogation, I was not about to argue. I said, "We'll begin with Plato. The *Apology*. A little of the Crito. A few pages of the *Phaedo*, so they know what happened to Socrates. Then we'll read the *Nicomachean Ethics*. I want them to read Pericles' Funeral Oration to make the connection between ethics and politics, to lead them in the direction I hope the course will take them. Then we'll end with *Antigone*, but read as moral and political philosophy as well as drama."

"There's something missing," she said, leaning back in her chair, taking on an air of superiority.

The drive had been long, the day was hot, the air in the room was dead and damp. "Oh, yeah," I said, "and what's that?"

"The Allegory of the Cave. How can you teach philosophy to poor people without the Allegory of the Cave? The ghetto is the cave. Education is the light. Poor people can understand that."

6

A few days before the course was to begin, Leon Botstein, president of Bard College, an excellent liberal arts college about two hours north of New York City, offered to place the course under the academic aegis of Bard. After ascertaining that Bard would incur no costs, he said, "Good! We'll get the publicity, and you'll get the credit before God." A week later, a letter arrived from Dr. Robert Martin, associate dean of the college and dean of the Graduate Center. He promised that Bard would provide a certificate of accomplishment to those who completed the course, but reserved any decision on course credit until the faculty executive committee could evaluate the curriculum, the faculty, and the progress of the students.

A copy of his letter was included in the packet of materials handed out to the thirty-one students who came to the orientation meeting on October 12, 1995. There were no secrets; the students knew as much about the issue of college credit as I did.

At the beginning of the orientation, Rafael Pizarro told the class about the effect of the humanities on his life. Then each of the teachers spoke for a minute or two. Dr. Inclán administered the questionnaire that he and Ramon Maisonet had devised, using various standardized scales to measure, as best we could, the role of force and the amount of reflection in the lives of our students.[5]

When they had completed the questionnaires, I explained to them that the sections of the course would be given in rotating sequence, beginning with philosophy, then art, logic, poetry, and history, and starting the sequence again with philosophy. I said the purpose was to integrate the disciplines, but I did not tell them the other advantage of the rotation. Since poor people suffer more health and personal problems than the rest of the population, I expected their attendance to be spotty. With the five-course rotation and two sessions a week, a student could be out for as long as two and a half weeks and still miss only one class in each subject. The alterna-

---

[5] See Appendix C for Dr. Inclán's evaluation of the effect of the Clemente Course in the Humanities.

tive was to teach the sections one at a time, which meant that a two-week absence would almost certainly lead to an incomplete.

At the end of the orientation I gave them their first assignment: "In preparation for our next meeting, I would like you to read a brief selection from Plato's *Republic*: The Allegory of the Cave."

The first class started badly. The young fellow who had volunteered to videotape the sessions (with an eye to making a "brilliant" documentary) telephoned to say he was going to be late, because he was on his way down from Martha's Vineyard where he had been visiting dear friends whom he had not seen for the longest time. I fired him.

Following the orientation meeting, I tried to guess how many of the students would return for the first class. I hoped for twenty, expected fifteen, and feared ten. Sylvia had agreed to share the administrative tasks of the course, and she and I prepared coffee and cookies for twenty-five. We had a plastic container filled with tokens. Thanks to Starling Lawrence, we had thirty copies of Bernard Knox's *Norton Book of Classical Literature,* which contained all of the texts for the philosophy section except *The Republic* and the *Nicomachean Ethics.*

At six o'clock there were only ten students seated around the long table, but by six-fifteen the number had doubled, and a few minutes later two more straggled in out of the dusk. I had written a timeline on the blackboard, showing them the temporal progress of thinking from the role of myth in Neolithic societies to *Gilgamesh* and forward to the Bible, the Greeks, Confucius, the New Testament, the Koran, the *Epic of Son-Jara,* and ending with Nahua and Maya poems, which took us up to the contact between Europe and America, where the history course began. It served as context, geography and time, inclusively: no race, no major culture was ignored. "Let's agree," I told them, "that we are all human, whatever our origins. And now let's go into Plato's Cave."

I told them there would be no lectures in the philosophy section of the course; we would use the Socratic method, which is called *maieutic* dialogue. "*Maieutic* comes from the Greek word for midwifery. I'll take the role of midwife in our dialogue. Now, what do I mean by that? What does a midwife do?"

It was the beginning of a love affair, the first moment of their infatuation with Socrates. If it is true that he was the first one to bring philosophy down to earth, it is also true that he was the first one to raise these students up to seriousness. Once he told them that the answer, the truth, was inside them and had only to be brought forth through dialogue, they were never again to see themselves in the same way. The humanities became a mirror in which they saw their human worth, and, like all lovers, they were transformed by love.

Later, Abel Lomas would characterize that moment in his no-nonsense fashion, saying that it was the first time anyone had ever paid attention to their opinions. Keeping to the metaphor Socrates preferred, they were born.

7

What is the life of man? A thing not fixed
For good or evil, fashioned for praise or blame.
—*Sophocles,* Antigone

The first meeting at Bedford Hills went almost as well. About forty women gathered in one of the largest classrooms at the prison. They were older than the students in the city, a complexity of skeptics and innocents, women who had acquiesced to the dark green uniform of the prison and others who wore only the one required piece of the uniform, and completed their attire with sweaters, blouses, fashionable shoes, the symbols of the "free world." Yet others, who had adopted the masculine role in their prison relations, cut their hair short and turned their prison uniforms into military-style fatigues, sharply creased, with the trousers bloused over jump boots. A roomful of accommodations gathered there, awaiting, perhaps with trepidation, another view of life.

My wife and Tom Wallace came to that first meeting in the prison. It was the only time either of them would go to Bedford Hills. I had described the prison to Sylvia, but nothing written, said, or pictured can reproduce the oppressive atmosphere of a maximum-security prison. It is not the clang of gates or the weapons trained on the prisoners, but the weight of remorse and the grieving of women separated from their children that is unbearable. Sharon Smolick characterized it in a single image: "The sound of a women's prison at night is of weeping."

When they found out that I could not guarantee college credit, the Bedford Hills women made a devastating response: Twenty-five of them dropped the course. There were two stages in winning over the small number who remained. The first was intellectual: *The Consolation of Philosophy.* Boethius is hardly a thinker to place alongside Plato or Aristotle, but the idea of Philosophy personified, the nurse of his childhood, coming to visit Boethius in his cell opened a discussion about freedom, pagan and Christian, before and after St. Paul.

Boethius, whose thought lives somewhere in the middle between the pagan and Christian ideas, was the best example, for to one side were the

Greeks and to the other the martyrs of Christianity. I do not know whether Philosophy was a consolation to the women in Bedford Hills, but they considered it, for one woman, Ada Velásquez, said in response to Boethius that in the night, after lockdown, she lay awake in her room to think of what she had done with her life. "We did crimes," she said, "but we're still human." She did not say whether she expected Philosophy to visit her cell.

The second part was more difficult. Terri McNair, who worked as a counselor to the women, said that I would have to tell them about myself, convince them that I was not merely a condescending rich white man.

"You mean a confession?"

"Yes."

On the way up to Bedford Hills to teach the next class, I decided to chance it, to tell the students of my mother's addiction to barbiturates and morphine, and of my own troubles in school and in the military. I did not lie to them: I said that for a while, when I was very young, a friend and I had imported marijuana through New Mexico and sold it in East St. Louis, Illinois.

"You don't look like a drug dealer," one woman said. And another called out, "Where you gold chains?"

Terri had been correct. After the laughter faded, the course began. The humanities had moved from the ivory tower to the world. In the end, however, it was not enough. Only a few women completed the course and only a handful earned college credit. And one of those women, Judy Clark, already held a master's degree and did not need the credit. She and I had both been undergraduates at the University of Chicago—although not at the same time; she is much younger than I—and we had both had our troubles there. It helped to have her and Niecie in the class, for there was never that deadly silence when the teacher must supply the answer, never a time when one of them did not break the silence with the next line in the dialogue.

Now and then the world was too much with us in the prison. Near the end of the year, I met with the women to review what they had seen on the videotapes and discussed in class. When we came to *Antigone*, I gave them the assignment for the final paper, which was to be about the play, using what they knew of Socrates, Sojourner Truth, Henry David Thoreau, and the poetry they had read with Charles Simmons to reflect on it, and then offer their own opinion of Antigone's decision.

One of the older women in the class spoke about the conflict in the play between family and state. She said she had experienced the same conflict. "You see," she said, rocking back and forth in her chair, "I had that situation with my daughter. I had to turn my daughter in to the FBI."

Her face swelled with tears and her voice died away, although she continued to speak. Something in the "situation" with her daughter had brought her to this place, but I could not imagine what it had been, and the etiquette of prison does not permit asking questions about a person's crime. All I could do was ask, "Can you write about it? You know more about Antigone than any of the rest of us can ever hope to know. You can teach us. Will you do that?"

"Oh, I don't know if I could," she said very softly.

"Will you try? Never mind the rest of the final assignment. Just write about Antigone as you understand her. Or just write about your own decision. Do that. Teach us. Teach me about Antigone."

She said she would. She is a shy, sweet, soft woman, whose skin is gray beneath the brown, as if she had been underpainted with sorrow or with age. She told me later that she had tried to write the essay, and then she lowered her eyes and collapsed inside herself.

8

Grace Glueck began in a darkened room, leading them across the centuries into the caves of Lascaux to imagine early men in firelight, dressed in animal skins, drawing out their dreams or hungry hopes on the vast subterranean walls. And then she took them out again to Egypt—first to the sun, then to the netherworld where the painted figures waited to arise again, whole and happy, perfect in every line. They stayed long in Egypt, not so much to look at the antiquities as to imagine them, to talk about them. Seeing this, Grace arranged for them to visit the Metropolitan Museum of Art, where Felicia Blum led them first to the Temple of Dendur, and then through the Egyptian Collection.

The students arrived at the museum on a Friday evening. Darlene Codd brought her two-year-old son, Yaro. Pearl Lau was late, as usual. One of the students, who had told me how much he was looking forward to the museum visit, did not show up, which surprised me. Later, I learned that he had been arrested for jumping a turnstile in a subway station on his way to the museum, and was being held in a prison cell under the Brooklyn Courthouse.

Had he come to the museum, he might have been in the thrall of the Egyptians, but it was not his luck. It was Samantha Smoot who was transformed by the humanities that night. And it happened while she was standing in the Temple of Dendur.

She is alternately possessed by fear or wishing; at times as carefree and stylish as the images mannikins project, and the next day old bones and chopped-off hair. I have seen her dreaming. One night, after I had taken a group of students to an Italian restaurant in Greenwich Village, Samantha was the last to leave. She walked up a few steps to the door, then turned back to the dining room with a regal air and waved to the eaters, as if they had looked up from their piccata or primavera to adore the young woman who told them of her importance by the deep dimples that graced her smile. "My fans," she said, and with a sweeping gesture of celebrity, turned and went out the door to where her classmates waited, shivering, inadequately dressed for the winter night.

"Did you finish high school?" I had asked in the initial interview.
She said she had not, because she "fell in with the wrong crowd."
"Do you live at home?"
"Yes."
"With your parents?"
"My father's not in the picture."
"Brothers or sisters?"
"My brother is upstate."
"For a long time?"
"Yes."

It was she who had said, announced, burst out with the news, in one of the first sessions of the course, that people in her neighborhood believed it "wasn't no use goin to school, because the white man wouldn't let you up no matter what."

She could read, but she could not write. The first paper she turned in was almost incomprehensible. Patricia Chui, a young editorial assistant on her way to becoming an editor at W. W. Norton, had offered to tutor someone in the course. I sent Samantha to her, and they worked together all through the rest of the year: The daughter of a physician, educated at the University of California at Berkeley, and the fearful dreamer from Brooklyn found common ground in the English language. They met twice a week, once in the offices of W. W. Norton and once in a coffeeshop in Greenwich Village, to discuss grammar, syntax, and the organization of the mind on paper. At the end of the course, Samantha was not yet ready for publication, but the young editor had made a success of her work, for Samantha's final paper would have earned a decent grade at any college.

Perhaps it was the influence of Patricia Chui or the visits to the offices of the publishing house or the humanities entering into her life, but I think that all of this came together for Samantha in ancient Egypt. In the Temple of Dendur it was she who asked the questions of Felicia Blum, and when they went on to a hall where the statuary was of half-human, half-animal female figures, it was Samantha who asked what the glyphs meant. As Felicia Blum read them, translating the incised stone into English words, Samantha dreamed a dream of Africa. This was her ancient mirror, not forests or savanna, but the splendor along the Nile.

Toward the end of the evening, Grace took over the tour, leading the students out of the halls of antiquities into the Rockefeller Wing, where she told them of the connections of culture and art in Mali, Benin, the Pacific Islands. At the end of the tour the students collected their coats and stood together near the entrance to the museum, preparing to leave. All but Samantha, who stood apart from us, posed in loftly serenity. We left her there—a tall, slim young woman, only a few days older than a girl, dressed in a deerstalker cap and a dark blue peacoat. She smiled at us, dimples of innocence and joy, made an exaggerated wave of farewell, and returned to ancient Egypt whence she had come.

9

Charles Simmons began the poetry class with poems as puzzles and laughs, tiny poems, jokes in form or language, puns. His plan was to surprise the class, and he did, again and again throughout the year. At first he read the poems aloud to them, interrupting himself with footnotes to bring them along. He showed them poems of love, seduction, commentaries on poems they read in the form of satire by later poets. "Let us read," the students demanded. And he refused.

A tug-of-war began between Simmons and the students, particularly Laura and Carmen. He withheld the reading from them, tantalizing them with the opportunity to say the poems aloud. In his third class, the students were arguing over a D. H. Lawrence poem about America when Henry Jones rose from his chair, pointed his finger at Laura, who sat across the table from him, and said, in an accusing tone, "Define your terms!"

The gate to poetry was finally opened not by Simmons directly but by Hector Anderson. When Simmons asked if anyone in the class wrote poetry, Hector raised his hand. "Can you recite one of your poems for us?"

Until that moment, Hector had never volunteered a comment, although he had spoken well and intelligently when asked. He preferred to slouch in his chair, dressed in full camouflage gear, wearing a nylon stocking over his hair, and eating slices of fresh cantaloupe or honeydew melon.

In response to Simmons's question, Hector slid back up to a sitting position. "If you turn that camera off," he said. "I don't want anybody using my lyrics." When he was sure the red light on the camera was off, Hector stood up and recited verse after verse of a poem that belonged somewhere in the triangle formed by Ginsberg's *Howl*, the Book of Lamentations, and hip-hop. Simmons was delighted. Later he told me, "That kid is the real thing." In the classroom, he joined in the applause. When the room finally grew quiet, Simmons and the students asked Hector to say the poem again, and he did it gladly.

Like some ancient poet, exalted by his art, Hector Anderson ascended to a new place in the class. His discomfort with Sylvia and me turned to ease. He came to our house. We spoke on the telephone. As a student, he began quietly, almost secretly, to surpass many of his classmates. But it was always at poetry that he excelled, asking Charles Simmons writerly questions about a poet's choice of alliteration or sudden rhyme. He wanted to know the surface as well as the sinew of poetry. Anderson and Simmons stood at opposite ends of a long table of age and ethnicity, but they engaged never-theless, in the way that artists can.

The first questions about Laura arose in the poetry class. She asked to read a Langston Hughes poem in which he describes a park in Harlem, announcing at the start her familiarity with the park, which was across the street from the shelter where she lived. She read well, and Simmons was impressed, but there was grumbling in the room.

Laura asked again for permission to bring her girlfriend to class. I said no visitors were permitted in the classroom. "I have turned away the ABC Television network and the *New York Times,* as well as many curiosity seekers, Laura. The only people who audit our course are the women in Bedford Hills."

At the beginning of the next class, a young black woman sat in a chair against the wall. She wore her hair in cornrows pulled so tight that streams of shining scalp showed between. The skin of her face was tighter still, stretched across her bones, revealing in embarrassing intimacy the details of her skull. "This is my friend," Laura said.

The girl and I shook hands. I told her she could stay this time, but that she could not come again. She smiled, but she made sure I understood the unpleasantness she intended.

Laura missed the next few classes. When next I spoke to her, she said there had been a problem in the shelter; someone had set her room on fire.

ONE POEM AFFECTED AND INTERESTED the students more than any other. At Bedford Hills, Niecie Walker and Aisha Elliott argued about it night after night. In the classroom, the students understood it perfectly, including the ambiguity, which they found intriguing. More than Maya Angelou or even Lawrence and Housman, whose work came so easily to them; more than anything they responded to this poem by William Blake.

The Little Black Boy
My mother bore me in the southern wild,
And I am black, but O! my soul is white;
White as an angel is the English child;
But I am black as if bereaved of light.

My mother taught me underneath a tree,
And sitting down before the heat of day,
She took me on her lap and kissed me,
And pointing to the east, began to say:

"Look on the rising sun; there God does live,
And gives his light, and gives his heat away;
And flowers and trees and beasts and men receive
Comfort in morning, joy in the noon day.

"And we are put on earth a little space,
That we may learn to bear the beams of love,
And these black bodies and this sun-burnt face
Is but a cloud, and like a shady grove.

"For when our souls have learned the heat to bear,
The cloud will vanish; we shall hear his voice,
Saying: 'Come out from the grove, my love & care,
And round my golden tent like lambs rejoice.'"

Thus did my mother say, and kissed me;
And thus I say to little English boy:
When I from black and he from white cloud free,
And round the tent of God like lambs we joy,

I'll shade him from the heat till he can bear
To lean in joy upon our father's knee;
And then I'll stand and stroke his silver hair,
And be like him, and he will then love me.

The students were torn between Blake's suggestion of the protective power of blackness and his setting of the poem in a racist world. In Bedford Hills, Aisha took the view that Blake loved blacks and wanted to show how powerful and close to God they were. Niecie saw only the racism evoked by Blake. It was their first experience with a literary ambiguity that touched their own lives. Simmons drew their feelings out, asking and asking, "Do you like the poem? What does he mean by 'the heat to bear'? Who is closer to God?"

He made the dialogue like the poem, and they were aware of what he was doing, complicit. The dialogue was at once about both beauty and ugliness, dreaming and the moment, hope and anger, and no harsh word was said.

10

David Howell telephoned on a Saturday afternoon in January. "Mister Shores," he said, anglicizing my name, as many of the students did.

"Mister Howell," I responded, recognizing his voice.

"How you doin, Mister Shores?"

"I'm fine. How are you?"

"I had a little problem at work."

"Uh-oh," I thought. Bad news was coming. David is a big man, generally good-humored, but with a quick temper. According to his mother, he had a history of violent behavior. In the classroom he had been one of the best students, a steady man, twenty-six years old, who always did the reading assignments and who often made interesting connections between the humanities and daily life. "What happened?"

"Mister Shores, there's a woman at my job, she said some things to me and I said some things to her. And she told my supervisor I had said things to her and he called me in about it. She's forty years old and she don't have no social life, and I have a good social life, and she's jealous of me."

"And then what happened?" The tone of his voice and the timing of the call—Saturday morning—did not portend good news.

"Mr. Shores, she made me so mad, I wanted to smack her up against the wall. I tried to talk to some friends to calm myself down a little, but nobody was around."

"And what did you do?" I asked, fearing the worst, hoping this was not his one telephone call from the city jail.

"Mr. Shores, I asked myself, 'What would Socrates do?'"

It was the first concrete example of a person thinking differently because of the course. David Howell had reflected on the situation, and made a decision that differed from his instinctive reaction.

The anecdote was important, but it was only an anecdote, one case. At the end of the year, Dr. Inclán would administer the questionnaire again.

THERE WERE OTHER MOMENTS in the classroom that gave some indication of the progress the students were making in understanding and integrating what they learned. One evening, in the American History section, which I had taken over from Tom Wallace, I was telling the students about Gordon Wood's ideas in *The Radicalism of the American Revolution.* We were talking about the revolt against classicism at the turn of the century, including Benjamin Franklin's change of heart, when Henry Jones raised his hand.

"If the founders loved the humanities so much, how come they treated the natives so badly?"

There were confounding answers to offer about changing attitudes toward the Native Americans, vaguely useful references to views of Rousseau, James Fenimore Cooper, and so on, but simply to confound the issue would have been unfair, dishonest. Henry had discovered the terrible flaw in the life of the mind, which is that knowledge does not always produce goodness.

I did not know how to answer his question. For a moment I wondered if I should tell them about Heidegger's Nazi past, confirming his view. Then I saw Abel Lomas at the far end of the table. His hand was raised. "Mister Lomas," I said, hoping that his comment would give me another moment to think about Henry's question. I had made promises about the humanities; Henry was now calling for me to defend those promises in the face of hard evidence to the contrary.

Abel said, "That's what Aristotle means by incontinence, when you know what's morally right, but you don't do it, because you're overcome by your passions."

The other students nodded in agreement. They were all of them inheritors of wounds caused by the incontinence of educated men. But now they had an ally in Aristotle, who had given them a way to analyze the actions of their antagonists.

TIMOTHY KORANDA WAS THE MOST PROFESSORIAL of the professors, arriving for each session just as the class was to begin. He always wore a hat of many styles, part fedora, part Borsalino, part Stetson, and at least one-half World War I campaign hat. From their first encounter the students recognized in their portly, formal professor what could be said to be a kind of zen sweetness; that is, not love, but a connection in that cool, empty realm where egos have been banished and inequalities cannot exist.

He taught them logic during the appointed hours, and afterward he spoke to them of zen. When the class was over, he walked with them to the subway, chatting all the way about zen or logic or Heisenberg. They did not share intimacies; he initiated them into the incorporeal world of pure thinking.

In the classroom he filled the blackboard from floor to ceiling, wall to wall, drawing the intersections of sets here and truth tables there and a great square of oppositions in the middle of it all.

One winter night, Koranda introduced them to logic problems stated in ordinary language that they could solve by reducing the phrases to symbols. He passed out copies of a problem, which was two pages long, and then wrote out some of the key phrases on the blackboard. "Take this home with you," he said, "and at our next meeting we shall see who has solved it. I shall also attempt to find the answer."

By the time he finished writing out the key phrases, however, David Iskhakov raised his hand. Although they listened attentively, neither David nor his sister Susana spoke often in class, for she was shy and he was embarrassed at his inability to speak perfect English.

"May I go to blackboard?" David said. "And will see if I have found correct answer to zis problem."

"Please, sir," said Koranda, stepping aside and holding out the chalk to David.

"May I erase?" David asked, pointing to the phrases Koranda had written.

"Be my guest. In fact, I shall assist you." And Koranda and his student together wiped the board clean.

David began writing signs and symbols on the board. "If first man is earning this money, and second man is closer to this town . . ." he said, carefully laying out the conditions. After five minutes or so, he said, "And the answer is: B will get first to Cleveland!"

Samantha Smoot shouted, "That's not the answer. The mistake you made is in the first part there, where it says who earns more money."

Koranda folded his arms across his chest, and smiled. "I shall let you all take the problem home to think about it," he said. "Meanwhile, I shall do the same, and at our next meeting we shall review the answer."

The scene took place during one of the coldest nights of that winter. When Sylvia and I left the Clemente Center a few minutes before eight o'clock, a knot of students was gathered outside in the icy night, huddled together against the wind. Snow had begun to fall again, a slippery powder on the hard gray ice that covered all but a narrow space down the center of the sidewalk. Samantha Smoot and David Iskhakov stood in the middle of the group, still arguing over the answer to the problem. I leaned in for a moment to catch the character of the argument. It was as polite as it had been inside the classroom, perhaps more so, for now they governed themselves.

11

I do not know when the course became an avenue to college. Perhaps it was at the instigation of Candace Reyes D'Andrea, the college counselor at The Door, but I think it is more likely to have occurred after two of the students who had enrolled in community college courses reported that the Clemente Course was far more demanding. Within a few weeks after that, the students began visiting with college admissions counselors from Bard, New York University, and Columbia University.

Since Bard is two hours by train from New York City, Donna Ford, who directs the Higher Education Opportunity Program (HEOP) there, and a group of students met over lunch at my house. They were astonished by her. The associate dean for academic services was young, fashionable, and easy to be with. She gave straight answers in plainspoken English. By the end of the lunch, all the students but Samantha Smoot wanted to go to Bard. Samantha said she was afraid she could not keep up.

Five students were accepted at Bard. Hector Anderson and Jacqueline Martin could not qualify for HEOP scholarships under the federal guidelines, but Henry Jones and Susana and David Iskhakov were offered complete scholarship packages.

Laura, whose GED test score was high enough to make her a candidate for admission at either Bard or NYU, chose to apply only to NYU, because she did not want to be far from her girlfriend. As the weeks passed, she missed classes now and then. Once, after she missed several classes, I telephoned her. There had been a problem, she said; she had to look for an apartment and a job, because she had to move out of the shelter.

Late in the year, after she was accepted at NYU, she stopped coming to class. Her social worker told me that Laura and her roommate had moved out into their own apartment. "We have no more control over them," the social worker said. "She does come back to pick up her mail. That's the only time I expect to see her."

"If you have her new telephone number, I'll phone her about coming back to class. There is only one session left before the final exam, and I would hate to see her lose the course credit now."

"She left specific instructions not to give the telephone number to you or anyone else from the Clemente Course," the social worker said. "I think she's afraid of what will happen if you call there."

"When you see her, please tell her that if NYU inquires about her grade in the course, I will answer truthfully."

"I'll tell her," the social worker said.

Although I never saw Laura again, I did speak to the social worker once more. She told me then that Laura's girlfriend had been noncompliant. When I said I did not know what she meant by that, she spoke about the fire, and added that there had been other problems as well. "I saw Laura two days ago. She passed by my office on the way to get her mail. Her face was bruised. I think she couldn't come to school because of the bruises."

"The girlfriend?"

"Yes."

12

During the last meeting before graduation, the students answered the same set of questions they had encountered during orientation. Sylvia and I, the people who knew them best, believed they had been changed by the humanities, but anecdotal evidence and our own goodwill toward them did not prove the efficacy of the humanities in leading people toward reflection and politics. Granted, the sample was small. Students had fallen to AIDS, pregnancy, job opportunities, pernicious anemia, clinical depression, a schizophrenic child, and even to poverty itself. In three of the seventeen instances we did not have both pre- and post-course tests; one or the other was missing.

Dr. Inclán's full report of the results appears in Appendix C. In summary, these were the significant changes he reported:

1. Improved Self-Esteem ($p<.05$)[6]
2. Decrease in Verbal Aggression ($p<.05$)
3. Improved Problem Definition & Formulation ($p<.001$)

---

[6] The letter p represents the probability that the results happened by chance. According to Dr. Inclán, when the probability is less than $<.05$, there is little doubt about the results. When p is $<.10$, the results are still useful, even though the risk of error is higher.

4. Increase in Values of
   Benevolence (p<.05)
   Spirituality (p<.05)
   Universalism (p<.10)
   Collectivism (p<.10)

The scales and inventories Dr. Inclán and his staff used are all well known and widely used. In his judgment, the quantitative results corroborated the anecdotal evidence. Something happened.

There was one last piece of anecdotal evidence. It came on the night of graduation. The staff of the Roberto Clemente Center had turned the waiting room/lobby of the center into a bar and buffet. A neighborhood restaurant delivered a Puerto Rican–style feast of fried chicken, roast pork (*pernil*), plantains and onions, flattened and fried plantains with garlic sauce (*tostones*). The students brought enough guests to fill every one of the eighty-five chairs we had been able to crowd into the conference room.

The registrar of Bard College had prepared certificates of accomplishment, as she called them, to be awarded by Dean Robert Martin. He was to speak briefly, as were Dr. Inclán and I. The main speaker was David Dinkins, former mayor of New York City. Halfway through the exercise, the mayor swept in, slightly out of breath, wearing a dinner jacket and looking more confident and important than he had during his years in City Hall.

He spoke for perhaps fifteen minutes, mainly offering anecdotes about himself and his friends. There was no Golden Age of poverty in Mayor Dinkins's stories; he and U.S. Representative Charles Rangel and others had all pulled themselves up by their bootstraps. But the words did not matter so much to the students as the fact that the former mayor of New York had come to the Lower East Side to the room in which they had studied. He had chosen to come there, to be late for his own law school fortieth reunion, he told them, because he thought they were important.

When it came time to conclude the exercise, I spoke a few words about each of them, congratulated them, and said finally, "This is what I wish for you: May you never be more active than when you are doing nothing. . . ." I saw their smiles of recognition. The words of Cato, which Hannah Arendt so loved, were there again, as when I had first written them on the blackboard. The end of that brilliantly constructed thriller, the *Nicomachean Ethics,* was there again, too. They could recall the moment when we had come to Aristotle's denouement, the idea that in the contemplative life man was most like God.

One or two, perhaps more of them, closed their eyes. I saw tears beginning in their eyes, I saw through tears of my own. In the momentary stillness of the room it was possible to think.

"But is this what Aristotle means by action?" someone had asked.

"Yes," I had answered. "Yes, exactly!"

After a breath, I finished Cato's thought, ". . . and may you never be less lonely than when you are by yourself.

"Godspeed."

Follow-Up
1

Dr. Inclán said that there would have to be three stages to the measurement of the effect of the humanities on the students: the pre- and post-course tests, and a follow-up "to see if the inoculation took."

Six months after graduation, only one of the students was not enrolled in an accredited college or working full time or both. The remaining student, Hector Anderson, was writing occasional pieces for a New York radio station and preparing to apply again to Bard College. Carmen Quiñones was going to school and working part-time as a counselor at Riker's Island. In October 1996, five students met in a New York recording studio to participate in a series of programs based on this book for the Public Radio International program *Marketplace*. Samantha Smoot delivered a passionate extemporaneous speech on poverty and the humanities, and she and Hector Anderson, David Howell, Jacqueline Martin, and Abel Lomas held an impromptu discussion of *Antigone*. They had not forgotten the play. If anything, their understanding of Antigone had ripened over time.

In December 1996, Henry Jones was nominated to head the black students' organization at Bard College. David Iskhakov was cross-breeding fruit flies in his biology course. His sister Susana was still planning to be a chemist, but a course with an excellent professor had led her to consider biology as a possible alternative.

Only Abel Lomas had not fared well. On Mother's Day, 1996, he was arrested for drinking a can of beer on the street outside the shelter where he lived. The police ran his name through their computer system and found a federal warrant for Abel Lomas. Several months before the Clemente Course began, Abel had been in his cousin's apartment when federal agents arrested his cousin and three other men for selling cocaine.

The federal agents, who were acting on information supplied by confidential informants, knew that Abel was not part of the drug ring. They did not arrest him. But a few weeks later, two of the men who had been arrested told the U.S. Attorney they would give him the name of another member of the conspiracy in return for a lesser sentence. Both men named Abel, and he was indicted in absentia.

Under the federal guidelines Abel Lomas will receive the same sentence as the other men who were in the room, a sentence based upon the amount of cocaine found by the federal agents. Had Abel been arrested by New York City police, it is almost certain that an assistant district attorney would have charged him with a misdemeanor, if he had charged him at all, and sent him home. Because his case comes up in federal court, neither the judge nor the U.S. Attorney has discretion. Abel Lomas faces at least ten years in prison with no chance for parole.

In a meeting with Assistant U.S. Attorney Patrick Smith arranged by Lomas's pro bono attorney, Peter Neufeld, two people from The Door and I spoke in support of fair treatment for a young man who had learned reflection and politics, asking the prosecutor to consider the case in light of the man and of justice. In the course of the conversation I asked Abel about his understanding of law. He spoke about the decision reached by Socrates in the *Crito* and about *Antigone*.

The Assistant U.S. Attorney said he had never read the classics and did not understand the references, which caused him to be confused about Antigone's decision, even though Abel explained it. All the young prosecutor could say was that the law should be applied equally to all persons. Although he would later reflect on the meeting and what Abel had said, justice was not then the issue uppermost in his mind, and in that sense he did not participate in legitimate power, he was merely an instrument of power, like the outside chiefs of the Pueblos—force. And no one can engage in dialogue with force.

2

The Clemente Course in the Humanities began its second year in 1996. It is more formal now, taught mainly by professional teachers. A new director and a new faculty are working under the supervision of Dr. Robert Martin of Bard College, with the participation of the Clemente Family Guidance Center staff and the staff of The Door.

Dr. Martin Kempner is the new director, as well as the instructor in moral philosophy.

We had trouble raising money again, but everyone is willing to continue the experiment, even if it means getting paid less or not getting paid at all.

Twenty-six students have enrolled, the demographics are the same, and the new art teacher also has problems with the slide projector. However, the miraculous effect of the humanities has not diminished: Once again, the teachers and the students astonish each other in the presence of the great malcontents, and the radical process begins—dialogue, reflection, politics.

3

A year after graduation of the first class, two more students had been accepted at Bard College: Hector Anderson and Abel Lomas, who had avoided going to prison by pleading guilty to a crime he did not commit. Samantha Smoot had won a full scholarship to the Fashion Institute of Technology, and Jacqueline Martin was studying to be a registered nurse. Only one of the students who had completed the course was not either employed or attending college. Pearl Lau had been fired from her job in a fast-food restaurant for attempting to start a union.

There was, however, one irony of tragic proportion. On May 14, 1997, the parole board met at Bedford Hills Correctional Facility to hear the case of Viniece Walker. She was a model prisoner and she had served more than ten years of an eight and one-third to twenty-five sentence. That afternoon the woman whose belief in the humanities had given rise to the Clemente Course was denied parole and condemned to two more years in prison.

XIX.

Conclusion: Good-Bye Blues

1. New American Blues

MANY YEARS AGO, in a third-rate nightclub on the South Side of Chicago, where Billie Holiday was working, I heard a man say that she did not sing jazz any more. "She sings blues," he explained. "Blues is when you know you can't get out of it."

There is no accepted definition of the blues, nor does anyone know exactly when the blues began. The first recordings were made around 1920, but the blues had been around for a long time by then. Although the early history of the blues was vague, the evolved form was purely American, southern, and black. Form and content blended easily in the early versions of the blues, which were more like chants than what we think of as songs. The blues came out of the music of laboring, and like laboring, the first blues were repetitions: one line said to fit the form, the sad mechanics of life.

People of entirely European descent did not sing the blues, unless perhaps some indentured servants or prisoners sang beside slaves or the descendants of slaves. The blues belonged to one race. They were so identified with the African-American experience that James Baldwin, in an essay about "The Discovery of What It Means to Be an American," told of finding his identity in the blues. He arrived in Switzerland with nothing American but a couple of Bessie Smith records, he said, and that was all he needed. The tone and cadence of the music were his madeleine. Out of the blues he was able to recall his childhood, the meaning of color, segregation, race and race hatred, America as only a black man could see America.

For James Baldwin, the blues represented race. He could not recall poverty based on the blues for he was not born in poverty. *Go Tell It on the Mountain,* his autobiographical novel about childhood in Harlem, begins: "Everyone had always said that John would be a preacher when he grew up, just like his father." Baldwin's young hero was raised in the ambiance of the church, studying the Bible, listening to the exegesis of sermons and discussions, singing the songs. The political life that grows out of the humanities was his from birth. When he heard the blues in Switzerland, James Baldwin heard two songs: the music he associated with race and the music and poetry any student of the humanities might hear.

For over two hundred years it had been virtually impossible to separate race from poverty in America. James Baldwin was born into one of the first generations where any sizable number of blacks could draw the distinction. The blues still belonged to people like him racially, but not economically or culturally or politically.

Baldwin was certainly right about the blues as American music, but the origin of the blues was not only racial. The blues are American in another way as well. They are made of many cultures: the iambic pentameter of the verse is English, as is the language; the African rhythms are abetted by those of Spain, Europe, and the Americas. The blues are a syncretism of woes, all the loneliness in the world concentrated in a single voice.

The essence of the blues has always been the same. It is the music of the aftermath, love lost, happiness gone, dead broke, door closed, good-bye. It is not hungry music, but it is always a song about hungers.

The blues come out of the realization that nothing will change. There is no sign of surrender in the blues, but there is no hope either. The blues are about the way it is: So you might as well. There are no blues for winners. The blues belong to those who begin as equals in the game of the modern world and end up less than equal; the blues sing of the irretrievable, irreparable, unredeemable, unlovable, lost and lonely Americans, the poor.

The blues are never a result of nature. There are no desert blues, flood blues, snow blues. There are only insurmountable blues, because everybody else got dealt a better hand. The blues are based on the undeniable truth that life is a game, and the game is unfair. There are lamentation blues and supplication blues, but nobody ever wrote a blues about justice.

There are old blues, and those are best, because they are the nearly forgotten blues. And there are this morning's blues, which do not necessarily belong to one race or another, but to all those people who do not know how to get out of the isolation of life inside a surround of force. Those are the do or die blues, the new American blues.

2. A Dangerous Corollary

The success of America has always rested on the certainty that the poor are not dangerous. If that seems an overstatement, said for shock value or merely to gain the reader's attention again at the end of a long book, that was not my intention. I want only to show that poverty and the blues, the feeling that "you can't get out of it," live in the same house.

They have lived there for generations, since the founding of the country in a revolution different from any other in history. In all the others, the people, mainly the poor, took power away from the rich. The lesson of those revolutions was simple and memorable: The poor can be dangerous. Watch out for the poor.

In the British colonies in America, it was not the poor but the aristocracy who revolted. The poor fought and died in the war—they always do—but they did not make the revolution. They were not dangerous. When it came time to write a constitution, it did not have to address the problems of the poor. With its Lockean origins, the Constitution had great concern about property rights, but no interest at all in distributing the wealth of the nation in some way that included the poor.

The dominant view of the poor in the young nation, and still the view in many quarters, was that of Herbert Spencer, who coined the phrase "survival of the fittest." The social Darwinists, following Spencer, believed that the only reason to give charity to the poor was to improve the character of the donor.[1] That took care of the moral question. And with no reason to fear a violent uprising, it made no sense to those in power even to consider sharing the wealth of the nation with the poor. There were dissenting voices, of course, socialists and do-gooders, but they had no power; they were not dangerous either.

In the South, slaveholders worried about runaways but not about revolt, even when blacks vastly outnumbered the whites on plantations in isolated areas far from any town or military installation. On the way west, the

---

[1] See Richard Hofstader, *Social Darwinism in American Thought,* (Boston: Beacon Press, rev. edn 1955).

Indians offered some resistance, but their destiny was manifest. William Graham Sumner expressed the popular view: Either the Indians became "civilized" or they became extinct.

When civil war did come to the United States, it was not between the rich and poor, although the immediate cause of the war was economic. The poor did not ever gain anything in the United States by threatening to overthrow the established order.

The poor are timid, conditioned by life within a surround of force; they kill each other. Even during the morally and politically tumultuous sixties, when McGeorge Bundy of Harvard and the National Security Council returned from seeing the American dead on the battlefields of Vietnam, and said to send more Americans to die, the poor shouldered their rifles and went. And died. They did not want to die. The unfairness of rich men choosing to send the poor to die enraged them, so in Watts, in Detroit, and in Chicago they burned down their own houses and killed their brothers.

Americans do not like such civil disorder, even when it does not touch them, but the response to disorder has not been to close the income gap between rich and poor. It is, in fact, far greater now than it was during the riots of the sixties. The response to public disorder among the poor is not to end or even to alleviate poverty. It is more like the sentiment expressed by Lieutenant David I. Harris of the Riviera Beach, Florida, Police Department, who said, "If we don't do something about poverty in the next twenty or thirty years, my job will be to shoot people down in the street." Lieutenant Harris does not fear the overthrow of the government by the poor so much as he fears the effect of killing people on his own character. Herbert Spencer again, but in a mirror image:

Poverty is a problem in America because exposure to it may coarsen the rest of the population. That is why the poor are generally kept hidden and why the homeless and the mendicants, who wander among the affluent, are both feared and detested.

The fear of mendicants and other visible poor has to do with the only real danger the poor have ever posed in America, which is to our sense of our own moral worth. Franklin Delano Roosevelt, for all that he is said to have wanted to save capitalism, also sought to salvage the nation's sense of itself as capable of goodness. A generation later, Lyndon Johnson and the War on Poverty, misguided and underfunded as it was, took the same path.

It was not until the rise to moral dominance of Ronald Reagan that the poor ceased to be a danger to our sense of our own moral worth. Reagan dismissed all moral questions in his own life and that of the nation through the deceits of charm. Now, at the end of the century, under cover of being a Democrat, Bill Clinton has turned the nation's attitude toward the poor back to the time before Roosevelt. He has made them morally and politically inconsequential. Only the poor are not covered by the quilt of political correctness that intends the protection of all persons who are, in truth or imagination, deprived of their natural or civil rights.

Since no one will help them, the poor have no alternative but to learn politics. It is the way out of poverty, and into a successful, self-governing life, based upon reflection and the ability to negotiate a safe path between the polar opposites of liberty and order. But to learn politics may also be a way for the poor in America to become dangerous at last.

Coming into possession of the faculty of reflection and the skills of politics leads to a choice for the poor: They may use politics to get along in a society based on the game, to escape from the surround of force into a gentler life, and nothing more. Or they may choose to oppose the game itself. If it is the latter, if the poor enter the circle of legitimate power and then oppose the cruelty of the game, they will pose a real danger to the established order.

No one can predict the effect of politics, although we would all like to think that wisdom goes our way. In their newfound autonomy people may turn to the left or right or choose to live smugly, disinterestedly, in the middle. That is why the poor are so often mobilized and so rarely politicized. The possibility that they will adopt a moral view other than that of their mentors can never be discounted. And no one wants to run that risk.

Tens of thousands or even millions of poor people entering the public world may not endanger the established order at all. But the possibility that it could must perforce change the view of the poor held in America since the eighteenth century: The rest of the citizens would have to pay heed. Then the remaining poor might be spared some of the forces that make misery of their lives. And that, in turn, would make it easier for more of the poor to move out of the private life and into the public world, where all persons may think of themselves as having effect.

If the poor who learn politics do not become dangerous, if they choose to survive modestly in peace and comfort, that is surely good enough. The goal is to end poverty, to consign the blues to history and romance, to make citizens of the poor. If that can be accomplished, the question of danger changes, for then the poor will be dangerous in the way that all citizens are dangerous in a democracy—they will be power.

In one way or the other, politics will make dangerous persons of the poor. The certainty of that has worried the elites of this earth since politics was invented. But Plato was wrong about politics then and his fundamentalist followers are wrong now. The happiness of others is a goal worth pursuing, and the method for achieving it, democracy, is a risk worth taking.

Appendix A: Three Lists

1. Statistics

A. Between 40 and 80 million people live in poverty in the United States, depending upon the definition of poverty. How and where to draw the line is a basic demographic problem, involving politics, economics, and ethics. In any case, the number receiving welfare should not be confused with the number living in poverty—only a small percentage of the poor receive welfare.

B. Poverty has undergone a major shift in the last half of this century: The elderly and children have exchanged places as the most impoverished group, and the number of poor children continues to grow.

C. The number of single-parent families has grown enormously during the last third of a century, with the rate of increase now higher among whites than blacks, although the overall percentage of black single-parent families remains far higher.

D. Poverty declined during the late sixties and early seventies and then rose continuously until 1994, when it began to decline for blacks and whites, while rising for Latinos.

E. The number of working poor, according to federal income standards, increased rapidly during certain periods; for example, between 1975 and 1986, it went up by 52%.

F. In absolute numbers, there are more poor whites than members of any other racial group. Proportionally, more Latinos are poor, with blacks close by.

G. The number of people in poverty does not correlate with the unemployment rate, which declined from 9.7% in 1982 to nearly 5% in 1996.[1] A decline in the poverty rate in 1994 and 1995 came at the end of the decline in unemployment and was not of equal magnitude. As the various provisions of the Welfare Reform Bill of 1996 take effect, the poverty rate will rise again, but no one knows to what extent. Some predictions are catastrophic. The great fear of experts who study the provisions of the Bill is that when the buoyant U.S. economy enters the inevitable down period of the business cycle there will be no federal safety net for the victims of the cycle. It is not yet known how the new bill will affect those who leave the welfare rolls and Medicaid benefits for low-paying jobs with no medical benefits, but the prognosis is not difficult to imagine.

H. In dollars adjusted for inflation, entitlements—except for the largest programs, Social Security (including Medicare), and mortgage interest deductions—have declined during the last part of the century, with transfer payments to those identified as poor planned to decrease precipitously in the future.

In the eight places from which examples are drawn in this book, welfare payments declined in real terms between 1970 and 1996. The inflation adjusted decline, according to the U.S. House of Representatives Ways and Means Committee, was:

> 18%—California
> 33%—Florida
> 46%—Mississippi
> 48%—New York City
> 49%—Oklahoma
> 58%—Tennessee
> 59%—Illinois
> 68%—Texas

---

[1] For a useful examination of inner-city ghetto poverty based on research done over a long period in Chicago, see William Julius Wilson, *When Work Disappears* (New York: Knopf, 1996).

In 1995, the maximum welfare payment was only 8.6% of average per capita income in Mississippi. Tennessee and Texas both paid a maximum of less than 11%. Twenty-one states and the District of Columbia reported 14% or more of their population living below the poverty line.

I. By virtually any measure, the percentage and the absolute number of children living in poverty in the United States reached its highest level in more than thirty years in 1993, declined slightly in the following two years, but remained above 20%.

J. The number of blacks living comfortable lives, in purely economic terms, quadrupled between 1970 and 1990; however, the increase was from a small base. Even so, black poverty has fallen from 55.1% in 1959 to 29.3% in 1995. The increase in the black population over that same period leaves the absolute numbers of blacks living in poverty very large.

K. Unemployment among black men, particularly the young, is between two and four times that among whites of comparable ages, with the greatest difference in the inner cities, where labor force participation has fallen precipitously during the last quarter of the century.

L. The gap between rich and poor in the United States increased rapidly from 1980 to 1994, with a slight decrease in 1995. Top executives typically earn 190 times as much as the average worker in the same companies. The richest 1% of the population owns nearly 40% of the wealth of the nation, while the poorest third have virtually no meaningful assets.

M. In the three years 1980, 1981, and 1982, poverty increased from 18% to 24% among children under six, and from 16% to 21% for children six to seventeen years old. This 33% increase in the efficiency of the game for children six and under remains one of the best examples of the effect of public policy on poverty.

All of the statistics (most of which were provided by the U.S. Census Bureau) have been disputed by one group or another, but the picture they draw of American society during the last third of a century is generally conceded to be correct.

Employment is considered the best antidote to welfare, but less often mentioned as a solution to poverty. Much of this discrepancy grows out of the kind of work and the reliability of work available to the poor. Workfare, for example, does not promise a rise out of poverty; it merely demands that those who receive state or federal aid labor according to the wishes of the state in return for what was previously an "entitlement."

2. Interpretations

A list of the qualitative aspects of relative poverty always provokes controversy, but more than a few of them are apparent, especially those that relate to employment:

A. Global competition for jobs and low wage rates outside the industrialized nations combine to take what had been relatively high-paying but low-skill jobs from the United States. Assembly-line labor, especially in the garment industry, is an example of this kind of work.

B. The use of technology in the workplace requires higher skills, eliminating many kinds of high-paying, low-skill jobs, adding to the problem caused by global competition, forcing the people who had held those jobs into unemployment or lower-paying jobs. In the past, the highest-paying low-skill jobs in America were concentrated in the automobile industry. After the Japanese took a large percentage of the U.S. auto market, U.S. workers were forced to accept Japanese management methods. Those who accepted jobs with Japanese assemblers in the United States could not join unions. Meanwhile, the entire industry was made over by a technological revolution that enabled the companies to eliminate many jobs at all levels.

C. A shift to service jobs from manufacturing jobs lowers wages and forces many people to identify themselves as poor.

D. The number of discouraged workers remains high. Labor force participation does not always correlate with a falling unemployment rate.

E. Downsizing, the reduction of the labor force to increase profits, increases the efficiency of the game by reducing the size of the middle.

F. A greatly increased number of women in the workforce reduces upward pressure on wages by creating a larger labor pool. Moreover, women continue to be paid less than men for the same work, making them more desirable employees in many industries. Families with two or three incomes move toward the middle, while families with one income are more likely to find themselves in poverty.

G. Migrants and immigrants compete for low-end jobs, pushing down wage rates. This effect may often be overstated, since many recent immigrants work at jobs citizens refuse.

H. Mechanization and rationalization in agriculture have eliminated some jobs—picking cotton, for example, which can now be done by machine. The farm labor that remains, however, continues to pay low wages while forcing people to work in the worst, most dangerous conditions. Most citizens now reject such pay and working conditions, leading agricultural interests to favor the establishment of a semi-permanent peasantry made up largely of undocumented immigrants.

I. A rise in what the government considers full employment, from 2% unemployed at the middle of the century to 5% (not including discouraged or underemployed workers), avoids triggering Keynesian measures, such as supplementary benefits for the unemployed or the large-scale government employment programs suggested by William Julius Wilson, Mickey Kaus, and others.

J. Even when minimum wage or dead-end jobs are available, a significant number of people refuse to work for what they call "chump change," which is often a euphemism for holding on to the health-care provisions of welfare as opposed to accepting employment at low wages without benefits.

K. The economy fails to grow at a rate and in a manner that produces a sufficient number of jobs that pay a living wage, which, according to the federal government, is between $7.80 and $11.70 an hour for a family of four, depending upon where they live.

L. Desegregation and affirmative action help to raise some blacks and Latinos into the economic middle, but do not solve the problem of poverty. While affirmative action does little to harm white men, it improves the lot of educated white women far more than any other group. Latinos claim they have gained very little through affirmative action.

M. Racism continues despite laws protecting the civil rights of minorities. Blacks and Latinos suffer more than any other group, from before they are born until they take their last breath, beginning with the improper diet of pregnant women and small children, through inadequate schools, dangerous neighborhoods, unemployment and job discrimination, and limited access to health care.

N. Declines in social life occur most commonly among the poor and those on the borderline between the middle and the poor: the divorce rate goes up; in some areas a majority of children are born out of wedlock; literacy rates fall; crime increases, although the murder rate has fallen in some areas; the number and percentage of citizens in jails and prisons reaches new highs; drug use increases as crack cocaine comes into popular use and competes with heroin, amphetamines, barbiturates, and synthetic drugs; and the number of people owning guns for no other purpose than to threaten or kill human beings goes up every day.

O. The mood of the country since 1980 has moved toward sanctions against the poor rather than assistance to them.

P. The situation that gave rise to the Works Progress Administration (WPA) and other programs during the Depression is not available to policy makers at the end of the twentieth century. When poverty is understood as relative rather than absolute, the citizenry sets different limits on government.

Q. The effect of the employment situation at the end of the century has been to relieve most of the upward pressure at the lower end of the wage scale, meaning that the working poor, the greatest percentage of poor people by far, have no purely economic tools to improve their situation. In Marxist terms, any increase in the value of their labor accrues to the surplus. For the working poor to move out of poverty, as some have in the middle of the decade, generally means taking on another job or moving from part-time to full-time work in the second or third job held by a family member.

R. There are as many Americans in prisons and jails as there are residents of Houston, Texas, an indication of the increasing success of the prison system in "farming" the poor.

3. Education

The United Negro College Fund advertises the role of education in the rise of blacks from poverty with these statistics:

> 1900—1,700 Negroes attend college.
> 1944—40,000 Colored People attend college.
> 1950—520,000 blacks attend college.
> 1992—1,393,000 African Americans attend college.

The other news is not quite so cheering.

A. There is a direct correlation between education and income levels, with the poorest and least educated at the bottom.

B. The school dropout rate in inner-city neighborhoods in some large cities has reached and even passed 50%.

C. Funds per pupil for poor school districts in many parts of the country are lower than those for rich districts in the same state. A suit in the state of Texas to overturn this inequity there was won by the plaintiff, but no system to equalize the districts had been devised by the legislature and accepted by courts years after the judgment. Money originally earmarked for education in some states, especially earnings from state lotteries, is being used instead to construct prisons. The state of Florida has pursued this policy for several years.

D. Schools have not been desegregated as envisioned by the *Brown v. Board of Education* decision. Private schools have taken the place of all-white schools in the South. In the rest of the country, private academies have separated the rich and those in the middle from the poor. Tuition for one year in a non-resident private school in or near a large city can be $15,000, which was close to the federal poverty line for a family of four in 1995.

In some cities in the South, textbooks, computers, and school supplies for children attending largely black schools are so meager that Frank Clarke, a retired executive, has established the Educate the Children Foundation to bring millions of dollars in educational materials to these schools in Mississippi, Arkansas, Louisiana, and Alabama.

E. The nature of education for the poor differs from that provided to the rest of the population, particularly the affluent. Allan Bloom, the author of a best-selling book about elitism, argued in favor of the difference, claiming that only the elite were fit to undertake a liberal education.

Mr. Bloom's dream has come true. Thomas G. Mortenson of the National Council of Educational Opportunity compared the ratio of rich to poor college graduates in 1979 and 1994. The rich were from families in the top income quartile and the poor from the bottom quartile. Bloom's elite, the rich, were four times as likely as the poor to graduate in 1979. By 1994, the rich were ten times as likely as the poor to complete four years of college. (*New York Times,* Jan. 27, 1997)

F. High school teachers and counselors frequently advise the poor to pursue training rather than education.

G. Inner-city schools attended by the poor are dangerous, chaotic places in which education cannot easily take place. Assaults on teachers are not uncommon, and in many junior high schools and high schools students must submit to physical or electronic searches for concealed weapons.

H. Tens of millions of Americans, including many of the poor, are functionally illiterate.

I. Standardized tests to measure the knowledge of high school students have shown a steady decline for most of the country, with the poorest children in the poorest school districts consistently at the bottom.

Early in the sixteenth century the government of England took responsibility for guaranteeing a minimum standard of relief for the poor. Since then, governmental definitions of poverty and public responsibility for the poor have expanded and contracted. During the Great Depression, the U.S. government became convinced of its role in the relief of poverty, but toward the end of that period, as unemployment declined and the gross national product began to rise, however slowly, governmental relief decreased.[2]

The definition of poverty affects both the amount of relief and the method. The casework approach was institutionalized during the late 1960s and early 1970s by federal law. In this approach to poverty, a single caseworker made home visits during which he or she attempted to work with all the aspects of a family problem, from the lack of a crib for the baby to education or training for the parents to the physical and mental health of the entire family. Laws in effect at the time, such as the man in the house rule, had a devastating effect on the concept of family by forcing the men to leave home before the women and children could receive benefits.

The casework approach as defined by government regulations had so many problems that it was soon abandoned. Neither the poor nor government nor the caseworkers themselves could manage it. The caseworkers burned out very quickly when they had to deal with all of the problems that confront the poor. The government saw the welfare rolls growing instead of decreasing. But it was the poor themselves who claimed to be most injured by the system. Not only the man in the house rule, but the intrusion of the caseworker into the client's home bothered them. And not all caseworkers were competent or compassionate.

Meanwhile, the number of people applying for welfare was increasing at the rate of more than 16% a year as welfare rights organizers and a new sense of entitlement spurred by the liberal character of the country during the 1960s sent more people to the welfare offices. In the early 1970s, when the poor retreated into quiet again after the riots and the protest marches, the casework model was discarded and a new, more monetarily oriented system was put in place. Caseworkers became bank clerks; the poor had to qualify according to the strict rules of the system. The definition of poverty bore less and less relation to the actual lives of the poor. That shred of autonomy, which was no more than to declare the human detail of their own suffering, disappeared. The physician had become a rulebook and the clients were no longer permitted to say where it hurt. To be poor was now to be a thing, as undifferentiated as sand or the drops that fall on the third day of rain. Poverty itself had been added to the problems of the poor.

---

[2] See Piven and Cloward, *Regulating the Poor: The Functions of Public Welfare,* for a view of relief as a response to civil disorder.

Appendix B:
Multigenerational Poverty
and Slavery

In a narrow legal sense, multigenerational poverty cannot be equated with chattel slavery, in which humans can be bought and sold like other tangible goods. But to limit the concept of slavery to chattel may be an error. According to Cynthia Farrar, "The beginnings of Athenian self-rule coincided with Solon's liberation in the sixth century B.C. of those who had been 'enslaved' to the rich," by which she means his attempt to avoid civil war by reducing the gap between rich and poor, not the freeing of chattel slaves.[1]

It is not only chattel slavery but also the enslavement Solon spoke about that compares to the lives of the multigenerational poor. The two forms of slavery share these attributes:

(1) their circumstances are enduring, often lifelong, and passed on to the next generation;

(2) they are excluded from citizenship;

(3) they are ruled without recourse;

(4) their situation leaves them subject to coercion;

[1] Farrar, The Origins of Democratic Thinking; p. 7.

(5) they are despised (not hated) by the rich or freeborn;

(6) their death is not mourned by the state;

(7) they and their families are limited in choices of food, clothing, housing, employment, and recreation;

(8) their circumstances reduce them to pleasures of the body;

(9) they respond passively to the master or the establishment;

(10) circumstances deter them from marriage and family ties;

(11) they are excluded from education, limited to training;

(12) in economic terms, they are fungible, more like goods than persons.

Since the comparison of slavery and poverty, even of Solon's idea of enslavement to the rich, seems outrageous when applied to contemporary America, a brief defense of each of the twelve points may be helpful:

(1) by definition, multigenerational;

(2) see Chapter XII;

(3) there is no constitutional guarantee of representation in civil cases, and the current Clinton/Congress administration has cut back the scope and funding of the Legal Services Corporation to reduce even further the recourse of the poor;

(4) workfare, for example;

(5) see Auletta on the "underclass";

(6) poor and people of color killed and wounded in Vietnam, the 1996 Welfare Reform Bill and the effect it will have on children;

(7) by definition;

(8) see Oscar Lewis, *La Vida*; President Clinton's, 1992 campaign promise to "end welfare as we know it"; code for ending AFDC;

(9) slaves have seldom revolted in the U.S. or anywhere else, and the poor in democratic societies do not participate in the public life;

(10) divorce rate, out of wedlock births, etc.;

(11) high school dropout rates among the poor approach 50% in some cities;

(12) see 1996 legislative debate on minimum wage, workfare provisions of the 1996 Welfare Reform Bill.

The salient of so limited a life is the lack of leisure. The poor have no time to be free. Slaves, prisoners, and poor people are deprived of reflection; they can only react, a condition that robs them of their human life.

Slavery, like poverty and prison, occurs within a surround of force, a place where panic prevents action, which takes place in measured stages: reflection, choice, and implementation. The passivity of slaves and poor people results from the lack of time, the impossibility of action. There have been few revolts in all the long history of slavery, and the revolt of the poor is so rare, so very nearly impossible, that even Marx gave the task to the intelligentsia instead of leaving it for the poor.

Revolt requires politics, which comes of action. Only those who have a fully human life, who recognize the capacity to begin, can revolt against enslavement or poverty.

Harvard Professor Orlando Patterson claims that the social construction of freedom, which the Greeks considered a fully human life, grew out of five revolutions.[2] They were

> *Economic*: "The creation of a complex preindustrial economy."
>
> *Social:* "On the one side . . . a relatively large slave population which sustained the aristocratic . . . population. On the other side . . . the majority of a population entirely emancipated from ties of economic and social dependency on its ruling class."
>
> *Political:* ". . . the invention of the democratic state. . . ."
>
> *Intellectual:* ". . . the generation of secular philosophy and the social and moral sciences."

All of which resulted in a fifth revolution: ". . . the social construction of freedom as a central value, in the course of which we find the creation of personal freedom. . . ."

Professor Patterson concludes that four of the five revolutions depended upon slavery and are unimaginable without large-scale chattel slavery. An earlier academic, Plato, disagreed, claiming that philosophy was the child of Thaumezein, the goddess of Wonder. But one could make a tortuous argument in which wonder was not possible without the time to wonder, which grew out of the release from the duties of private life granted the male citizens by slavery and misogyny.

Patterson's point, that freedom in Athens was enabled by slavery, can hardly be disputed. Aristotle made the same point somewhat earlier when he wrote about the need for leisure in order to engage in the *vita activa*.

---

[2] See his *Freedom* (New York: Basic Books, 1997), p. 47.

Appendix C:
Evaluation of the
Clemente Course

by Jaime E. Inclán, Ph.D.

The team of psychologists was not interested in evaluating the extent to which the students acquired knowledge or skill.[1] This was the faculty's responsibility. Our task was to assess the potential of the course for personal transformation. Therefore, we sought to identify measures that would reflect such changes, if they occurred.

The course was intended to develop the capacity for reflective thinking, according to Earl Shorris. Furthermore, we wanted to ascertain whether a change toward greater reflective thinking would have an effect on the public, i.e., the political life of the students. The group agreed on assessing four dimensions: (1) changes in self-view—how highly the students valued

---

[1] In public mental health centers like the Roberto Clemente Center, the mission and funds allocation are intended for "direct services." To evaluate a program like this, we had therefore to depend on volunteers. Patricia Vargas, an NYU undergraduate student, Ramon Maisonet, a psychology intern at the clinic, and Sandra Martinez, a psychology extern, and I set out to establish some way of evaluating the course. We worked as a team to design and implement the evaluation I report on here.

themselves; (2) cognitive changes—how the students approached problems; (3) interpersonal changes—how they handled conflict with others; and (4) values framework—the way the students viewed the world.

The next task was to identify reliable measures. Students' views of themselves could find their most distilled representation in the level of *self-esteem*. Positive self-esteem has been linked to increased competency at personal and social levels. The measure used to assess self-esteem was the Index of Self-Esteem [W. Hudson, 1992].

The Problem Solving Skills Scale (problem definition and formulation and decision-making sub-scales) of the Social Problem Solving inventory [D'Zurilla and Nezu, 1990] was used to assess cognitive approaches to problem solving. According to its authors, social problem solving refers to the *cognitive-affective process* by which a person attempts to identify, discover, or invent effective or adaptive coping responses for specific problematic situations encountered in everyday living. As such, positive changes in social problem solving would be an indication of greater reflective thinking.

We also wanted to include a more direct measure of *interpersonal problem solving* strategies. For this, we used the Conflict Tactics Scale [M. Strauss, 1979]. This instrument asks the subject to define a family relationship for analysis (for example, father/subject) and measures the extent to which reasoning, verbal aggression, and physical aggression were used in a determined period of time to solve differences.

Values were assessed by use of the Values Survey [S. Schwartz, 1992]. Schwartz asks subjects to rate fifty-six value questions on a nine-point Likert scale (supreme importance to opposed to my values). The fifty-six value questions represent eleven value types: self-direction, stimulation, hedonism, achievement, power, security, conformity, tradition, spirituality, benevolence, and universalism.

Finally, a demographics inventory was developed to identify the students' general characteristics. The measures were administered at the first orientation session, prior to course commencement, and subsequently upon termination, at the last course session. Tests are commonly used to determine the significance of differences between group mean. T-test comparisons of the pre- and post-course tests were conducted.

A midterm narrative evaluation of the students' own views of the course was also conducted. We wanted, through this vehicle, to find out if the students felt they were (1) learning; (2) learning useful material; and (3) satisfied with the course.

A problem that concerned us from the beginning, but that we felt unable to address in this pilot study, was the contribution that the specific course faculty (the course director, Earl Shorris; the other four faculty members; and assistant staff) might have in the results obtained. Furthermore, if change was observed, what effect could be attributed exclusively to the students having become a group with consistency over time, or to "some attention" (psychological, programmatic, personal, etc.) being paid to them. The decision was to assess, in this pilot phase, if there were any positive effects obtained. Further specific inquiry as to the relative role of each program component—specifically, course content, group process, and faculty impact—would be considered in succeeding years.

The students ranged in age from seventeen to thirty-three; 76 percent were between seventeen and twenty-six years of age. Sixty-eight percent were females and 32 percent males. Eighty-seven percent were single, 3 percent separated; 10 percent did not respond to this question. Forty-six percent defined themselves as African American, 36 percent as Latino, 14 percent as White, 4 percent as Asian. Forty-three percent had completed eleventh grade or less; and 80 percent of the students had completed high school (or GED) or less.

Thirty-one students started the course, seventeen completed it (55%), and fourteen (45%) completed the course successfully and received six college credits from Bard College on the basis of their high scholastic level of performance. While the course organizer expected a high rate of attrition early in the course (when most dropouts occurred), selection criteria and retention strategies would seem to need further review.

At midcourse point, the students were asked to complete a brief five-point Likert scale (1=poor; 3=average; 5=excellent) evaluation. The group mean scores obtained were:

increased my knowledge and skills	3.94
usefulness of material in everyday life	3.76
experience was worth my time and expense	4.18
overall course rating	4.53
overall (average) teacher rating	4.06

The midcourse ratings for each of the teachers were: Art, 3.71; Logic, 3.84; History & Philosophy, 4.69; Literature & Poetry, 4.00. Significantly, the students expressed an overall rating of the course at the midpoint level of 4.53. This would suggest that they valued the course content highly and gave it a score above that obtained by the teachers (4.06). Selected comments about aspects of the class that the students liked the most included:

The diversity of art, the different cultures that it came from

Learning things I never thought of

Puzzles

Learn to look at life in more than one way

The way he discusses things in the class

Wide variety of poems—good discussions

All

Analysis of the pre- and post-course test results showed that significant changes were obtained in some aspect of each of the four levels of assessment considered. The students' self-esteem improved significantly: $p < .051$. The students' use of verbal aggression as a conflict resolution tactic decreased significantly:$p < .061$. With regard to cognitive strategies for problem resolution, the students improved significantly—$p < .001$—in one of the areas assessed, problem definition and formulation. With regard to their values orientation, the students had developed a higher valuation ($p < .10$) of collectivism, as well as registering significant changes in the same direction for the specific values of benevolence ($p < .051$), spirituality ($p < .051$), and universalism ($p < .101$).

The results offer insights on the impact of the course. First, the course significantly increased the students' self-esteem. The pre-test group mean of 28 fell below the criterion (scores above 30) for clinically significant problems in this area. The significant improvement in self-esteem indicates that the course increased a "protective factor," i.e. self-esteem, in a non-clinically deficient population. The course's ability to impact positively the self-esteem of youngsters who were not "deficient" in this area suggests that the course may be a powerful intervention in mental health promotion.

The importance of a significant improvement in self-esteem derives from the centrality that self-esteem has for everyday functioning.

I believe that our self-esteem guides and motivates our actions and, in turn, the outcome of our actions impacts on our self-esteem, so that a reciprocal process is always operating. Cycles of either low self-esteem, despair, and the avoidance of challenges, or high self-esteem, hope, and the confrontation of challenges will result. Thus, I view self-esteem as interwoven with resilience, a view shared by a number of researchers and clinicians. For example, Michael Rutter (1985) has written: "Resilience . . . seems to involve several related elements. Firstly, a sense of self-esteem and self-confidence; secondly, a belief in one's own self-efficacy and ability to deal with change and adaption; and thirdly, a repertoire of social problem solving approaches."

The psychologist Nathaniel Branden (1987), who conceptualizes self-esteem as having two main components—a feeling of personal competence (self-confidence) and a feeling of personal worth (self-respect)—notes: "The higher our self-esteem, the better equipped we are to cope with life's adversities; the more resilient we are, the more we resist pressure to succumb to despair or defeat."

Another researcher in this area, R. Brooks (1991), described the following interrelationships:

The significant increase in self-esteem poses an interesting challenge for mental health professionals, because it suggests that psychological growth and self-valuation, as measured in self-esteem, can be improved by educational interventions. This finding, if further corroborated, would open the door further for an enhanced integration of educational and other "ecological level" interventions in mental health care. More importantly it reaffirms the value and role of education in the development of self-esteem, and challenges society to invest in sound education as a protective factor against emotional dysfunction.

It has been said that 90% of successfully engaging an issue depends on the framework used to address the problem. Students in the course significantly improved their problem definition and formulation skills. These gains have broader applicability and generalizability than skills training or task-mastery competencies. Decision-making scores, however, did not significantly increase at the time of the second assessment. This suggests that problem definition and formulation changes might precede decision-making changes. It may also be that decision making might involve a kind of choice making in the real world that may require further support and working through. To this end, we are recommending that in future implementations of the course students have access also to group and/or individual discussion and counseling forums, where the personal challenges and consequences of these emerging changes can be aired and their implications in the students' lives considered.

The finding concerning the students' decrease in verbal aggression as a conflict resolution tactic is very encouraging. It confirms the observations made routinely of very cordial and respectful behavior within the class setting. This finding suggests very persuasively that reflective thinking gained ascendance in the lives of the students, and that its inverse, force-driven cognitive and interpersonal methods, lost much of the centrality, certainly the hegemony, that they might have occupied in the students' lives. No significant changes were observed in the subjects' use of reasoning or physical aggression as conflict resolution tactics. In fact, the student's use of "reasoning" as a conflict resolution tactic decreased in the post-course test. This was an unexpected finding. There is a possibility that their defintion of "reasoning" was raised to a more exacting level by the course material.

Changes were not only observed at the personal and family levels but also included significant changes in the students' values outlook. At the completion of the course, the students valued collectivism more highly (p<.101). To better understand the meaning of this increase in the cluster of values representing collective interests, some familiarity with the values scale is necessary. The author of the values schedule aggregated values into several value clusters: individual interests (power, achievement, hedonism, stimulation, self-direction), and those that served primarily collective interests (benevolence, tradition, conformity); and he considered universalism and security to be "at the border," serving both individual and collective interests. Spirituality, depending on how it is defined subjectively, may lie in either domain, and the author considers them independently.

The "border" value of universalism, and the independent value of spirituality, increased significantly in the direction of greater valuation for each. Universalism has been associated with Maslow's notion of the self-actualized person. A post-course test improvement in spirituality as a value is also significant. Schwartz emphasizes spirituality in the Buber sense of a basic human need for endowing life with meaning in the face of the seeming meaninglessness of everyday existence. It would appear that a positive increase in spirituality conformed to the objectives of the course.

It is also worth noting the significance of the higher valuation of benevolence that resulted in the post-course test. Benevolence, as defined by Schwartz in the values schedule, is one component of the former pro-social value type. "Whereas pro-social referred to concerns for the welfare of all people in all settings represented in Schwartz's Universalism, benevolence focuses on concern for the welfare of close others in everyday interaction." Further, he states that "the motivational goal of benevolence values is presentation and enhancement of the welfare of people with whom one is in frequent personal contact (helpful, loyal, forgiving, honest, responsible, true, friendship, mature love)." Again, higher valuation of benevolence as a value would support accomplishment of the course objectives.

Some of the values findings are not as robust statistically (p<.10) and require caution in their interpretation and generalization. However, it would seem that the results suggest dimensions and depths of change that warrant very serious consideration and attention.

In sum, the Clemente Course in the Humanities had a significant impact on the lives of the students who participated in it. The impact was captured by the evaluation of the course. Significant increases in self-esteem, cognitive problem solving, interpersonal conflict resolution tactics, and pro-social values indicate that the course in the humanities increased protective factors associated with mental health.

The results obtained challenge mental health practioners to review our assumptions concerning the nature of behavioral difficulties and the pathways available for intervention. While much of the field is looking toward biological intervention models and toward symptom-remission strategies, the experience of this pilot study suggests that in a non-clinical population, results associated with mental health promotion were obtained through a high-level course in the humanities. The strict emphasis on education (versus training or skills development) challenges us to rethink the assumptions, process, results, and consequences associatied with "training" initiatives. In particular, could it be that imbedded in the "training" model and process is a perpetuation of the problem of dependency and "lesser" status? Indirectly, the results of this pilot study suggest that mental health practitioners pay attention to the difference between dependency-generating training strategies and the autonomy-promoting, thus liberating, educational strategies and approaches.

If a course in the humanities helped to improve the way the students felt about themselves and the way they interact with others, could this open an institutional, group-oriented strategy to address the problem of the poor and their continued marginalization? The experience of this course suggests that mental health centers would do well to understand the underlying conditions in the ecological field of their clients (like immigration transition, or, in this case, poverty), and to establish programs to address the conditions themselves that affect the behavior and feelings of the group of clients.

Acknowledgments

I T S E E M S U N F A I R , A K I N D of theft, to put only one name on this book, for so many people risked time and reputation in hope that the work might be useful. But I cannot properly credit a hundred people as co-authors, for which I apologize.

First, to Sylvia. After more than forty years, we have only joint projects. We are not apart even when we are in different cities. Her burden has been my great good luck.

These are some of the other people I slighted:

New York City: The Clemente Course in the Humanities was largely the work of those to whom this book is dedicated. Neither I nor the students will ever forget the gift of time and talent they made to us.

Although he taught but one session, the Hon. Bruce Wright, retired New York jurist, made an indelible impression on the students.

In addition to Dr. Inclán, others at the Clemente Center helped with evaluations, making videotapes, caring for the children of the students, and creating an environment in which the students felt safe and welcome: Patricia Vargas, Ramon Maisonet, Luis Gonzalez, David Rodriguez, Rashid Sherif, M.D., Manuel Muñoz, and Elizabeth and Daisy Cruz. Of course there cannot be a school without students, including those who do not appear in the main text: Lisette Nazario, Katidra Felder, Freddy Ariel Santos, Marlen Malaj, Jessica Franco, Pearl Lau, and Ahmed Waddell. Without my friend, Jaime, there would have been no course. I am grateful to him for his help and for his presentation of wisdom with a happy face.

Attorney Peter J. Neufeld gave his time and considerable talent *pro bono* to our student, Abel Lomas.

For Mayor David Dinkins to come to the Lower East Side of New York to speak to a graduating class of only seventeen persons is entirely in character. It was not a campaign appearance; he is a decent and caring man.

Since the list is so long, I will not, for the most part, repeat the names of the people who appear in the body of the book. I am grateful to them all.

In the Bronx, Nancy Mamis-King's imprimatur led to help not only from her, but from Filomena Rosario, Barbara Bianculli, Kathleen Gilbert-Nabakaba, Hermina Thornhill, Alicia Dean, Carmen Quiñones, Jacqueline Rodriguez, Debra Alston, Jesica Burton, Madeline Rivera, Alicia Lyons, Charlotte Perry, Mary Vasquez, Bernadette Carter, and Ben Powell.

The Clemente Course was organized with the assistance of many people at The Door, including fund-raiser Kathleen Connolly. At Grand Street, Rachel Connolly and her staff, including Sheila Johnson and Calvin Patterson. Susan Matloff, Jacquetta Cole, and Les Ford also recruited students.

Introductions were provided by William Rapfogel, executive director of the Metropolitan New York Coordinating Council on Jewish Poverty, and his staff.

At Bedford Hills Correctional Facility, Superintendent Elaine Lord, Deputy Superintendent Joseph Smith, Sharon Smolick, and Roberta Falk helped, but no one helped as much as Terri McNair, who has been named a hero by the U.S. House of Representatives for her work in the community and who deserves that accolade again for her work at Bedford Hills. Many other women helped. Niecie Walker and Judy Clark, of course, but also Ann Marie Truscio, Nicole Pappas, Diane Smith, Christina Nankervis, Tracy Schwartz, Elaine Bartlett, Ada Velásquez, Georgette Reed, Carole Marcotte, Nadine Simmons, Rosalie Cutting, Iris Bowen, Deloris Harrison, June Benson, and Cherie Gallipoli.

Annandale-on-Hudson, New York: The students and I are grateful to many people at Bard College: Peter Sourian, Leon Botstein, Matthew Deady, Donna Ford, and Ellen Jetto. But the most extraordinary event occurred when Dr. Botstein gave responsibility for Bard's involvement to Robert Martin. There could not have been anyone better or more able than the cellist/philosopher/administrator Bob Martin.

Oklahoma: Visiting with R. C. and Vickie Morrison in Bixby was a welcome respite from long days in Tulsa. Gary Dart introduced me to his staff at Legal Services, among them B. Joyce Smith and Cindy Hodges Cunningham—two bright, compassionate women without whose help my work in Oklahoma would have taken many more weeks.

Texas: My sister MaryJean and her husband Hal Roberts are always my happy starting point in El Paso. Many other people helped: Leona Lakehomer, Mary Fernández yet again, Eriqueta Peña, Ceci Murillo and her clients (whose names I cannot use), John Estrada, Sister Mary Beth Larkin, David Gonzalez, Joe Aguilar, Chevo Quiroga, Alfredo Baca, The Latin Pride Car Club, Guadalupe Dueñez, Jr., Henry Irigoyen, Ray Tillis, Bobby Mendez, Raúl Carrasco, Merle Navarro, Los Blue Diamonds and The Flaming Angels and their families, and the residents of the Salazar Projects.

Mississippi: Frank Clarke and I are fond of telling people that we've been friends for so long we can remember when we both had hair. Even so, for him to travel to Mississippi with me was an act of great generosity.

On our last day in Greenville, Thelma Giles, whom Frank and I always addressed as Miss Giles, stopped by to wish us well. She had been so helpful I hardly knew how to thank her. "Miss Giles," I said, "would you mind if I kissed you on the cheek in saying good-bye?"

"Oh, no, I would not mind," she said, turning away a little, and smiling shyly as I kissed the air.

On our way back to Memphis, Frank and I were invited to lunch with Mrs. Barbara Bacon-Quinn at her home. We had enjoyed many meals with Mrs. Bacon-Quinn and Miss Giles, but none so warm or gracious as that. Both women are retired teachers. Each is, in her own way, complex and interesting. I miss their company.

Many other people were helpful in Mississippi. In Tchula, Charles Washington, Napoleon Young, Mayor Banks, the Jolly Family, Ethel and Irma Anderson, Johnny Dale, and Blanche Brown. In Lexington, Dr. Goldie Wells and Phyllis Epp introduced me to many people. Millie Russell Holmes, her daughter Herlene, her sons and grandchildren, do not appear in the body of the book, although we spent a great deal of time together.

In Mound Bayou, William Crockett, superintendent of schools, and Mayor Nerissa Norman extended the imprimatur of their positions in the community to Frank and me.

In Greenville, it seemed that everyone in the town was willing to help, beginning with all of Mrs. Bacon-Quinn's family: Corliss Goree, George

Bacon, and everyone they knew from the clinic, where Corliss is the chief nurse, to Frankel Street, which George and I visited together until I got to know people there. Dr. Kelly Mills, director of the clinic, laid out the health issues of the poor, including those out in the country, many of whom had never seen a doctor until Kelly Mills came knocking at the door on one of his Thursday afternoon excursions. Sophronia Triplett, Lorene Liggins, Tony Mitchell, Mrs. Ethel Brown, and the trustees from Parchman Farms also helped.

Chicago: George Lakehomer and Earl Watson welcomed me to the city where I was born and put me in contact with Rita Ashford, who knows practically everyone in North Lawndale. When Theodore Roethke said, "My heart holds open house," it was art; for Rita it is reality. She is a professional peacemaker; that is, she collects a paycheck for keeping the New Breed and the Black Gangsters and the police from killing each other and anyone who happens to get caught in the crossfire.

One terribly hot afternoon Rita confessed her great fear to me: Sooner or later, her work and her son's gang affiliations would come into conflict. And she did not know how she would deal with it. I wish her well.

Sun River Terrace, Illinois: My thanks to Reverend Lorenzo T. Thompson of the Rock Foundation Ministry, and Reverend Alex T. Bond, Jr., and his congregation.

Tennessee: John Cooper made it all happen. He asked Dr. Joyce Hopson to be my guide in eastern Tennessee. No one could have been more knowledgeable, helpful, or fearless. After a while in Claiborne and Hancock counties I felt very much at home, especially at dinner with the Hopson family and sitting on the front porch at Wayland and Ruth Kinsler's house outside Sneedville near the Kentucky line. I was there for a long time, and it would have been very lonely without them.

In Sneedville, Jack Stapleton, Wayne Waller, George Hunley, and I ate lunch together often, buying sandwiches in the market and sitting on piles of lumber in the shed across the street to trade war stories. They were good companions, good teachers.

In Cedar Fork, Philip Noah generously made one of the chairs in the corner of his general store available to me whenever I stoppped by.

On Straight Creek I did business with George Jones, who makes the finest moonshine and gives the best medical advice in the county. Jones told me he drinks a quart of moonshine a day to keep his cholesterol low. I did not meet his mother, but he said she was ninety-four years old and was down to drinking only a pint a day. On the subject of moonshine, I thank

Judge David Ray for his gift of a pint. It may not have been an act of jurisprudence, but it was tasty.

In Clairfield, one of the gentlest and most admirable men I met while working on this book, Shelby York, founder of the main social services organization in the Clear Fork Valley, opened up a world that I could not otherwise have found.

There was a strike at the Colquest Mines going into its fourth year when I first went to Clairfield. I met a great many of the miners and their wives, including William and Cora Perry, who had suffered a long time on the picket lines only to be betrayed by the United Mine Workers Union. I wrote about the strike, but no one was interested. My apologies to the strikers and their families and supporters: Alan and Sue King, Riley Parton, Troy Hatfield, David and Debby Hatfield, Danny Muse, David and Sharon King, Lonnie Webb, George Morgan, Charlie Black, and especially Kay Rose. The miners were not poor until the UMW convinced them to go out on strike and the mine owners refused to give in. The miners would not have become poor if Richard Trumka, then president of the union, had not broken his promise to stand by them.

Florida: Grace Darling is still magical. David Griffin took time out from his work on Socrates to play host and instructor. Sally Schmidt of Florida Rural Legal Services and I met in a soup kitchen, where she counseled poor and homeless people; if it were not for her help and guidance, I do not know what I would have done in that part of the country. Anne Harvin in Riviera Beach and Mary Ellen Beaver and Gregory Schell in Belle Glade oriented me to the local issues. George Feldman, Ingrid French, Ulysses Demetrius "Pop" Winn, Bernard McDonald, and the people of St. George's Episcopal Church also helped.

California: Ethel Long-Scott, her sister Caroline, her staff, their children, and the members and clients of the Women's Economic Agenda Project (WEAP) in Oakland and the allied group down the hall, the African-American Contractor's Association, launched much of the work and many of the ideas in this book. They are good friends, with much to tell.

My thanks also to Dr. Lois Goodwill, Dr. Charles Martin, and Dr. Evelyn Lee for frank and brilliant conversation, and to Rene Picot, Arthur O'Neal, Betty McCullough, Barbara Montgomery, Vernon Long, and the young people of Visitation Valley.

Anthony and James Shorris explained issues of health care and law, correcting my technical errors. To be able to ask advice of sons is one of the best rewards of fatherhood.

My friend and soon to be co-author of a Norton anthology of indigenous Mesoamerican literature, Jorge Klor de Alva, and I argued over many of the ideas in this book, some of which were presented to a graduate seminar he was teaching at U.C. Berkeley. The best of our conversations were nurtured by red wine and laughter.

Parts of this book formed the basis for a series of pieces on *Marketplace*, a program aired on public radio stations around the country. J. J. Yore, the senior producer of the program, took the risk, turned the work into radio, and through brilliant coaching lifted the quality of my reading to the lowest rung of semi-professionalism. He and his accomplice David Brancaccio turn out a first-rate program, and I was pleased to be part of it.

The book got sustenance along the way from the good wishes and interesting comments of Rick MacArthur, Lewis Lapham, Colin Harrison, and Anne Navasky. Richard Simon, editor of *The Networker*, gave Jaime Inclán, Patricia Vargas, and me the opportunity to discuss the thesis of the book and the Clemente Course at a *Networker*-sponsored workshop for social work and psychotherapy professionals in Washington, D.C. Roberta Pryor has proved again to be a good matchmaker.

Ann Adelman and I have never met, but I like her.

There is a new and very talented faculty at the Clemente Course. I am grateful for their acceptance of the idea of the course and their willingness to carry it on: Donna Ford in Literature, Susan Weisser in Poetry, Marci Reaven in American History, Zainub Bahrani in Art History, Anita Kawatra in Composition, and in Moral Philosophy, the director of the course, the wise and gentle Mickey Kempner, a first baseman who chose philosophy over the chance to play professional baseball.

This work began in conversation with Starling Lawrence, was carried on with the help of his friendship, enjoyed his editorial comments, and ends with his having the last word, as usual: Thanks.

Index